AMERICAN MARKETING ASSOCIATION

AMA HANDBOOK FOR

MANAGING

BUSINESS TO

BUSINESS

MARKETING

COMMUNICATIONS

J. Nicholas De Bonis   Roger S. Peterson

American Marketing Association
Chicago, Illinois

Printed on recyclable paper

NTC Business Books
a division of *NTC Publishing Group* • Lincolnwood, Illinois USA

De Bonis, J. Nicholas.
    The AMA handbook for managing business to business marketing
communications / J. Nicholas De Bonis, Roger S. Peterson.
        p.   cm.
    Includes bibliographical references and index.
    ISBN 0–8442–3595–4 (alk. paper)
        1. Industrial marketing—Management.   I. Peterson, Roger S., 1945– .
    II. Title.
HF5415.1263.D43   1997
658.8—dc20   96–21980
                                                                            CIP

Published in conjunction with the American Marketing Association,
250 South Wacker Drive, Chicago, Illinois, 60606.

Published by NTC Business Books, a division of NTC Publishing Group
4255 West Touhy Avenue
Lincolnwood (Chicago), Illinois 60606–1975, U.S.A.

7 8 9 0 BC 9 8 7 6 5 4 3 2 1

DEDICATIONS

To Susan and Andrew for their continual patience, support, and understanding.

—J.N.D.

To Chuck Ritley, Karl Niemuller, Steve Nilan, and Al Edwards for having confidence in the process and giving me the slack to do it right.

—R.S.P.

CONTENTS

Acknowledgments   xvii
Introduction   xix

PART 1

Of Birth—Or Rebirth   1

CHAPTER 1

Marcom in Relationship Marketing: The Who, What, Where, When, Why and How   3

Not Seeing the Forest for the Trees   4
A Marketing Model for the 21st Century   6
Staking the Claim: Becoming the Manager of External
   Perceptions   10
The Master of Mix:The Marcom Professional as
   Integrator and Generalist   10
Of Mr. No and the Devil's Advocate: The Marcom
   Professional as Perpetual Teacher   11
Never Get Stale: The Marcom Professional as a
   Perpetual Student   11
Resources   12

CHAPTER 2

The Warfare of Perceptions: Marketing Is a Noun, Selling Is a Verb   13

Internal Objectivity and External Perceptions   14
Getting the Big Picture Straight from the Start   15
Who Needs the Big Picture and Who Needs Smaller
   Pictures?   16
How Perceptions Kill Ideas: Mind-sets and Mine Fields   16
Preceptions and Problem Solving   17
Levels of Knowledge and Knowing   18
Resources   19

CHAPTER 3

Tomorrow's Agenda: Damn the Torpedoes!   20

What's on Deadline? Your Introduction to
     Juggling   21
The Marketing Plan and Where Marcom Fits   21
Marketing Organizations: Corporate versus
     Divisions   24
Who's on First?   27
Reading the Agencies' Minds   27
Gathering Available Information   29
General Needs Assessment: Inherited Projects and
     Staff   29
Resetting the Marcom Budget to Zero   30
Resources   30

CHAPTER 4

*Defining Markets and Matching Messages:
     What Business Are You In?*   31

Just What Do You Sell and in Which Market?   32
The Competition: Who Else Is in the Game?   33
How Do You Compare?   34
What Do They Read? Target Infographics   34
What Do They Attend?   35
What Independent Consultants Do They Use or
     Follow?   36
What Training Are They Searching For?   36
Who Else Is Involved in Specifying and
     Deciding?   37
Creating a Budget That Sells   37
Resources   37

PART 2

*Building a Macro Platform
     for Marcom*   39

CHAPTER 5

*Research and Evaluation:
     No More Wet Fingers in the Air*   41

Checklist of Do's and Don'ts   42
Objectives of Marcom Research   43
A General Marcom Research Process   44
Some Cost-Effective Research Ideas   49
Measuring the Effectiveness of Marcom
    Activities   49
The Debriefing: Evaluating the Effectiveness of an
    Integrated Campaign   50
Justifying the Expense of Research   51
Resources   52

CHAPTER 6

Building the Foundation:
The Communications Audit   54

Checklist of Do's and Don'ts   56
Developing the Preliminary MIP   56
The Communications Audit   57
Conducting the Audit   57
Communications Audit Matrix   60
Resources   60

CHAPTER 7

Building Consensus for Action:
The Marcom Summit   62

Checklist of Do's and Don'ts   63
Summit Attendees and Summit Setting   64
The Agenda: Reviewing the Audit in Detail   65
The Anatomy of Problem Solving   66
Getting Consensus and Sign-off   67
Selling MIP Discipline Internally   68
Resources   69

CHAPTER 8

Identity and Design: Of Icons and Images   70

Checklist of Do's and Don'ts   71
Project Names: How Bad Product Names Take
    Root   72
Of Ownership and Misplaced Affection   72

Types of Names   73

Procedures for Getting Good Names   74

Employee Name Contests   77

Symbols and Icons   78

Designing for Future Impact   78

Understanding Creative Directors and Designers   79

Tips for Integrating Your Program   80

Measurement and Evaluation   80

Resources   81

PART 3

Managing the Micro Tools   83

CHAPTER 9

Advertising and Collateral Sales Literature: Customizing Marcom in the Information Age   87

Checklist of Do's and Don'ts   89

The Message: What to Say   89

The Medium: Where to Say It   94

Media Schedule: When to Say It   97

The Budget: What to Spend   99

Collateral Sales Materials   101

Marcom of the Future   103

Tips for Integrating Your Program   104

Measurement and Evaluation   105

Resources   107

CHAPTER 10

Relationship Database Marketing: Spending $20 to Make a Dollar   108

Checklist of Do's and Don'ts   109

Database Marketing   110

Information As Part of the Overall Marketing
    Strategy   111

The Functions of Progressive Databases   115

Tips for Integrating Your Program   117

Measurement and Evaluation   117

Resources   118

CHAPTER 11

*Direct Response Marketing:
Laser Strikes on the Targets*   119

Checklist of Do's and Don'ts   120
When to Use Direct Marketing   121
Basic Direct Marketing Strategic Decisions   121
Direct Marketing Media   122
Tips for Integrating Your Program   135
Measurement and Evaluation   138
Resources   139

CHAPTER 12

*Trade Show and Exhibit Marketing:
Military Staging for Closing Sales*   140

Checklist of Do's and Don'ts   142
Exhibit Marketing Myths   143
Of von Clausewitz and the Order of Battle   144
Exhibit Systems, Materials, and Construction   145
The Exhibit Medium as the Message   146
Reorienting the Sales Staff   150
Demonstration Management   155
Managing Exhibit Traffic: The Role of Preshow
     Promotion and Show Literature   157
Managing Inquiries from the Show   157
Tips for Integrating Your Program   160
Measurement and Evaluation   164
Resources   165

CHAPTER 13

*Event and Seminar Marketing:
There's No Business Like Show Business*   167

The Difference Between Event and Exhibit
     Marketing   168
Checklist of Do's and Don'ts   169
The Cards You Want versus the Cards You Are
     Dealt   170
Adopting an Event: Sponsorships and Special
     Events   172
Seminars and Tutorials   175

Agenda Essentials   177
Road Shows   178
Sales Meetings: Your Primary Event Market   181
Tips for Integrating Your Program   181
Measurement and Evaluation   184
Resources   184

CHAPTER 14

Telemarketing: Creating a Second Sales Staff   187

Checklist of Do's and Don'ts   188
Where Does Telemarketing Fit in the Overall Marketing
     Plan?   189
Hiring from the Inside or the Outside   193
Training   195
Quality Control   198
Motivation   199
Making Successful Telemarketing Calls   201
Telemarketing Costs Checklist   206
Future Technologies: Telemarketing in the
     21st Century   207
Tips for Integrating Your Program   207
Measurement and Evaluation   208
Resources   209

PART 4

Managing Important Relationships   211

CHAPTER 15

Public Relations:
The Best Defense Is a Good Offense   213

Checklist of Do's and Don'ts   214
Public Relations Objectives   214
Public Relations Is More than "Firefighting"   216
The Best Defense: Proactive Public Relations   217
The 4 A's of PR: A Public Relations Checklist   219
Other Tactical Considerations   220
Objectives and Strategies for Media Relations   221
Two Other Public Relations Functions   224
Internal Public Relations   225

Tips for Integrating Your Program   226
Measurement and Evaluation   226
Resources   227

CHAPTER 16

Financial Relations:
Of Stockholders and Stakeholders   228

Checklist of Do's and Don'ts   229
The SEC and Its Agenda   230
Management As Message—And the Chairman's
    Agenda   232
Information Management: Understanding versus
    Facts   234
The Investor Relations Message Management Task
    Force   236
Relationship Investing: Investor Relations or Speculator
    Relations?   237
Investor Relations: Two Approaches   238
Analysts: High-Stakes Poker   239
Of Stockholders and Stakeholders: IR's Integrated
    Audiences   242
The Basics: Factors, Problem Definition, Objectives,
    Setting   246
What Is News and How to Report It   248
The Initial Public Offering Checklist   249
Handling a Takeover Bid   251
Handling Chapter 11 Restructuring   254
Tips for Integrating Your Program   257
Measurement and Evaluation   263
Resources   264

CHAPTER 17

Employee Relations: Creating Company
Loyalty That Customers Notice   267

Checklist of Do's and Don'ts   268
Ownership and Motivation   269
Departmental Marketing   270
Internal Merchandising of Communication
    Programs   274
Tips for Integrating Your Program   276

Measurement and Evaluation   279
Resources   281

CHAPTER 18

Community and Government Relations: Don't Forget to Call Home   282

Checklist of Do's and Don'ts   284
Setting the Objectives   285
Your Accounts Payable Department   286
Local Government Officials   287
True Power: Finding the Key Influences in
    Town   288
Corporate Support: "We're Sure Your Firm Would Want
    To . . ."   288
Influencing Governmental Changes   290
Trade Schools and Universities   290
Local Reporters and Editors   291
Big Ideas for Little Budgets   292
Tips for Integrating Your Program   293
Measurement and Evaluation   295
Resources   296

CHAPTER 19

Crises and Contingencies: Communicating During Times of Trouble   297

Checklist of Do's and Don'ts   298
Preparing and Planning Ahead: Taking the Grim
    Inventory   299
Assembling the Crisis Team   300
Remembering Crisis Context: A Company Crisis and
    Your Marketing Plan   301
Crisis Context: An Industry-wide Crisis   306
A Marketing Problem—Or Something Else?   307
Admissions and Precautions: "I'm the Corporate
    Attorney and I'm Here to Help You."   308
Media Relations During a Crisis   309
After the Crisis: Refining Plans for the Future   311
Tips for Integrating Your Program   312
Measurement and Evaluation   314
Resources   316

Appendices 317

A   Marketing Information Platform (MIP)™ Sample
    Template   317
B   Project Platform Worksheet   324
C   News Release Worksheet   327
D   Trade Show Management Checklist   329
E   Legalities of Copywriting   334
F   Legalities and Trademarks   336
G   *Business Marketing's* "Copy Chasers" Guidelines
    for Good Advertising   342
H   Ketchum Public Relations–Pittsburgh's Crisis
    Marketing Message Action Plan (MAP)   345
I   Event Marketing Site Inspection Checklist   348
J   De Bonis and Peterson Results/Efforts (R/E) Ratio™:
    Analysis of Marcom Results versus Effort Expended
    in Marcom Dollars   354

Index   361

ACKNOWLEDGMENTS

This is the hardest part of the book to write—it's like being an Oscar winner who has 30 seconds to thank everyone who contributed to his or her winning the award. There are so many people past and present, friends and colleagues, mentors and teachers, students and trainees who have individually and collectively contributed to not only the material for this book, but to my development as a professional and as a person. The book is an extension of their support. And I thank them all. To my coauthor, Roger, thanks for being the engine that could. To Susan, my business and life partner, thank you for your insights and expertise. And to my son, Andrew, thanks for taking me away from the computer when I needed a break.

—J. Nicholas De Bonis
Peachtree City, Georgia

Many thanks to Francesca Van Gorp of the American Marketing Association for believing in the book idea and urging NTC Business Books to copublish, and thanks to Anne Knudsen at NTC for agreeing with Francesca. Rich Hagle at NTC deserves some thanks for putting up with us. Thanks also to Amy Wenshe, Lorraine Caliendo, and their colleagues at AMA's Kent Library for gathering so many resources for me. AMA's library alone is worth the price of membership.

Various professionals contributed elements to the book: Michael Anderson and Ray Solone of Anderson/Solone Marketing Communications of Sacramento; Eugene Winther of 360 Designers & Producers of Sacramento; D. James Sabraw, Sacramento's "Mr. Marketing"; Daniel K. Mannisto, my favorite CFO; Heidi Foran of Dana/Foran Marketing Communications; Janice Rosenthal of Rosenthal Communications; Rivian Bell and Lance Ignon of Sitrick and Company, Los Angeles; Lawrence Werner of Ketchum Public Relations/Pittsburgh; Bud Frankel of Frankel & Company, Chicago; Joe Williams of Joe Williams Communications of Bartlesville, Oklahoma; and Serena E. Leiser, conference director at the College of the Holy Cross in Worcester, Massachusetts. And, of course, the most thanks to Nick De Bonis for agreeing to work with me in writing this much-needed book.

Personal thanks are in order to many. My parents, Fred and Joan Peterson, put up with all my diverse interests and never discouraged any. Were it not for John Boben, my ninth grade English teacher, I never would have discovered the fun of writing. Paul Pease, Silicon Valley's first high-technology ad man, once gave me sage advice as we walked around a Palo Alto park. It was at a time I needed a book just like this. Your advice made sense, Paul, and it's in the book. Lastly I want to thank Heidi and Bret for their patience and understanding. And, guys . . . you no longer have to knock before entering my study.

—Roger S. Peterson
Rocklin, California

INTRODUCTION

In a nutshell, this is a practical, nonthreatening guide to understanding and executing effective marketing communications (marcom) programs in the business-to-business arena. Our point of view is simple and direct—people and businesses fighting to survive in markets with commodity mentalities must use an integrated approach to marketing communications.

In short, the *AMA Handbook for Managing Business-to-Business Marketing Communications* is about marcom that works—integrated marketing communications, and how to do it.

WHO WOULD BENEFIT FROM THIS BOOK?

✔ CEOs—If you're a CEO and seem to be getting the impression that marcom is some kind of "black art," this book will unlock the mystery.

✔ Marketing communications professionals—If you are a marcom operative, this book will help fill in the connections.

✔ Sales professionals, engineers, and product managers—If you've just been thrown into marketing, this is your book! Just start reading.

✔ Agency professionals—If you already understand the idea behind integrated marketing communications, this book will help you open up the process so you can start billing for it.

✔ Professors—We know it's hard when courses have locked-up titles such as Principles of Advertising and Intro to Public Relations, or Marketing 101. Restrictive, isn't it? Adopt De Bonis & Peterson—your students won't sell this one back!

But aren't there other marketing books? Sure, there are many good books on marketing and public relations and advertising. Textbooks for college courses on principles of advertising and introductory marketing and basic public relations number in scores.

There are also many "pop" business books that focus on concepts such as positioning and guerilla marketing, and professional reference books that go into great detail on mechanics.

In any of these books you might find reproductions of famous ad campaigns, fascinating war stories, some theory and research, guidelines to managing client accounts, overviews of important areas such as media and market research, or primers on producing an ad or designing a brochure. And these topics are all important. If you work for an ad agency or public relations firm, your library would be well-stocked with all such books. But that is not what this book does.

So just how is this book different? This is not a college textbook or three-pound reference tome. As our title indicates, this is a "how-to" guide for soldiers deep in the jungle of marketing warfare.

In these pages we will introduce you to the main concepts CEOs and even marketing professionals may miss about marketing communications. We'll also introduce you to the marketing communications process without burying you in mechanical details.

How do you read this book? Basically, you can jump around to the topics you need to know. The chapters on communications tools (Chapters 8 through 19) can be read in any order you want. What's more, each of these tactical chapters has the same generic chapter structure. However, regardless of the order in which you read those chapters, we urge you to read Chapters 1 through 7 first.

STRUCTURE OF INTERIOR CHAPTERS

The readability and practicality of this book are important. That's why all chapters, beginning in Part 2, share this format:

Chapter Opening Quotes

We've searched for a pithy relevant quote on each topic. Some are from contemporary experts, some are from people outside marketing, and some are very old. In addition, each chapter starts with a "grab-you-by-the-neck" scenario. Some are true and actually happened to someone just like you. Others are scenes you very well could experience in your career.

Checklist of Do's and Don'ts

This section gives you a quick sanity check on handling the topic in real life. The do's and don'ts are designed to get your attention and persuade you to read each chapter. You will find some of the do's and don'ts rather surprising—so read on!

Text of Chapter

Whenever possible we have included vignettes or short case histories to show how real people have handled the chapter topic.

In Chapters 8 through 19, the marcom tactical chapters, we have added:

Tips for Integrating Your Program

After all, this is a book on integrating all communications modalities into a total promotion package for your company. So we have tried in each chapter to show how to do just that.

Measurement and Evaluation

We know that your CEO and CFO always try to nail you with, "How do we know it works? How do we know we got our money's worth?" So in addition to Chapter 5 on Research and Evaluation, we've included a section on measurement in each tactical chapter (8 through 19).

All chapters end with:

Resources

You need help, and we don't end our assistance with just the chapter. At the end of each interior chapter you will find a list of books, software packages, organizations, newsletters, services, and directories related to the chapter topic.

But will this book put you to sleep? No, because we won't bury you in details of production, esoteric theory, or dense scholarly research findings. We will frequently cite places to find in-depth coverage of mechanics. But we prefer to focus your attention on basic practical concepts—*concepts to use tomorrow.* If you are managing marketing communication professionals, this book will also help you assess the way they handle their roles.

We believe marketing communications people often focus too heavily on mechanics and, thus, lose the big picture. You can also get someone to help you understand production or research findings. But you must know the logical process of managing the overall marketing communication mix. Being an expert in mechanics may win you creative awards, but it won't help your sales reps sell. We believe a balance of concepts and details is needed. That's why this book is . . .

A "forest and trees" book: We believe the forest is as important as the individual trees. We want to help you see the broad mix of marketing communication tools available to you.

Therefore, we frequently use the terms *macro* and *micro*. No, this has nothing to do with economics. With macro and micro comparisons, we are merely drawing distinctions between big picture or "forest" issues and the subsets or "trees" within. The basic idea is that you have to recognize the sets and subsets in a marketing communications plan. By balancing macro with micro, issues with details, problems and solutions, you see **how integrated marcom works.**

We see this as a way to avoid the curse suffered by many marketers who fall back too easily on *just* trade shows, or *just* public relations, or *just* direct mail. You shouldn't get tied to only one marcom tool, so we offer you . . .

A survival guide: Frankly, many practitioners—on both the agency and corporate side—find themselves walking down the sidewalks of marcom, stepping in all the puddles and wondering why their shoes get wet. This book helps you step around those puddles. This book is intended to *help people survive and prosper in marcom roles.*

We stress process: We deal with the developmental process in these pages. By process we mean the sequence of building a marketing communication program, not the things (deliverables, as some call them) that are produced. This is a practical process that will unfold as you turn these pages.

A process approach to marketing communication involves wiping the slate clean of assumptions about your company's position. It involves asking fundamental questions of everyone. It means precisely identifying and isolating problems, and then building a consensus about how to proceed against those problems. We borrow a term from accountants and call this "zero-based marcom."

And we stress platform: Understanding the developmental process helps you build the right platform for success. Prepare yourself—we will talk frequently about process and platform.

The term *platform* comes from ad agency copywriters. The copywriter starts a writing assignment by first summarizing the objectives of the copy and outlining the main points the copy will employ to solve the problem at hand. Typically, this summary is called the *copy platform,* and it is reviewed by the client to see if the copywriter is heading in the right direction.

Curiously, most agencies and most corporations don't take the copy platform idea and build backwards to the real beginning. That's what we do: we take the idea of a copy platform and greatly expand on its use. We show you how to create the right platform upon which to build your overall marketing communications plan. When you understand the process of building the correct platform, you will be well prepared to handle the marcom assignments placed in your lap.

Is there any jargon in this book? As you've noticed, even marketing communications has its shorthand. Sometimes it's called *mar/com,* sometimes *mar-comm*. We call it marcom. That's a fairly common term in the business world. We also use *IMC* to refer to integrated marcom. Otherwise, we've worked very hard to make this book as jargon-free as possible. But we have included our "rules of the road," which we call *De Bonis & Peterson's 10 New Rules for Business Marcom Success*™

RULE #1:   "THE INTEGRATED WHOLE OF MARCOM TOOLS IS GREATER THAN THE SUM OF ITS PARTS." CHAPTER 1

RULE #2:   "BEWARE OF THE 'NOT INVENTED HERE' SYNDROME. RESIST BECOMING A CLONE." CHAPTER 2

RULE #3:   "NEVER ASSUME ANYTHING ABOUT YOUR MARKET, BECAUSE YOU CAN'T KNOW IT THAT WELL." CHAPTER 2

RULE #4:   "INTEGRATED MARKETING COMMUNICATIONS IS NOT A QUICK FIX. IT, TOO, TAKES TIME." CHAPTER 3

RULE #5:   "IT ISN'T IMPORTANT WHETHER YOU LIKE THE PRODUCT OR COMPANY NAME YOU SELECT. BUT IT DOES HAVE TO WORK." CHAPTER 8

RULE #6:   "IN DATABASE MARKETING, THE ONE THING THAT'S MOST IMPORTANT IS THE 'ONE.'" CHAPTER 10

RULE #7:   "LOSE THE SALE, BUT KEEP THE RELATIONSHIP." CHAPTER 10

RULE #8:   "THE SUCCESS OR FAILURE OF A DIRECT MARKETING CAMPAIGN ISN'T DEPENDENT UPON THE RESPONSE RATE." CHAPTER 11

RULE #9:   "TRADE SHOW EXHIBITS ARE ALL ABOUT STRATEGY AND TACTICS. OWNING ONE, HOWEVER, IS NOTHING BUT EGO." CHAPTER 12

RULE #10:   "NEVER MAKING A MISTAKE IS A BAD SIGN." CHAPTER 19

Still doubting if this book is for you? Well then

✔ Do you think it's advertising that sells products or services?
✔ Do you think the essence of a public relations program is cranking out a press release on something every week?
✔ Do you wonder if the reason for your big trade show is just to make an annual appearance and watch people eat shrimp?
✔ Do you think that the way to evaluate a direct mail campaign is to compare your response rate to some generic standard?
✔ Is your four-color literature going out-of-date too soon?
✔ Are you having trouble retaining repeat customers?

If you even so much as squeaked a "yes" to any of these questions, you could use this book.

General notes: When we use the terms prospects, buyers, or customers, we also mean dealers, members, and donors. When we say targets, we mean companies, institutions, and government agencies. We alternated the use of "he" and "she" just to keep you alive, and sometimes we shortened it by using "s/he."

In summary: We'll help you take more control of your firm's communications program. In the process, we'll help you to "own your job" rather than just puddle-jump through mechanics. We hope you recognize that, unless you are the CEO, it will be hard to be in absolute command of marcom. Lots of circumstances have influence on a business, so it would be puffery on our part to say we guarantee you success. But if you read the book in its entirety, we offer you more success than you are having now. So let's begin.

About the Authors

J. NICHOLAS DE BONIS, PH.D.

Dr. Nick De Bonis is a consultant with the Strategic Management Group, Inc. (SMG), based in Atlanta. Prior to joining SMG in the Spring of 1996, he was a consulting partner of De Bonis & Peterson Marketing Consultants, which has offices in Atlanta and Sacramento. The Atlanta office number is 1-800-631-8864. Nick continues to conduct research and publish in the area of relationship marketing communications.

He is co-author of *Top Dog* with David Pincus, a unique business book which is half fiction and half nonfiction. Published by McGraw-Hill Business Books in 1994, it is a comprehensive look at how top managers' communications skills affect leadership. *Top Dog* has been published in five international editions and became a paperback in early 1996.

Nick's doctorate is in advertising and marketing from the University of Tennessee-Knoxville. From 1992–96, he was a full-time adjunct associate professor of marketing at the Goizueta Business School at Emory University in Atlanta. He has also been on the faculty at Louisiana State, Texas A&M, California State-Fullerton and Pepperdine universities.

ROGER S. PETERSON

Roger S. Peterson has spent 25 years in sales, product management, and corporate marketing communications, working in the book publishing, computer software, and ad agency industries.

Peterson's business career followed two years of teaching high school social studies in Minnesota and active duty in the U.S. Navy. He is a graduate of Macalester College of St. Paul, Minnesota, and currently teaches introductory marketing for the University of California/Davis Extension Program in Sacramento.

Peterson has published articles on topics ranging from humor to history, from technology to marketing, from education to politics. Peterson is vice president of the American Marketing Association/Sacramento Chapter. He is a business writer and operates the West Coast Office of De Bonis & Peterson Marketing Communications in Rocklin (suburban Sacramento), California.

J. Nicholas De Bonis
800-631-8864

Roger S. Peterson
800-484-2799, ext. 2707

PART 1

Of Birth — or Rebirth

Have you ever joked about wanting to go back in time and start something over because you finally realized what went wrong? If you've dabbled in some aspect of marketing communications and had something that went wrong or you know could have been better, Part 1 is all about starting over. Reorientation, if you will. In a sense we are about to untrain you first so that we can properly retrain you. If you're entering or being trained in marcom, this book is a primer on how not to make the mistakes that make you wish you had a "do over."

In marketing warfare, as with real war, the fog of battle can be deceiving. In Part 1, we will try to get you in sync with a new plan of attack to stay ahead of the fog. To be sure, this is not a pure exercise or one which carries a guarantee of success. Just like real war, unexpected things can take control. But we believe by merely raising the concept of reorientation, we make a solid point not soon lost, even in the fog.

CHAPTER 1

Marcom in Relationship Marketing: The Who, What, Where, When, Why, and How

"It's a new ball game ... every company's marketers, no matter how large or how small the company, must now consider every channel of advertising and distribution with completely open minds."

—Stan Rapp & Tom Collins

Many marketing communications professionals miss the real point of what they do. They often see their jobs as managing various projects with the goal of producing the "deliverables." Admittedly, those deliverables are very visible to your coworkers. Likewise, the absence of things such as adequate brochures and so on can be equally visible. The cold reality is that the marcom function finds its operatives knee-deep in details of projects and even lists of projects.

Therein lies a problem. Unless you keep the big picture in mind, you might begin to believe that getting "things" done is what marketing communications is all about. That leads to living the fiction that ads and brochures sell products. The ending to that short story is that you will find yourself stunned and speechless when the CEO or vice president of sales wonders why nothing is working.

NOT SEEING THE FOREST FOR THE TREES

What's happening in such a scenario? Basically, it's an imbalance between the big picture and the details. Trees are getting the attention, and the forest is lost for the trees. The view is too microscopic and inadequately "macroscopic."

The evolution of integrated marketing communications (IMC) as a marcom strategy was a matter of survival. As more and more markets became dominated by a commodity mentality, the survivors discovered that the ability to communicate with prospects and customers could create a sustainable competitive advantage in the marketplace. Lewis Grizzard said it best—"If you're not the lead dog, the scenery never changes."

A DEFINITION OF MARKETING COMMUNICATIONS

It's important to provide a working definition of marketing communications so that you understand the scope of this function as it relates to the overall marketing strategy. This is what marcom is, what it does.[1]

Why	This is the macro marcom objective—to satisfy the customers' decision-making information needs.
Who	"Who" describes not only the source of the marcom messages, but the source's credibility, and its equity or liability. For some target segments, a company official may have more credibility than a third-party spokesperson. For others, an ad campaign may be perceived as manipulative and have a negative behavioral effect.
says **What**	These are the discrete message(s) in the marcom, both explicit and implicit.
to **Whom,**	Marcom is intended to be "segment-of-one" communication, which understands the demographics, psychographics, and infographics of the target.
How,	These are the multiple channels which are used to communicate the marcom message. All customer touchpoints communicate something, implicitly or explicitly, good, bad, or indifferent.
When,	The timing of marcom should be determined by the information user. This means providing the message when it's needed, including on demand.
Where,	Marcom message delivery should be at the location most desired by the audience. Placing ads on the back of stall doors in restaurant restrooms, for example, may guarantee a captive audience, but the intrusion can create a strong negative effect.

They also learned that effective marcom didn't mean simply managing a traditional promotional mix; every element of the marketing mix, every touchpoint with the customer communicates something about the company and its marketing strategies. What's more, it became apparent that a company has to tie (integrate) all these tools together so that each one interacts and supports the others.

You might ask, "That all makes sense but why is it so unique now?" The answer is that company structures and fiefdoms often separated these functions in ways that *prevented them from being thematically integrated.*

Take trade shows, for example. Often this function is placed in sales departments. Telemarketing as an outbound sales tool is typically placed in

through what **Noise**	Marcom doesn't take place in a vacuum. You have to anticipate that there will be interference, called *noise* or *clutter,* for your marcom from a variety of sources, either external—competing messages of information overload—or internal—a function of distractions in the customer's personal life. Noise affects the ability of the communication to get through to the target and can hinder the desired effect. Noise can also interrupt the feedback process; you don't "hear" what the customer is saying, because her response to your marcom is filtered through too many levels in the organization.
with what behavioral **Effect**	This acknowledges that there is an intended outcome, a behavioral return on investment (ROI) as a result of the marcom: did the target respond, satisfy the marcom objective? Determining effect means research or tracking. It also requires a mind-set that understands that which of the specific marcom elements was "responsible" for the behavior isn't relevant; what is relevant is the outcome generated by the total marcom effort. An analogy would be the Gulf War in which each military branch and each country had specific military objectives. The end result didn't depend upon the success of just one; it depended on the total effort.
generating what **Feedback**	Marcom isn't monologue; it's dialogue. Attending to, receiving, analyzing, and responding to customers' communications is a necessary closure to the marcom process

---

[1] Modeled after Lasswell's communication model. Lasswell, H. D. (1948). "The Structure and Function of Communication in Society." Reprinted in Schramm, W. (1960). *Mass Communications.* Urbana, IL: University of Illinois Press.

the sales department, too, but direct mail promotions are sent by marketing. Inbound customer support call centers are housed in customer service departments, but 800-line inbound information queries are taken in marketing.

In Chapter 2, we discuss the differences in perspective between sales and marketing. If you haven't already discovered it, these and other departments often develop a sense of territoriality. Should it be that way? Not if they are all working for the same company. Shouldn't all communications functions be integrated and mutually supportive?

A MARKETING MODEL FOR THE 21ST CENTURY

The dominant U.S. marketing philosophy for the past 40 years has been sales-driven, successfully negotiating a series of transactions. A major premise of this book is that transaction-based marketing has been replaced by *total relationship marketing* (*TRM*), depicted in Figure 1.1.

The objective of TRM is to create long-term relationships with customers. One way we demonstrate the concept of relationship marketing to a group is to try to sell a $1 bill which represents $1 worth of business. The opening bids are usually less than 15 cents. And no one is willing to give

FIGURE 1.1. *Total Relationship Marketing Model*

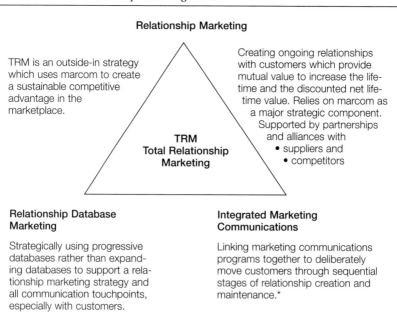

Relationship Marketing

TRM is an outside-in strategy which uses marcom to create a sustainable competitive advantage in the marketplace.

Creating ongoing relationships with customers which provide mutual value to increase the lifetime and the discounted net lifetime value. Relies on marcom as a major strategic component. Supported by partnerships and alliances with
* suppliers and
* competitors

**TRM
Total Relationship
Marketing**

Relationship Database Marketing

Strategically using progressive databases rather than expanding databases to support a relationship marketing strategy and all communication touchpoints, especially with customers.

Integrated Marketing Communications

Linking marketing communications programs together to deliberately move customers through sequential stages of relationship creation and maintenance.*

*Adapted from John Deighton and Kent Grayson, "Marketing and seduction: Building exchange relationships by managing social consensus." *Journal of Consumer Research* 21 (4), 660 (March 1995).

us the $5, $10, or $20 we're asking. That's the transaction mentality—I'm not willing to spend $1 to acquire $1 in revenue.

The responses quickly change when we suggest that whoever buys the dollar will receive an additional $100 during the next 60 minutes. The bids jump to $20, $40, and even $60. Participants begin to understand that what they could acquire isn't $1 worth of business; it's a *net lifetime value* (*NLTV*) of a relationship which has both a time dimension and a revenue component. The NLTV we are most interested in is the *discounted* net lifetime value, because an anticipated dollar of revenue gained 12, 18, 24, or 36 months in the future doesn't have the same net value as it would if the dollar were acquired today. We've always relied on the financial experts to define what the discounted net lifetime value of a future relationship is today.

As with any relationship, communication is an essential factor in not only creating, but sustaining and growing that relationship. This is the relationship communication component of the diagram in Figure 1.1 and the major emphasis of this book.

The databases are the tool used to sustain micromarketing and marcom efforts. This concept is discussed at length in Chapter 10, "Database Marketing."

Overview of What Integrated Marcom Entails

A basic premise of any integrated marcom strategy is that all elements of the marketing mix communicate something to customers. With this in mind, we introduce you to:

DE BONIS & PETERSON BUSINESS MARCOM RULE #1:
"The integrated whole of marcom tools is greater than the sum of its parts."

The traditional marketing mix has included the 4 Ps: product, price, placement, and promotion. Each had a discrete function and marcom was relegated to the promotional mix, which includes sales, sales promotions, advertising, public relations, and direct response. In a broader sense, every element of the marketing mix communicates something about the company. Products offered may be innovative or "me, too," which communicates something relevant to the buyer about the company's leadership role in an industry. A low-ball pricing strategy communicates something different about an organization than a parity pricing strategy. Product distribution using fleet trucks communicates one message; using an independent carrier communicates something entirely different.

Marcom also includes not only intended explicit messages, but implicit messages that are communicated, intentionally or not. A copier company may sell itself, for example, as a quick-response service-oriented organization. While the service rep may arrive quickly on the scene, however, he or she may spend more time drinking coffee and dawdling with employees than actually repairing the equipment, thus communicating an entirely different message.

Since the 4 Ps model became the accepted marketing standard in 1956, additional Ps have been added: planning, perception, packaging, and people.

Planning. It's not enough to build a better mousetrap if you want the market to beat a path to your door. You'd better determine if a better mousetrap is what the market wants and, if it does, then what kind, shape, color, and so on.

Perception. Tom Peters said it best: "Perception is everything." When the perception of the marketplace fails to match the marketer's reality or desired reality, the resulting dissonance results in the loss of business. Marcom is a major element in creating, reinforcing, or modifying perception.

Packaging. This refers more to the bundling of products and services than physical packaging. How products and services are packaged provides important value-added dimensions for the buyer.

People. Each touchpoint with the customer—whether it is sales or customer service, shipping or maintenance, billing or reception—represents an opportunity to communicate something positive or negative about the organization, its products or services, and its people. Customer service, for example, is typically an entry-level position staffed by less experienced company newcomers at low wages with few incentives for helping to sustain customer relationships the organization has spent a lot of money to acquire. This is why many companies are redefining the customer service position, increasing the qualifications, the pay, and the incentives; it is one of the most critical communication touchpoints in the organization.

Working Definition of Integrated Marcom (IMC)

Don Schultz, the Northwestern professor who is inarguably the father of integrated marketing communications (IMC), has said that defining this concept is analogous to the parable of the six blind men and the elephant. Each had hold of a different part of the animal and was trying to describe it to the others. The blind man holding the leg reported that it was like the trunk of a tree. To the one holding an ear, it was like a giant leaf, and so forth.

For some organizations, IMC means combining advertising, public relations and other marcom functions into a single unit. It's been our experience that this is frequently done as part of an organization downsizing strategy, not necessarily to achieve more efficient, integrated communications. Developing a company slogan which is consistently used in all communications is how another client defines IMC, while a third sees IMC as a coordinated multimedia campaign.

These are certainly components of an integrated marcom strategy. But an integrated strategy is more comprehensive, part system, part process and part how the company defines the marcom element as part of the overall marketing strategy. Our working definition of an integrated marcom approach includes the following elements:

- *Synchronized management*—marcom doesn't just happen, it's managed and coordinated. The sales people need to know what PR is planning, PR should be plugged into sales promotions, sales promotions should be aware of what advertising is going to be run, advertising has to coordinate with customer service, and so on. How many times has your organization run a business-to-business ad with a toll-free number as the response device, but when inquirers called, the people answering the phone had no idea what the campaign was all about? It's axiomatic that all elements of the traditional marketing mix communicate something to the market. Production decisions, pricing strategy, distribution channels and promotions all say something about the company and its products and services.

- *Multichannel communication flow*—all formal and informal communications channels and touchpoints should be used to get the marcom message across. And as we discussed in the Marcom Sidebar, these channels should be determined by the customer, not the seller. Markets are no longer willing to be subjected to the "we'll speak, you'll listen" philosophy. They're more receptive to communications which satisfy their time, location and format needs. If a buying center wants marketing information available on interactive CD or through an interactive on-line computer network, it's counterproductive to continue outbound telemarketing, direct mail or other marcom activities because it's more convenient for you.

- *Consistency*—inconsistent messages create a perceptual dissonance about the organization and its ability to meet the customers' information if not product needs. What happens when sales makes promises that shipping can't or won't meet?

- *Measurement*—marcom should be accountable in a behavioral ROI sense. Marcom has an objective: to help create, modify or reinforce customer behavior. Effort must be measurable against outcome.

- *Tailored relationship-building messages*—the messages should reinforce the idea that customer relationships are central to the company's marketing strategy, even to the point of expressly stating that message in both formal and informal communications.

- *Internal & external focus*—marcom must be shared with the internal stakeholders, as well as the prospects and customers. If there's not an internal buy-in to the marcom message, it will be difficult to sustain that message to the external marketplace.

STAKING THE CLAIM: BECOMING THE MANAGER OF EXTERNAL PERCEPTIONS

"Marketing communications" is not as descriptive or functional as it could or should be. External perception management is a far more functional way of putting it. Thus, for purposes of discussion, whether you are a CEO or a sales manager or marketing manager, think of your communications function as managing external perceptions.

Why? Because if you can get external perceptions from largely negative values to largely positive values, your communication plan is working. Then it's up to sales to sell and close and fulfillment to ship and customer service to support.

As much as possible, describe your communications program in terms of managing external perceptions, and that compass will greatly improve how everyone understands its role.

THE MASTER OF MIX: THE MARCOM PROFESSIONAL AS INTEGRATOR AND GENERALIST

You or your communications manager should remain a generalist. It is important not to think of yourself as just an advertising manager or just the public relations manager. The preferable way to view the role is marketing generalist or marketing communications generalist.

What is our point? Basically, you shouldn't strap yourself with a structure or title that presupposes the kind of communication tactic or tool to use. Consider this example. Say you're having a problem with customers who got the impression your management is dropping a product line the customer just bought. If you went to an ad agency for assistance, what solution do you think they might suggest? Likely, it would be an ad campaign because that is what they do: advertising. Suppose you take the same problem to a public relations agency. Their suggestion isn't likely to be advertising. You will get a public relations program because that is their specialty.

You need to be familiar with the strengths and weaknesses of all communication modalities so that you can pick and choose the right, integrated blend to solve the problem at hand.

OF MR. NO AND THE DEVIL'S ADVOCATE: THE MARCOM PROFESSIONAL AS PERPETUAL TEACHER

Like it or not, communications professionals are often second-guessed by product managers, CFOs, CEOs, and other departments. It comes with the territory.

So rather than fight it, enjoy it! If you always wanted to be a teacher, this is your chance. But don't be "preachy."

You will be surprised how much you can open discussion and thinking traditionally closed simply by asking "Why do we do it that way?" or "Let me be a devil's advocate—what if we did it this way?" The answers will fill in some blanks for you and provoke some thinking. Organizations, especially as they grow in size and number, tend to develop a habit-forming inertia.

Remember what IBM's Thomas J. Watson once said about thinking: "All the problems of the world could be settled easily if men were only willing to think. The trouble is that men very often resort to all sorts of devices in order not to think, because thinking is such hard work."

Playing the role of teacher can open the discussion a little—provoke a little thinking.

NEVER GET STALE: THE MARCOM PROFESSIONAL AS A PERPETUAL STUDENT

Never stop learning new tricks. With the proliferation of commodity marketplaces and the arrival of integrated marketing communications, you need as much leverage and training as possible. Here are some tips on where to get it:

Associations. You can join lots of national and local groups, especially if you sell into vertical markets. But two groups are important for communications operatives in the business-to-business arena. The Business Marketing Association (formerly Business/Professional Advertising Association) is a strong, vital group that made the obvious IMC adjustment inherent in its name change. Likewise, the American Marketing Association is an outstanding resource for marketing professionals throughout North America. AMA publishes several journals, including the valuable biweekly *Marketing News.* AMA also publishes books and copublishes books (such as this one) with NTC Business Books. Publications from both these associations are valuable professional reading, and the cost of membership is money well spent. Get your CEO to join them too.

Publications. For the business-to-business professional, one publication stands out among all others—*Business Marketing,* a monthly published by

Crain Communications. Another monthly worth getting is *Sales and Marketing Management,* a Bill Communications journal.

Seminars. Several seminar groups provide one-day intensive training in various software tools important to marketing. These seminars, often costing less than $200, are a great way to become familiar with the latest technology. Likewise, various universities have developed regional and national courses and programs on various aspects of marketing. These programs are aimed at working professionals who need "booster education" or new training.

Marketing Trade Shows. The Exhibitor Show, an annual Las Vegas show for exhibit marketers produced by *Exhibitor* magazine, is an intensive three-day event of vendors and seminars. Similarly, TS/2, another exhibit marketing trade show run by the International Exhibitors Association, provides outstanding programs and vendor exhibits. With the rising importance of trade shows and exhibit marketing, these are good investments.

RESOURCES

1. Rapp, S., and Collins, T. (1988). *Maximarketing: The New Direction in Advertising, Promotion, and Marketing Strategy.* New York: McGraw-Hill.
2. Debelak, D. (1989). *Total Marketing: Capturing Customers with Marketing Plans That Work.* Homewood, IL: Dow Jones-Irwin.
3. Griffin, S. B. (1963). *Sun Tzu's The Art of War.* Oxford University Press. This is only one production of the ancient Chinese general's thoughts on strategy. An interesting read similar to Trout and Ries' *Marketing Warfare.*
4. Schultz, D. E., Tannenbaum, S. I., and Lauterborn, R. F. (1993). *Integrated Marketing Communications: Pulling It Together and Making It Work.* Lincolnwood, IL: NTC Business Books. This book's a good companion to the book you are reading.
5. *Marketing Masters,* 1991. Edited by the American Marketing Association, Chicago, Illinois. These are article reprints on core marketing topics authored by some of the field's best minds. Good reading.
6. Theodore Levitt (1986). *The Marketing Imagination.* New York: The Free Press/Macmillan. Levitt is one of the great minds of marketing, and this book is one of the wisest in the field.

CHAPTER 2

The Warfare of Perceptions: Marketing Is a Noun, Selling Is a Verb

> "A problem properly stated finds its own solution."
>
> —French architect
> Charles E. J. Le Corbusier

Problem solving is the generic task inherent in marketing's role in any organization. But the task of problem solving runs into the roadblocks of conflicting perceptions.

Take two related functions that many people think are the same thing: sales and marketing. Sales and marketing are really very different functions. Most people in the business world really don't understand that. You must. The goal of this chapter is to show you why such differences are important. It's fundamental to reorienting the way you face marketing communications.

- Sales focuses on the close; marketing focuses on the build.
- Sales looks for trees; marketing looks at the forest.
- Marketing is caught up in process and definition. Sales is more concerned with completion.
- Sales gets nervous about tools and fit, while marketing gets nervous about consistency and message.
- Sales tends to be microscopic, while marketing is more "macroscopic."

- In a metaphoric sense, marketing is the noun while sales is the verb. But both are needed to make a complete sentence.

Reduced to one simple axiom, the focus of marketing is on perceptions with the goal of solving problems.

How does your target audience perceive its needs? How does the audience perceive your company's product or service? Tom Peters said it best: "Perception is all there is."

Marketing people who don't understand this rarely succeed. Whether it's product definition, pricing, packaging, or communications, in marketing tasks we must recognize that perception is the soil that nurtures both rose and ragweed.

Gerald A. Michaelson, a leader in American marketing, made an interesting observation to an American Marketing Association leadership conference. He suggested that American marketing has too much impatience. "We just want to plant the seed and then pick the fruit—doing nothing in between." The in-between, he said, is process. We would add to that wisdom that the process involves careful attention to perceptions, be they correct or incorrect.

Marketing communication operatives must understand that they are the ones charged with managing perceptions. In fact, *perception management* is a more functional description of the profession than marketing communications, and the profession's operatives should really be called managers of external perceptions.

INTERNAL OBJECTIVITY AND EXTERNAL PERCEPTIONS

The marketing communication function must, of necessity, deal with two elusive factors: internal objectivity and external perceptions. The true marcom professional is the devil's advocate for spotlighting and interpreting each of these domains.

Internal objectivity is the ability to analyze your firm's communications problem in an unfettered manner. You may have created a good ad campaign but after one year the results show it didn't work. Your name for a product may not be the one that best works for that product. More so, the name your CEO has fallen in love with may not work. Guess what—it's up to you to show the CEO that the name won't work. The same is true if the trade show exhibit you had last year doesn't fit the plan and theme you want this year.

As a marketing or marcom person, you must maintain your objectivity. The worst thing you can do is to blindly convert to the established party line about products, competitors, and the dynamics of your marketplace. Sometimes you will be the bearer of news no one wants to hear, or you may need to use information in a devil's advocate role. Be sure management and colleagues understand the value such objectivity will bring to the overall marketing effort. In short, never marry the natives. This brings us to:

> **DE BONIS & PETERSON BUSINESS MARCOM RULE #2:**
> **"Beware of the 'not invented here' syndrome. Resist becoming a clone."**

Likewise, you must champion the validity of external perceptions. You may think your target audience is wrong about the product they chose for the long term; yours may well be the better long-term buy. The customer may have held on too long to perceptions of your firm generated by past management practices. It is difficult to face such dissonance.

Nonetheless, that is what they think, and you ignore such perceptions at your own risk. The storage bins of American business history, particularly the area of high technology, are crowded with homeless products and failed ventures based on superior ideas that failed one test: perception.

That is not to say you cannot set about to change incorrect perceptions. That is a major goal of many communications plans. We cover such situations in this book. But initially you must help your organization to recognize perceptions in their raw and pristine reality.

GETTING THE BIG PICTURE STRAIGHT FROM THE START

Ralph Waldo Emerson once wisely observed, "The field cannot well be seen from within the field."

How true. Marketers must step out of the field to see it properly, and that takes market research. We devote an entire chapter to research and evaluation, and each "tools" chapter has an ending section on measurement and evaluation. But we thought a word on research is appropriate at this stage if for no other reason but to make you conscious of its importance from the start.

It has become an axiom of business to know your marketplace and know it well. Yet, many business-to-business firms, especially those operating in small niches, believe their original market knowledge plus feedback from field sales will give them adequate information to make decisions. For some companies that can work for a long time. Sadly, however, many markets change underneath companies so fast that nuances are missed while companies attend to everyday operations.

With this in mind, we introduce

> **DE BONIS & PETERSON BUSINESS MARCOM RULE #3:**
> **"Never assume anything about your market, because you can't know it that well."**

By this we mean, you—by yourself—cannot do it. You are too close to the situation and may fall into the danger of believing your own promotional messages. CEOs are great for saying "Hey, I know this market inside and out!" But reality is that CEOs may get caught up in public stock offerings and stockholder issues and bank issues and legal issues and, suddenly, one day they are out of touch.

The remedy? Make sure your communications budget includes some form of market or customer research. We're not saying you have to have a vice president of research. There are many research firms listed with the American Marketing Association. Some specialize in survey research, some on focus groups, and others handle other forms of research. There are also university professors who consult to companies on research, and graduate students who are eager for experience in doing custom research. There are also many companies that provide on-line research reports or do customized collections of secondary research already done in your marketplace. Even if your research largely confirms your intuitions, isn't that insurance money well spent?

WHO NEEDS THE BIG PICTURE AND WHO NEEDS SMALLER PICTURES?

The big picture/small picture dichotomy is important in marketing communications. The reason is that marcom involves managing lots of different projects such as brochures, photo shoots, ads, trade shows, mailers, events. And each project needs project management. The project managers can quickly get lost in each project. Attention to the details is important. Marcom is all about getting the details right so that the project succeeds. But marcom is also about the big picture.

If no one else in your firm can keep the big picture in sight, namely your corporate goals and marketing plan, then you should. The chairman, the CEO, the COO, the CFO—they all have their own distractions away from the big picture. If you are involved in marcom, then you must maintain the balance of the big picture with all the details, the macro view of things as well as the micro view of things. Throughout this book, we will remind you of the macro/micro dichotomy. It's almost analogous to the concept in Eastern philosophy about the inherent balance of life called yin and yang.

HOW PERCEPTIONS KILL IDEAS: MIND-SETS AND MINE FIELDS

One usually doesn't think of Albert Einstein and marketing in the same breath. Yet Einstein said, "Great spirits have always encountered violent opposition from mediocre minds."

We quickly add here that we don't want you to go forward labeling every idea you get as genius and opposing others' ideas as dumb—even if they are. We also don't want you to label all who disagree with you as cursed with mediocre minds.

Arthur Schopenhauer once observed, "Every man takes the limits of his own field of vision for the limits of the world."

Managing communications in a business-to-business firm is often like wading through a sunny pond in summer. All looks well. The weather's nice, the birds are chirping, and the water feels cool and alive. Until you step on someone's discarded broken bottle.

The reality of highly competitive business today is that management finds it difficult to take a long-term view of things. Let's do quick fixes, today—and it better not cost very much either. Sadly, marketing isn't an antibiotic that works overnight. It's a process, a sequence of steps, each needing to work its way through the problem before the next step kicks in.

But if you're the chairman with stockholders upset about a quarterly earnings report, or a CFO looking at overhead costs and the interest rates, you're not very attentive to long-term fixes. That's where the communications professional becomes a teacher of sorts. We'll return to this topic in Chapters 6 and 7, which deal with the communications audit and audit summit. There we will help you learn how to show short-term thinkers the wisdom of long-term programs.

PERCEPTIONS AND PROBLEM SOLVING

The authors of this book are very interested in how people solve problems—CEOs, marketers, anyone for that matter. In marketing you are always solving some problem. It could be the problem of inadequate leads for which a direct response campaign or exhibit training is needed. Maybe it's a pricing problem. But some problem is at the heart of any marketing task.

The key question to ask, however, is what exactly is the problem that needs solving. Charles Kettering, the famed General Motors engineer, put it rather pointedly by asserting, "A problem well stated is a problem half-solved."

Here is where the most fundamental mistakes are made in marketing: The problem isn't precisely defined, or the wrong problem is attacked, or there is a root problem, hidden underneath the surface problem, that no one recognizes or wants to admit exists.

The last of the three is also a perception problem. G. K. Chesterton hit it on the nail, saying "It isn't that they can't see the solution. It's that they can't see the problem."

Let's use a couple of examples. Suppose your sales staff, in an upheaval of frustration, pleads that they need a new brochure—they can't sell without it. Salespeople frequently look for problems to explain away the cold reality of selling: *sales people sell, not brochures.*

As the person responsible for marketing or communications, you must dig further to find out the real problem—the root problem. To do otherwise is to spend lots of time and money on a brochure that isn't attacking the right problem.

To continue the example, here are some problems that might be keeping the sales staff from closing deals:

- The sales staff may need training in closing.
- They may not be reaching the true decision makers or key influences.
- The product line may be out-of-sync with marketplace demands (and this one means that marketing and product development are at fault).
- Product development, engineering, or R&D may not be working closely with marketing.
- Existing literature is features-oriented rather than benefits-oriented (this one means the development of the literature is incorrectly cast).
- The entire lead development program is inadequate, from generating suspects to qualifying them as prospects to adequately responding to requests for proposals (RFPs).
- The customer base may be responding to a negative rumor about company stability and longevity—and you don't know it.
- Competitors may be spreading a rumor about company stability.

We hope you see the point here. It is relatively easy to verbalize a surface problem, but it takes some digging, some customer research, and some analysis to get to the root problem. War-time industrialist Henry J. Kaiser cheerfully claimed that "Problems are only opportunities in work clothes." If you don't solve the root problem, just about everything you do will be incorrectly focused on some surface problem. Why spend time and money that way?

So step one in any marketing task is to precisely and fully state the problem. Agonize over the problem definition, if necessary. Edward Hodnett summarized this particular process well: "A good problem statement often includes: a) what's known, b) what's unknown, and c) what's sought." By designing the problem process this way, you dovetail the discussion with the need to make clear statements of objective.

LEVELS OF KNOWLEDGE AND KNOWING

Take another look at Hodnett's first two elements. Think about the concept of knowledge for a second. There's knowledge, but there also is "un-knowledge." Actually, look at knowledge and knowing in four distinct ways:

1. Knowing something
2. *Thinking* you know something
3. *Knowing* you don't know something
4. *Not knowing* you don't know something.

Which is the worst level of knowledge? Clearly, the fourth; not knowing what you don't know means you are taking actions without regard to factors or events that are invisible to you. Clearly it is better to first find out *what* you don't know, then proceed to understand that information and know it well, and *then* take action. Yet, many companies take actions without being fully aware of important factors—solely for their own lack of inquiry. Remember the words that Arthur Conan Doyle placed in Detective Holmes's mouth: "How dangerous it is to reason from insufficient data."

RESOURCES

1. The team of Al Ries and Jack Trout has written several books which are important marketing manifestos: *Positioning: The Battle for Your Mind* (1986) and *Marketing Warfare* (1986). Another Reis and Trout work is *Bottom-Up Marketing* (1989). All three are published by McGraw-Hill.
2. Levinson, J. C. (1984). *Guerrilla Marketing: Secrets for Making Big Profits from Your Small Business*. Boston: Houghton-Mifflin.
3. Nadler, G., and S. Hibino (1990). *Breakthrough Thinking: Why We Must Change the Way We Solve Problems, and the Seven Principles to Achieve This*. Rocklin, CA: Prima Publishing.
4. Nadler, G. and S. Hibino (1995). *Creative Solution Finding: The Triumph of Full-Spectrum Creativity over Conventional Thinking*. Rocklin, CA: Prima Publishing, Rocklin.
5. Ruchlis, H. (1990). *Clear Thinking: A Practical Introduction*. Buffalo, NY: Prometheus Books.

CHAPTER 3

Tomorrow's Agenda: Damn the Torpedoes!

> "Management by objectives works if you know the objectives. Ninety percent of the time you don't."
>
> —Peter Drucker

This chapter is about making the break. Turning a new leaf. Whether it's the realization that your past approach hasn't worked, a new job you are soon starting, or just an additional assignment handed you, this chapter's for you.

Much of what you can accomplish for your company in the long term will be determined by how you handle marketing communications in the short term. If you are starting a new job, how you handle your first week is critical. In fact, you should begin the process before you start the new position. The moment you accept the offer and determine the start date, specify to the department secretary or to department colleagues the information you would like collected and readied for your arrival. The information we have in mind is covered in this and the next five chapters. Such preplanning sends the clear message that you are a "take charge" communications manager and sets up a positive impression.

This will also help keep you from getting lost your first week on the job. It is very easy for marketing communication people to get lost their first week because of the many inherited projects in production. Some of those who get lost still manage to produce lots of flashy brochures, even for years. But what their colleagues perceive is "seat-of-the-pants" paper shuffling as the company loses control of the big picture: *positive external perception.* You can rise above that.

This chapter will also give you a new appreciation of objectives. Reread Peter Drucker's opening quote. It is appropriate to this chapter, especially when you use the word *objective* in the same context as the word *agenda*. Within companies, different executives often have different objectives or agendas. You need to know what they are.

WHAT'S ON DEADLINE?
YOUR INTRODUCTION TO JUGGLING

If you're starting a new job, have an up-to-date production schedule available for your first day. It can be organized in two ways: category-driven or event-driven.

A category-driven production schedule simply lists each project under the various forms of marcom, for example, ads, collateral, trade shows, special events, media relations, financial relations, and so on. Using computer spreadsheets, you can outline deadlines, costs, delivery dates, press checks, photo shoots, check request dates—whatever you need to manage the project.

An event-driven production schedule lists all projects of whatever kind under the event or activity that requires them. For example, an upcoming analyst tour for your chairman would list all the financial reports, product literature, press interviews, and so on needed to support that tour. Your attendance and exhibit at an expo will list all the exhibit construction deadlines, lead forms, data sheets, presentations, demo scripts, press interviews, hosted meals, sales training, and hospitality room requirements.

A word of recommendation: go for the event-driven schedule. It is much easier to see what's missing using that approach.

THE MARKETING PLAN AND WHERE MARCOM FITS

If you work for the top marketer, by all means try to get a copy of the company marketing plan to study before starting the job. It will tell you a lot about the presumptions the company is making.

If market research has been done, such research is likely summarized in the plan. If no market research has been done, that's a bad news/good news scenario. The absence of any research says either they believe their knowledge is so faultless they only need a wet finger in the air, or the budget is so low that research never gets included. The good news is that you can be the hero who argues successfully for doing market research.

The general marketing plan and its budget will also tell you how much they have thought about the role of and expectations for marketing communications.

- Given management's expectations, is marcom adequately funded?

- Is the timeline for change too ambitious and unrealistic?
- Does the plan spotlight prejudices they have for or against one or another marcom tool (for example, direct mail)?

The budget will tell you a great deal, because in many ways the power is in the budget. You quickly need to determine if that budget is hard or soft—in other words, does management live and plan by it, or is it something submitted to the CFO once per year and then ignored? In general, do the budget and their expectations have realistic presumptions? Conveniently, budgets and expectations bring us to:

DE BONIS & PETERSON BUSINESS MARCOM RULE #4:
"Integrated marketing communications is not a quick fix. It, too, takes time."

A Marcom Timetable

Implementing a marketing communications program, especially one that is integrated, requires planning and management. It's a 9-step process, which is outlined below. The individual components of this plan are discussed throughout the book.

1. Review the marcom objectives. This is discussed in Chapters 1 and 2.
   - Where does marcom fit in the overall marketing plan: internal and external dimensions?
   - Each campaign is then executed for each specific group of customers using a set of marcom tools that are uniquely appropriate to satisfying the objectives.
2. Establish marcom strategy(ies). This is discussed in Chapter 4.
   - What are the short- and long-term external objectives for each customer segment? What are the customers doing now in terms of buying behavior? What do we want them to do?
     For example, the objective for loyal customers may be to maintain their present level of usage, to increase their level of usage, or to create new business usages. Additional objectives may be set for prospects, influences, and so on.
   - What are the short- and long-term internal objectives? What are the individual agendas of management, sales, marketing, communications, legal, and so on.
   - How should the marcom budget be established?
3. Perform relevant target market research. This is discussed in Chapter 5.
   - What's the net lifetime value for each market segment?
   - What are the relevant demographics?
   - What are the relevant psychographics?

- What are the relevant infographics?

4. Conduct a thorough marcom audit. This is discussed in Chapter 6. An audit tells you what is currently being communicated internally and externally, through both formal and informal communications, at all touchpoints within the organization and with customers.

5. Draft a preliminary MIP™ (Marketing Information Platform). The MIP is discussed in several chapters, specifically Chapters 6 and 7. An MIP outline template is provided in Appendix A.

   The marketing information platform is the framework on which all marcom is based. It provides not only strategic guidelines for meeting marcom objectives, but creative guidelines as well.

6. Hold an integrated marketing communication (IMC) summit meeting. This is the focus of Chapter 7. The major functions of the summit meeting are to

   - Review the MIP
   - Validate, adjust, or create the organizational base positioning statement
   - Review and create a final draft of the MIP
   - Achieve consensus and sign-off
   - Distribute the results internally so that there is marcom consistency in all internal and external communications

7. Execute the marcom strategies and tactics. Chapters 9 through 19 are the "how to" chapters, each keying on a specific marcom activity.

   A major key to successfully implementing an IMC strategy is to develop what would typically be defined as a production management chart or a Gantt chart, named after the efficiency expert who designed it, depicted in Figure 3.1. Each of the marcom activities is scheduled and coordinated with all of the other activities across a

FIGURE 3.1 *Marcom Management Chart*

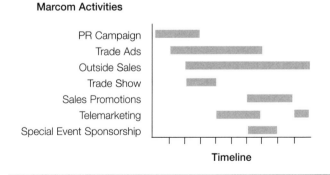

timeline, which could be days, weeks, months, or years. This will also be relevant when assessing the impact of the marcom program.

8. Conduct follow-up research and evaluation. This is also discussed in Chapter 5. This includes a marcom return-on-investment analysis, which attempts to provide a way to demonstrate accountability for marcom activities.

9. Reset the marcom strategy(ies) and tactic(s) to zero. This is discussed later in this chapter. The implication is that each project or fiscal year's marcom shouldn't simply be a repeat of what was done before, but should be planned and justified as if no marcom had occurred previously.

MARKETING ORGANIZATIONS: CORPORATE VERSUS DIVISIONS

As companies press into international markets, the job of corporate marketing becomes much more complex. Issues of market peculiarities, nationalism, cultural differences, language differences, legal differences, and local loyalties are the factors of this complexity.

Likewise, corporate acquisition programs add to the complexity of marketing as competitors are purchased and their product lines absorbed. Chapter 8, "Product Identity," deals partly with this topic.

Ask for an organizational chart of corporate marketing to determine who controls the marketing for international operations as well as the acquired divisions and subsidiaries. This has significant impact on everything from print runs to local project management, from travel obligations to design implications.

What Is the Chairman's Real Agenda?

If your firm is a publicly-held corporation, you already realize how much more complex all communications issues are. We have included an entire chapter on financial/investor relations to show you the issues (Chapter 16).

The Japanese are critical of American corporations, in part, for what they perceive as a preoccupation with short-term performance versus long-term growth. We believe this criticism is true. In a sense, publicly-held corporations almost have dual marketing personalities. There's the product-oriented personality concerned with beating the competition, gaining market share, and growing in its category. The other side is the Wall Street personality concerned with quarterly numbers and stockholder smiles. Each personality often seems to fight the other for dominance.

The chairman of the board of your company is the person primarily focused on the Wall Street side. In short, you need to know the chairman's agenda. Is the chairman's agenda increasing the stock's price? Is it showing increasingly higher revenue numbers for the next three quarters? Is the chairman primarily concerned with pleasing the venture capitalists on the board who merely want to sell the company when the stock value hits a magic number?

If you don't know the chairman's agenda, it can have an impact on a number of your activities. First and foremost, it affects your management of the annual report and financial press tours. But it can also have an effect on product promotions and sales announcements.

If you are interviewing for a job, it is a good idea to meet the chairman and the CEO. Show your awareness of the dual personality implications on communications. Try to identify the chairman's agenda. You may not learn that agenda the first week, but try to show your genuine interest in such a way that superiors realize you have logic and process behind your inquiry.

The CEO's Agenda

The president/CEO is also concerned with Wall Street and board politics, but product and sales rank right up at the top, too. The most important thing you need to know is the CEO's attitude toward both marketing and the marketing department. You won't find it out quickly, but it will prove handy when you do. For example, is marketing adequately funded given the organizational chart and the revenue projections? Did the CEO come from marketing, sales management, customer service, manufacturing, product development, or human resources? This tells you something of the CEO's professional training and orientation. It also might suggest something about the company's plans and agenda, such as whether the company is sales-driven or contract-driven, engineering-driven or marketing-driven.

How much does the CEO know about marketing? In the initial meeting, ask the CEO what he or she thinks of marketing and what his or her reservations are. It may be the first time such a question has ever been asked! Just asking the question may make a good impression.

Your Visit with the VP of Sales

Never accept a job in marketing without at least talking with the sales manager on the phone. You will work very closely with this person and you need to know the person's background, training, experience, and management style.

The sales manager's attitude toward marketing and the marketing department is important information.

- What do the salespeople think of marketing and the marketing department?
- Ask about sales philosophy, and find out which sales training programs new field reps are required to complete.
- Can you work with reps in the field?

- Can you attend the sales training class?
- Better yet, can you be included in sales meetings?
- Who's the best field rep and why?
- What's the single biggest reason for a sales rep's failure in this company, other than the obvious lack of closes?
- Which field rep has the keenest awareness of competitive advantages and disadvantages?

These questions will help you understand the scope of the communications task you are embracing, and they show the sales manager the depth of inquiry you see necessary for handling the job.

Your Visit with the Company Attorney

Marketers often develop conflicts with their corporate attorneys, but there really is no need for it. The attorney is concerned that corporate assets not be compromised by product liabilities suits, stockholder actions, SEC actions, or trademark issues. Thus, what the company says in its external communications has an impact on the attorney's responsibilities.

In your first meeting with the corporate attorney, identify where there have been past problems. Make known your awareness of how copy in advertising can be overly promissory and thus expose the company to lawsuits. (See Appendix E on legal guidelines for copywriting). Make known your awareness of financial issues such as prior knowledge, material disclosure, insider information, and the SEC requirements for equitable news distribution (see Chapter 16).

Ask if a corporate style guide is available to give guidance on the treatment of logos, company descriptions, copyright and trademark issues, and so on. If the attorney sighs and says no, you have a "bird-in-the-hand" opportunity to ask if you can lead the way in developing such a guide in collaboration with the attorney.

Handled correctly, you can leave this meeting with the attorney believing he or she finally has someone in marketing who understands the legal implications of external communications.

Your Visit with the CFO

We wish we could make big promises to you regarding the CFO. Although some people in accounting and finance may be more broadly educated than their colleagues, those with narrower focus are still found in many firms.

But in all fairness, part of the problem is on marketing's side, too. Marketing, as a profession, doesn't have the certification and licensing requirements of the financial professions. Measurement and evaluation of marketing programs is often incomplete or nonexistent. Marketing has its own perception problems in corporate life, where some colleagues dismiss marketers as the guys who deal in happy talk and imprinted golf shirts. And as we have said elsewhere in this book, marketing budgets are typically big and therefore conspicuous to the CFO.

There are two important things you can do in your first meeting with the CFO, a meeting you should request. First, indicate to the CFO the process approach you will take to external communications. Chapters 6 and 7 deal with this process by showing you how to conduct a communications audit and how to develop a consensus platform for action. Indicate to the CFO your desire for his or her participation in the audit process.

Second, find out the CFO's attitude toward and problems with marketing in general. It could be the budgeting process or a constant stream of surprise check requests that throw off cash management.

Maybe the CFO has no problem and the relationship with your department is fine. That can happen. One of the authors of this book once dealt with a comptroller who walked into his office one day to announce that marketing was underfunded. (You will experience this not more than once in your career!)

WHO'S ON FIRST?

The visits you make with all these executives should give you a fairly good idea of what makes the company tick. Is it sales- or transaction-driven, or is it relationship-driven? The former is a common phenomenon.

After you reach some assessment of what drives the company, meet with your colleagues and your superior to see if they agree with your assessment. Since you are giving them something to react to, you will get a reaction. Their nodding agreement, their quick denial—or their defensiveness—will tell you more than you knew before.

Why is all this important? Quite simply, you need to know the corporate culture in order to represent it to the outside world. If you proceed to describe the company in external communications as relationship-driven when management and the world perceive it as transaction-driven, your efforts won't work. In the business-to-business arena, corporate customers and the trade press that follows an industry can't be fooled easily.

READING THE AGENCIES' MINDS

Once you have a comfortable assessment of the corporate culture and marketing's role within it, it is time to meet with the firm's marketing agencies and get their view of things.

Ask the ad agency to describe the approval process for advertising. Their answer will tell you a great deal about what it's like to get things done in your firm.

- Are six or seven different executives' signatures needed, or is approval handled by the top marketer and the CEO?
- Is the first-draft copy and art "comp" (comprehensive) approved immediately or, on the other hand, do numerous first-draft comps have to be paraded before a committee before approval is reached?
- Does the agency believe they are getting all the information they need, i.e., the whole story, before they go to creative?
- Has the agency ever considered resigning the account and, if so, when and for what reasons?

The maturity and sophistication of a marketing department is really spotlighted by the relationship with its ad agency.

Much is also learned by examining the firm's relationship to its public relations firm and exhibit vendor.

- Ask the public relations firm if they believe they are given all the information they need to adequately represent the client.
- Ask them to grade the marketing department on media interviews and media credibility.
- How difficult is it for the public relations firm to convince the client of the need for such time-consuming activities as a press tour?
- How does the client react to question-and-answer (Q & A) briefings and rehearsals?
- Is the client willing to rehearse for interviews, or do the executives bluster that they know what to say and can handle any reporter?
- Is management in love with outdated ideas such as press conferences and the "release-per-week-no-matter-what" style of media relations?
- Similarly, ask the exhibit vendor if the firm is tied emotionally to the outdated notion that a company must own its own trade show exhibit.
- Does the client listen to recommendations about exhibit layout, traffic flow, and graphics?
- Does the vendor think the exhibit personnel have the right training for trade show selling and qualifying?

These questions will tell you a great deal about how long it takes to get things done, and what the "threshold of pain" is regarding projects, changes, and new ideas.

GATHERING AVAILABLE INFORMATION

At the beginning of the chapter we mentioned the need to collect information before you even arrive on the job. Aside from the items already mentioned, here are other items you will need:

- A summary of the industry and its history
- Copies of the key trade publications and their year-end wrap-ups
- Exhibitor directories from the key trade shows attended
- Organizational structure of the company
- Organizational structure of the marketing department
- Last two annual reports
- Last employee annual report (if they have one)
- Corporate capabilities brochure
- Product catalog or data sheets
- Employee newsletters
- Customer newsletters and magazines
- Profiles or resumes of your staff members

GENERAL NEEDS ASSESSMENT: INHERITED PROJECTS AND STAFF

Early in your tenure, you will need to assess staff strengths and weaknesses. Asking staff for their resumes will definitely not build morale, but your first staff meeting can start with something like this: "I'm new, we don't know each other, but I would like to get an understanding of your backgrounds. Please provide me with whatever you feel will do that, and also let me know what you believe is your best work here. Oh, and here's my resume so you can know more about me."

After you get a packet or portfolio from each staffer, schedule a time to meet with each one for coffee or lunch. The place should be relatively private and nonthreatening. Give them a chance to talk extemporaneously with little interruption from you. Get a sense for their frustrations and their work style, and what personal workplace pet-peeves they have.

Lastly, try to schedule a regular, weekly time to meet with each person. Instead of discussing projects, this set weekly appointment is for the staffer to talk about whatever is on his or her mind. These "one-on-ones," used so effectively at Intel Corporation, for example, will become an important element in managing your new team members.

These management tools will help you assess the right match between staff people and projects.

RESETTING THE MARCOM BUDGET TO ZERO

One important caveat should be noted. These marcom guidelines and integrated marketing communications strategy are not intended to provide an absolute formula for your organization's marketing communications strategies or tactics. A formula implies two things: a lack of flexibility and guaranteed results.

Any marcom program must be tailored to the individual organization. Some strategies and tactics are going to be more important than others. Some elements of an IMC strategy are going to be less applicable. The key is to select those components that work best for your organization. Through a process of constant testing and review, you will develop the ability to modify marcom programs to achieve desired—not guaranteed—results.

It is important that each annual marcom plan and each individual marcom project be planned using a "zero-based" marcom approach, a concept borrowed from the "zero-based" budgeting technique. Zero-based budgets start from the presumption that there were no expenditures the previous year. Many times budgeting is done by simply increasing last year's expenditures by a percentage. This year you budgeted $500 for paper clips; the paper clip budget for next year is 10 percent more, $550. This despite the fact that there's a $200 paper clip inventory remaining at the end of the year or that your company has gone to a completely paperless environment in which paper clips won't be needed.

A zero-based marcom plan or budget doesn't assume that, because your company was an exhibitor in a trade show last year, you should participate in the same show this year, or spend the same amount of money. A zero-based approach determines whether being at the trade show is important for your customers, as is discussed in Chapter 12, and rejustifies the expense. Each planned marcom activity goes through the same justification process. This makes it easier to establish a budget, which we discuss more in Chapter 4.

RESOURCES

1. Pincus, J. D., and J. N. De Bonis (1994). *Top Dog*. New York: McGraw-Hill. This is a fascinating study of CEOs and CEO "wannabes" and how they can and should become chief communications officers for their firms.
2. Ryans, J. K., Jr., and P. A. Rau (1990). *Marketing Strategies for the New Europe: A North American Perspective on 1992*. Chicago: The American Marketing Association. Granted, the subtitle about 1992 dates the book, but the contents provide good information nonetheless.

CHAPTER 4

Defining Markets and Matching Messages: What Business Are You In?

> "Precision of communications is important, more important than ever, in our era of hair-trigger balances, when a false or misunderstood word may create as much disaster as a sudden thoughtless act."
>
> —author James Thurber

As a marketing communication professional, preciseness is essential at all steps. Today's market niches are too narrow to operate with inexact assumptions and definitions. That includes imprecise definitions of target audiences, media, and the integrated tailored messages sent to those audiences using those media.

One reason for being precise is that it makes the later creative process more responsive. Also, many business people just don't perceive advertising and public relations people as being logical, precise thinkers. Another reason is that measurement and evaluation opportunities are enhanced if the reference points have been carefully crafted.

This chapter deals with defining audiences. Such an exercise is essential to the communication audit process and the resulting communication strategy and tactics.

Let's consider an example of the implications of imprecise definitions. Public relations is a term crying out for preciseness. For many companies, especially in the business-to-business arena, the term just doesn't work very well. It is also a term encumbered by misplaced glamour and untrue images.

If your marketplace is the general public, as is the case for a supermarket, you have an interest in public relations. But if your market is a business-to-business environment, the general public as such is a secondary concern. We recommend breaking down various relationships using terms such as community relations, media relations, dealer relations, government relations, investor relations, and so on. This enables you to craft messages that fit the task. Nonetheless, Chapter 15 in this book is titled "Public Relations" and covers the broad sense of the term, especially media relations. This is necessary because the term *public relations* is familiar to you, the reader, and we must deal with it first on that basis before we introduce more specific definitions.

The following sections ask questions about target audiences and their habits. These questions can be found in the Marketing Information Platform (MIP) we introduce you to in the upcoming chapters on the communication audit and marcom summit.

JUST WHAT DO YOU SELL AND IN WHICH MARKET?

The question "Just what do you sell and in which market?" can prompt very long discussions for companies in dynamic markets. It is not unusual for management to be unaware of the real motivators for customer purchases. Identifying the real, perceived "value-added" is often the answer to this important, albeit time-consuming, question.

It is well worth the time. The CEO, vice president of marketing, and vice president of sales will consider it a very valuable exercise. Changes will be made as a result of this one question.

Why is this question so important? Let's use an example from a consumer packaged goods company. Acme Foods manufactures and sells a variety of snack foods and packaged meals to distributors and retailers, including frozen mini-pizzas, TV dinners, and dinner vegetable entrees. Acme's TV dinners, for example, are rated the highest in taste tests. The company's trade ads and promotions, and consumer advertising focus on this attribute. In certain metro areas, however, Acme is losing TV dinner sales. The distributors and store managers can't offer much of an explanation.

Acme's product management structure and promotions are based on the assumption that consumers think in terms of an Acme TV dinner versus other TV dinner brands. But the consumer doesn't think that way. The consumer gets home late and doesn't want to cook anything. Instead, the consumer calls Domino's Pizza to order one large combo special to be delivered. The question of competing TV dinners never comes up!

The competition for Acme TV dinners isn't other TV dinners. It is fast-food alternatives. This marketing myopia, or lack of understanding of the market, is one of the inherent flaws in consumer brand and product management. Remember our discussion in Chapter 2 on the warfare of perceptions?

The lesson is that, as you analyze what your business-to-business firm really sells, you should try to break down categories. Think the way your customer thinks and, if you don't know how your customer thinks, read Chapter 5 on research and evaluation. Mentally turn around your presumed categories and industry niche descriptions. Look at them vertically instead of horizontally, from the top rather than from the bottom. Acme's challenge is to convince consumers that the TV dinner or frozen pizza in the freezer is a better alternative to a pizza delivery store, and to work with distributors and retailers to get that message not only to the end user, but to all members of the distribution chain.

Even in large-ticket capital equipment purchases, the equipment you sell may not *really* be what the customer is buying. There was an expression in the 1970s that "you can't get fired buying IBM." Were IBM's business mainframes technologically superior to other computers? Some believe Univac and Control Data had superior products. What was the guy in the MIS center really buying in those days? It wasn't the computers themselves, but rather career safety and security.

As far as the MIS manager is concerned, those qualities are part of the invisible packaging, the value-added bundle. Never underestimate the role that emotions and fear play in large capital purchases where you would think quantitative analysis and logic rule the decision.

THE COMPETITION: WHO ELSE IS IN THE GAME?

The business-to-business world is no less competitive than consumer/packaged goods markets. New competitors, often smaller and more agile, can undercut the prices of established firms whose overhead and thinking compel higher prices. New technology based on industry standards can make life difficult for firms that once ruled the domain with proprietary offerings.

You can analyze competition in the following ways:

- What firms are direct competitors with the same package offering of product and support? A tell-tale sign is that your management used to be with ABC Corp. or your best field reps came from XYZ Inc.

- What firms are attacking only one of your flanks, for example, post-sale support, repairs, international?
- What new firms are using more common industry standards to offer customers the same results you offer?
- What firms are one-country competitors only, for example, a dominant competitor in France only or another one in England only?

HOW DO YOU COMPARE?

You need to determine the strengths and weaknesses of each competitor. List them market by market, region by region, nation by nation. A firm that is a strong competitor in Europe may be a weak one in Australia. Find out why. The field sales reps and management in the various subsidiaries can offer this analysis. They will know which competitor always makes customer "short lists" of vendor candidates.

The other half of the competitive analysis is to compare your firm's relative strengths and weaknesses against each competitor *in each market*. Given tight budgets, it may be necessary to spend less on marketing communications in, say, the Germanic markets and put that promotional clout into the Asia Pacific markets. You will seldom be dominant in all markets and you will seldom have the budget to promote heavily in all markets. You need this analysis to make prudent choices.

This exercise can be fruitless if you, your management, and your field sales reps gloss over your firm's weaknesses. The discussion of strengths and weaknesses is one of the main tasks of the communications audit and the summit meeting you will read about in the next chapters. If your product offering is not making the short list in one market, you may need to withdraw from it or consider developing a special product line for that market.

WHAT DO THEY READ? TARGET INFOGRAPHICS

Your firm's target audience likely has several professional trade publications that keep customers informed about industry developments and industry politics. These publications are obvious candidates for corporate image advertising and product advertising, plus their mailing lists can be used for direct response marketing. The term we use to define the information usage characteristics of market segments is *infographics*.

Infographics identifies what sources of information buyers in a segment seek out, utilize and rely upon to make or validate buying decisions, and when and where those sources are used. This is different than mediagraphics, which describes the characteristics of the readers, viewers or listeners of a specific media outlet. Infographic data includes

- Traditional descriptors reflecting prospect and customer media habits
- The relative weight assigned to these information resources
- Other characteristics such as source credibility and the impact of one- versus two-sided information.

Sources could also include trade shows or other major events the target might attend. (Infographics is discussed more completely in Chapter 9.)

Of course, the editorial content is what the readers want, and herein lie some important considerations. In researching your target audience, you need to ask two fundamentally different questions about trade publications: What trade publication do you regularly read? And what trade publication is a "must read" to keep up-to-date with your field?

There is a big difference between these two questions. The answer to the first may well be a newsletter or weekly newspaper with industry gossip and personnel moves. It gets picked up quickly, read in small time slots during the first day, but probably doesn't have much shelf life. The answer to the second question is likely to be a more in-depth treatment of the profession or industry developments, typically with longer articles the reader may keep on the shelf for months or even a year.

Application articles or technical articles favoring your firm's product or service might be better aimed at the second publication, but management and contract announcements will be read faster in the former publication.

What Would They Read If It Were Available:

In spite of the thousands of trade publications servicing every SIC code imaginable, you may one day find yourself in a niche that really isn't served well by any publication that exactly matches your advertising and editorial needs. Should you grin and bear it? Use slightly off-the-bubble publications? Or should you produce your own publication?

We don't mean the typical customer newsletter here, but rather a substantive publication with feature articles that has shelf life and truly serves the needs of your target audience. It might even solicit articles from customers, providing them a chance for recognition unavailable in the existing magazines. Obviously launching such a publication is a major expense and commitment. You should do it only when market research clearly spotlights the void and only after gathering a representative sampling of customers in a focus group to identify their editorial wishes.

WHAT DO THEY ATTEND?

Every industry has at least one annual trade show that attracts all the companies. In addition, many regional shows servicing local marketing differences provide less expensive selling opportunities.

Find out what shows your customers attend. You also need to find out why they attend a show. It may well differ depending on the person's job title. For example, going to a trade show might be considered a reward for a lower-level manager who has little purchase influence, but it could be a must-show for an upper-level manager. If presentations at general sessions or seminars is your main marketing tactic at a show, you must find out if your customers attend such sessions or prefer to walk around the exhibition hall where you don't display. The same is true for the reverse situation. Be sure you read Chapter 12 on trade shows and exhibit marketing.

What Would They Attend If It Were Available?

As we say in Chapter 13 on event marketing, you don't have to play cards with the deck dealt to you. If your market research indicates there is no clear match between your kind of customer and the trade shows servicing their industry, you might consider producing your own event.

It could be a small trade show, a series of regional shows, a seminar road show at major airport hubs, or a single annual event. It's a big investment. However, you control the elements, the costs, and the agenda, rather than tolerating the agenda of a trade show producer.

WHAT INDEPENDENT CONSULTANTS DO THEY USE OR FOLLOW?

Most industries have consultants with years of corporate experience who now offer their expertise for a fee. Many publish newsletters. Customers tend to gravitate to such consultants because of perceived objectivity. Whether they are objective or not is another story, but you need to find out who the gurus are and why. At the very least, you will want to include them in news announcements and press tours, or even feature them as speakers in a road show seminar series.

WHAT TRAINING ARE THEY SEARCHING FOR?

Your market research may identify gaps in customer understanding or education, especially if fast technological developments are influencing customer environments. It may be worth the effort to do further research to find a training niche you can enter. Focus groups of representative customers can help to identify these training gaps. In such instances, positioning your company as a leader is made easier by the industry training seminars you offer.

WHO ELSE IS INVOLVED IN SPECIFYING AND DECIDING?

In any survey research of your customer base, you need to clearly differentiate those who specify products or services for purchase, those who make the decisions, and those who merely complain. Database marketing can then tailor the company message according to key influence factors.

Is a purchasing committee assembled, and how long does the committee operate before making a decision? Depending on price and the company's legal status, a board of directors' decision may also be necessary.

CREATING A BUDGET THAT SELLS

Too often, a client's marcom budget seems to be arbitrarily set or based on some sense of "what we can afford." A budget number is provided— $100,000 for a direct mail lead-generation campaign, for example—and the marcom activities are squeezed and trimmed and poked and prodded to fit into that budget straightjacket.

That's like your boss allotting you $100 to fly from Chicago to Los Angeles, which would normally cost $400. You respond, "I need another $300 to get to L.A." and your boss says, "Well, that's all I can allow, so go as far as you can." And you end up in St. Louis, a long way from Southern California.

Marcom budgeting should be objective and task-based. Marcom objectives that support the overall marketing strategy have been established. Each objective is going to require an integrated combination of marcom activities. These marcom activities are going to each require X amount of budget dollars. For example, using our previous scenario, a lead-generation direct mail campaign using a highly targeted business list, a well-designed, high-quality brochure, and a 24-hour-a-day inbound customer service center 800 number may cost $135,000. The budget should be $135,000.

Projecting budgets becomes easier as the management of the marcom integration becomes more efficient and uses the zero-based marcom approach described in Chapter 3. It also becomes easier to develop and request budgets if a return-on-investment analysis is conducted for marcom projects, as we discuss in Chapter 5.

RESOURCES

1. Roger Von Oech wrote two great books on creative thinking strategies: *A Whack on the Side of the Head* (1983), Menlo Park, CA: Creative Think; and *A Kick in the Seat of the Pants* (1986), New York: Harper & Row. We suggest these books on creative thinking to help you with question number one in this chapter: What is it that you really sell? Both books are quick reads with reflective questions and activities.

Building a Macro Platform for Marcom

Part 2 is about the necessary step of collecting the right information and sorting through it to build a foundation for action. Properly constructed, this foundation or platform for action helps you to build a consensus in your organization that will give you the latitude to act effectively—and relatively independently.

You need to master several roles to build the consensus and construct the communication platform. Diplomacy helps, but being a devil's advocate helps more. At this stage of the game, you are primarily asking lots of questions. You are challenging assumptions. You will use all you know about marketing communication in a teaching role as well. You will be the disinterested observer who can step back and raise a red flag when something doesn't make sense. Otherwise, you might blindly believe everything you hear. Keep in mind, vested interests and "turf" mentalities often have viral effects on the corporate body. You are there to do things differently—to show them a new way. You must never "marry the natives." In a very real sense, you are engaging in what we call "zero-based marcom."

Done correctly, you will have the chance to build respect for what you are doing so that your "helicopter" colleagues will realize they no longer need to hover over everything in marketing communications.

The final chapter in this part deals with corporate and product identity. These are really the totality of all of a company's perceived image—the macro of all macros—but here we will discuss identity in terms of names, logos, and design factors.

CHAPTER 5

Research and Evaluation: No More Wet Fingers in the Air

> "Most new discoveries are suddenly seen things that were always there."
>
> —philosopher Suzanne Langer

Your marcom budget proposal for next fiscal year includes money for marcom research activities, an item that has traditionally fallen to the budget ax despite the fact that funds are allocated for marketing research. This year you are determined to sell the expenditures by providing justification for your request.

What is your argument?

Measurement and evaluation is a subtopic in each of the tactical nuts-and-bolts chapters that follow because research should be an ongoing, integral part of the marcom decision-making and post-implementation review processes.

This chapter talks about selling research internally and about some basic research procedures that are important to obtaining valid, reliable results.[1]

Management typically doesn't want to spend money on research. It's one of the first things cut from the budget. Not only is it hard to demonstrate a direct, absolute return on investment (ROI) for the research dollars, but management in many cases believes that research is redundant. Managers may say, "We know this business, we know the market, and our reps are in touch with our buyers. So why do we need research—especially research that is contracted out to a third party who doesn't know as much as we do?" It's almost as if management believes that admitting there is a need for research compromises its management potency.

The result is what we call the "wet finger in the air" decision-making style—"If I wet my finger and stick it up in the air, I can tell which way the wind is blowing. That's all I need."

Figure 5.1 shows the top five activities on which 1992 business-to-business promotional dollars were spent, according to the Business Marketing Association (BMA).

In contrast, only 18 percent of the business-to-business marketers surveyed indicated that they spent money on marcom research; marcom research budgets represented less than five percent of their annual promotional budgets.

CHECKLIST OF DO'S AND DON'TS

- Do's:
    1. Do abandon the "wet finger in the air" decision-making style.
    2. Do make sure that the research has a specific objective and that the method used satisfies that objective.
    3. Do research one issue at a time.
    4. Do use someone who knows research and can help construct valid, reliable research projects.

FIGURE 5.1   *The Top Five Business-to-Business Promotional Activities for 1992*

1992 BMA Survey of Business-to-Business Marketers	*Percentage of Companies Surveyed Engaged in This Marcom Channel*	*Estimated Percentage of Promotional Budget Spent on Marcom Activities in This Channel*
Narrowly Targeted Special Trade Publications	80%	25%
Trade Shows and Exhibits	74%	13.2%
Direct Mail	66%	6.8%
Company Catalogs	61%	6.2%
Publicity and Public Relations	60%	4.7%

Source: Adapted from George E. Belch and Michael A. Belch, *Introduction to Advertising and Public Relations* (Burr Ridge, IL: Irwin, 1993), p. 722.

- Don'ts:
  1. Don't jump into marcom research at the last minute. Make research a part of the integral long-range marcom plan.
  2. Don't put too much into one study. One big omnibus study doesn't equal several small, well-targeted, well-defined studies.
  3. Don't rely on focus groups as the sole source of data for decision making or for posttest analysis. Focus groups are overused as a research tool; focus group data should be augmented when feasible and possible with other research.

OBJECTIVES OF MARCOM RESEARCH

Marcom research presumes that marcom objectives have been established, as described in the example provided in Figure 5.2. These objectives aren't only necessary for developing marcom activities, but are essential for both pre- and post-testing to take place.

Marcom research pretesting benchmarks the present status of the target, including information already possessed, attitudes held, and intended behavior. Pretesting also seeks to understand the information needs and expectations of opinion leaders, users, deciders, buyers, key influences, and gatekeepers in both the internal and external environments, and what to say to these people, how best to say it, when to say it, and where to say it. This includes identifying the demographics, psychographics, and infographics of these targets as we have discussed in earlier chapters.

Benchmarking allows you to develop objectives for desired change and degree of change as a result of marcom and to subsequently test the effectiveness of the marcom against that standard.

If for no other reason, marcom research determines top-of-mind attitudes among your targets so that your communications are congruent, regardless of whether you like those attitudes or not. It is absurd to develop sales materials and trade ads that loudly proclaim your company's quality standard when the components you ship have a reputation of having one of the highest rejection rates in the industry.

It is important to understand that research is not the end, but the means to an end. Research doesn't make the decision. It is another tool for gathering information to help those who ultimately have the decision-making responsibility. Marcom research should provide accurate and useful information for better decision making in planning marcom activities, as well as providing a post-measure of effectiveness, both powerful strategic justification for research dollars. And it helps satisfy top management's need for data, not guesses.

FIGURE 5.2   *An Example of Measurable Marcom Objectives*

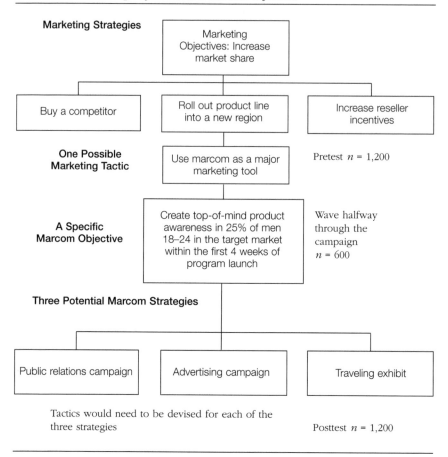

A GENERAL MARCOM RESEARCH PROCESS

Any type of research uses a relatively standard procedure, which is briefly discussed here not only as a primer, but for a checklist to evaluate vendors that may be conducting studies on your behalf.[2]

Define the Problem.   What is it you need or want to know and why? Is it to develop a marcom plan, identify marcom opportunities, solve a marcom problem, or evaluate a marcom activity's effectiveness? This will help formulate what information is needed and how to obtain that information.

If it's to create a marcom message, the concern may be what should be said. Possible research questions would include what message and marcom would be most effective. Pretest methodologies might include those in Figure 5.3.

FIGURE 5.3 *Matrix of Possible Pretest and Posttest Marcom Research*

Potential Marcom Pretests
- Attention-getting value
- Awareness tests
- Comprehension tests
- Concept tests
- Source credibility tests
- Reaction tests: attitude, like or dislike of the concept
- Purchase intent
- Readability of the marcom message
- Media mix acceptability

Potential Pretest Methodologies
- Descriptive surveys: phone, mail, in person
- Analytical surveys [1]
- Content analysis of marcom messages
- Personal interviews
- Focus groups
- Field experiments: market tests, split-run tests
- Lab experiments: theater tests, lab store tests
- Field observations
- Physiological testing

Potential Marcom Posttests
- Awareness tests
- Recognition tests
- Recall tests
- Behavioral results: inquiries, sales, attendance, and so on
- Attitude changes

Potential Posttest Methodologies
- Surveys
- Personal interviews
- Store audits
- Focus groups
- Field observation
- Case studies

[1] A descriptive survey describes current attitudes, perceptions, or conditions. An analytical survey attempts to explain why the attitudes, perceptions, or conditions exist.

If the objective is to create a more customer service–oriented attitude company-wide, one research question would be what the current attitudes toward customer service are; another might be what are the levels of customer service perceived from within the organization compared with what the customers say they experience. Another research question might be which managers or employees are important opinion leaders who should be targeted.

Collect Secondary Information. A lot of data already exist, either internally or external to your organization. Company files and reports, sales reports and other transaction data, marketing reports, and general archival information may answer some of the questions without further research. Secondary data—compiled outside the organization—are available from a variety of sources: syndicated research organizations, libraries and other on-line resources, government agencies, trade associations, trade and academic publications, or general business trades publications, to name a few.

Select and Design the Research Method.   If primary data *are* to be collected, the research method should be one which efficiently collects valid and reliable data. Valid data means that it answers the questions you need answered. Reliable data means that statistically comparable results would be achieved measuring the same group or situation with similar methods. A key consideration is which data collection method will most efficiently, accurately and reliably gather the needed data. Some primary research designs would include:

- descriptive survey: identifies current attitudes, perceptions or conditions.
- analytical survey: attempts to explain why the attitudes, perceptions or conditions exist.
- content analysis of marcom messages
- personal interviews
- focus groups
- field experiment: market tests, split-run tests
- lab experiment: theater tests, lab store tests
- field observations
- physiological testing

Design the Data Collection Instruments.   Once the research method has been designed, the data collection instrument needs to be constructed. This is a very specialized task, which requires someone with research expertise to assure that the data obtained isn't biased by the questionnaire construction, for example.

Identify and Select the Sample.   Who the members of the sample are going to be is the next step, and a crucial one. In most cases, you are not interested in a convenience sample. You want one that is stratified to be representative of your target market and that is randomly selected. The number of people or companies in the sample is also critical. Different experts have different targets, but a good rule of thumb for any marcom research project is that an n (sample size) of 100 is the smallest base that will provide valid data. The ideal objective is to justify and collect data from more than this minimum.

Conduct the Research.   Put the project into the field and collect the data. If you are a client, maintain contact with the research organization; listen to some of the phone surveys that are being collected, review information as it is received, be actively involved rather than simply sitting back and waiting for results to be laid on your desk. Do not, however, micromanage or change the research parameters midstream.

Analyze and Interpret the Data. The data are only as good as your ability to understand what they mean. The basic principle is to look for the answers to the research questions for which the study was designed. Be careful with the interpretation. If 20 people answer "5—Strongly Agree" on a five-point scale, 12 answer "4—Agree," eight answer "3—Neither Agree nor Disagree," five answer "2—Agree," and two answer "1—Strongly Disagree," that doesn't mean that the average response was 3.91489 or almost "Agree." It does mean that, out of 47 respondents, 32 or slightly more than two-thirds agree or strongly agree with that item.

Prepare the Report. The report should answer the research questions and make appropriate recommendations. Develop it in such a way that the readers or the people to whom you present the report will understand what you are talking about. Tables, charts, figures, and graphs should be used to supplement the written portion of the report, which should discuss only the relevant findings.

Focus Groups as a Research Tool

Focus groups are overused and abused as a marcom research tool. They are fun, can be put together relatively quickly, and provide a lot of anecdotal information. But the information obtained from focus groups is either relied upon too heavily without other more rigorous research data to back it up, or the participants' perspectives and comments are discounted as irrelevant or incorrect. We have seen situations where clients expected the focus groups to simply validate decisions that had already been made. When the groups failed to do that, their input was dismissed.

Since focus groups are relatively small, averaging 10 to 12 people, the results are not generalizable to the target population. Some researchers try to combine the results of a series of focus groups, and claim that the data are quantifiable because of the large aggregate number of people who participated. There is no set number of focus groups that is required to have valid data. If you have a well-balanced group, you ask the right questions, and you are satisfied that the responses answer your research questions, one focus group could suit your needs. It may also be necessary to do four to six groups. Doing more groups, however, doesn't necessarily increase the validity of the results or make the results any more quantifiable.

One of the biggest problems with focus groups is researchers who try to quantify the focus group results, which is qualitative data. They take a single focus group and note that eight out of 10 participants said "green is better," which supposedly makes "green" the correct answer.

For what is obtained, focus groups can be extremely expensive compared to the same amount of money spent conducting a good solid survey. For example, $4,000 spent on one focus group could be more effectively used to help underwrite a quantitative phone survey that would yield richer data. Some managers are captivated by focus groups; they don't necessarily think through what is the most appropriate method to answer their research questions.

Working with the Research Supplier

When using an outside vendor for primary or secondary research, the following steps will make your relationship more effective and productive. Unless it's a quick-and-dirty project, ask for bids for each research project, even those that are ongoing or repeat projects. There is little need to have a research firm or consultant on retainer.

1. Write a thorough description of what you need to accomplish with your research.

2. Establish a reasonable, but firm, deadline for the bids to be received. A supplier that can't meet the deadline will usually have difficulty meeting project deadlines.

3. How well do what the vendors propose match your needs? If they are recommending a different direction for your research, review their recommendations to see if there are valid reasons for the changes. If they are off on their own tangent, they will be difficult to control when the project is underway. In some cases, the supplier may have a trademarked research software or method that they want to use that may not meet your needs. In some cases, their research method may be overkill, but they can't modify their approach to only provide what you want.

4. Check references.

5. Look at the project prices. If a vendor's price is significantly higher or lower than the average, they probably won't meet your needs. You get what you pay for. In many cases, there are good, solid local firms that can do your research at a more reasonable cost than nationally known firms, unless you need the national group's prestige attached to your research project.

6. Consultants brought in to do one specific job—designing a corporate image campaign, for example—may decide that they can do everything from product research to marketing research to marcom research. These are usually specialists, however, whose effectiveness is limited to their area of expertise. Trying to use them in broader areas is dangerous.

If the consultant only wants to deal with top executives and not with the managers who will actually oversee the projects, raise a red flag. You will quickly lose control of not only the project, but the research agenda. As a manager, it may be difficult to monitor their work, because they won't be inclined to accept or return your phone calls or to include you in basic strategy meetings. This type of arrogance can result in your company agreeing to research that you don't need, discounting solid research that has previously been done, and it can result in flawed data because everyone is afraid to point out any errors.

SOME COST-EFFECTIVE RESEARCH IDEAS

Many of the objections we hear about funding marcom research relate first of all to the cost of the research and second to the idea of having to hire someone outside of the organization to do the research.

There is a major plus to having someone outside the company do the research, even if there is an internal project director or manager. The independent researcher or company hasn't "married the natives," so to speak, and gotten caught up in company groupthink. They can in most cases more objectively define the research problems, select the proper methodology, and frame the questions the appropriate way. While using the same outside research provider repeatedly does result in their understanding your needs and industry more clearly, it can also mean that they end up doing the research that will provide the answers you want to hear, rather than objective answers that you need to hear.

One way of saving some research dollars is to tap into the local academic pool. There are several departments on any college campus that can usually offer research expertise, including business, political science, and sociology. Many times the project can be used by a faculty member as a site-based learning experience for students. Or the faculty member would accept a consultant's fee that is more reasonable than a research agency might charge. Graduate students are another source of experienced research talent at a reasonable stipend; the practical experience looks good on the postgraduate resume. At least one school we know has a student practitioners' group that takes on projects referred to it by agencies that consider the projects to be too small for their interests.

MEASURING THE EFFECTIVENESS
OF MARCOM ACTIVITIES

One function of research is to gather data during and after marcom campaigns, including information that can be used to assess marcom effectiveness. There's an old advertising maxim which says, "I know that my advertising works half the time—I just don't know which half."

Marketing communications should be accountable for results in a true behavioral ROI sense based on a simple ratio of results to effort expended.

This requires a major change in measurement mind-set, as was discussed briefly in the marcom model in Chapter 1.

The elements in the traditional promotional mix are sales, sales promotions, advertising, public relations, and direct response. While there are a number of ways to objectively measure sales and direct response effectiveness, it has always been more difficult to measure the effectiveness of advertising, public relations, and promotions.

Measurement tools and techniques attempt to measure how much "bang" was netted per buck by each specific promotional mix element. The net result is data that supposedly shows how much more important one promotional tool is than another—for example, that advertising is more valuable than a sales promotion, or that a direct mail campaign is more successful than a public relations campaign. The data is used to justify, gain increases in, or protect budgets for individual marketing communications departments. A by-product is difficulty in getting departments to cooperate, because they are busy protecting their budgets and areas of expertise.

The general objective of any marketing communications effort is to change, modify, or reinforce the customer's behavior, not to justify a budget or to determine accountability for each discrete promotional mix element. In an integrated marcom strategy, the issue of which promotional element worked best is moot. It is which combination of marcom activities achieved the desired customer behavioral response that is important. This is based on the assumptions that 1) the buyer can't tell you which of the many marketing messages she received was responsible for the buying behavior and 2) the behavior is a result of the cumulative effects of information from the total marcom strategy.

To illustrate, consider the first time you asked your spouse or significant other, "What was it that first attracted you to me?" You want to know whether it was your suave and debonair attitude, your wheels, your physical features, or your "social pedigree." The typical answer is, "It wasn't any one thing, it was a combination of things." The same is true for customer responses.

For this reason, it is suggested that marcom measurement be based on the effects of combinations of marcom activities using the De Bonis & Peterson Results/Efforts (R/E)™ ratio. An example of a complete marcom campaign analysis using the R/E ratio approach included in Appendix J.

THE DEBRIEFING: EVALUATING THE EFFECTIVENESS OF AN INTEGRATED CAMPAIGN

Marcom research has two distinct functions. One is to help develop the marcom strategies and tactics before the fact by identifying important demographic, psychographic, and infographic characteristics of the target businesses and individuals involved in the buying decisions within those businesses. The second is to evaluate the effectiveness of the completed marcom activities to provide some guidelines for future marcom. Think of it as data for a campaign "debriefing," which analyzes what worked and what didn't.

Marcom research is perhaps the most complex management task you will undertake for a variety of reasons. First, many people are math, data, or statistic phobic. They are not only afraid of the numbers, they are afraid of how the numbers might be interpreted, what sort of spin might be put on the data to make it look better. It's an old axiom: "Statistics don't lie, but liars know how to use statistics."

It is important to determine not only how the data is going to be gathered, but what information is essential and necessary to the marcom management process. Defining this beforehand not only makes it easier to gather the data, but can reduce some of the fears about how the data is going to be used.

Another issue, perhaps the more critical one, is getting access to the data you will need for assessment. This is not only a procedural or systems issue, but one of trust and cooperation. It is important that the data be provided to you in a form and format you can use, whether it's through a network or by disk or by hard copy. But some departments will be reluctant to give up what they consider to be proprietary information to an "outsider," even though you all ostensibly work on the same team. If push comes to shove, negotiate a way for the department to provide you with the numbers you need.

JUSTIFYING THE EXPENSE OF RESEARCH

Research doesn't necessarily mean quantitative procedures and statistical tests for significance. Much of the research which is necessary is qualitative or descriptive in nature, and can be conducted relatively simply while providing valid information. The key is formulating a research design that will satisfy the research objectives. Time and budget are important considerations; unfortunately, too much research is done on a shoestring budget with a "needed it yesterday" deadline.

The following basic questions should be asked:

1. What is the purpose of the research? What are we trying to determine? How will the results be used?
2. What kind of data or information will satisfy the research objectives or answer the research questions?
3. Where is that data or information?
4. How soon are the results needed?

5. What research technique will most efficiently gather that data or information?

 Techniques would typically include mail, phone, e-mail, or FAX surveys, depth interviews, focus groups, panels, MBWA input, and copy testing, for example, content analysis, fog index, comprehension tests.

6. Should an outside agency be used?

7. How is the information or data to be analyzed and reported?

8. What is the required budget?

The answers to these questions will help determine the nature of the research that is needed and define the research process. The ultimate goal is to develop useful information from the data that can be used in decision making, helping to justify the research expense.

RESOURCES

1. Bearden. W. O., R. Netemeyer, and M. F. Mobley (1993). *Handbook of Marketing Scales: Multi-item Measures for Marketing and Consumer Behavior Research.* Newbury Park, CA: Sage Publications.
2. Blankenship, A. B., and G. E. Breen (1993). *State of the Art Marketing Research.* Chicago: AMA and NTC Books.
3. *The Green Book* (1993). New York: New York Chapter, American Marketing Association. (Formerly *The International Directory of Marketing Research Houses and Services.*)
4. Pope, J. L. (1993). *Practical Marketing Research, Updated.* New York: AMACOM.
5. Skinner, Richard N. (1994). *Integrated Marketing: Making Marketing Work in Industrial and Business-to-Business Companies.* New York: McGraw-Hill.
6. Templeton, J. F. (1994). *The Focus Group: A Strategic Guide to Organizing, Conducting and Analyzing the Focus Group Interview.* Chicago: Probus Publications.
7. Tull, D. S., and D. I. Hawkins (1993). *Marketing Research: Measurement and Method. A Text with Cases.* 6th ed. New York: Maxwell Macmillan International. (This may not be available in a bookstore, but should be available at a well-stocked regional library or university or college library or bookstore. It is a valuable research resource that should be sought out.)
8. Wimmer, R. D., and J. R. Dominick (1994). *Mass Media Research.* 4th ed. Belmont, CA: Wadsworth. (This college textbook may not be available in a regular bookstore, but should be available at a well-stocked regional library or university or college library or bookstore. It is a valuable research resource that should be sought out.)

NOTES

1. Valid means the research measures what is intended to be measured or measures true differences in the characteristics it seeks to measure. Reliable means that the results would be comparable or consistent when measured repeatedly in independent research studies.
2. Our thanks to Susan J. De Bonis, Ph.D., a media research consultant based in Atlanta and full-time adjunct faculty member at the Goizueta Business School, Emory University, for her assistance in writing this chapter.

CHAPTER 6

Building the Foundation: The Communications Audit

> "Understanding is the beginning of approving."
>
> —André Gide, *Journals,* 1902

You are responsible for developing the preliminary Marketing Information Platform (MIP) for the coming fiscal year. The final MIP will be instrumental in assuring that your organization effectively and efficiently communicates company and product or service messages.

What should the MIP include and how will you obtain that information?

Communications—both internal and external—must be a defining element of any marketing strategy. This means that marcom must have specific objectives and tasks. This planning is necessary for appropriate marcom decision making to occur. It also permits and guides the measurement and analysis of the marcom activities. Measurable objectives means that the measurement method and the criteria for success are established. Many organizations, however, perceive marcom as a natural outgrowth of other marketing activities, so planning is more *ad hoc* than preplanned, a myopic perspective which fails to incorporate and fully utilize marcom strengths.

Marcom must start with a clearly defined target, which is critical in planning what will be communicated, when, where, how, and by whom. This established, the marcom objectives can be created. As will be discussed throughout this book, these objectives should be practicable, behavioral, and measurable.

Practicable means that they are capable of being achieved. The ultimate behavior is purchase response, but there may be some intermediate behaviors that are also relevant. The objective when targeting prospects, for example, would be to generate a response to a toll-free number. When targeting a customer, the behavioral objective could be to get that customer to provide a referral. Objectives may also be cognitive—creating knowledge in the target's mind—or affective—influencing the target's feelings and attitudes. Measurable means that there is a means by which response behaviors can objectively be assessed.

The document that provides the foundation for integrating the various marcom activities within the organization is what we call the Marketing Information Platform™ (MIP). The term is borrowed from advertising, where a copy platform provides the functional framework on which the creative concepts are hung. A copy platform addresses the advertising objectives, the target audience, the key selling points that need to be communicated, the general theme or appeal to be used, and any additional information that supports the creative process.

The MIP performs the same function—but for all marcom activities. The result is that everyone in the company is "singing off the same sheet of music." The development of the MIP has other functional purposes, as well. For example, it has a way of smoking out internal disagreements about the company image and its products that management frequently doesn't know exist. It also provides a sanity check on organizational unity: "Is this who we are and what we sell?"

The MIP is also essential to the development of a zero-based marcom strategy, which will be discussed in depth in the next chapter. In short, in a zero-based marcom approach, all projected marcom activities are justified and budgets developed using the previous year's MIP only as a guide. As the company and products or services change, so should the MIP. The existing MIP should be reviewed and revised as necessary, and signed off as a totally new document.

It should also be stressed that the MIP is a process, not a form or format. It is not a document that is filed away. It's the underpinning for daily marcom. A complete MIP outline template is included in Appendix A. This template may be used as it is, or adapted for your own organization's needs.

CHECKLIST OF DO'S AND DON'TS

- Do's:
    1. Do a complete communications audit annually. The initial audit is onerous and time-consuming. Each successive audit becomes less so.
    2. Everyone in the organization should participate in the development of the MIP, from rank-and-file employees to top management.
    3. The final MIP should be signed off by representatives of all of the organization's divisions, departments, or companies, and then followed.

- Don'ts:
    1. Don't change the audit significantly from year to year. The objective is to have a consistent baseline, rather than comparing "apples" marcom with "oranges" marcom.
    2. Don't simply lift out our sample MIP profile and slap it into your organization. Modify, expand, or shrink it depending upon your organization's marcom needs and expectations.

DEVELOPING THE PRELIMINARY MIP

The development of a Marketing Information Platform starts with a draft, which then passes through several revisions and finally becomes the focus of the marcom summit discussed in Chapter 7, "Building Consensus for Action: The Marcom Summit." *Draft* is an operative word, because the MIP can't become an official, final document until everyone agrees to it. In fact, we have used the following terminology on an MIP: "Once the final version of this MIP has been agreed to and acknowledged by the sign-offs below, this MIP becomes the official company platform for all marcom, internal and external, until such time that changes in the company's status or profile, marketing strategy, or relevant facts contained in the MIP require elements of the MIP to be amended and signed off."

As the marcom specialist, you are responsible for drafting the first MIP based on your knowledge and perceptions of the organization.

The MIP developed by an organization must be unique to that company's marketing strategies and objectives, and to the marcom strategies and objectives. There is a general framework, however, that we suggest as a starting point; modifications should then be made as necessary. Be brutally honest and objective, and ask the respondents to do the same. Without honesty and objectivity, the MIP will be useless.

Circulation of your first draft allows you to probe the assumptions and perceptions of people within the organization. Readers will be eager to correct the errors or gaps in your work, and this feedback is critical to being able to write the necessary revisions and to perform successfully the important function of marcom consensus builder. A byproduct of this process is that your subordinates, colleagues, and superiors will become much clearer about the MIP's function and the essence of an integrated marcom approach. They will also see the logic and discipline you are bringing to the task, which creates an important comfort-level factor in this sometimes overwhelming activity.

THE COMMUNICATIONS AUDIT

The development of a Marketing Information Platform also means a thorough communications audit. This can provide an important benchmark for future marcom and MIPs, and will either validate or refute current perceptions about the types of internal and external communications taking place and their effectiveness.

An important first step is to determine what communications are currently taking place and what attitudes and opinions about the company and its products currently exist. This is achieved through a communication audit, which should be conducted at least once a year to assure that marcom activities are on target. Figure 6.1 provides an outline of the communication audit process.

An audit should also be conducted whenever current marcom activities don't seem to be producing results, and whenever a company changes management, adds or changes product or service lines, or changes its status—for example, merges with or acquires another company, or goes from private to public.

The marcom audit not only assesses current marcom activities but should identify strengths and weaknesses of marcom programs, assess the long-term effects of marcom, and provide an adjustment of future marcom goals and objectives.

CONDUCTING THE AUDIT

All touch points should be reviewed in as many ways as are practicably possible, including a communications audit, an audit of internal data, and external interviews.

Conduct a thorough communications audit.

1. Where are the "touch points" with the organization's
   - Internal publics? For example, consider the following:
     Personnel forms
     Personnel policies and policy statements

FIGURE 6.1 *Communication Audit Process*

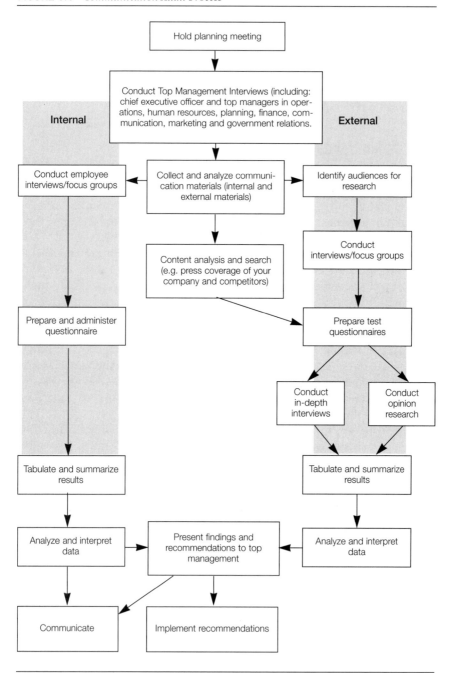

Adapted from Hill and Knowlton, Inc., *Business Marketing,* January 1989, p. 32. Copyright, Crain Communications, Inc. Reprinted with permission of the publisher.

Personnel communications: newsletters, memos, e-mail,
   VOX mail

Break and lunch room posters and flyers

Restroom conversations

The grapevine

- External publics? For example, consider the following:

Sales: outside field reps and telemarketers

Customer service

Finance: accounts payable, accounts receivable

Shipping

Service reps

Sales collateral materials: brochures, annual reports

Public relations: press releases, events, newsletters

Advertising: graphics, logos

Sales promotions

Media contacts, media kits

Receptionist contacts, waiting rooms

Parking

Security

Voice mail or answering machines or services

2. Who is responsible for those communications? Where is the collection point or clearinghouse

- For internal marcom?
- For external marcom?

3. What are the marcom objectives?

- Internally?
- Externally?

4. What is being communicated to meet these objectives?

- Explicit messages
- Implicit messages
- Boilerplate information

5. How is the information being communicated? With which media or channels?

- Press releases
- Annual reports
- Customer newsletters
- Advertising
- Collateral sales materials
- Trade articles or other publications by company personnel

Collect internal audit data.

1. From rank-and-file employees, mid- and upper-level management

2. From short- and long-term customers; prospects; inquirers; influencers; business, institutional, governmental, consumers

3. From formal communications such as newsletters, employee handbooks and policy statements, memos, and personnel forms, including performance reviews

Conduct external interviews.

1. Community leaders: local, state, regional and national

2. Industry leaders in your industry

3. Industry leaders from the major industries to which your company markets

4. Security analysts

5. Wholesalers, distributors, and resellers

6. Editors and general managers of media

COMMUNICATIONS AUDIT MATRIX

Figure 6.2 represents a potential microsegment marcom matrix for a telecommunications company. Four potential service categories for this company would be local telephone service, long distance service, cellular service, and equipment sales. Within each service category, five types of transmissions could be offered, either separately or as bundled services: voice, FAX, video, data and messaging. In each category, there could be multiple subtargets—for example, the consumer group, the business group, the government group, and the institutional group. Each cell in the matrix represents a discrete target that has unique informational needs.

Each marcom strategy could be targeted to each cell in the matrix, but the more likely scenario is that different combinations of activities will be more productive in different cells. This requires a tremendous amount of management and integration, but the end result is seamless communication with the groups in the target cells.

RESOURCES

We could not locate any primary resources concerning communication audits. The audit format we use is flexible enough to be used in different environments but is not intended to be an all-inclusive list. Relevant resources in this process would those dealing with human resources management and interpersonal relationships, group dynamics, and negotiating.

FIGURE 6.2 *Matrix of Potential Marcom Targets in the Telecommunications Industry*

Local Service	Long Distance Service		Cellular Service		Equipment
	Voice	*Fax*	*Video*	*Data*	*Messaging*
Consumer					
Personal					
Work at Home					
Business					
Small Business					
Med. Business					
Large Business					
Government					
Local					
State					
Federal					
International					
Institutions					

1. *Marketing Audit: Over 100 Questions Designed to Improve Your Marketing Plan by Building your Strengths and Eliminating your Weaknesses* (1988). Chicago: American Marketing Association.
2. Jandt, F. E. (1985). *Win-Win Negotiating: Turning Conflict into Agreement.* New York: John Wiley and Sons.
3. Kolb, D. M., and J. D. Bartunek, eds. (1992). *Hidden Conflict in Organizations: Uncovering Behind the Scenes Disputes.* Newbury Park, CA: SAGE Publications.
4. Larson, F. E., and F. M. J. LaFrasto (1989). Teamwork. Newbury Park, CA: SAGE Publications.
5. O'Brian, J. D. (January 1992). "Negotiating with Peers: Consensus, Not Power." *Supervisory Management.*

CHAPTER 7

Building Consensus for Action: The Marcom Summit

> "Of all men's miseries the bitterest is this, to know so much and to have control over nothing."
>
> —Greek historian Herodotus

You've had a great Friday. After much coaxing, you have convinced your management that it is important to get everyone together for a one-hour meeting in the conference room to discuss company mission and the need to have a coordinated communications policy everyone can adhere to.

Then Monday morning comes. You get two e-mail messages. The CEO has decided not to attend your meeting, reminding you that he has a vice president of marketing who is responsible for running those functions . . . but he does want the opportunity to approve the results of the meeting. To top it off, the head of product development has decided that communications isn't her domain, but she wants to continue approving all product names that come out of marketing.

What two mistakes did you make in trying to sell consensus and its benefits to the vice president of marketing, the CEO, and the product development chief?

The previous chapter introduced you to the concept of the communication audit. A thorough audit of all aspects of internal and external communications will provide you with a baseline for determining the size and scope of your communication task.

Your colleagues and management can make corrections to the first draft of the Marketing Information Platform (MIP), filling in answers that you left blank and providing additional information as needed. (See the sample MIP in Appendix A). After you incorporate those edits and other information gathered in your communications audit, you proceed to a second draft of the MIP. This second draft is now complete enough to be the focal point or agenda for a marcom summit meeting dedicated solely to your organization's internal and external communication issues. By this time you can begin to see a general direction for communications—a course of action.

This marcom summit is no ordinary meeting. The players are few. The venue is important. The time allotted is critical. The success of the summit can determine the latitude and authority you will be given to handle your company's marketing communications. The result of your efforts is a foundation or platform for future communication strategies and tactics. (That is why we call that foundation a Marketing Information *Platform*.)

CHECKLIST OF DO'S AND DON'TS

- Do's:
    1. Do, in your communications about corporate marcom policy, ask if there is a corporate mission statement and ask when was the last time management took quality time to reflect on strategy, the competition, and your volatile niche in the market.
    2. Do ask management what, in one sentence, is the single unique value that the company brings to its marketplace. If the answer is all nouns and no verbs, be suspicious.
    3. Do ask what is the worst possible and plausible thing that could happen to the product or service, and ask what contingency plan you are charged with executing should that event take place.
    4. Do ask management what customers, in confidence, likely say about the company behind the backs of sales reps and management and customer service.
    5. Do ask management to answer the question "what is it that we sell?" and ask if all executives agree with the same answer.
    6. Do in strategic planning meetings, always play the devil's advocate. Remember—you are stuck with the results if you don't.

- Don'ts:
    1. Never schedule something like a strategy session at the office during regular work hours—it is a waste of time.

2. Never assume that any area of company business is outside your responsibilities if that one area could produce negative external exposure or perceptions.

3. Never use your own four-color brochures to brief agencies or new employees on your firm's value added. Brochures are mere attachments to the real document you should give them.

4. Never stop gathering research, formal or anecdotal, about external perceptions. Always use social and business opportunities to ask how the company is perceived.

SUMMIT ATTENDEES AND SUMMIT SETTING

For marcom to operate with any validity going forward, top management must be involved in the communications summit. Although the vice president of marketing and the vice president of sales might think their presence is all you need, such limited attendance will largely prove a waste of time.

The reason is rather simple. Let's say a summit of just three or four marketing and sales leaders decides that the company should take a new strategy of attack and develop a new product line. The chairman and the CEO, often the company founders, would find such an announcement startling, if not downright presumptuous. "How in the world did they come up with that?" is the likely response. In companies that are swimming in highly competitive waters, top management is very "hands on" and unlikely to relegate strategic decisions to sales and marketing executives.

If you have shown management the logical process you are using to develop a marcom plan, you already have their attention. If their reaction indicates no such process has been used before, selling them on the investment of time required for the summit meeting should be easy. The toughest part will be getting a date compatible with everyone's schedule.

In your memos and recommendations concerning the audit, the MIP, and the summit, be sure to indicate that the goal of the summit meeting is to involve all management in the formulation of a communications strategy and tactics. The MIP, used as the information collection tool, will clearly show the depth of your inquiry and what it all leads to. Recipients will also see the sign-off section that you will ask everyone to initial once the final draft is composed following the summit meeting.

Aside from the top executives and the sales and marketing chiefs, you should invite the CFO. The CFO has considerable power over your budget. As we mentioned earlier, CFOs don't all have a favorable view of marketing. Involving the CFO in this process may be the best way to show this person how logical marketing can be—at least when you are in charge. Because the summit and the MIP end with discussion of communications strategy and tactics, the CFO will see the logical reasoning behind each communications expenditure. In fact, the summit and the MIP could make you a real hero to the sales and marketing chiefs if they have had unco-operative relations with the CFO.

If post-scale customer service is a major part of your unique selling proposition (USP) in your market, the executive in charge of this area is also an important attender at the summit.

The setting for the communications summit is very important. Here are the possible settings, ranging from most ideal to unsatisfactory:

1. A Saturday/Sunday at a remote cabin or retreat facility
2. The company board room on a Saturday/Sunday
3. A hotel meeting room during the week
4. The company headquarters during the week

Holding a communications summit meeting at the company during work-ing hours is ill-advised. The executives are too accessible and the phone calls are too easy to take. It is easy for everyone to "just interrupt for a quick second."

The key, as you can see, is to reduce interruptions and allow the strate-gic thinking process to unfold. A weekend summit at the company head-quarters is fine, except that staffers working on weekends might be curious enough to pop in "just to say hello." Even a meeting during the week at a local hotel will still be interrupted by calls from executives' secretaries.

The first time you hold a communications audit summit meeting at your firm, it is highly unlikely you will finish in one day. That's another reason why a weekend retreat setting is a good plan.

Packaging the communications summit as a weekend retreat may make it very attractive indeed. Executives and you can bring spouses, thus removing part of the sting of being away from families. Your memo can suggest an informal meeting, casual attire, quiet pastoral surroundings—and the time and space to think out strategy.

THE AGENDA: REVIEWING THE AUDIT IN DETAIL

Just so it won't surprise you, you should know that very few companies ever go through such a process to develop communications strategy and tactics. Actually, very few ad agencies or public relations firms go through this exercise with clients. Large agencies such as Ogilvy & Mather have a creative briefing aimed at accomplishing something similar. J. Walter Thompson has their "T-plan" composed of four basic questions:

1. Where are we (the client) now? (current market standing)
2. Where do we want to be? (objectives)

3. How do we get there? (strategy, tactics)

4. How will we know when we get there? (measurement)

The MIP is a more elaborate communications inquiry, and one that you conduct yourself. As mentioned, your second-draft MIP becomes your agenda for the summit meeting. From the second draft you refine points *and get thoughtful discussion going.* Up to this point your interaction with people about the MIP has been only one-on-one. At the summit, they get to listen to each other, hearing both agreements and disagreements.

As we said, you will likely spend more time on the broader questions such as "What is it that we really sell?" Don't stop discussion on such points prematurely. As you look over the MIP, you will notice it starts with broad-brush general questions that address the "macro" and moves eventually to fairly specific "micro" questions.

The marcom summit needs a beginning that puts people at ease and heads off potential problems. Two problems in particular can happen: Executive X may discover that executive Z has been operating with totally different assumptions about the company, and be surprised. Or, in your role as devil's advocate, you may pose a question that gets a negative reaction such as "How can you conclude such a thing?"

One of the authors, when conducting these summit meetings, places a large rock in the middle of the conference table. He announces that the summit is intended to foster deep, provocative thinking and to provide an open, honest forum where all negative realities can be aired and real company problems discussed. If anyone gets upset about part of the discussion, he suggests they get mad at the rock rather than the speaker. It works. It sets the tone and seems to head off both kinds of problems.

THE ANATOMY OF PROBLEM SOLVING

Throughout the communications summit meeting, strive to help participants understand the inherent differences in two concepts that are widely used but often confused: strategy and tactics.

On a white board or flip chart, write the following six concepts and keep this list visible throughout the meeting: factors, problem definition, objective, audience, strategy, and tactics.

Factors.   Factors are conditions that exist, good or bad, and immutable situations that you must accommodate. Factors are just there, both favorable and unfavorable, and that's the way it is.

Problem Definition.   We devoted a whole chapter to perceptions and problems, and here's where the rubber meets the road. In precise, exacting terms, what is the problem you need to solve? This could be related to a factor you want to change. The problem definition could well be a long statement.

Objective(s). You want to accomplish X by Z time-frame. The objective must be specific, but it also must be reasonable for the time-frame specified. If the objective and its deadline are not specific, you cannot measure the success of the objective.

Audience. You have identified a problem and an objective, but whom do you want to hit with the objective? That's the target audience. You could have several objectives and corresponding audiences.

Strategy. How will you accomplish the objective? The answer to that question is your strategy, expressed in conceptual terms and used to unite and direct your organization almost like a road sign. The strategy statement centers on a verb that implies real action, for example, promote, stress, emphasize, build. For example, your strategy may be to build brand awareness with the target audience.

Tactics. Unlike the conceptual compass and sextant the strategy statement provides, tactics are the things you do to execute the strategy. In our example earlier regarding brand awareness, two tactics might be to initiate a corporate image campaign using advertising and a seminar series. The ad campaign and the seminar series are tactics.

Strategy and tactics are terms often used interchangeably—and they shouldn't be. Marketing guru Gerald A. Michaelson told an American Marketing Association leadership conference that strategy is all about doing the right thing, and tactics are all about doing things right. We would add another juxtaposition: strategy is how you think about your marketing task, while tactics are what you do about that thought. In another way of looking at these important terms, strategy is the mental conceptualization and organizing glue for your marketing plan, and tactics are the actions and physical tools you create to execute that conceptualization.

GETTING CONSENSUS AND SIGN-OFF

The end of the summit meeting finds you with a general consensus about the answers to your questions as well as the direction communications should take. The best summary of the summit discussion is to edit the information into draft three of the MIP, ideally the final draft, and distribute that draft for sign-off.

Your cover memo to the final draft should indicate that the MIP now takes on a new role. It becomes much more than a long, printed document. It is now the platform for all company communications (advertising, media relations, exhibit themes, and so on). Indicate how much you appreciate their participation in the drafting of the MIP. The time they spent will eliminate the need for repetitious approvals of all communications efforts. You can tell them that now the ad agency and the public relations firm have a clearer notion of what they are expected to do, thus preventing them from falling on the excuse "Well, we didn't know."

Lastly you ask the summit participants to sign off. This is an important psychological exercise. It gets them to commit, not just to the document, but to the process you put them through and a new way of handling communications. Their sign-off is virtually an endorsement of you and your efforts. It is also some insurance against them second-guessing everything you do from there on out.

What if something changes? Let's say in six months a new competitor emerges or a new product line is introduced by your firm. Or after your attendance at a big expo, everyone notices subtle changes in the industry or in customer expectations.

The best way to handle this is a shorter summit meeting involving the same people. This meeting also provides the opportunity to have a post-show debriefing as well as adjust the MIP and its communications plans. This doesn't have to be another weekend retreat, but an off-site meeting place is still important. Such discussions or post-show debriefings, especially if a trade show is a major benchmark in your marketing year, quickly become perceived as the proper role of good communications management—with you in charge. But as before, distribute the amended MIP and get a new sign-off.

SELLING MIP DISCIPLINE INTERNALLY

The results of the summit need to reach beyond the summit attenders. After all, why keep a good thing secret after all that work! Ideally the MIP will specify certain strategies and tactics for areas such as investor relations, community relations, and even employee relations. This book has separate chapters for these areas of communications. Company managers in the relevant areas, such as the human resources manager, need to see the MIP and buy in to the process and results. You may need to conduct summary meetings with these managers to show them the breadth of the program and why it is important in their respective areas.

The sales executive may want each field rep to have a copy of the MIP. Internal designers, documentation managers, human resources managers, stockholder relations managers, and others may need copies. There's a risk here that the MIP, complete with confidential information and analyses, could fall in the hands of someone who is ready to leave the company and work for a competitor. It is best to serialize the copies and keep the serial numbers on file with your human resources department. That way departing employees who have been privileged to get a copy are asked to surrender it and are reminded that the information in the MIP is company property. The serialization, like the executive sign-offs, also serves as a psychological reminder that this is something special.

One of the important company guides that can result from the MIP is a corporate style manual or standards guide. This manual or guide covers company copyrights and trademarks, such as logos, and details how they should be rendered in all uses.

RESOURCES

1. Porter, M. E. (1980). *Competitive Strategy: Techniques for Analyzing Industries and Competitors*. New York: The Free Press/Macmillan.
2. Goetsch, H. (1993). *Developing, Implementing, and Managing an Effective Marketing Plan*. Lincolnwood, IL: NTC Business Books and the American Marketing Association.
3. Ames, B. C., and J. D. Hlavacek (1989). *Marketing Driven Management: Prescriptions for Survival in a Turbulent World*. Homewood, IL: Dow-Jones/Irwin.

CHAPTER 8

Identity and Design: of Icons and Images

> "A good symbol is the best argument, and is a missionary to persuade thousands."
>
> —Ralph Waldo Emerson

A product manager decides she wants to hold an employee contest to choose a name for the company's top product offering for the new sales season. She thinks this is the best way to choose a name because it will get employees excited and involved.

Employees are getting wind of the contest. What is the inherent problem with this approach and how can you direct it safely without dismantling the contest and disappointing the employees?

Of all the communication mistakes that marketers make, none make better stories to the outside world than corporate or product identity goofs. Corporate names or product names that have to be changed, often for embarrassing reasons, usually make the front page of the *Wall Street Journal*. Probably no other communication area is less amenable to quantitative certainty than corporate and product identity.

Some definition is necessary. Although used in a varied way, *corporate identity* is really the totality of how a corporation is perceived by its customers. That includes its public statements, its advertising, how the media views the company, the company's brands, the quality of those products or services, the corporation's name, the corporate logo or logotype, and that elusive area called corporate culture.

All those ingredients of identity are discussed in this book, in one chapter or another. In this chapter we want to talk about identity in terms of corporate names, corporate logos, and product names and logos. An aspect of this is the naming process and the design process that results in a name, a logo and, ideally, a recognized brand. So, as the title implies, this chapter is about image, icons—symbols, if you wish—and design. We believe this aspect of marketing deserves a chapter all its own.

In product identity you will find everyone has an opinion but few want to take care to do it correctly. Or safely. The corporate attorney will be ever-so-careful, and marketing demands may prompt you to move more quickly than the attorney finds comfortable. In corporate identity and design, things can get cast in concrete (literally, in some cases) before all long-term factors are considered.

You will make mistakes in product identity—but so have others. In the folklore of marketing is the story of General Motors and Nova. General Motors thought Nova might be as good a name for its South American showrooms as it was in the United States. It soon discovered, however, that in the Latin dialects of Spanish, nova sounds like "won't go." And it didn't, either.

CHECKLIST OF DO'S AND DON'TS

- Do's:

    1. Do make sure the CEO understands the process and guidelines you want to use for naming a product.
    2. Employee name contests are a good news/bad news approach. An open-ended contest without guidance and direction can be a costly and time-consuming distraction.
    3. Do involve a designer early in the naming process, long before you ask a trademark attorney to seek protection.
    4. If the name is for a premier product that will lead the company for years, investing in the expertise of a psycholinguist is as important as paying a lawyer's bill.

- Don'ts:

    1. Don't choose a name without checking how it translates, literally, figuratively, colloquially, and in the auditory sound into the languages of all the countries in which you plan to market.
    2. Don't assume a good designer can make up for a mediocre or bad name.

PROJECT NAMES: HOW BAD PRODUCT NAMES TAKE ROOT

In business-to-business, just as in consumer/packaged goods markets, the development cycle for a new product is long and complex. During that period of gestation, before marketing's work becomes visible to the external world, projects often acquire names as well as project numbers. The reason is simple: it is easier to remember a project nickname than to memorize a project number.

What happens, however, is that the project name often takes on a life of its own. Then project managers and their staff fall in love with the project name. After all, it's their baby and they want to name it. Regrettably, the project name rarely has any marketing value.

For this reason it is important that marketing be involved in the development of projects and their identity, with full understanding that the final marketing name is a function of positioning and sales potential.

OF OWNERSHIP AND MISPLACED AFFECTION

We are about to describe to you one of the most difficult tasks you will undertake in marketing: telling a product manager or, worse, a CEO that it doesn't matter if he or she likes a name or logo.

Obviously, this has to be handled diplomatically. It should also be handled in the beginning of the identity/naming process. In the first meeting you conduct about choosing a name, outline for all concerned how important it is *that the name work well.*

To work well, a name has to fit the marketplace for that product or service. It has to mesh with the naming conventions of other product or services in the product line, or at least not cause confusion with other names. The product name has to blend well with the corporate name, or at least not be conspicuously contradictory or negative.

More importantly, an ideal name for a product is one that:

1. Captures the value-added position of that product relative to competing products

2. Is easy to trademark

3. Is adaptable to all design applications, including color designs

Now, you would think that everyone at your presentation will nod their agreement, turn to colleagues and say "of course." They probably will—for the moment. Until such a time as they come up with their own favorite name. That's when the problem begins. If the CEO, for example, excitedly offers a name, chances are the name will develop a life of its own and suddenly the CEO will be in love with it. She owns it. It's hers. She wants that name. After all, she's the CEO, she owns a big block of stock, so why can't she own the name, too. Our point should be obvious: It is hard to fight with ownership, whether it's owning of a corporation or "owning" a name.

So head off the problem before you get to the pass. During your first identity/naming meeting, use an example such as this. Turn to the CEO and product manager and ask them to imagine opening up a new restaurant or office supplies store. It would be tempting to name the place after themselves, as in "Nick 'n Rog's Bar and Grill" or "De Bonis and Peterson Office Supplies." The problem is that the downtown area is filled with restaurants, stationery shops, card shops, office supplies marts—you name it. Wouldn't it be better to call the store Elm Street Office Supplies, or Parkside Deli (if near a city park), or Sutter Street Top Stop (if near the Sutter Street subway station)? Those names *work better.* You may not personally like the name, but you do want the name to help drive sales.

It is tough to put ego aside, but sales are more important than ego. Of course, these examples don't apply if you are already a famous restaurateur or office supplies kingpin with name identity. For the rest of the world, remember this:

> DE BONIS & PETERSON BUSINESS MARCOM RULE #5:
> **"It isn't important whether you like the product or company name you select. But it does have to work."**

TYPES OF NAMES

There are naming groups or conventions that can help prompt names for you. Here are some of those groups:

Acronym and Lettered Names. IBM, DEC, and so on. These acronyms are trademarked along with the words they stand for, often becoming a primary logo on products. Sometimes the letters really don't stand for anything. This approach is frequently used by companies that change the corporate name because of broad acquisition programs that take the parent firm far afield from its original roots. AMR is the parent of American Airlines. Do you know what TRW stands for in that corporation's name?

Descriptive Names. These words tell what the corporation or product does, but they often lack excitement or distinctiveness. As a name, they can be downright boring. What's more, it is relatively hard to gain trademark protection for them. Nonetheless, this is an approach that has been frequently used and still is used today. It hasn't hurt International Business Machines or Minnesota Mining and Manufacturing much, even if they are more frequently known as IBM and 3M.

Phrases Used as Names. This is popular in consumer/packaged goods markets—for example, Milky Way, Banana Republic, My Sin. Business-to-business companies also use it, such as State of the Art Software.

Manufactured or Custom Names. This approach is becoming popular with all types of companies because the name is so easily trademarked. Some examples are Exxon, Intel, Compaq, Texaco, Bufferin, CompuServe, MicroSoft, and so on. You cannot find these words *as common nouns* in the dictionary because they are not words. But as *names* that establish *identity,* these words develop great meaning.

Borrowed or Fanciful Names. The best example of such identity is Apple Computer. What does the common noun *apple* have to do with computers? Nothing. But what if Jobs and Wozniak had named their company Silicon Tech Inc. and the computer the STI x25. These names are off-putting and sound hard to use and unfriendly. But a computer and company called Apple sounded approachable, easy, and fun—and ultimately successful, too. Chevron, the name of the former Standard Oil Company of California, is more consumer-friendly than the older name. But the word chevron, a word for military striping, has nothing to do with gasoline retailing.

Attribute or Fitted Names. Supposing your product, in its category, has the most power by anyone's objective measure. You might then choose a word that spotlights that feature, such as czar, dynamo, boss, top dog, and so on. These are all common nouns or terms or phrases, but they take on a new meaning as a proper noun or name.

Audience Targeted Names. Similar to an attribute name, this is an approach used when the product is clearly aimed at a specific profession-al level or group. Supposing your company produces games, gadgets, and services for high-IQ people such as members of Mensa. You might call the corporation Cognoscenti, Inc., based on an Italian word that means people who are very knowledgeable about something. It breaks the rule about pronunciation—but not for the Mensa crowd.

PROCEDURES FOR GETTING GOOD NAMES

Make sure that all product development schedules include a time for the project to be given a product name. Indicate that you want to assemble a product identity committee (conveniently, PIC is the acronym) to study the process and task. This should occur at last six months before product release, because the trademark process and literature development task need time to run their courses.

The PIC should include the product manager, the heads of sales, marketing, and marketing communication, your in-house attorney or paraprofessional, and eventually your logo designer.

If your sales and distribution involves a dealer network, involving a key dealer may be necessary. They are close to the marketplace and may understand the politics of the sales environment better than you do.

It is advisable to invite your CEO as well. You want to show the CEO that you are taking command of the task with a logical, process approach. At that point, the CEO may be sufficiently comfortable with your approach and the PIC meetings to forgo further attendance until you get down to testable name candidates, but you need to be certain of that comfort level. If the CEO doesn't endorse the process and make that endorsement known to all its participants, there is a good chance he or she won't accept the final recommendation. So get that endorsement stated, clearly and up-front, perhaps in the form of a memo over the CEO's signature that outlines the naming process and PIC members.

Depending on the importance of the product you are naming, you may need the outside assistance of a psycholinguist. This is a professional with multidisciplinary training who studies language, its perceived meaning, and its relationship to the speaker. Psycholinguists are typically multilingual, and their foreign language skills are usually not restricted to Romance languages either. A psycholinguist, once fully informed of your objectives and product attributes, can help you isolate word parts, called morphemes, that might lead to a custom name. This expert's language skills can also help ensure that translations of the name will work in all your markets.

Have an agenda for the first PIC meeting. The first item on that agenda should be "factors to consider in finding a name that will work well for us." There are several factors you should outline for the PIC members:

1. List the competitive realities and marketplace trends that affect the selection process.

2. What product or service attribute is the unique selling proposition (USP)? What is the value added?

3. What are the international markets in which this product or service name must work?

4. In general, how do we want to be perceived with this new product or service? What do we want the name to say about the overall company?

By listing such factors, the complexity of the task is laid out for all to see. You have defined the rules of the name game; it's now your game. Personal names then become contradictory to the logic of the process and are less likely to take hold.

There are also some generic factors common to any identity/naming task:

Credibility.   Does the name blend with the corporate culture, or is it so far afield that journalists might be compelled to spotlight the disparity? In short, the name has to be believable.

Editorial Twisting.   This is a variation on credibility because it involves the trade and business press. Journalists love to have fun by taking advantage of a name when the company has a bad quarter or the product fails some big customer. To avoid this, try writing some negative headlines using the word to see if you are handing a cynical writer more ammunition than you care to give away.

Pronunciation.   Ideally, the word should be easy to pronounce, or at least easy for your target audience.

The Sound of the Word.   Ideally, a name should be mellifluous or sonorous, meaning that the word should have a smooth, pleasant flow to it when pronounced. Some consonants, such as Z and X, don't always lend themselves to mellifluous names. Many technology companies come up with names that almost offend the ears.

Syllable Count.   Ideally, the word used as a name should contain very few syllables, easing pronunciation.

Interpretation and Recall.   Ideally, you want a name that customers can recognize as meaningful to them. Likewise, you want a name that, once recognized as meaningful, is also easy to recall.

Translation and Dialect.   If you plan to market this product or service in other countries, you must test the word in that language. Some very amusing stories of error have occurred when a seemingly innocuous word, translated into French or another language, sounds insulting or off-color. With translation calculators and university language professors in abundance, this isn't a mistake a careful company will make.

Dialect comes into play here, too. A word that works well in the North American market may fall flat in England due to differences in dialect. A highway in America is a motorway in England. Suspenders here mean fasteners on women's underwear in England. A truck is a lorry. An elevator is a lift. A presidential *administration* here means government bureaucracy there, while *government* here means a prime minister's majority there. While we are on this topic, British business people go out of their way to use American words when here, but Americans find the differences amusing and are slow to adapt when in Britain.

Ease of Trademark.   Last but hardly least, you have to protect your use of the word as a name by seeking trademark protection. This is increasingly difficult and complex. Trademark challenges are common. Some companies have chosen words as names in markets quite remote from the companies that challenge the mark. Even if the two companies really don't cross paths in the same customer's domain, it often isn't worth the cost of fighting the challenge. Trademarks lawyers love fanciful and manufactured names because of the ease of protection. All this is apparently nothing new. Shakespeare once observed "I would to God thou and I knew where a commodity of good names were to be bought."

EMPLOYEE NAME CONTESTS

Asking employees to submit name candidates is a commonplace approach. That's why we set the stage in the beginning of this chapter with such a scenario.

Obviously, employees will enjoy such a contest. It's a good way to involve employees. Product enthusiasm will surely be enhanced. But any contest without rules is a bad contest. If your product identity committee

DO YOU ALWAYS NEED A TRADEMARK ATTORNEY FROM THE START?

We will probably get more flack for the following comment than anything else in this book! The answer is no, you do not have to use a trademark attorney from the very beginning of a naming project. You certainly do need one for the final trademark application, however. But you can test a name earlier at considerably less expense.

Many trade magazine publishers are developing large CD-based access files of all their publications. Ziff-Davis's Computer Select CD service is an example. With this service, you can check a name to see if it has appeared in any article published in your industry by that publisher. If no one is using that word as a name, you have the first indicator that a good name may be available.

Many trademark attorneys use the Dialog Information Service (a Knight-Ridder company) to check existing protected marks. You can do that yourself. If you are a member of the American Marketing Association, the AMA Kent Library can run the names through its Dialog access. If the word isn't found protected by someone else, you have passed another checkpoint.

Now it is time to turn to a trademark attorney, but make sure you inform the attorney that you have already checked Dialog. You don't want to be invoiced hundreds of dollars for something you already did for far less.

should suggest a naming contest, just make sure the factors listed above are made known to the employees. They will understand the importance of rules, marketing realities, and legalities—*if you tell them.* But a naming contest without such guidance could derail the process you want to set into motion with the PIC, and therein lies long-term danger and unnecessary costs.

SYMBOLS AND ICONS

Trademark history is a fascinating topic. Actually, using pictures or symbols to represent families, countries, and businesses is a human enterprise going back centuries in time. The use of symbols to represent businesses really came into wide commercial use in the nineteenth century, probably because few customers were literate. If the customer couldn't read the label, it was a good idea to develop a symbol for your products or company. That way the customer could easily spot your packages or cans on the shelf.

Prominent sociobiologist Edmund O. Wilson explained it this way: "Human beings live—literally live, as if life is equated with the mind—by symbols, particularly words, because the brain is constructed to process information almost exclusively in their terms." We're not sure if Dr. Wilson had trademarks in mind when he made that observation, but a trademark is a symbol specifically developed to give customers a sense of consistency and comfort with your company and products.

Consider Ford Motor Company for a moment. Ford's script logo in a circle is one of the most famous logos in the world. By their own admission they made some poor vehicles in the 1970s and paid for it dearly. So they set about designing a car with total quality in mind. They came up with the Ford Taurus, a good car by an reasonable measure. We are not suggesting the Ford logo made Taurus a success. But Ford's overall identity, and stated commitment to excellence ("Ford . . . where quality is job one"), got them past all the bad years to a point where the Taurus is one of the best-selling American-made cars. Likewise, on the business-to-business side of life, Intel seems to have survived the early problems with some Pentium processors. You cannot open a newspaper without seeing "Intel Inside" on nearly every IBM PC clone. An old Ashanti proverb says it best: "Rain beats a leopard's skin, but it doesn't wash out the spots."

DESIGNING FOR FUTURE IMPACT

Finnish designer Eliel Saarinen once commented, "Always design a thing by considering it in its next larger context—a chair in a room, a room in a house, a house in an environment, an environment in a city plan."

The same observation applies to designing a name into a physical asset such as a logo or logotype (the name rendered only in a specific typeface or stylized typeface). As with other topics you have read about in this book, it is a matter of elements in their context—trees inside the forest, the micro within the macro.

A design for a name must be based on three important factors: What are all the physical applications the design will have to serve? How long is the name intended? and How does that name and design fit within the marketing plan and the corporate image?

Aside from the marketing reasons for a name, there is the critical element of cost. Changing the name of your corporation may well be the most expensive marketing task you will ever undertake.

Look around your company site for a moment. Think of all the physical and nonphysical implications. The biggest nonphysical factor is the legal and trademark processes. On the physical side is an iceberg of costs: letterhead and business cards, product literature, documentation, invoicing and other accounting needs, trucks, uniforms, trade show exhibits, and building signage. The cost of corporate entryway signage, often in concrete and other durable materials, is very expensive. It is much easier to choose the right name for the company at the very beginning.

UNDERSTANDING CREATIVE DIRECTORS AND DESIGNERS

The designer has the task of making a word into a symbol that will enhance your corporate or product image. At the same time, the logo cannot be in conflict with the existing perceptions and image of the corporation, unless of course the assignment is to change the corporate image entirely.

In short, this is a complex task. The logo design assignment is far more important than designing a brochure. Brochures, even annual reports, have a shelf life far shorter than a logo. Therefore, don't hesitate to find a specialist if you sense your in-house designer is uncomfortable with the task.

Aside from visual appeal, the designer has to consider all the factors we have already discussed. That is why the designer really needs to become involved in the selection process once you have narrowed your list to words that fit the criteria discussed earlier. Even the best designer cannot take an inferior or weak name and design it into glory. Remember the old maxim, "You can't make a silk purse out of a sow's ear."

The cost of application is a big factor for the designer. He or she may well point out severe cost restraints with one name or another because of the difficulty of rendering it in all applications. The best example here is color. If you direct the designer to develop both color and black-and-white renderings, as you should, she may come back with the observation that a particular name or logo really requires four or more colors to be truly workable. Suddenly a name has increased your printing costs by 30, 40, or 50 percent. Do you want to find that out early, or too late? In short, brief the designer fully and listen carefully when she cites potential problems with a particular name.

Suppose you are down to the wire and have two name candidates for a product you will introduce at BigExpo. Your trade show exhibit vendor's designer mentions how dramatically name X can be rendered into a rising archway entrance to the exhibit. But she has no such dramatic suggestion for name Z. If all things are equal and you have otherwise studied the application advantages of both name candidates, this may be a solid reason for going with name X.

TIPS FOR INTEGRATING YOUR PROGRAM

It should be obvious that a product name and its logo affect every aspect of marketing communications. Rather than belabor the obvious, we will point out a few examples.

An ad campaign for a new product will combine the minimum copy necessary to fulfill the promise of the headline tied to the appeal of the graphics. Your name must be one that can give a creative director fertile ideas for this combination, recognizing that the reader makes an instantaneous judgement to read one ad and pass over the next. Final name candidates should therefore be reviewed by your advertising agency to see what strengths and weaknesses they see.

A product roll-out doesn't have to be restricted to an expo. If you have a dealer network, they should be involved early in the roll-out process. A dealer meeting should be executed with all the guidelines in our event marketing chapter, with the new product name explained, featured, spotlighted, and reinforced for all it's worth. If the dealers don't thoroughly understand the name and its value-added, there will be many problems down the line.

MEASUREMENT AND EVALUATION

Measurement of a name or logo's potential success is really referenced in all the selection criteria and guidelines we outlined in this chapter. Measurement after the fact is far more ellusive.

✔ Do dealers or field salespeople use the name enthusiastically, or do they tend to bury the name for some reason?

✔ Does editorial coverage of the product seem to be accepting or neutral toward the name, or is the name itself analyzed negatively or flippantly?

✔ What is the reaction at BigExpo? Does the name direct the visiting prospects correctly, or is confusion making it difficult to explain the product features? If you do product demonstrations at BigExpo, what do the demonstrators sense about the name's success?

✔ How many qualified responses are your direct marketing efforts yielding? If Product X is producing too many prospects seeking a solution to Problem Y, something is amiss in the mailer or package.

RESOURCES

1. Olins, W. (1990). *Corporate Identity: Making Business Strategy Visible through Design*. New York: Harvard Business School Press/McGraw-Hill.
2. Sauerhaft, S., and C. Atkins (1989). *Image Wars: Protecting Your Company When There's No Place to Hide*. New York: John Wiley & Sons. The first chapter of this book is entitled "Perception versus Reality."
3. Selame, E., and J. Selame (1975). *Developing a Corporate Identity: How to Stand Out in the Crowd*. New York: Lebhar-Friedman Books.
4. Gregory, J. R., with J. G. Wiechmann (1991). *Marketing Corporate Image: The Company as Your Number One Product*. Lincolnwood, IL: NTC Business Books.
5. Garbett, T. (1988). *How to Build a Corporation's Identity and Project Good Image*. Lexington, MA: Lexington Books/D. C. Heath and Company.
6. Aaker, D. A. (1991). *Managing Brand Equity: Capitalizing on the Value of a Brand Name*. New York: The Free Press/MacMillan.
7. Deal, T., and A. Kennedy (1982). *Corporate Cultures: The Rites and Rituals of Corporate Life*. Reading, MA: Addison-Wesley Publishing Co. This book is an old standby on company cultures and their impact on image and identity. If no longer in a bookstore, check your local library.

PART 3

Managing the Micro Tools

In this part, we discuss important marcom tools and processes in the external marcom program. We focus on the basic concepts behind these marcom tools without getting academic or burying you in production details. Part 3 helps you move from the macro to the micro, from wheel to spokes, from the overview to the particulars. In a general sense, you now move from the strategic to more tactical tools.

By micro, we don't mean the details or mechanics. But we do mean some more specific aspects of the communication message and how they are best handled.

How you distinguish among the marcom elements is critical. Most of your colleagues outside of marketing will confuse them. Even product or brand managers inside marketing get them confused. When a CFO gets them confused, your budget can be adversely affected.

It is your job to keep the marcom weapons straight. You are the keeper of the ammo dump in the warfare of marketing. You are also the "guard on-duty" to make sure the communication audit you hammered out and the resulting Marketing Information Platform (MIP) are carefully observed with each tool.

We look at these concepts while observing a well-known truth that often gets lost in marketing operations: some things are more important than other things. Sounds trite, doesn't it? But the business world is full of stories of companies that missed that simple truth. (Many of their telephone numbers have since been disconnected.)

An important lesson is the need to define the really essential elements needed to develop effective external communications. Overall messages. Messages intended more for the long term. Messages to anchor audiences when the image gets garbled by transitory events or occasional changes. We call these the macro messages. What generally get distributed, however, are micro-level messages.

In reality, integrated marketing communications can be thought of as a distribution or delivery system. It is a mix of carriers, each bringing the goods to the target audiences in different ways. But the end goal is always to move product or sell services. That is why marcom must work closely with sales to make sure the message gets to the destination at the right time to help sales reps close.

In a sense, the structure of this part of the book is somewhat arbitrary. Direct mail is so closely related to telemarketing that they really could be in a category together. But we are making an organizational point by placing them separately. We are making the distinction here that exhibit marketing and telemarketing are face-to-face or voice-to-voice communication settings that provide instant feedback on the receptiveness of the message delivered. But please don't forget that you should be using the total arsenal of marcom tools—all working together.

The Marketing Information Platform (MIP)™ we introduced you to in Part 2 will help you decide how to distribute the macro messages and the micro messages. But until those main problems and messages are identified, asking an ad agency or public relations firm for a creative campaign or program is a waste of time.

Advertising and Collateral Sales Literature: Customizing Marcom in the Information Age

> "I know half the money I spend on advertising is wasted, but I can never find out which half."
>
> —John Wanamaker

Your company has just released its advertising agency, primarily due to the fact that its local office has undergone some major management changes and other personnel upheavals, which have resulted in the agency being less responsive to your company's concerns and needs. Your marketing director has agency management experience working primarily on consumer accounts and there is other creative talent in your company upon which you can draw. You are responsible for organizing an in-house agency and integrating its functions with the other marcom activities.

What are your priorities and concerns?

Advertising's a marcom tool, not a cause of behavior, but an effect of the need for a marketer to communicate with a target market about its products and services. It's the messenger, the means and not the end.[1] And while most advertising discussions ultimately end up focusing on creativity, we're going to suggest that creativity's not only overrated, but frequently gets in the way of business-to-business marcom.

The most important point is that mass market advertising's dead, a victim of information overload, road kill on the information superhighway. It's no longer an efficient marcom tool. Markets are no longer defined in terms of mass, but in terms of microsegments. Segment-of-one marketing and mass customization are the buzz words for the 21st century. As a result, marcom has to adapt to satisfy its role in the traditional promotional mix.

Ideally, communications need to be designed for and directed at segments of one. The sole buyer in the small company who has previous experience with your product category doesn't have the same informational needs as the buyer in the medium-sized company's buying center who has no product category experience.

The reality is that mass communications has evolved into the mass customization of communications; unique marcom messages are transmitted to groups of target companies that have been clustered to the lowest homogenous information denominator possible. You have one marcom mix for knowledgeable sole buyers in small companies and another mix for inexperienced buying-center buyers in medium-sized companies.

Advertising is an essential component of the marcom mix in business-to-business marketing. The traditional function of advertising was to inform the buyer about products and services and persuade them to think about and, we hope, choose our brand when making a buying decision. Today, the business advertising function is integrated into a series of marcom activities and has several specific functions to perform:

1. To create awareness among target markets of the product or service
2. To promote comprehension about what the product or service can do for the buyer
3. To encourage a conviction that this product or service is not only necessary, but should be purchased from the advertiser
4. To stimulate action or buying behavior

There are 4 Ms in the advertising mix that help meet these objectives—the message, the media mix, money, and the media schedule. This chapter examines each. As we have suggested elsewhere in this book, producing ads and commercials is something that can be outsourced. Developing the strategic functions advertising is to play in the integrated marcom mix cannot be outsourced.

CHECKLIST OF DO'S AND DON'TS

- Do's:
    1. Do understand that the mass market no longer exists. It has been replaced by microsegments that expect one-to-one marcom.
    2. Do develop specific, measurable objectives for advertising campaigns and collateral materials that are integrated into the marcom mix.
    3. Do create ads which are functional for the target.
    4. Do include research and testing as an integral part of the strategy and the budget. This provides both foresight and hindsight, both of which are necessary for effective marcom strategies.

- Don'ts:
    1. Don't require a single ad to create awareness, comprehension, conviction, and action across a broad spectrum of different targets. An ad should have one target and one message for that target. An ad that tries to do all things to all audiences will be significantly less effective.
    2. Don't establish an advertising budget and then make creative, placement, and other decisions. Decide what the objectives are, what advertising will have to be done to satisfy those objectives, and how much those activities will cost.
    3. Don't use a howitzer to kill a fly, which means don't bury the inquirer with information she doesn't ask for, want, or need, or have a field sales force distribute bounce back lead-generation cards. On the other hand, make sure that the information provided is sufficient to satisfy the inquirer's needs.
    4. Don't get caught in "formula" thinking when it comes to advertising or any marcom activity. Your markets are constantly shifting and realigning, and their information needs today are not the same needs they had yesterday.

THE MESSAGE: WHAT TO SAY

In the late 1980s, Joe Isuzu was one of the most identifiable pitchmen on TV. The campaign won a handful of creative awards for Della Famina McNamee, but it was scrapped in 1990, because Joe wasn't selling Isuzu cars as well as he was the trucks. As creative as the campaign was, it didn't sell product.[2]

To the average individual advertising means the creative concept. We would like to argue that creativity should be the last aspect of advertising messages developed. David Ogilvy perhaps said it best. "The first ad I ever produced showed a naked woman. It was a mistake, not because it was sexy, but because it was irrelevant to the product—a cooking stove. The test is relevance."[3]

Our rule: It's more creative to be functional in what you are writing and designing than it is to be purely creative and miss getting the message across to the target audience. The ad must be functional for the message recipient first; functional is defined as providing the message in a way that is quickly understood by the audience. The one element of the business buyer's day that is not expandable is time; there are only 24 hours in which to cram all of the business and personal responsibilities and functions, and still have time for sleep. That said, there are some strategies and tactics that will help you to write and design more effective marcom ads.

The business-to-business advertising copywriting style is significantly different from journalistic and creative writing styles. In journalistic writing, the goal ideally is the presentation of information from an objective perspective; creative writing implies self-expression—putting one's emotions, impressions, feelings, and arguments into words.

Business advertising is neither objective nor self-expressive. It is intended to be a biased, persuasive communication based on a single marcom objective established for the ad. That objective is based on the target's information needs, not the marketer's. The ad is written and designed according to this specific objective, which requires disciplined creativity. The ad copy is quick, to the point, and states the product, service, or idea benefits clearly and concisely. It is more factual and perhaps less creative than consumer advertising.

It is important to state explicitly that the ad should have one target and one message for that target. An ad that is intended to accomplish all four of the objectives above and is targeted to a broad spectrum of different targets will be significantly less effective.

There are five simple strategies that will help you create more effective business ads.

1. Start with a strategy statement: what is it the ad needs to say? Creative tactics are how you say it.
   - Preparation is the major key to success. Don't just start designing or writing. Think about the marcom objective, and outline the argument or make a list of the major copy points in descending order of importance. Then start writing.
   - Brainstorm all possible ideas, including those that seem at first blush to be too far "out of the box." Then start to eliminate approaches or concepts until you get to the one that seems to be the most functional.
   - Check and double check all of your facts and information. That prevents dumb mistakes.

2. Know your target audience.
   - Who is your target? Are they product users, initiators, influencers, information gatekeepers, deciders, buyers, or a combination of these roles?
   - What are their information needs? The message for targets who are unaware of your product or service, but whom you wish to initiate an inquiry about your product or service from their companies' buying centers will be dramatically different than the message for current product or service buyers.
   - Business buyers don't avoid business ads. They seek out relevant information that will make them more efficient in the buying process and reduce the amount of risk in their decision making. One key is to meet and satisfy those expectations. That means more copy than you would generally find in consumer ads. This balance is determined, however, by the ad's objective. A message that is intended to generate an inquiry for more product information from an unaware audience should rely on visuals to hook the reader's interest; one that is intended to make a direct sale would have to provide more information in a copy format supplemented with visuals.
   - You are asking the target to pay attention to, take in, and respond to information.

     The basic question that has to be answered for the reader or listener or viewer is the WIIFM (wiff-em)—"What's in it for me?" What is the benefit if the person does what the copy suggests or asks?

3. Understand the strengths and limitations of the medium for which the ad is being designed. While some ideas may translate efficiently from one medium to another, some messages have to be redesigned or rewritten for the specific medium in which the ad is going to be placed.

   A majority of business-to-business advertising dollars are spent in specialized trade publications. Readers of these publications are a captive audience—they sought out that information source and are highly involved, highly interested readers. As a result, the marcom message can be longer, more complex, and have a specific call to action targeted at the audience.

4. There is an old saying that a camel is a horse designed by a committee. Writing and designing ads by committee can result in the same effect: a camel when a racehorse was wanted. While there may be input from a variety of sources within the organization, there needs to be one manager for the design and writing of the ad.

EFFECTIVE COPYWRITING HINTS

1. Make a checklist of what you want to get across and stick to it. That makes sure that you don't forget anything and don't overdo it.

2. Write to one person—the target profile. Write in the second person; use the term "you" to personalize the message.

3. Establish the opening thought. The rest of the copy should flow logically and smoothly from one idea to the next.

4. "Set the hook" and hold the reader/listener/viewer by offering a benefit or a reward. Don't take too long to get to the point. The reader/listener/viewer will lose interest. Keep the ideas simple and to the point. You don't have much time to hold the reader's attention.

5. Stick to one main idea that satisfies the ad's objective. One major idea is more effective than ten little ones.

6. Write clearly. Write shorter, concise sentences. Long-winded copy isn't read. You are not writing the great American novel.

7. Pick your words carefully. There is a big difference for a hospital nutritionist between a product that is "sugar free" (no sugar added) and one that is "sugarless" (ingredients contain no natural sugars).

8. Use present tense, active-voice language to foster the sense of response immediacy.

9. Write with word pictures. There is a difference between a LAN (local area network) that uses "fiber optic wire" and "fiber optic wire with clarity that would let you hear a pin drop."

10. Avoid the traditional marketing cliches.

11. Highlight the unique aspects of the product or service: What gives that product or service a sustainable advantage over the competition and provides a reason for buying.

12. Identify the product early and repeat it often. If the advertiser is more recognizable than the product, identify the advertiser early and often.

- If you can, write alone. Copy written by one person has a more personal, more cohesive rhythm.

- There is no such thing as "writer's block," and there is no such thing as a "pure" or "natural" copywriter. The best copywriters are those who are superior copy editors. If you feel blocked, write anything, good, bad, or indifferent. Your ability to put words on paper isn't blocked; it is your ability to put what you think are the best or correct words on the paper. Where is copy improved? In the editing. You've never heard someone say, "I

13. Don't be ambiguous, be explicit. Don't let the readers/listeners/viewers decide what the message is. Make up their minds for them. Tell the viewers/readers/listeners what to do and how to do it. Don't assume that the target audience will know what you want them to do.

14. Tailor the copy to the audience; communicate at their level in their language.

    • What is the average education and reading level of your target audiences? Write to that level. The average reading level of the general population in the United States is somewhere between the eighth and tenth grades.

    • Use proper grammar, even though you are writing in the vernacular, or "the way people talk." (How do people perceive others who speak poorly?)

    • Use the jargon of your industry only if the users understand the terms. If they don't, provide a translation.

15. Make sure the ad is appropriate for the product or service. Does it reflect favorably on the advertiser's image? As Ogilvy advised, don't use sexual innuendo to sell crematory services.

16. Test the copy. Ask for people's opinions, especially those in the target market. See if you are hitting the mark.

17. Write the copy to match the medium. Radio copy isn't effective in videos. Magazine copy doesn't work in direct mail.

18. Have fun with the writing and design process. You will write better copy if you are interested in what you are doing.

19. Role play being the target reader or listener or viewer. Would the copy interest you? Hold your attention? Encourage you to buy?

20. Read all copy aloud. It sounds different than when it is read silently. You may hear something other than what you intended.

---

have editor's block." Write a lot. Then edit. It is easier than wrestling with your "block," and it is also easier to delete than to add words.

5. Give yourself sufficient time to write and let it sit. Then edit what you have designed and written, and let it sit again. This process, which is more typically the ideal than the reality, results in a more polished communication.

From a different perspective, Reva Korda of Ogilvy and Mather suggests that the faster copy is written, the better it is. A copywriter with too much time gets "too darn smart," according to Korda, and loses contact with his or her own natural, intuitive reactions to a product and what might make another human being want to buy it. Here is a quick five-point checklist to test for effective copy.

✔ Can the message be quickly and easily understood?

✔ Are the benefits stated clearly, concisely, succinctly? Does it inform?

✔ Is the copy honest and believable? A series of smaller, believable claims are always more effective than one large claim which—though true—isn't believable.

✔ Is the copy memorable without detracting from the message?

✔ Does it motivate the reader/listener/viewer to action?

THE MEDIUM: WHERE TO SAY IT

Deciding which media to use for advertising is frequently a function of historical precedent and/or budget constraints. The proper method, however, is to select the medium or media mix which most effectively reaches the specific micro-segments to which the message is being targeted. This is based on the *infographics* of the target markets, the decision-makers, buying centers and the buyers. Like demographics or psychographics, infographics is a descriptive tool which defines a target audience along six current dimensions, which are described below: media usage, frequency, setting, time frame, influence and credibility.

Media Usage.   There are two dimensions to media usage. The first is the sources of information to which the business buyer exposes him or herself: which trade publications and other business media does he or she read or watch, or which trade shows and exhibits does he or she attend? This is more of a passive activity, perhaps described as media habit or media inertia. The buyer may, for example, subscribe to *Sales and Marketing Management,* which arrives every month and is perused.

The second dimension of media usage is the information sources the business buyer actively seeks on a regular basis: which media does he or she actively seek out? If *Purchasing* magazine is supposed to be in Monday's mail and it is not there, does the buyer actively go searching for the magazine to determine why it wasn't delivered?

Frequency.   How often they use these sources. There is a difference between a casual reader and one who routinely builds in time during the week for intelligence gathering by reading the trades and the catalogs and the direct mail, for example, to see what's new, what's on sale, what may be in short supply in the future.

Setting. Where they use these sources. Are these media used specifically in the influencer's individual office, or is a publication put on the table in a common area for access to all?

We have traditionally made a clear distinction in marketing between the consumer and the business buyer. While there are some minor differences in how buyers make purchase decisions, the buying needs, and risks in the respective environments, there are more similarities than dissimilarities. It's the same individual making a decision in both situations. The roles are not cleanly separated; the individual isn't schizophrenic, defined as suffering from mutually contradictory or antagonistic objectives.

As a result, some consumer marketers are targeting people at work. The consumer doesn't have enough time to review the offers at home, but is more willing to take the time to do so in the workplace. This does, however, create a problem for managers who object to the use of company time for personal buying, despite the fact that their children come to the office to solicit donations for a youth group on company time.

There are some reports of success in targeting the business buyer at home, where the offer can stand out against the backdrop of the consumer mail. This obviously works especially well with the telecommuter and the work-at-home market.

Time Frame. When an information source is used is another infographic descriptor. Although calendar or day-part time are relevant, time frame refers to seeking out and using the information source relative to the user's stage in the decision-making sequence. Different media sources are used for information acquisition, for decision making, and in post-purchase learning. Understanding which medium or media mix is used by the information seeker in which circumstance is crucial to meeting that individual's needs.

Influence. Information obtained from which sources are more likely to create, modify, or reinforce a target's attitude or behavior?

Credibility. What is the relative credibility of the information sources? If the buyer receives conflicting information from two sources, which is most likely to be believed and make a difference in information acquisition or behavior? Does a report about automatic data systems in the *Wall Street Journal* have less, the same, or more impact than the same report carried in *MIS Week* or *OR/MS Today?*

Individual media not only have images that can contribute to their credibility, but there are other inherent characteristics that are compatible or incompatible with certain products and messages.

For example, the quality of color reproduction and the paper used by some trade magazines means that the ads can be more visually oriented and less copy heavy than ads in a trade newspaper where the reproductive

Defense Mechanisms for Information Overload[4]

A major modern-day affliction suffered by the individual in both work and home environments is information anxiety caused by information overload. It has been estimated that the average American adult is exposed to over 600 advertising messages in a single 24-hour period. The amount of information that exists today is expected to double within five years. As John Naisbitt noted in *Megatrends,* running out of information isn't a problem—but drowning in it is.

When the amount of information to which an individual is exposed and the rate of exposure exceeds his or her intake capacity, the person's mind initiates defensive behavioral adaptation strategies, which creates problems for marketing communications, which are then more carefully screened or blocked out altogether.

The buyer decreases the number of information sources to which he or she pays attention, eliminating low-priority information. This results in less of an opportunity for the marketer to successfully attract the buyer's attention; if no attention is given, no message gets through and no buying behavior occurs. The buyer also expends less of an effort and spends less time shopping for information alternatives, which makes it more difficult to hit the target with a shotgun multimedia strategy.

The buyer drastically reduces the amount of exposure to information. This is like the CEO who says, "Give me a 30-second rundown on this project." Compare the amount of time you spend today with trade publications compared with the amount of time you might have had to read these same publications ten years ago. This makes it more difficult for the marketer to establish message relevance, much less to get the entire message across.

The buyer also decreases the effort of comparing the quality of the information received from multiple sources, which results in more reliance on whichever message gets there first. As a result, subsequent communications that contradict the original message are discounted. This means it is important to be first with succinct buying information when the business buyer is gathering relevant information for decision making.

Information overload means the buyer is less able to distinguish between communication sources. When was the last time you said, "I don't remember where I heard or read or saw such and such?" And then you qualified the information by indicating that you didn't really know whether it was true or not? Being unable to recall the source or remember from which of several sources the information could have come results in less source credibility and reduces the likelihood that the information will be relevant to a decision. Credible communications rely on the individual's ability to identify the source.

The challenge for marcom is to provide relevant information to the appropriate buyer when that buyer needs it, where the buyer needs it and in the medium to which the buyer is paying attention. Much of this responsibility, as is briefly discussed at the end of this chapter, will be assumed by the information seeker as interactive communications on demand becomes a technological reality.

quality and paper are poorer. Designing a full-page magazine ad that is all copy fails to utilize the reproduction strengths of magazines, unless the user's information needs demand the amount of information included in the copy to the exclusion of visuals.

A trade magazine might have more credibility than a regional general business newspaper, but it is a monthly publication; the ad campaign needs to hit the target audience six times in the next six weeks and the newspaper is a weekly publication. Use the newspaper.

Or the sales offer is extremely complex and requires collateral materials for the offer to be completely understood. While a trade magazine may offer the most readership, even a double truck ad can't convey the entire message. The only medium that can handle the information requirement is a multi-component direct mail piece.

While these considerations are important, it is the infographics of the target that is more important and that contributes to your ability to package unique messages to discrete microsegments of your target universe.

MEDIA SCHEDULE: WHEN TO SAY IT

Reach, effective frequency, and continuity are the major objectives of any media schedule. While it is important to understand these concepts, it is also recommended that media buying is a specialized undertaking that should be assigned to a media planner.

Reach refers to the total number of different prospects (companies or people) exposed to the ad or a series of ads during a given time period.

Average frequency is the number of times the target is reached by the ad series over a specified period of time. In advertising, as a general rule of thumb anything fewer than three exposures is considered ineffective and anything over 10 exposures is considered excessive and, therefore, also ineffective.

There is a problem with focusing on average frequency, however, which is explained in the following example. Your target audience is 10 people and you are running an ad 10 times. Five people are exposed to the ad twice, which equals 10 exposures. Three of the 10 are exposed to the ad five times, which equals 15 exposures. And two people in the target are exposed to the ad all 10 times, which equals 20 exposures. The total number of exposures is 10 + 15 + 20 = 45, which, divided by the 10 people in the target, equals an average frequency of 4.5 exposures. In this example, however, half of the target was only exposed twice, which is below the rule-of-thumb number for effectiveness. Average frequency has to be interpreted very carefully.

Effective frequency is the number of times the target must be exposed to the ad series for it to accomplish its objective. While there is no magic number, there is an optimal frequency rate that can be discovered through testing. The optimal frequency lies between the minimum number of ads needed to achieve awareness and the number of ads at which wearout occurs, i.e., the audience becomes irritated at seeing the ads. Frequency is also a function of the number of times an ad runs, which is another media schedule decision.

Frequently, media placement is a trade-off between reach and frequency: should the objective be to have more people exposed to the ad or to have fewer people exposed on a more frequent basis? There is no hard-and-fast rule.

It depends again on the advertising objective. If the objective is to create awareness, the general rule of thumb is to achieve a high reach to get as many potential buyers as possible to become aware of the product or service. Similarly, if what is being offered is a high-risk, high-involvement product whose benefits aren't easily explained to or identified by the target, a higher level of frequency may be necessary to achieve effective reach.[5]

Continuity refers to the actual advertising schedule in terms of the number of weeks or months the ad will run. The general rule is that frequency creates message retention, continuity sustains it. Continuity is a function of your advertising budget, your customers' use cycles, and the competitive environment.

Given a choice, most of us would advertise 24 hours a day, 365 days a year. Since that is not usually possible from a budgeting perspective, scheduling strategies are necessary. Customer buying patterns provide one yardstick determining the advertising schedule. If your product has a high usage rate and is repurchased monthly, for example, your schedule would need to be more constant than a product that is reordered quarterly. In the latter example, you would want your advertising to reach the target buyers slightly ahead of their decision-making time frame.

Schedules have different industry names. A continuous schedule means a regular advertising pattern without gaps or periods of nonadvertising with relatively constant spending during the duration of the campaign, whether it's weeks, months, or the year.

A *flighting strategy* is characterized by a period of intense advertising followed by a period of no advertising. This on-off-on schedule takes its name from flocks of birds that fly for hours, then land and rest for hours. It is similar to an intermittent reinforcement schedule in behavior modification. When the reinforcement is withdrawn, the behavior continues, it is hoped until reinforcement resumes. Once the ad message is stopped, there is a carry-over effect—the message is retained until the next series of ads begins.

A *pulsing pattern* is a combination of the continuous and flighting strategies. A pulsing campaign has peaks and valleys. For example, the first month, $1,000 is spent for advertising, $4,000 the next month, and then $15,000 during the window when reaching the buyers is most critical. The fourth month the ad expenditures would drop to $1,000 again.

Bursting, roadblocking and blinking are additional strategies that are used to increase the impact of advertising. *Bursting* means running the same trade ad every week in the same publication for six months. *Roadblocking* is running the same ad in the three major publications read by your target audience; wherever they read, you are "blocking the road." Ramada Inns used a *blinking* technique, limiting ads to Sunday television to reach business travelers at home before they left for the week.[6]

It is also important to be aware of the competitors' advertising schedules. One strategy is to match their schedules so that the potential customer has comparative information. Another is to advertise during the gaps in the competitors' advertising schedules so that your advertising voice isn't competing with other messages.

We've worked with clients who, when asked, said their advertising scheduling was based on what the competition was doing. When we surveyed the competition, they indicated that their advertising schedules were based on what our client's schedule appeared to be. No one seemed to be a leader with a specific strategy; they were all followers, an example of the tail wagging the dog.

THE BUDGET: WHAT TO SPEND

There's an apocryphal marcom story about the entrepreneur who builds a successful business from scratch and then reads in the business trades that a recession is being forecast for the next year. She decides to proactively take some measures to reduce operating expenses in anticipation of the recession and, like most businesses, decides that one of the easiest areas to make cuts is in advertising and promotions. And she finds the economists were right. Business does start to fall off. Anticipating a continued business decline, she decides to make further cuts in marcom expenditures and sure enough, business continues to suffer. And so on.

According to a study conducted by the Wayman Group, business-to-business marketers budgeted almost 3.5 percent of their sales to marketing in 1994, most of that—2.14 percent of sales—committed to direct sales. Marcom was the second largest spending category with 0.88 percent of sales spent on marketing communications. Roughly 24 percent of the marcom expenditures went for print ads and 24 percent for direct mail, according to the report. Trade shows and exhibits represented 12.9 percent of marcom expenditures; sales literature, coupons and POP accounted for 9.3 percent; public relations was 5.3 percent; dealer and distributor materials accounted for 3.3 percent; TV and radio expenditures were 2.7 percent and .8 percent respectively; and .5 percent was spent on out-of-home media.[7]

It is a given in business that promotional mix dollars—money spent for direct sales, advertising, public relations, sales promotions, and even direct response—are some of the least defensible from a return-on-investment perspective and are often where the first budget cuts are made when business declines. But it is also a given that companies that either hold the line or even increase expenditures in these areas during downtime are the ones that come out of the recession healthier, more competitive, and holding more market share than those who didn't.

In many cases, the advertising budget is set before the advertising objectives are established—a cart-before-the-horse budgeting method. The result is that advertising decisions are made on the basis of "How much do we have to spend?" rather than "What is it we need to do and what will it cost to do it?"

Budgeting methods are top-down or bottom-up. In the former, allocations are determined by management based on a particular method; in the latter, the advertising objectives drive the budget.

Among the top-down methods are the dartboard method, an ill-defined arbitrary budgeting process; the "all-we-can-afford" method, which allocates promotional dollars from what is left after budgets have been set for production and operations, for example; the percentage of sales method, which bases advertising allocations on sales; and the competitive parity method, which matches the competitors' advertising expenditures.

Another method is the share-of-market method, which evolved from work by J. O. Peckham for A. C. Nielsen. Using market share data collected for a number of years, Peckham derived a relationship that suggested that market share and share of advertising expenditures were correlated. A company that wanted to maintain a 10 percent market share, for example, should spend 10 percent of the industry's advertising expenditures promoting that product. The formula changes for new product entry; the advertising budget should be about 1.5 times the brand's target market share objective for the first two years. For example, if the two-year goal is a 10 percent market share for the new brand, the company should spend 15 percent of the total industry advertising expenditures during those two years.[8] While Peckham's work was done primarily in consumer markets, the same share of mind-share of market ratio also applies to business marketing.

Based on the fact that advertising is an integrated marcom tool with specific objectives established in the overall marcom mix, we recommend an objective and task, zero-based bottom-up budgeting method. This is a three-step process that 1) sets the advertising objectives, 2) identifies the strategies and tactics that will be necessary to meet the objectives, and 3) sets the costs for the tactical components. The sum is the budget.

Zero-based budgeting means that each ad campaign starts with no budget, even if a similar campaign has been run previously. The previous campaign simply provides guidelines about which strategies and tactics were previously employed; each needs to be reviewed and justified in the context of the current campaign. Once the new objectives, strategies, and tasks have been established, their costs are recalculated based not on what was spent previously, but on what current costs would be.

An important benefit of the objective and task method is that the expected outcomes of the tactics are measurable, which allows you to start to develop an ROI accountability for the ad campaign.

COLLATERAL SALES MATERIALS

Collateral sales materials are devices that supplement other marcom activities, including pamphlets, booklets, brochures, catalogs, manuals, technical specs sheets, newsletters, videos, CDs, sales and press kits, trade show handouts, and point-of-purchase displays, to name a few of the major sales and marcom aids.

Traditionally, these have referred to printed materials, but today they include such things as software, videos and CDs, and information supplied on interactive bulletin boards and networks.

The design of a collateral tool is defined by its function. There are four basic things these materials are designed to do.

- The collateral could be a stand-alone sales device delivered through the mail as a sales offer or fulfillment piece, handed out at a trade show, or left by a delivery person. Its purpose is to make the offer, overcome objections and close the sale. Its format and design must replace the direct sales call.
- The collateral could be used as a door-opener, something which is going to create an inquiry from a prospect, to create a lead-in for a telemarketing call to set up a sales appointment or to encourage the client to accept a sales appointment. Its objective is to get attention. Its format and design must have stopping power and immediately get the door open.
- The collateral piece could be used as a sales aid intended to be used by the field sales force or telemarketing rep to augment the sales presentation.
- The device could be a leave-behind, something which is left with the prospect to which they can refer after the sales presentation to gain additional information or to review what they learned about your company's product or service.

Design Considerations

We met a marketing promotions director some years ago who said she couldn't decide whether to develop a sales presentation portfolio or an easel presentation tool for the sales force to use when making a sales call. We told her that wasn't her decision. She assured us that it was; she was the project director.

So we had to make our point more explicit. It wasn't her decision. It was a decision that needed to be made by the salespeople and their clients. Which format would best enhance the sales presentation for both the sales rep and the person or group to whom he or she was talking?

As it turned out, the easel design was chosen without input from the sales force. Unfortunately, when the easel was stood on the buyer's desk with the product pictures facing the buyer, the technical product specs were hidden underneath on the back side of the page, rather than being printed on the back of the next page facing the salesperson where they could easily be referred to. As a result, the salespeople each requested two easels—which doubled the cost of the job—and then tore the easel apart. They put the pages into a portfolio so that, when the portfolio was lying on the customer's desk, the page on the customer's right had the product photos, but the page on the left had the product specs which could be read by the sales rep.

Many of the design considerations will be dictated by what the collateral piece's objective is and what format will most effectively achieve that objective. Any device designed as a door-opener, for example, needs to be relatively simple and nonthreatening, attention-getting, colorful, enticing, and easy to understand. The objective of the door-opener is to arouse interest without necessarily persuading the prospect to buy. In that sense, its objective is similar to that of advertising and is intended to move the recipient to an actual sales presentation. An example would be a lead-generating brochure designed to solicit names and phone numbers for a telemarketing contact.

A stand-alone sales device must make a sales call. It has to state the benefits, handle objections, and close. This typically means a more sophisticated, involving piece. If the collateral, however, is a sales aid—like the easel discussed in the example—it should supplement, not supplant the sales presentation and should not be used as a leave-behind.

Much of the collateral carried in by salespeople and used during the sales presentation are stand-alones, which is an expensive redundancy. There is little rationale for sending a salesperson in to run a videotape that makes a complete sales pitch, reducing the rep's role to little more than asking, "Are there any questions?"

A leave-behind should also be something that quickly summarizes the major sales points made in the sales presentation. It is intended to be a reference guide for the buyer, not a full-blown recreation of the sales pitch, and it is not a presentation aid.

Some clients argue that they don't have the time, resources, or where-withal to develop distinct collateral for each cell in the matrix. The answer is to creatively design a piece that performs multiple, but distinctive, functions. For example, a twelve-page 5 × 7-inch minicatalog could use the cover as the door-opener; the options, which are addressed on the inside cover, are to keep reading or to call a toll-free number.

Page 3 is a table of contents option menu. This tells the reader what's ahead either by making the phone call or by continuing to read. A check-list of pertinent product features and benefits to be discussed with a tele-marketing rep if the prospect calls could occupy pages 4 and 5. Pages 6 through 9 contain an expanded, self-contained sales presentation. Pages 10 and 11 summarize the main selling points, and the back of the cover (page 12) contains additional contact and response information.

The device could be mailed to the organization prior to or after a tele-marketing call, or carried in by a salesperson. It could be used as a pre-sentation aid or a leave-behind.

A relationship tool should be substantive enough to represent the value of the relationship to your organization. Developing a special newsletter for these clients, which could wrap around your internal newsletter, indicates that you consider them to be an integral part of your business, and that regular and relevant communications with them are indicative of that value.

The most important considerations are: where does the collateral fit in the marcom mix, and what would be most functional for the target? Does the target have CD capability? If the collateral is software, are both PC and Mac disks available?

MARCOM OF THE FUTURE

Defensive responses to information overload and new technology have forever changed the character of mass media advertising. To combat these trends, advertisers are looking to alternative media and new technologies to distribute their messages.

Infomercials on VHS tape and audio cassettes, computer software and CDs, broadcast FAX, and the Internet are all being successfully used in business marketing.

Interactive media will be an increasingly large part of the new advertising environment (see Figure 9–1). Information will be resident in the marketer's computer system, accessible to and accessed by the information user when she wants it. The system will allow the user to seek out the information she wants and to ignore the rest. This will also provide important tracking information for the marketer's progressive database, identifying what information is most relevant to particular user segments, when that information is accessed, and what formats are most effective.

FIGURE 9.1.   *How Much Bang for the Buck?*

Web advertising is relatively expensive, unless the advertiser can find the narrow information channels used by the target market. There has been a rush to join the Internet home page bandwagon, but preliminary results are disappointing. Estimates are that nearly 10 million people surf the Web regularly, but there's no indication that Web advertising has been widely successful as an advertising medium to the consumer market, much less the business market. There are a few exceptions, but the general consensus is that the market is taking a "wait and see" attitude, responding to more traditional media sales pitches rather than those seen on the Web.

	Cost	Audience	Cost per 1,000 Consumers
Television			
30-second spot, network news	$65,000	12,000,000	$5.42
Magazine			
Full-page color ad, national weekly	$135,000	3,100,000	$43.55
Newspaper			
Full-page ad, midsized city	$31,000	514,000	$60.31
World Wide Web			
Online magazine, one-month placement	$15,000	200,000	$75.00

Reprinted with permission of Forrester Research, Inc., Cambridge, Massachusetts.

As a *caveat,* each new medium must prove itself based on results. A new medium must both fit with the marketer and the audience, and offer something other media do not. In some cases, the decision will have to be "gut reaction" due to a lack of history. What works today won't work tomorrow. Figure 9.2 provides an overview of current communications expenditures in business-to-business marketing.

TIPS FOR INTEGRATING YOUR PROGRAM

In order for an advertising campaign to be fully integrated into a marcom strategy, there needs to be a clear understanding of who the target is, what the target's information needs are, and what behavioral outcome is desired. This information comes from a variety of departments within the organization.

The advertising theme should also be echoed in all of the other marcom communications, in every customer touchpoint. This provides the element of consistency, which was one of the components of the integrated marketing communications definition in Chapter 1. The advertising theme should be understood by the internal audience as well. Place a call to the headquarters of motivational guru Zig Ziglar and hear the company's promotional theme repeated: "Good morning. It's a great day here at Zig Ziglar. How may I help you?"

MEASUREMENT AND EVALUATION

There are three components to effective testing of advertising and collateral materials:

1. Specific objectives for the ad campaign or the collateral must be established.
2. Both pre- and posttests should be used.
3. Proper research methods should be followed.

Pretesting is a way of assessing the potential effectiveness of the ad campaign or the collateral materials before money is spent to produce and place them, and includes testing several message variables:

FIGURE 9.2. *Business-to-Business Marketing Communications Expenditures*

After direct selling, most money spent on business-to-business marketing goes toward marketing communications, with print advertising and direct mail the two largest expenses. More than half of the communications budget is split equally between these two items. Expenditures for marketing communications are shown in the graph below.

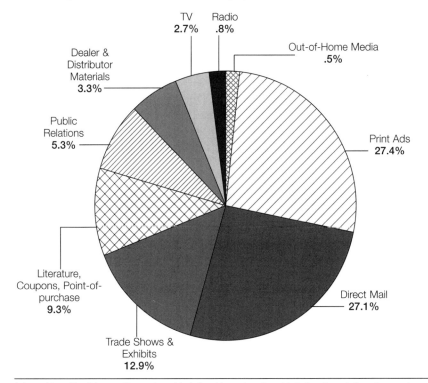

Adapted from The Wayman Group, Inc., *Marketing News,* American Marketing Association, January 1, 1996, p.1.

- Message concepts—does the ad impart the information needed by the target clearly and use the proper image?
- Message comprehension—does the target understand the message?
- Message impact—does the target react positively, negatively, or with indifference to the message and the product or service to which it relates?
- Message retention—does the target recall the major message points?
- Message reaction—what is the target's buying intent as a result of the message?

If the ad or the collateral device fails to deliver on any of these dimensions, it should be redesigned until it does.

Proposed media strategies can also be tested. This relates to researching audience infographics and them testing the impact of information delivered through what would seem to be the prime media channels. It should be emphasized that how people perceive ads and the products they hawk is affected by not only the medium in which the ads appear, but the context in which they appear. Consider the perceptual aura generated by television ads paid for by advertisers who put up $1 million for a spot in the 1995 Super Bowl.

Posttesting is necessary to validate or discount precampaign decisions and to provide important information for future decision making. Both of these methodologies and research procedures are discussed more in depth in Chapter 19.

It should be noted that posttesting can lead to either elimination of posttests when the data seem to consistently validate that proper decisions have been made or to the development of formula thinking in the development of advertising and collateral materials. The posttests indicated that this was a powerful sales supplement, so let's continue to use it. Both circumstances are attractive, since they ultimately lead to a major reduction in budget requests for research dollars.

They are both equally dangerous, however. Sometimes simply making a change in an ad campaign can result in a successful effort that isn't sustained over time. The spike in increased inquiries or sales appointments or sales was a result of the change itself, not of the message. And the successful formula is constantly changing. Using the same "proven" strategies and tactics repeatedly implies a static target, one that is standing still. Today's targets are dynamic ones, shifting and changing shape as you design ways to communicate with them. What works today won't work tomorrow.

RESOURCES

1. Barban, A. M., D. W. Jugenheimer, and P. B. Turk (1996). *Advertising Media Sourcebook*. Lincolnwood, IL: NTC Business Books.
2. Cox, G. R., and E. J. McGee (1990). *The Ad Game. Playing to Win*. Englewood Cliffs, NJ: Prentice-Hall.
3. Hall, R. W. (1991). *Media Math. Basic Techniques of Media Evaluation*. Lincolnwood, IL: NTC Business Books.
4. Lancaster, K. M., and H. E. Katz (1989). *Strategic Media Planning: A Complete Text with Integrated Software*. Lincolnwood, IL: NTC Business Books.
5. Ogilvy, D. (1985). *Ogilvy on Advertising*. New York: Vintage Books/Random House.
6. Schudson, M. (1984). *Advertising, the Uneasy Persuasion. Its Dubious Impact on American Society*. New York: Basic Books.
7. Schultz, D. E., S. I. Tannenbaum, and R. R. Lauterborn (1993). *Integrated Marketing Communications*. Lincolnwood, IL: NTC Publishing.
8. Wurman, R. S. (1989). *Information Anxiety*. New York: Doubleday.

NOTES

1. For someone interested in the historical perspective, three books are recommended: Marshall McLuhan's *The Medium Is the Message* and *Understanding Media,* and Vance Packard's *The Hidden Persuaders*.
2. King, Thomas R. (August 2, 1990). "Isuzu Ends Its Popular Liar Campaign." *Wall Street Journal,* B4.
3. Ogilvy, David (1983). *Ogilvy on Advertising*. New York: Crown Publishers.
4. Material in this section is adapted from Richard Saul Wurman's definitive 1989 book *Information Anxiety,* a must-read for anyone concerned with marcom or any mass communication endeavor.
5. Naples, Michael J. (1979). *Effective Frequency: The Relationship between Frequency and Advertising Effectiveness*. New York: Association of National Advertisers.
6. Rothman, Andrea (February 3, 1989). "Timing Techniques Can Make Small Ad Budgets Seem Bigger." *Wall Street Journal,* B4.
7. Miller, Cyndee. (January 1, 1996). "Marketing industry report: Who's spending what on biz-to-biz marketing." *Marketing News,* 30 (1), p. 1.
8. Bogart, Leo (1995). *Strategy in Advertising*. Lincolnwood: NTC Publishing.

CHAPTER 10

Relationship Database Marketing: Spending $20 to Make a Dollar

> "We have for the first time an economy based on information, a key resource which is not only renewable, but self-generating."
>
> —John Naisbitt, *Megatrends*

Customer data have been amassed which are resident in different areas of the organization. Customer databases exist, for example, in marketing, sales, finance, distribution, and customer service, each originally designed for different purposes and uses. None of these lists are on the same network, or accessible through the same hardware or software. There is no central information collection point, no standard information format, and no guidelines that indicate what information is desirable. Now your organization has decided to implement database marketing or, at the minimum, to revamp its databases. Management wants decisions about what the hardware and software costs are going to be.

What is your first step?

Database marketing is one of the hottest buttons in marketing today, but perhaps one of the least efficiently utilized marketing tools. This is due to a frequent misconception that a database is a tactical resource, not a strategic one, and that database marketing is simply the management of large databases of names and other transaction data which have been accumulated about customers or prospects. These databases expand quickly, but just as quickly become choked with irrelevant information. The lists that are generated are used in shotgun marketing, which is not only more expensive for the marketer, but adds to the excessive "information noise" clients already experience. As a result, an organization's strategic database marketing decisions typically focus on which hardware and software will provide the most efficient list generation, storage, and retrieval.

But focusing on hardware and software decisions is a seriously inefficient example of a cart-before-the-horse strategy. Before these system decisions can be made, an organization needs to define

- How information fits into its overall marketing strategy,
- What information is relevant,
- How that information is to be acquired and brought into the organization,
- Who needs to have access to which parts of the information,
- How the information is to be disseminated and in what format,
- When, where, why, and how it is to be used, and
- Who is going to have ultimate responsibility as the information czar within the organization.

Once these decisions have been made, most of the hardware and software decisions are less difficult to make and can be turned over to an external consultant who specializes in recommending appropriate workstations, networks, software, and servers.

This chapter provides some guidelines to answering the questions raised above in the context of a relationship marketing strategy that uses progressive databases to support the communications functions of micromarketing.

CHECKLIST OF DO'S AND DON'TS

- Do's:
    1. Do develop a marketing perspective that recognizes that customer relationships, not products or services, are the organization's primary asset.
    2. Do make marcom a major defining element of any marketing strategy. The strategy should include who the information target is, what information the target requires to make the appropriate response, and when, where, and how that message should be delivered.
    3. Do get a commitment from management that says it has understood that the initial investment establishing a sophisticated

    regional or national database can be substantial, and that little
    return on investment will be realized normally until the second
    year, when the database reaches critical mass and the in-house
    technology improves.

4. Do establish a protocol so that all marketing, sales, finance, distribution, and customer services activities work off the same
   major unduplicated database.

5. Do adopt a "segment of one" communications strategy that focuses on the information needs of the customer. This also means
   replacing the term "database marketing" with "relationship database marketing."

6. Do walk before attempting to run. Start with the most critical seg-
   ment(s) and establish a relationship micromarketing strategy and
   database for that segment. Then progressively expand the strategy and the database to include other segments.

- Don'ts:

  1. Don't make hardware and software decisions until it is deter-
    mined what information is necessary to fulfill marketing objec-
    tives and how that information is to be accumulated, where it is
    to be stored, and who is intended to have access.

  2. Irrelevant information should not be collected, much less stored.
    Relevancy is determined by whether or not the information will
    support the marketing objectives, strategies, and tactics.

  3. Progressive databases are infinitely more complex than transac-
    tional databases and require tremendous resource commitments.
    Don't abandon relationship database marketing before it has had
    a chance to establish itself.

  4. Marketing communications isn't managing projects and produc-
    ing materials. These activities can be outsourced; strategic plan-
    ning can't be.

  5. The database isn't the end; it is the means.

DATABASE MARKETING

Database marketing, according to Dun & Bradstreet Information Services of
Chicago, is operationally defined as merging primary (internal) customer
information with third-party data that can be used to drive the focus of marketing efforts and future marketing decisions. Database marketing implies
management of hardware systems and software. "Merging" internal and
external information focuses on process and the systems requisite to
accomplish that process. The end result is that the utilization of database
information takes a back seat to the acquisition, storage, and retrieval of
the data.

We'd like to suggest that the term database marketing be revised to relationship database marketing, which operates on the premise that the more that is known about a customer or prospect, the better a product or service can be provided to satisfy the customer's expectations. Relationship database marketing uses data to communicate more effectively with microsegments to establish mutually beneficial long-term buying and selling relationships. It suggests an operational definition that focuses on the strategic necessity for developing relationships with microsegments of the marketplace. The database is simply another tool that supports this strategy.

DE BONIS & PETERSON BUSINESS MARCOM RULE #6:
"In database marketing, the one thing that's most important is the 'one.'"

The emphasis shifts to the marketing activities and the resulting relationships rather than the database itself. A usable progressive database facilitates the execution of the myriad marcom activities marketers use to establish customer relationships. This is an important conceptual hurdle for an organization to clear before it can effectively begin to use primary and third-party data to reach its markets.

INFORMATION AS PART OF THE OVERALL MARKETING STRATEGY

As we have discussed throughout this book, the quantity and quality of information shared with internal stakeholders and external audiences largely determines the quality of relationship the organization has with both internal and external stakeholders.

Communication is an integral part of any marketing strategy, and effective communication requires an understanding of the audience. For people who have done outside sales, understanding the potential customer's information needs is always critical to establishing communication. Customer service requires knowing who the customer is and how to communicate with that customer. Collections is also an information-based activity.

The key to successful database marketing is identifying what is useful information and what is irrelevant, and then developing processes that allow that information to be collected, stored, and retrieved when necessary.

Those decisions are grounded in the most basic decisions about what business an organization is in. A sales-driven organization, for example, which measures success in the number of transactions made per time period, has information needs that are different from an organization that is relationship driven.

For sales-focused organizations, relevant primary data are defined as transaction data: buying center or buyer contact information and transaction histories, including what is purchased and order quantities, when it is bought and the price paid, account payment information and credit terms, service records, and promotions to which the customer responded. Third-party data are mail and telephone lists bought or rented for prospecting purposes. Niche marketers have relied heavily on databases, but mainly for finding new customers instead of retaining current ones.

A transaction strategy fails to exploit a fundamental principle of marketing—*that it is exponentially more profitable to keep existing customers than it is to acquire new ones.*

DE BONIS & PETERSON BUSINESS MARCOM RULE #7: "Lose the sale, but keep the relationship."

As a general rule of thumb, for example, it costs five times as much to acquire a new customer than to keep an existing one. An organization that has a 30 percent attrition rate among its customer base will not be as profitable as one that doesn't add a single new account, but that has only a five percent customer attrition annually. For banks, reducing credit card customer loss by two percent has the same effect on margin as a 10 percent cut in costs.

A relationship marketing philosophy, in contrast, stresses customer retention rather than new customer acquisition. It counts on the fact that a current customer has a net lifetime value (NLTV); customer profits are received over the lifetime of the relationship, which is usually defined in years. (Again, the NLTV is a discounted value; the revenue received in future years isn't worth as much today as money received today. The company's accountants can provide the formula for determining the discounted NLTV of the customer's future purchasing stream.)

An important corollary is that higher margins are achieved by increasing the NLTV of current clients by extending the life of the relationship and increasing the number and value of the purchases made during that lifetime. A seven-year customer, for example, is six times more profitable for a bank than a customer the bank keeps for only one year.

Relationships are important for the buyer as well; they help reduce or minimize decision-making risk. In the traditional laissez-faire marketplace, *caveat emptor* was a workable concept, because the buyer had face-to-face knowledge of the seller. Today, the seller and buyer are not geographically close, but new technologies allow one-to-one contact that mimics the segment of one or one-to-one marketing of the pre–Industrial Revolution era.

Customers need and seek out relevant, accurate information for appropriate buying decisions, information that provides a better knowledge of the marketplace and its products, is clear and easy to understand, and which doesn't add to the customer's already oppressive information overload. A company's marketing communications should be generated to satisfy these expectations.

For relationship-driven companies, relevant primary data go beyond buying center or buyer contact information and transaction histories, as is discussed in the next section. Mail and telephone lists are also bought or rented for prospecting purposes, but the lists are purchased on the basis of the information they are able to provide about prospective buyers.

Defining Relevant Information

Maintaining the customer relationships requires an effective relationship communications strategy and programs. Customer contact should be based on relevance, not frequency. This strategy requires understanding the information needs of the customer, which is a primary function of a progressive database.

Relevant information is situationally defined as information that is going to help the marketer better understand the customer or potential customer and how to communicate more effectively with that individual or organization. Hispanic buyers, for example, will generally read an advertisement or direct mail piece in English. But they prefer to read the fine print—i.e., the specific offer information, guarantees, warranties, and other qualification information—in their native language.

A notation that a business customer is hard of hearing is relevant so the next time that customer calls, the customer service rep can speak clearly and loudly on the phone. A record may indicate that the customer works a late shift so that package deliveries need to be geared for a late afternoon delivery.

A progressive database includes not only basic transaction data about an account, but also relevant behavioral information about buying habits, including who the decision maker was, what influenced the buying decision, and which decision-making strategy the buyer used.

This information is invaluable in creating products or service offerings, pricing strategy, distribution decisions, and promotional strategies. Attachmate Corp., for example, a company that develops PC communications software, uses data from the more than 165,000 annual customer service support calls it receives to plan upgrades for current software and identify market needs for new products.

Psychographic data—also known as lifestyle or activities, interests, and opinions (AIO) information—is also important, not just for segmentation or positioning, but to understand what messages would be important to the audience. A business can also be psychographically classified by its business activities, its public programs (interests), and political activism (opinions), for example, as well as by the psychographics of its management, shareholders, and other stakeholders, including employees.

Infographics of the target audience are also important, as was discussed in Chapter 4. *Infographics* means the information usage characteristics of market segments—what sources of information buyers in a segment utilize and rely upon to make or validate buying decisions, and when and where those sources are used. These would include traditional descriptors reflecting prospect and customer media habits, the relative weight assigned to these information resources, and other characteristics such as source credibility, the impact of one- versus two-sided information.

Segmenting a target marketing infographically allows for unique messages to be directed to microsegments using the communications channels or media that are appropriate. In this day of information overload, knowing when, where, and how to deliver a marketing message is critical. Information that appears in a customer's preferred information source has tremendous credibility.

How to Capture Relevant Information

Once "relevant information" has been defined, organizational resources can be assigned to be responsible for capturing and reporting that information. The basic rule of thumb is that any customer "touch point," i.e., contact with the customer, is an opportunity to gather information.

Sales information is perhaps the most obvious opportunity to capture customer information whether in the outside sales, telemarketing, retail, or direct response environments, or through the sales call sheets completed by an outside sales force. While the transaction information is important, so is other qualitative information about the account. Salespeople know, for example, who to contact at an account; what the best time is to reach that individual or group and when to schedule an appointment; what information is usually requested before a decision is made; and how to close the sale.

Customer service is a critical touch point, as are credit and collections departments. The former tracks customer concerns and complaints, and what was required to resolve the complaint. The latter could provide important information about how and when to approach an account and what financial information would be pertinent to the relationship.

Shipping, and installation and service departments might seem unusual modes for gathering customer information, but each represents a touch point. A shipping clerk talking to a receiving clerk may learn about a proposed expansion into a new sales territory by the receiving clerk's company. This would be important for marketing and sales in planning for future servicing and communication with this account. Or it might present an opportunity for sales to partner with the customer in developing more efficient ordering and distribution systems. An installer or service rep might also hear about how a recent sales promotions campaign had been perceived by clients, feedback that might not have been available through more formal, established channels.

The public relations department, in scanning the economic or business environment, might come across marketing intelligence that is going to have a drastic financial impact on a series of major customers, information that would be relevant to the current and future relationships.

Customer-initiated communications are also relevant. Tracking should include not only the reason for the communication, but who initiated it, when it was initiated, how it was transmitted to the organization and when, and what the response was.

It would be impossible to create a listing of all the touch point scenarios which occur during a typical (even a nontypical) business day. Suffice it to say that each touch point is an opportunity to learn something more about the customer, the decision maker, end user, influencer, or prospect. This information helps to maintain and extend the value of the relationships for both parties, and provides critical insight into the informational needs of the target. An organization needs to "get out of the box" and expand its conventional information gathering to include these myriad touch points.

An important corollary that needs to be established here is that each touch point represents a two-way communication opportunity. What is being said by the sales person, the customer service rep, the installer or service person, the shipping clerk, or the collections agent communicates a tremendous amount of information about a company.

Consider the local copier company that touts itself as a customer driven-organization, a message repeated in its trade ads, sales calls, and direct mail sales letters, all of which feature the CEO as spokesperson. Imagine the dissonance created in the mind of the customer when the service rep is consistently late for routine service calls, takes a smoke break every 20 minutes, and constantly complains about his job and belittles the organization for which he works. Nor is the rep responsive to the customer's questions about company services or knowledgeable about or interested in that aspect of his job. The intelligence gathering in this situation is by the customer and will clearly affect future purchase or lease decisions.

THE FUNCTIONS OF PROGRESSIVE DATABASES

A major function of a progressive database is to provide data with which customers and potential customers can be profiled, segmented, and targeted. Without databases that can tell you who your customers already are and to which customers items can be cross-sold, it is difficult for a company to increase a customer's NLTV.

For example, the FCC National Bank of Elgin, Illinois, which issues a credit card called FirstCard, initiated a multimillion-dollar project in 1994 to develop an integrated, relational credit-processing system. The objective was to create a progressive database that could be used to target FirstCard customers more precisely. Using software specifically designed to create a relationship database, the bank can track and analyze its customer relationships.

One major benefit would be to segment out and track the cards issued to businesses for their employees or to segment out and track personal cards that are used for business purposes. A business may have one or more accounts with the bank, including not only the credit cards, but checking accounts, commercial lines of credit, certificates of deposit, and other bank services. Information about all these accounts is linked into one marketing customer information file (MCIF), allowing the bank to target promotions to specific card users and groups of users.

Depending on the marketer's customer information needs, an MCIF can be a compilation of all information accumulated about an account or a file that links account information from several files in the organization so the marketer knows they are related.

In their simplest form, these databases create an opportunity to recognize a purchase or interaction anniversary. Your telemarketing rep calls with a reminder that, based on the customer's consumption history, it's time to reorder pencils. On your hotel's sales office calls to find out if an industry association is holding its annual sales convention in your city next year, as it does every third year.

An important *caveat* is that these relationship communications must not be phony. One buyer we know is perturbed that one of the salespeople with whom he placed a modest printing order has sent him a birthday card, an employment anniversary card, and a get-well card during a brief illness, despite the fact that, in his mind, the purchase was simply a transaction. A relationship was not established, nor was one necessary for this straight rebuy situation. In the buyer's mind, a meaningful relationship communication from the salesperson would be notification that prices on the products ordered will be going up by 10 percent the next quarter, so a reorder now would save money.

In its most sophisticated form, a progressive database provides important business or ordering cycle information about accounts, order quantities, the type of merchandise or services purchased, information about the decision-making process and the key players, and what types of cross-selling or upgrading opportunities exist.

A progressive database is also essential for the establishment of proactive customer service. Having relevant on-line information about a customer allows the service rep who has been empowered to protect and enhance the organization's relationship marketing strategy.

Rosenbluth International Travel knows which airlines, class, auto rental agency, and hotel a business traveler prefers by destination city, the airport from which the client prefers to depart and at which airport the client prefers to arrive, and the usual time of day the client prefers to arrive. Other information that allows Rosenbluth to provide one-stop reservations service for the client includes whether the customer wants a special airline meal ordered, which credit cards the client prefers to use, and whether he wants a nonsmoking room at the hotel.

Progressive databases also represent a potential revenue stream through list rentals.

TIPS FOR INTEGRATING YOUR PROGRAM

A key start-up strategy for relationship database marketing databases is to initially track a limited number of customer buying histories to develop NLTV profiles for the most desirable customer segments.

Strong customer relationships should be established with these major key accounts. One of the goals is to extend the lifetime of customer relationships, which increases their NLTV. This is supported by a marcom mix designed to increase the frequency and relevance of marcom contacts based on the premise that they help to strengthen the relationship.

The next step would be to focus on the second tier of key accounts and then the third tier, and so on. In each case the objective is to extend and increase the NLTV of those accounts, and to move them to the next higher level. These profiles also provide information for developing profitable prospect targets and for determining which marcom mix elements are most likely to be relevant to the prospects.

The expense of relationship database marketing programs have to be justified by segment by making sure the NLTV is valuable. Otherwise, these programs may merely evolve into an expensive way to deliver advertising.

MEASUREMENT AND EVALUATION

It is very easy to quickly become bogged down in database research and evaluation. Keep in mind that crunching the numbers and sophisticated statistical programs are not the objectives. The objective is to keep the progressive profile a dynamic one, i.e., one that is evaluated and modified as necessary on a fairly regular basis, preferably quarterly, but certainly no less frequently than semiannually. The research objectives should be to track randomly selected samples of microsegments to maintain the quality of the profile for each segment and to verify the NLTV.

For example, we had a call recently from an organization concerned about the relative value of Customer A, which was acquired in 1989 with an initial purchase of $5,000, and Customer B, which made an initial purchase of $5,000 in 1994. The immediate response was that this was the proverbial pomegranate and kumquat comparison; these are not cohort accounts. And that philosophically, the 1989 customer remained the more valuable customer because its revenue stream was known, whereas the 1994 customer was still unproven in the long run.

The person making the inquiry understood those two perspectives, but wanted to be able to compare the discounted value of 1989 and 1994 dollars versus the discounted value of Customer B's projected five-year NLTV. We think this is splitting hairs, but it could be calculated by someone in finance.

RESOURCES

1. David Shepard Associates (1990). *The New Direct Marketing: How to Implement a Profit-Driven Database Marketing Strategy.* Homewood, IL: Dow Jones-Irwin.
2. Hlava, M. M., editor (1984). *Private File Creation/Database Construction: a Proceeding with Five Case Studies.* Washington, DC: Special Libraries Association.
3. Hughes, A. M. (1991). *The Complete Database Marketer: Tapping Your Customer Base to Maximize Sales and Increase Profits.* Chicago: Probus.
4. Nash, E. L. (1993). *Database Marketing: The Ultimate Marketing Tool.* New York: McGraw-Hill.
5. Shaw, R., and M. Stone (1988). *Database Marketing: Strategy and Implementation.* New York: John Wiley.
6. *The 1995 Cowles Report on Database Marketing.* 911 Hope Street, Box 4949, Stamford, CT 06907-0949. 1-800-775-3777. Suggested retail price is $245.

CHAPTER 11

Direct Response Marketing: Laser Strikes on the Targets

"The question is no longer whether a company will use direct marketing, but how it will be used."

—Stan Rapp, President,
Rapp and Collins, 1985

The successful implementation of a progressive database strategy has allowed your company to identify tightly defined microsegments for marketing a variety of products or services. Alternatives are being sought to the traditional sales and marcom activities that will maximize the ability of the organization to make unique offers to these microsegments. One recommendation has been more emphasis on a direct marketing approach. What does this strategy entail?

Spawned in the early 1870s when the Montgomery Ward catalog was initiated, direct response has been one of the fastest growth areas in marketing during the past decade. Direct marketing is a selling method that has application for virtually every consumer, business-to-business, governmental, and institutional target. Direct marketing gives the buyer the three things he or she wants: buying convenience, buying efficiency, ad reduction in buying time.

By definition, direct marketing involves communicating directly with customers to generate responses, bypassing the traditional distribution channel or reseller environment. In one-step direct marketing, the customer responds to a marcom message and receives the product or service directly from the seller. In a two-step direct marketing program the receipt of the product or service is dependent on a second response by the buyer. A customer may respond to a subscription offer, for example, but would not begin to receive the publication until the bill has been received and paid. A negative response option means that the buyer responds and continues to automatically receive a product or service until he or she initiates a cancellation or disconnect. Obvious examples are video, CD, and book-of-the-month clubs where the product is shipped unless the receiver indicates the shipper should withhold the product. Perhaps less obvious examples are insurance policies or telephone service, which are renewed or continued until the customer initiates a termination of the relationship.

The major advantages of direct marketing include the ability to achieve a selective target reach, something that is best described as laser marketing. Laser marketing locks on, in military jargon, to a segment of one and guides a marcom "smart bomb" to the target. This microsegmentation capability means increased frequency levels in "striking" the target and better control of timing when the marcom messages will hit. Communications are more personalized and, as a result of these increased marcom efficiencies, marcom costs are reduced. This is especially true for the organization that is focused on the NLTV of the direct marketing relationships; it is more interested in making a slow dime than a fast nickel.

Business-to-business direct response marketing has traditionally worked well. It provides a time-efficient buying avenue for the purchaser. The major disadvantage is not knowing how or when to integrate direct response into the marcom mix. The result is wasted communications and failure to provide the appropriate information to the respective business segments.

CHECKLIST OF DO'S AND DON'TS

- Do's:
    1. Do develop a specific strategy or direct response marketing and set objectives that are integrated into the overall marketing plan.
    2. Direct response marcom is, by definition, two-way. Each communication must provide for a response opportunity.

- Don'ts:
    1. Direct response marketing shouldn't be underestimated as a business-to-business marcom tool. Both direct mail and telemarketing

have been productive tools for business buyers for many years. They provide the means for the buyer to talk to a lot of salespeople, initiate purchases, gather product information, and negotiate deals with a minimum of effort, time, and energy. Direct marketing also provides the buyer with some control over the sales relationship.

2. Don't become so involved in moving on to the next target or phase or strategy that you don't build in the time or budget to evaluate current programs. That evaluative process is critical to future marketing decisions. This is discussed more completely in the research chapter.

WHEN TO USE DIRECT MARKETING

There are five key marketing situations in which direct marketing would be an appropriate strategy. These are not mutually exclusive; one or more could be used to justify a direct marketing plan.

- When potential buyers can be identified relatively easily and reached through a direct marketing medium/media
- When direct marketing is the most economical and profitable means of product or service distribution
- When time constraints make it critical to obtain quick initial sales or to adapt to quickly changing market needs or product innovations
- When it is important to test the potential of a market before making a large financial commitment to market entry
- When accurate measures of buying responses are desirable

BASIC DIRECT MARKETING STRATEGIC DECISIONS

As in any marketing plan, a direct marketing strategy needs to be developed. The first step is to identify what the primary objective of the direct marketing campaign is to be.

Is the campaign intended to be a door-opener for other marketing activities? Is the objective to generate an inquiry, a sales lead, or trade show, exhibit, or store traffic? Is a final sale the desired outcome of the direct marketing activity? Is it a follow-up to a sales call or for customer resolicitation? Is the direct response strategy to solicit referrals from current customers? Is it intended to develop and enhance the customer relationship by providing product news and information that informs and educates customers about their buying decisions? Or is it primarily image building for a product or brand?

These decisions suggest that direct marketing is intended to be integrated into an overall marketing plan, as are all marcom activities, a theme central to this book. Deciding where direct response fits makes subsequent decisions about which marcom channels or media to use more functional.

It also allows the desired response to be identified and a strategy for handling the responses put into place. One telecommunications company we know has rolled out new services without providing the inbound customer service operators with the information necessary to handle the inquiries that were generated by the direct marketing part of the roll-out.

Knowing what the desired response is and planning for the response also allows response to be tracked, which contributes to the essential evaluation of any marcom program. The behavioral response can be quickly identified and tracked, which allows future modifications or adjustments to similar direct marketing efforts.

DIRECT MARKETING MEDIA

A number of media can be used for a direct marketing campaign, including direct mail, telemarketing, and print, broadcast, and specialty media. This section, however, focuses on successful direct mail strategies and tactics; telemarketing and advertising are discussed in other chapters. Direct response advertising is only one of the marcom tools and represents marketing promotion in which a product or service is advertised for purchase directly from the manufacturer or service provider. In other words, advertising in which the call to action is to buy the item directly from the advertiser.

Direct Mail Campaigns

Perhaps the most important lesson in using direct mail as a direct marketing tool is to understand that direct mail isn't advertising. Advertising is marcom directed at mass audiences that is intended to inform or persuade. Direct mail is a highly targeted segment-of-one marcom which is intended to sell the recipient on making a response. It is a "sales call in print" delivered by a disinterested third party. The three major functions of direct mail as a direct marketing tool are 1) to acquire new customer relationships, and to 2) increase the NLTV and 3) extend the lifetime of current customer relationships.

Checklist of Direct Mail Do's and Don'ts:

- Do's:
    1. Direct response offers are made to individuals; the marcom strategy must be to generate segment-of-one communications.

2. The mail piece may be the only salesperson who has contact with the prospect or customer. Not only must the benefits be sold, but the offer must overcome the inherent negative feeling toward direct response devices. Emphasize the major benefits: what will the product do for the respondent?

3. The basic objective of a direct mail campaign is to elicit responses. Make an offer that can't be refused.

4. The direct mail piece is a substitute for a face-to-face sales call. Ask for the order.

5. Do use a two-sided message approach—overcome inherent objections in the sales offer.

6. Do make the desired response very clear and make it an easy, nonthreatening activity. Repeat it at every opportunity, on every device in the mailing.

- Don'ts:
  1. Don't repeat the same offer in the same format over and over. Vary the offer, the incentives, and the physical format

  2. Don't get into a "formula" box, which means that every campaign is based on the formula developed 15 years ago. Each campaign is unique, even one that is done on a repeat basis. Each direct mail campaign is an opportunity to test and retest the tried and true.

  3. Design shouldn't overpower the function of the direct mail device.

  4. Establishing the budget, and then determining what to mail and how, is backward. First determine the function of the direct mail device and how it needs to be delivered to meet the objectives, then establish a budget for the piece that will do that.

  5. Don't rely on response rate as the only determinant of the success or failure of the mailing. Response rate is simply an indicator. A more valid measure is the NLTV of the relationships that are engendered.

  6. Don't ignore current customers, who are a known direct response quantity. A customer retention program requires at least 12 different communications with customer segments during the year. Each should be a different physical format and a different offer in the customer's perception.

Responding to direct mail or any direct marketing marcom is a learned behavior. That is one reason that the profile of the best consumer direct mail responders is older, more educated people who have tested direct mail solicitations and learned over time that ordering via direct mail works. Interestingly, women are generally better direct mail consumer responders than males. Business buyers have long used direct marketing as a way of improving organizational buying efficiency; it is less time-consuming and affords more buyer control than sales calls.

Four Types of Direct Mail Campaigns

The four types of direct mail campaigns are completed transaction mailings, incomplete transaction mailings, nonresponse mailings, and research mailings. *Completed transaction mailings (CTMs)* are part of a one-step direct marketing program. This would include product or service purchases, subscriptions, memberships, and donations. The key to a successful CTM mailing is to make it explicitly clear in the copy, in every design element, and on every piece that a purchase decision is the desired outcome and to ask for the sale.

Incomplete transaction mailings (ITMs) are used in a two-step marketing program. They include applications, lead generation devices, trial offers, and mailings to generate trade show, event, exhibit, or store traffic. A two-step program implies that there is an additional qualification necessary before the buyer is given an opportunity to make a decision. "If you are interested in this product, call our sales rep and he or she will make an appointment to meet with you."

Nonresponse mailings (NRMs) are intended to support a customer retention program and would include product or service news announcements, customer newsletters, and anniversary mailings. *Research mailings (RMs)* are questionnaires or other instruments designed to gather marketing intelligence about customers or prospects that helps the company market more efficiently.

A couple of brief *caveats* about nonresponse and research mailings are important. Since direct mail response is a learned behavior, any direct mail marcom device that doesn't require a response teaches nonresponsive behavior. For example, a computer store mails five brief newsletters without asking for any response. The sixth mailing asks for a purchase. The recipient has learned not to respond, a behavior that is hard to overcome. If each of the five had asked for a response, the target would have learned that responding was the intended behavior of the mail piece. The asked-for response doesn't always have to be a sale; it could be a response that would result in additional customer information being supplied, or one which asks for referral names.

The most critical rule for research mailings is that they must be legitimate. They shouldn't be disguised sales offers or supplemented with a sales pitch. This tactic not only irritates the customer, but dilutes both the validity of any data which is collected and the strength of the sales offer.

Critical Factors in a Successful Direct Mail Campaign

The most critical factors in managing a direct mail campaign are, in a loosely defined descending order of consequence, as follows:

- The lists that are used
- The offer that is being made, including the ease of response and the risk reducers that are offered
- The postage
- The physical format or design of the direct mail piece(s) and the budgeting for these materials
- The research, analysis, and review stage

Perhaps the most misunderstood part of the entire process is determining whether the mailing was a winner or not. Too often that determination is made solely on the basis of the response rate, which averages two to five percent for any direct mail campaign. Response rates are relative, depending upon the offer and the objective. While response rate is an indicator of whether or not the campaign worked, the NLTV of the relationships that result from the campaign is actually a more relevant indicator.

DE BONIS & PETERSON BUSINESS MARCOM RULE #8:
"The success or failure of a direct marketing campaign isn't dependent upon the response rate."

For example, a bank that targets a high-quality, expensive direct mail campaign to a highly qualified list of investment managers who control multimillion dollar portfolios may only have a response rate of .5 percent, but may convert all of the responses into an investment. That is a successful direct mail campaign. The same response rate for a company selling a low-ticket, low margin item would be disastrous.

Response rate shouldn't be confused with opening rate. With a little imagination and the right incentive, any direct mail piece that is delivered can be guaranteed a 100 percent opening rate. Whether the 100 percent who open also respond is dependent upon a number of factors, including the relevance of the offer, its timing, and other factors beyond the mailer's control.

Another important lesson is that, too often, the only response option provided to the buyer is "Yes." If your campaign has a 4 percent "yes" response rate, what do you know about the other 96 percent? Nothing.

You don't know if they said, "Yes, I'm interested, but I'll respond tomorrow" and then they forgot. Or, "No, I'm not interested right now," or "No, I'm never going to buy this product or service." You don't know whether the offer was even received; perhaps it was lost in the mail or sabotaged when it got to the organization.

Direct Mail Lists

The single most critical element in any direct response strategy is the list which is being used. The list should be highly targeted, narrowly focused on a microsegment, rather than a general list that results in a shotgun marketing approach and tremendous circulation waste.

As an aside, there are those occasions when the target may not be clearly defined. A direct mail piece could be shot-gunned to a universe; the intent of the mailing would be to have interested prospects prequalify and identify themselves for follow-up marketing.

There are basically four types of lists available—house lists, cooperative lists, responder lists, and compiled lists, in descending order of quality.

House Lists. Lists derived from internal progressive databases and primarily comprised of current and past customers and inquirers are called house lists, as discussed in the database sections. To briefly reiterate, any organization—small, medium, or large—has within its own business records a substantial amount of information that contributes to understanding the needs and expectations of customers and future customers, information that is augmented with data from third-party sources.

These lists—if updated and purged regularly to make sure that the contact information is correct—provide some of the most successful direct marketing targets available to the organization. The respondents are a known quantity. The organization knows what sells this group and what doesn't, to what types of offers and incentives these people or businesses will respond, and what marcom messages are necessary to achieve that response, including the type of direct mail physical format most effectively achieves the target's information needs.

Consolidated lists are a type of in-house list which is generated from the merging of primary in-house databases and databases and lists purchased from third-party sources. They were developed in response to the inability of compiled and responder lists to, for example, identify bilingual red-headed ex-Air Force pilots who fly an ultralight, live north of the Mason-Dixon line, and manage companies with 50 or more employees.

Customers are also a source for developing prospect lists using a "tell a friend" or "get a friend" strategy alluded to in the direct marketing strategy section. Customers who are satisfied with your product or service are frequently willing to identify other potential customers. They also have the ability to prequalify these prospects based on first-hand knowledge of their needs and interests.

As a rule of thumb, we recommend to clients that they conduct a referral campaign with customers at least once a year based on the notion that birds of a feather flock together. If you've captured one bird, they can identify the others in the flock.

The referral campaign strategy is to tell customers what the prospect profile is and shows them the direct mail offer the referral will receive. Customers are informed that, unless otherwise directed, their name will be used in making the contact with the prospect. While incentive programs for referrals are generally discouraged, unexpected thank-yous or rewards for referrals who become customers are a powerful way of enhancing the existing relationship with the current customer who made the referral.

Cooperative Lists.   A permutation of house lists are cooperative lists; they are derived from a database owned jointly by several organizations. These organizations could be companies that sell collateral products or services, or direct competitors. Each company contributes primary names and information from its own customer data, and each also buys and contributes third-party lists and data to enrich the cooperative database. For some companies, participating in a cooperative database list is the only way they will permit their data to be traded. The use of a cooperative list is restricted to the co-owners, which limits how often the names are used and provides controlled access to sensitive marketing data. It also provides highly qualified, narrowly targeted audiences, and provides the target with purchasing access to a group of companies that provide products or services the target needs or uses.

Responder Lists.   One type of publicly available third-party lists are responder lists. The names are on the list because of an overt response by the business, e.g., the company made an inquiry, purchase, hosted or attended a demonstration, or made a trade show visit.

These lists are relatively expensive due to their quality, which is a function of several factors, including the cost of acquiring and maintaining the quality of the lists. Responder lists generally have very accurate contact information, which means a low nixie (nondeliverable) rate, due to the fact that they are frequently updated and purged.

This increases costs to the list owner or broker, an overhead expense passed on to the buyer in a relatively higher cost per thousand names. The lists are sold on a restricted basis, which means that the owner has to make profit on fewer sales. Restrictions are typically placed on the use of these names, including what offers may be made to those on the list and the number of times the names can be accessed. This protects the quality of the names, ensuring that they are not oversolicited, which reduces their value to the buyer.

Responder list sellers frequently summarize transaction data discussed in Chapter 10 into large, medium, or small buys, for example, to protect their own transaction histories. This is usually acceptable to a list buyer, who is typically more interested in indices of purchase interest and potential value.

Compiled Lists.   A compiled list is one of the simplest forms of database output, and is assembled by independent third parties in the compiled list business or by a membership group that uses its roster as a revenue source. The lists include either business or individual and household data and are usually created from some published source. Public sources include business licenses and yellow pages listings, while private sources include business transaction records, purchasing information, and professional association membership rosters—for example, active members of the American Institute of CPAs, segmented by job title, area of interest, and ZIP code.

Compiled lists are relatively inexpensive in terms of cost per thousand names. They are cheaper to generate than responder lists and very little maintenance is done to assure list quality. Compiled lists have a high nixie rate due to the fact that they are updated or purged infrequently. As a general rule, a list that is not self-updating, or updated or purged at least semi-annually, becomes nondeliverable at a rate of 15 to 50 percent per year.

Compiled lists also have a high duplication rate. A compiled yellow pages list, for example, may provide 120 percent coverage of a target city's businesses. It is usually desirable to pay an additional charge for a dupe elimination computer run to a list broker or computer company that specializes in eliminating list duplications or to develop an in-house procedure to cull out the duplicate names and addresses. Compiled lists are typically unrestricted in terms of who may buy and use them. As a result, these lists may be oversolicited by organizations using a shotgun marketing approach that makes the audience less responsive to relevant offers.

It is estimated that there are 10,000 to 20,000 responder lists available in the U.S. list market and between 40,000 and 60,000 compiled lists. The starting place for identifying third-party lists is the Standard Rate and Data Service (SRDS) direct mail list directory, published by SRDS in Des Plaines, Illinois. Another strategy is to identify the target profile, determine on what type of lists this target would most likely appear, and identify and go after those lists. A list buyer who knows how to locate, negotiate the purchase of, and manage lists is worth his or her weight in gold.

Renting, Buying, and Testing Lists

External third-party lists are typically rented, though the list industry and its customers frequently talk about "buying" and "selling" names. Buying a list implies immediate ownership of the name and collateral information; the buyer can contact the name as many times as the company wants to and make whatever offer it wants to.

Renting a list means that list use is subject to restrictions that limit the use to one or two contacts and, in many cases, restrict the solicitation. Once the list renter has elicited a response from a name, however, that name becomes the property of the organization that elicited the response. A basic rule of thumb when renting a list is to make an offer the respondents can't refuse, even if it's only to generate an inquiry for additional information.

FIGURE 11.1 *Comparison of Selectivity Characteristics of Two Mail Lists*

	Cost/1,000	No. of Names	Average Annual Catering Expenditure
List A	$12.50	10,000	$600
List B	$15.00	1,000	$250

That response and when it was made is added to the in-house database and the name becomes a proprietary asset.

The quality of a list is enhanced by the number of selectivity factors the broker can offer, *i.e.*, whether a desired segment can be identified and selected from a list. For example, let's say you want the names of 500 companies that bought more than $500 worth of catering services in the past 12 months.

In the comparison chart in Figure 11.1, List A would seem to be the better list: a cheaper CPM (cost per thousand), more names, and a larger average order size per name. However, the names and addresses of companies and buyers who match your target profile can't be identified on List A. These names can be pulled, however, from List B, which makes it a more valuable list.

The Offer, Risk-Reducers, and Response Options

The offer, first and foremost, should be relevant to the buyer—something he or she needs or wants, or—in business-to-business marketing—something the organization needs. The ability to make such a determination is based on the quality of the customer and prospect databases and information gleaned about the purchasing needs and decision patterns of an individual or an organization.

The best means for generating a response is to offer something for free or at no risk. The free item need not necessarily be a product or service—it could be additional buying information, a premium, a sales contact, or other activity that will move the individual closer to making a decision.

The timing of the offer is also important. Making a sales pitch for ski equipment to a ski resort in the middle of the ski season would be less effective than a price sale at the end of the ski season or a summer sale.

The biggest fear in making any decision—whether it's making a purchase, deciding whether to turn left or right at the corner, or what punishment to mete out to a child—is whether we made the right decision or the wrong one. This is especially true for a direct mail responder.

Remember that the direct mail piece is a sales call in print; approach the buyer the same way that you would in a face-to-face sales situation. Provide risk-reducers that eliminate in the buyer's mind the possibility of making the wrong decision.

Generally, free trial offers are more powerful than money-back guarantees. But a free trial offer on a medium- to high-ticket item places too much risk on the seller, a legitimate reason for explaining to the buyer why the product or service comes with a money-back guarantee. Such a guarantee should be explained thoroughly as a separate element in the direct mail piece or, to be even more effective, as a separate stand-alone piece. The key question the guarantee should answer is how the buyer can't lose.

Whenever a trial or money-back period is offered in direct mail, it is important to make several follow-up contacts with the buyer to make sure that the company is using the product and the buyer is deciding that he or she wants to pay for it. A quick follow-up would be to check that the product or service was received and is being used. It is also helpful to restate the benefits to be derived from the product or service and how to obtain those benefits. A reminder should also be included that the trial or money-back clock is running and that a decision is expected by some date. This reminder should also be sent two weeks before the end of the time period.

Otherwise, when the buyer is notified that time is running out and that payment is expected or that the money-back guarantee is expiring, the least risky thing for the buyer to do is to return the product or service. This also helps forestall claims that the buyer wasn't aware that the 60-day trial or money-back period had elapsed.

The ease of response can also contribute to decision making. Consider the bounce back card that is printed on a gloss-coated paper with very narrow lines that don't provide enough space to type, much less print, the buyer's name, job title, company, address, and ordering information. In contrast, the response device that is already filled out and requires only verification of the information simplifies the response.

There is also an ongoing discussion about whether to offer anything other than an 800 number for responses. Our rule is to offer both. Some people will want to call immediately. Others will perceive the response card as delaying the decision and will opt to mail it. The decision about which response mode should be used isn't yours; it's the responder's.

One problem with direct mail offers is that they are typically designed as one-way communications that say "We'll speak, you listen." The messages are typically one-sided; they only tell the good stuff. This adds to the responder's risk, because she knows that there are some downsides to the product or service. In a sales call, these are called objections; the axiom is that the sale doesn't begin until the objections are raised.

A direct mail campaign must overcome the objections just as a salesperson sitting face-to-face with the client would. That means raising and responding to the objections: "Here are the 10 reasons we hear most often about why people wouldn't buy our product or service and how we respond."

That approach reduces the buyer's risk, because it acknowledges questions or concerns likely to arise in the decision making. It demonstrates that these questions shouldn't be barriers to making a purchase. The response provides the information needed to overcome the objections.

Clients occasionally question the wisdom of using this strategy; "Doesn't it place objections in the buyer's mind that might not have surfaced?" The answer is "yes." But by raising and overcoming the objections, the seller has subtly indicated that the concerns and the information needs of the buyer are of primary importance. If we can't overcome your objections, don't make the purchase decision.

Postage Decisions

It is typically assumed that direct mail campaigns are mailed at the bulk mail rate because of the costs associated with first-class postage. While generally true, first class rates can be reduced to around 20 cents per piece with appropriate bar coding, labeling, and bundling. We recommend spending a day at one of the U.S. Postal Service's bulk mailing seminars to not only fully understand the bulk mailing system, but to learn more about how to utilize bulk- and first-class mail.

The actual costs for a first-class mailing are significantly higher than bulk rate; 1 million pieces at $.11 is $110,000, and 1 million pieces at $.205 is $205,000. But the amount in question is the *difference* between the first-class and bulk rates. Your company will spend a minimum of $110,000 on the million pieces. The question is, "What would justify spending $95,000 more to go first class?"

That's an 86 percent increase in postage costs. But it doesn't require an 86 percent increase in response rate to cover the cost of the additional expense. If the product being sold by direct mail results in a net profit of $50, then 1,900 units—$95,000 divided by $50—would have to be sold to cover the difference. The product may, for example, typically earn a 4.5 percent response rate, or 45,000 units sold off 1 million pieces. To sell the additional 1,900 units means the response rate would have to increase from 4.5 percent to 4.7 percent, or by .2 percent to cover the cost of the difference between first-class and bulk-rate postage. If first class will generate an additional .2 percent in sales, it should be used.

There are five basic circumstances when a first-class postage option should be considered.

1. When it is critical to control the timing of when the piece is received. If the mail piece is going to be integrated with other marcom activities and the timing of its impact is critical to the campaign, first class provides a way of more narrowly targeting delivery. If bulk mail is going to be used for budgetary reasons, the mail room, lettershop, or bulk mail center (BMC) should have delivery data. Or a

bulk mail test could be conducted to determine average delivery times of materials so that the actual mailing could be back-timed to hit on the appropriate day(s).

2. For improved delivery when address forwarding and address returns are important, especially for maintaining quality progressive databases. This strategy is perhaps less important for a customer database that is updated through an aggressive customer retention program. It would be beneficial for a reactivation of a merge campaign. But it can be an important strategy for a prospect list that has a high nixie rate; having materials forwarded and returned can be beneficial in the long run by contributing to the quality of the names on the list. This service is available at an additional cost at the bulk-mail rate, which again requires an analysis and assessment of the difference in cost between first-class and bulk-mail postage.

   There are two important psychological factors that can be used to support a decision to use first-class postage.

3. It reduces sabotage, both in the delivery system and by the receivers. There have been an increasing number of post office bulk mail horror stories the past few years in which tons of direct mail materials have been found hidden in carriers' homes or in post office loading dock dumpsters.

   The interesting sidelight to us is that these situations are usually uncovered by the postal authorities. We are not aware of a single complaint filed by a direct mailer who realized that one ZIP code in a city was a virtual black hole—mail went in, but nothing came out. This shows a lack of tracking by the mailers, who undoubtedly looked at average response rates and perhaps even wrote the campaign off as a loser.

   For both consumers and business customers, pass-through, i.e., the ability of the mail to get through the organization, is a little easier to achieve with first class postage. Psychologically, the gatekeeper, i.e., the individual screening the mail, perceives a direct mail offer with first-class postage as being more important than bulk mail, a value-added perspective that is important in getting through to the target.

4. To increase the opening rate, especially for prospect audiences. Keeping in mind the earlier *caveat* about opening rate, postage can be included on a direct mail envelope or piece three ways: stamp, metered imprint, or printed postage indicia. Research has repeatedly found that stamped pieces have a higher opening rate than do metered pieces, even if the stamp is a bulk-rate stamp and the metered rate is first class. Indicia mail has the lowest opening rate

of the three. The hint would be that the success of a bulk-rate mailing could potentially be increased by using stamps.

Consider the art gallery offering high-quality, limited edition lithographic prints to 1,500 selected domestic dealers. The consignment terms were generous, the direct mail piece was a high-quality 12-color job. The list had been ruled to represent the most likely buyers. Then the postage decision arose. The difference between bulk rate and first class was around $250. The gallery owners decided that their shoestring budget couldn't absorb that amount and so the offer was sent bulk mail. The response rate was less than one-half of one percent. A follow-up to the campaign discovered that sending that offer bulk mail seriously devalued it and created dissonance in the potential customers' minds. They decided that the offer couldn't be as good as it looked if the seller wasn't willing to spend the additional 15 cents to mail it first class.

The final circumstance when first class postage is important relates to situations where your organization may have shot-gunned into a market to find prequalified buyers.

5. For initial response to inquiries. Inquiries should be responded to within 24 hours of their receipt, either by telephone or with a direct mail response sent by first class. The reason is that the inquirer's interest was as its peak when she initiated the inquiry. If it took the inquirer's bounce-back card three or four days to reach your office, several weeks to be processed and returned, the inquirer's interest has waned, if not the reason for the initial inquiry. The individual's status may also have changed. Collecting all inquiries received during the month and then mailing out a bulk-mail response means that the inquirer who contacted your company at the beginning of March isn't likely to hear from you until the middle of April or later.

Consider the salesperson who received a three-month-old bounce-back lead from a buyer. He placed a call to the buyer, which was answered by the department's secretary. The salesperson identified himself and the reason for the call, and asked for Mr. Johnson, who sent in the response. There was a moment of silence and then the secretary informed the salesperson that Johnson had been killed in an auto accident more than six weeks before.

Format and Budgeting

Don't forget that a direct mail offer is a sales call—each piece has its function. The envelope asks for the appointment and gets through the gatekeepers. Its design should satisfy those objectives. The sales letter establishes the length of the appointment and sets the agenda in the opening paragraphs, makes the sales pitch, overcomes the objections, and asks for the sale.The other inserts support the argument by focusing on specific features and benefits, providing the guarantees and overcoming objections. The response devices close on the sale and provide a means for responding.

Prospect Mailing Campaign

It's axiomatic that one-step direct response marketing can't sell something to someone who doesn't already need or want it. Since prospects are not randomly aligned in terms of need, want or interest, it is important to identify the potential customers who are most in need, most want, or are most interested in the product or service that is being offered using the databases already discussed. The objective is to skim these people off the top of the market and then include them in a customer retention program designed to increase the NLTV of the relationship and increase the lifetime of the relationship. This is discussed in depth in the next section.

The most critical factor in prospecting is the list. The more highly qualified the target, the more successful the campaign will be. The second critical factor is understanding that the prospect is at risk for responding; there is no existing relationship, no previous experience with your organization on which to rely in making a buying decision. And the buyer may know little about your organization. Keys to overcoming these obstacles include quickly establishing the relevance of your product or service to the prospect and generating a response by making an offer she can't refuse.

The third critical factor is understanding the buying process. It doesn't move from product awareness to product purchase, but progresses through a series of steps. From awareness the buyer moves to gathering information about the product, including asking other people about the product, seeking additional information sources, perhaps even testing the product and comparing it to other products. The buyer then makes a tentative decision to make the purchase, weighs the buy–no buy options and it is hoped, makes the buy. At this point the purchaser is a trial buyer, not a customer. She evaluates the product or service; this learning will influence future information gathering and purchase decisions.

A stand-alone direct mail direct response campaign implies an increasingly complex series of offers, each intended to move the buyer closer to the actual purchase. The initial contact may simply be to create awareness of the product. The second could be to provide detailed information about product benefits. The third could be to overcome objections. The fourth could be to provide comparison information for competing products or services. The fifth could ask for the sale.

It should be stressed that the buyer should be given an opportunity to make a purchase at each stage of the campaign. Don't make the most interested buyer wait for the punchline. Each mailing should provide the individual with an opportunity to make a purchase decision or to defer the decision while moving to the next stage in the sales process.

If direct mail is one element of a marcom strategy, then the function of the direct mail offer would be dictated by where it is integrated into the sales process. It is important to include multiple response options for prospects, ideally on separate devices. For example, a green-bordered bounce-back is a "yes" response device. Send me the product, additional information, call me, have a salesperson call. A yellow-edged card is for someone who says, "Maybe. Send more information." Or "Maybe, but not in the immediate future." Follow up three weeks later with a modified offer in a physically different format. Again, include all three response options.

A red-bordered card would be for the prospect who says s/he'll never be interested in buying your product or service. Hit them six weeks later with a different offer and include all three response options. Three months later try a cross-selling offer to perhaps generate a purchase in a related product area. Six weeks after that use a purge offer. Three months later try a second product offering. Try a step-down offer; perhaps the buyer needs to grow a house plant before buying a prefab greenhouse.

If the name still hasn't produced a sale after a year, ask for referrals; who are companies they know who might be interested in the product or service being offered. Follow the rule established earlier in this chapter for referrals. The rule is, never give up on a name, even if it's simply to swap.

The follow-up time frames mentioned are only intended to be guidelines. Your organization should have primary data that will indicate what the time frames should be for your customer base.

TIPS FOR INTEGRATING YOUR PROGRAM

As we've already discussed, it is easier and more profitable to maintain a customer base than it is to replace an existing customer. The three keys to a successful customer retention program are dependent upon a fully developed marcom mix. The keys are a high solicitation frequency, a greater variety of solicitations, and a wider variety of product, service offerings. This requires coordination among all of the marcom team departments.

An effective customer retention program requires at least 12 different communications with customer segments during the year. This establishes an important relationship with the customer that reduces his or her risk in the buying decision. Which airline would you be most likely to recommend to your employees or your travel agency? One that worked and communicated with you regularly during the year to let you know how much your company had saved on its business travel, or the one that contacted only when it thought it could sell seats?

It should be emphasized that the contacts don't all have to be through one channel, which is where the integration of the marcom mix is important. Having someone from your organization stop and visit a major direct response customer may not result in an immediate transaction, but it does strengthen the relationship. It also gives you a chance to gather some first-hand marketing intelligence about this particular organization. Using customer service reps to make phone contacts during slower inbound call periods—do they exist?—is another way of maintaining an ongoing, integrated marcom mix.

Each direct mail contact with a customer should use a different physical format and a different offer so that it is perceived as a unique offer by the customer. A different offer mailed in the same format has little impact; it is perceived as being the "same old, same old" offer. A variety of solicitations implies that the response doesn't always have to entail a sales decision, as described in the list of different types of customer mailings which follows. This list also provides some ideas about widening and varying the product offerings.

Some of these examples are relatively self-explanatory; others require some definition.

1. Reselling the main item. If the product or service is a consumable or has an estimated usage life, it is relatively simple to track and anticipate when the customer is going to need to reorder.

2. Indoctrination mailing to new or long-term customers. This is one of the easiest customer mailings to justify and one of the best received by customers. The objective for the newest customers is to explain how to obtain maximum benefits from the product or service. Messages to long-term customers would include a review of these benefits and the features that provide them, and additional value-added product or features uses which the customer may have forgotten, not discovered, or not used regularly.

3. Product/service line expansion offer. Requires new product development or licensing for products in the same product line.

4. Upgrade offer. Offering the customer a better quality product or service than the one purchased or a newer product.

5. Cross-selling offers. Offering the customer products not directly associated with the initial product purchase. We will not only sell you the smoke detectors to put in the company's bathrooms, but the batteries to operate them, and fire extinguishers as well.

6. Retention materials. These are catalogs, magazines, or other direct mail devices which are thicker and more expensive to produce than other materials and, for those reasons, are more likely to be kept by the customer. These serve as constant reminders of the product or service categories which are available to the buyer. They are essential for the next type of customer mailing.

7. Refer back offers. These refer the customer back to the original catalog. "10 percent off anything ordered from the Spring, 1995 outdoor catalog" or "20 percent off anything ordered in the next two weeks from pages 52–55." If you are a not-for-profit organization that solicits from businesses, you can refer company sponsors or coordinators back to specific programs run or supported by the organization. "The Thai orphanage described on pages 24 and 25 of your donor's guide has recently opened a building with 25 additional beds. This requires $10,000 annually to provide appropriate medical support. If each current corporate sponsor would raise $1,000, this would cover operating expenses for three years."

8. Referral mailings. This is the "get-a-friend" program used so successfully for years by outside salespeople. The basic concept behind the strategy is that satisfied customers are willing to tell you about people they know who would be likely to buy your product or service. A key tactic is to ask for a reasonable number of contacts; five seems to be the average. But make it clear that even one name would be appreciated, and that if the responder knows more than five, the additional names are welcome. Give your customers an example of what will be mailed to the referrals, what the offer will be, and how they will be treated. Provide a negative response option that says, in the absence of your asking that we not do so, we are going to use your name as the one who referred us to the new potential buyer.

9. Monthly statement mailings. These bill stuffers have low readership, but high impact and import for those who do read them.

10. Relationship marcom mailings. These typically take the form of customer newsletters, which is a discussion for a second book. The rule of thumb is that relationship communications devices rarely ask for a response from the recipient, which leads to a learned pattern of nonresponse behavior, as discussed earlier. Make readers an offer they can't refuse for something that is relevant and low-risk for them, and inexpensive for you to provide when compared with the enhanced NLTV.

11. Sale bulletins, promotional item, or seasonal item offers. The danger with sales bulletins is that business buyers learn to anticipate and wait for the sales, just as retail buyers do. Sale bulletins shouldn't be mailed on a predictable schedule; they should appear to the buyer to be randomly spaced.

12. An anniversary mailing. This mailing corresponds to the anniversary of the customer's purchase decision. One strategy is to extend the lead time; if the purchase was made in October last year, mail

the end of August or the beginning of September as the customer's need and interest starts to build. This permits several mailings before the interest or need peaks.

13. Reactivation mailing. This is a way to say to the customer that s/he's been missed, that she hasn't ordered in *x* months. Ask the buyer, "Should we keep you on our active list, and could we take your order?"

14. A purge mailing. Don't just eliminate names and addresses from lists. Let the person most qualified to do so make that decision—the addressee. An average response rate can be as high as 40 percent— one quarter will say "take me off" the list; one quarter will say "we've expanded, moved, changed our name and we haven't received any mailings recently, but here we are"; one third will respond, "keep me on the list even if I haven't made a recent purchase"; and the rest will respond with a purchase, which normally pays for the mailing. For the 60 percent who don't respond, either purge after 18 months to two years, sell the names to or swap them with another company, or remail a second purge after two weeks. Be careful not to fall into the trap of threatening to drop nonresponders and then failing to follow through, as several major national magazine subscription direct mailers do.

MEASUREMENT AND EVALUATION

Edward Nash makes a distinction in his direct marketing texts that is extremely relevant, and that is the distinction between testing and research. Testing is the process of producing marcom materials or conducting a marcom program and then tracking the results. The objective is to find out what worked and what didn't. But testing doesn't tell us why some people responded, why some business buyers' attitudes were changed, why the activity was successful or unsuccessful. That's the role of research.

It is very easy to justify the nominal budgets required for testing; the results can be used to make decisions for future marcom activities. It is more difficult to justify the budget for more in-depth research; the results may not have an immediate or direct application, which means that the ROI isn't immediately clear. One researcher we know is constantly testing and producing recommendations for changes in marketing and marcom. But rarely does she have the time or the budget to really develop an understanding of the reasons for the outcomes and she never has the opportunity to do the follow-up to see if the changes that were made based on the test results worked. This is one of the main discussions in Chapter 5.

RESOURCES

1. *The Journal of Database Marketing.* London: Henry Stewart Publications.
2. Ljungren, R. G. (1989). *The Business to Business Direct Marketing Handbook.* New York: American Management Association.
3. Nash, E. L. (1992). *The Direct Marketing Handbook.* 2d ed. New York: McGraw-Hill.

CHAPTER 12

Trade Show and Exhibit Marketing: Military Staging for Closing Sales

> "The greatest possible number of troops should be brought into action at the decisive point."
>
> —General Karl von Clausewitz

You have just been assigned the task of handling an exhibit at a new trade show. You don't know if the choice of shows was correct or not, but you have to make it work. The sales reps say you have to have a big cocktail party—after all, it's expected because the competition does it. You have no idea what the company's exhibit looks like because it is in a warehouse and it will cost thousands just to preview it. The president wondered out loud if the company should dump the show. The CFO is aghast at the cost of trade shows, and no one can cite a single sale that came from the last one.

What's your next step?

If the gods of marketing conspire to cause your tumble into only one dark pit of trouble, pray they don't make it a trade show. Aside from the cost of exhibiting, the drain on human resources needed to properly plan and staff an exhibit can be substantial. Technology oriented companies may push R&D people for months prior to a show, to finish products or get shaky ones stable enough for demonstrations.

There is probably no other area of marketing so fraught with misunderstanding and anxiety as exhibit marketing. The problem is that just about anything you do regarding trade shows is expensive. Also, it's your baby yet you must yield parts of its upbringing to many vendors and some groups over which you will have little control, such as labor unions. Lives have been threatened in the frequent clashes between a nervous exhibitor desperately seeking a successful trade show and a recalcitrant union member who cares little about anything.

Few companies attend trade shows with the right orientation. Few send the correct mix of staff to meet the show objectives—if they even identified objectives in the first place. Few show staffers understand the critical issue of traffic flow and how that is tied to exhibit design. Yet those same companies are quick to complain that trade shows cost too much and don't produce the leads expected.

As with any marketing communications tool, you must evaluate each trade show as critically as you might consider a new trade journal for advertising. A well-chosen trade show coupled with a well-designed and properly staffed exhibit can shorten the sales cycle and actually produce the most cost-effective results of any communications medium. But it cannot be executed in a vacuum. There has to be a plan and it has to be tied to other marcom tactics.

Nonetheless, the strength and power of exhibit marketing shouldn't get lost in a discussion of its pitfalls. Trade show selling pays, according to the McGraw-Hill Laboratory of Advertising Performance. In 1991, McGraw-Hill reported that the average cost of contacting and closing a sale with a qualified trade show prospect was $334, compared to the $1,384 cost for closing a direct sales call.

Presuming it is included in your marketing plans for the right reason, a trade show is an opportunity for power selling using artificial turf. We all know that getting the prospect to the home office is getting them on the best turf possible. Your staff and management are there as well as a customer showroom—everything you need. So think of a trade show as artificial turf you can control for good team selling.

- Trade show exhibiting provides opportunities for sales training and product training.
- Your non-sales staff get a first-hand look at a little reality beyond their cloistered confines at the home office.
- You can introduce prospects to current customers.
- You can talk directly with unhappy customers to isolate and defuse problems before they fester.
- You can check out the competition, perhaps finding new sales reps to hire.

In this chapter we will provide you a conceptual and practical overview of the issues surrounding exhibit marketing and how it works with the other communications tools.

Note: We use the word "exhibit" or "display" rather than "booth," because you are at a trade show to exhibit or display the company, its products, and its values. You are not there "to booth." Leave booths at the county fair. The other reason is that Europeans say "stand" rather than "booth," but the word "exhibit" translates easily into both the European and Asian marketing cultures.

CHECKLIST OF DO'S AND DON'TS

- Do's:
  1. Do identify the single major problem you want each trade show to solve for you.
  2. Do develop a show theme or slogan to use in preshow promotion and in the exhibit graphics.
  3. Do remember that you are not the only exhibitor your prospects will see.
  4. Do listen to prospects carefully. Seek clues for needs and use them as the hooks for your solutions. Reciting rehearsed lines will sound uncaring and inattentive.
  5. Do concentrate on the benefits of your products or services. Features really don't mean much to the key influences who sign checks.
  6. Do follow up on leads within five working days of the show closing.

- Don'ts:
  1. Don't assume your field sales reps can handle trade show selling. There are big differences between the two selling environments.
  2. Don't throw lavish parties. They don't build mindshare or a purchase stream. They just build big questions from CFOs.
  3. The person who designs your literature isn't necessarily as good at designing exhibits.
  4. Don't do trade shows without preshow promotion.
  5. Don't let anyone tell you trade shows are no place for selling.
  6. You don't have to own an exhibit. Exhibits are selling tools, not ego trips for country club banter.
  7. Handing out lots of literature at shows is a mistake—unless of course your show goal is to pass out lots of literature.

EXHIBIT MARKETING MYTHS

A trade show is an expensive place to harbor myths, so we think you should be aware of them before you are assigned the duty of managing a trade show exhibit.

Some companies live a costly fiction: "This is a show we always go to. People expect us to be there. It's a big party, really, so the main thing is the cocktail party we throw for everyone in the evening. The booth is just part of the price of admission. We take them out on the golf course, feed them some shrimp, give their spouses a big night out. They love it!"

So what's wrong with this picture, you ask? Well, for one, if this isn't a trade show they can sell at, why rent exhibit space? As importantly, if this is just old home week in New Orleans once a year, at what show do they exhibit to sell these prospects? Worse yet, do they actually believe shoving shrimps in people's mouths will make quota for them? The old golf and glutton route might have worked in old industrial selling, but modern business-to-business marketing requires sophisticated selling to precisely targeted, qualified prospects.

To evaluate a trade show's potential for your company, ask some basic questions:

- What percentage of this show's attendance is our target group?
- Is this national show more effective than smaller regional shows (or vice versa)?
- Will key decision makers (i.e., check signers) attend this show, or merely the evaluation committee? If not, what other marcom medium will be used to reach those key decision makers after the show?
- What preshow promotion will be needed to break through to these prospects given that you have never attended the show before? Is our product up to the test this year?
- Given the expense and lack of mindshare, would it be better to first send a few key representatives who can work out of a hotel suite and evaluate the show for next year?

Even if you have attended a show before, a new product line or strategy may require a total reevaluation of your trade show program. Borrow the popular financial tactic of zero-based budgeting. Ask yourself these questions: Does this show fit into the new strategy or product line? Should you reevaluate the show attendance to see if this is the right group?

Trade shows have a life cycle just as products do. They tend to wear out over time, shifting focus or losing punch. Given the expense, it is important to know why you want to go to a show and to ask that regularly.

Mathematical myth abounds at trade shows. One is the attendance figure. There is virtually no trade show that's a 100 percent match for any exhibitor if you consider the total attendance. For one thing, the total attendance includes other exhibitors and often the spouses brought to the show. As an exhibit manager, you must zealously find out the attendance breakdown and match that to your target audience. Only that net audited figure should be considered in a cost-per-attendee analysis.

A numbers game might work for consumer products in the broadcast media, but not for business-to-business marketers at trade shows. It's ill-advised to assume that if you push more people through your exhibit, magical success will come your way. In fact, depending on the sales cycle and the cost of your product or service, you could mathematically show that fewer people will spell success much faster. Consider this. Do you want 500 people to walk in so you can show your management what a popular exhibit you had, or do you want to promote the exhibit to the 50 qualified prospects likely to buy? In short, be busy with the 50 known quantities rather than the 500 unknown quantities you just might get stuck handling. The numbers game is tricky in business exhibit marketing.

OF VON CLAUSEWITZ AND THE ORDER OF BATTLE

The chapter opener quotes Prussian general von Clausewitz. Perhaps the battlefield metaphor to marketing gets stretched somewhat for exhibiting— von Clausewitz probably never saw a trade show.

A battlefield is an attempt by two armies to control turf and the strategic passageways around it. When the order of battle is established, the controlling general briefs the staff on the specific objectives of that battle on that turf, which will be entirely different on the ground 10 miles away.

The same can largely be said of trade shows. Two shows in the same industry can draw slightly different audiences. Winning over the masses is important, but is not the main purpose of the battle. Inside the exhibit, control of the environment is important and is critical to the battle plan.

Like a general, an exhibit manager must lead his or her colleagues toward a couple of precise objectives. At a trade show, you will deal with several generic groups (i.e., current customers, new prospects, trade press, and business press). It would be difficult to effectively manage objectives for more than these four groups.

This is especially important given the trend in trade shows: the growing number of trade shows responding to the growing number of specific, discrete interest groups and customer niches. You can't say and do the same thing at all your trade shows, even if you have one product line.

As marketing strategies differ, so do their effectiveness under changing conditions. But the evidence has been clear for some time that both the cost-per-sale and the sales cycle are shortened through trade shows compared to a program relying solely on field sales calls. Again, it's the opportunity exhibits provide for setting up an artificial turf of your own control where an *ad hoc* selling team is ready to overcome every objection the prospect can throw at you.

A number of years ago a major computer maker chose not to attend a national computer show. Some time after the show, a considerable number of attendees said they had visited the absent exhibitor's exhibit! What this says about show surveys or attendee brand awareness or attendee attentiveness is for another discussion. But it should spotlight one thing: trade show attendees can be fickle. You must act to ensure your exhibit has the proper mindshare both to build traffic and to convey the right message.

EXHIBIT SYSTEMS, MATERIALS, AND CONSTRUCTION

In this section, we break some icons by challenging you with two fundamental questions—sort of a zero-based budgeting of the mind. As we have said before, exhibit marketing is expensive. In order to contain costs so the cost-per-attendee and cost-per-qualified lead makes it all worthwhile, you must be cognizant of the black holes of trade shows.

Trade show black holes are those ravenous accounts that seem to leave gaping bites in your budget—and invoices likely to make a CFO's hair singe. Those items are exhibit construction, freight, and drayage. Looking at those fearsome costs, you can see one thing shared in common. It's weight. Reduce weight and all three cost centers are reduced.

Let's put aside weight for now and examine another cost nightmare. If you do several shows per year and you are assigned the same space dimensions in each show, you are blessed with a consistent measurement for exhibit planning. If you do several shows per year but have little control over space dimensions, you have a severe cost control problem. You lack control because you must remake your exhibit to meet the dimension you drew in the booth selection lottery. Renovating a custom exhibit, which involves expensive carpentry and heavy plywood, can often cost 10 to 20 percent of the original exhibit's cost.

The first fundamental challenge is, Why have a custom exhibit? With changing markets and volatile economics, it makes much more sense to have some form of modular exhibit that can be reconfigured and easily installed and dismantled.

The flexibility of a modular system is only one advantage. Equally important are the materials used to construct the panels, connectors, and supports. The lighter the weight, the more easily your staff can assemble without outside labor. Freight and drayage costs are also reduced with most modular exhibits. When reviewing the proposals of exhibit houses, pay close attention to the weight of the materials, the simplicity of the connectors, and tools required to install and dismantle. These are as essential to the evaluation of the exhibit as its appearance.

The second fundamental challenge is, Why own an exhibit in the first place? "Well, we have to have an exhibit! What a silly question," you say. Of course you must have an exhibit. What we are posing is far more basic: why *own* one?

Let's go back to your exhibit program. You have several shows per year with no predictable control on the allotted space you draw at some or all of those shows. We have already discussed the advantages of modular exhibits. But what if you announce a new product line or service that requires a different sized exhibit than even your modular unit can handle? What if you have to run simultaneous shows, or start an exhibit program in Europe or Australia? Suddenly your modular exhibit can't be stretched. In short, your flexible exhibit isn't flexible enough.

DE BONIS & PETERSON BUSINESS MARCOM RULE #9:
"Trade show exhibits are all about strategy and tactics. Owning one, however, is nothing but ego."

The solution is a *flexible exhibiting capability* that eliminates the anxieties over space drawings plus offers you the option of a "new" exhibit annually.

The other part of this flexibility equation is alternative methods of financing. This could be a rental program or a leasing program. When most people think of rented exhibits, they think of the dented and tattered aluminum wonders offered for rent by convention centers or exposition management firms. This isn't what we are recommending. Instead, you must find an exhibit house that can plan your exhibit needs with a rental program or a long-term lease contract that covers the vendor's purchase of an inventory of components for all your possible needs.

Such an exhibit house should be viewed as a strategic marketing vendor, much like your advertising or public relations agency, who thoroughly understands your goals and with whom you foresee a long-term relationship. This chapter's sidebar, "A Professional Opinion," focuses on an exhibit vendor who is a true pioneer in such an arrangement.

THE EXHIBIT MEDIUM AS THE MESSAGE

As with all marcom activities in general and your trade show program in particular, you must be the owner of process. You must constantly guide your colleagues toward the goal of balancing the macro with the micro. With all the details involved in a trade show, it's very easy to forget the macro, i.e., the big picture.

Clearly, the big picture is the single perception or impression prospects will have as a result of visiting your exhibit. When attendees are surveyed, what single "top of mind" recollection do you want them to cite? Don't expect them to volunteer more than one impression.

As you consider materials and forms and shippers, also dwell on message. Agonize over it. Consider how and where that message should be displayed.

Remind yourself why your company wants or needs to be at this show this year. Examine each target group you anticipate in the exhibit. If fate could be with you, what precisely stated perception would you like each key influence to have when they leave?

Here's a simple exercise to help you. Draw a simple graph with prospect types listed on the vertical axis and the following words across the top: nouns, adjectives, and verbs. Try to reduce your show objective for each key influence into each sentence part. As you complete the exercise you should find it easier to develop one show theme that can be rendered and displayed in your exhibit, your show guide, and your literature,

An example follows:

- Reiterate (verb) to existing (adjective) customers (noun) that support to older products they purchased will be continued.
- Emphasize (verb) in our presentations to new (adjective) prospects (noun) that the announced products can accommodate later add-on modules to solve additional problems.
- For the trade press (noun) spotlight (verb) the new (adjective) products that reinforce our stated product direction.

Using this exercise, you might want to develop a simple "What's New at ACME" sheet for the trade press who might spend only five minutes in your exhibit. A piece that diagrams your product direction could help prospects follow your presentation. A service support summary for existing customers will make them comfortable if the new product lines are substantially different from what they bought from you. And the show theme? "Acme . . . where customer support and future direction work in tandem."

Designing the Exhibit's Message

It is essential that your exhibit house know well ahead of the show what message you want to convey. The various key influences who visit your exhibit may need the message and product information delivered in different locations of the exhibit. For example, a 5 to 10 minute video may be the appropriate place to direct the high-level executive who has appointed the specifying team but merely wants a once-over-lightly feel for your company. However, the hands-on members of that specifying team may require a full product demonstration. Exhibit design, therefore, must reflect these different pathways to the message, show theme, and show objective.

Connecting message to exhibit design requires consensus on the look and feel you want for the floor plan and facade. The exhibit design house needs to know if what you want to convey is the mystery of a product

A PROFESSIONAL OPINION

Eugene Winther is a man with many points of view. In fact, he has built his company, 360 Designers & Producers of Sacramento, California, into an international trendsetter by challenging some sacred cows of exhibiting. Once while setting up a 10,000 square foot exhibit in Las Vegas, he wondered out loud to the client why anyone needs an exhibit larger than 3,000 square feet. He hated building custom exhibits so much, he decided to get out of the business entirely when he bought the rights to the Expon modular technology. And heresy of heresies, he tries to talk clients out of owning any exhibit.

What follows are excerpts from "Winther on Exhibiting" from his address to the 1992 International Exhibitors Association (IEA) Conference and Exposition:

"There are two common reasons to buy a new exhibit. Either the current exhibit no longer fits within the company's marketing plans or the exhibit begins to show wear and tear. Identifying the reason for a new exhibit is pretty simple. But paying for a new one is often a complex problem. Even in good times, most companies watch capital expenditures closely. Capital purchases have to be justified on function and productivity but also the effects such purchases have on financial statements and tax liabilities.

"Many companies find the cost of a new exhibit too high for a lump-sum cash purchase. And this often brings the plans for a new exhibit to an end. However, some financing alternatives can uncover sound ways to fit the high cost to the company's budget.

"A good place to start is to review basic accounting. Buying an exhibit outright results in an asset on the balance sheet. Depending on the financial situation of the company, this may or may not be desirable.

"Also, unlike fine art and vintage automobiles, vintage exhibits don't appreciate in value. Although a company can depreciate the exhibit asset (deduct a certain portion of its value each year), the residual or salvage value will be a fraction of the original purchase price. What's more, there's the problem of how to dispose of the exhibit.

So let's expand our financing alternatives. To do so, you should realize that modern exhibit financing options are grounded in the notion that owning an exhibit

---

under wraps for only those special few who qualify, or an open design that invites all.

You might ask, "Why are you pushing the idea of an exhibit design house—the guy who does our ad collateral is a genius."

He very well may be—in a two-dimensional environment. But an exhibit is three dimensional. What's more, the layout must pay careful attention to the traffic flow issue of what you want people to do when they walk into your exhibit. As mentioned earlier, different types of prospects need to be routed differently. In addition, every show has rules against crowding aisle ways or distracting adjoining exhibitors with excessive noise. Such problems are addressed easily by a professional exhibit designer.

is less important than merely using it. In fact, alternative financing can result in treating the exhibit as an expense. This can be done through renting, but leasing is another option. A lease program can be set up that permits a company to treat the exhibit as a fixed and predictable expense over several years. That can make an ally of any CFO concerned about the rising costs of exhibits.

"Usage options can be considered. For example, a cooperative partnership can be formed between two companies or corporate divisions to rotate use of an exhibit. This works best when each company or division has a static show schedule and always uses the same space on the show floor. A good exhibit vendor can help make this a possibility.

"Co-occupancy is another option. Get a company with a complementary product line to exhibit with you each year, sharing the cost of space, exhibit, and other easily defined items. In fact, don't disregard out-of-hand the idea of sharing an exhibit with your competition. For the National Shopping Center Association show, my company constructs an annual "Pavilion of Shopping Center Contractors." Costs are split evenly. As significantly, the combined exhibit makes for a "must see" draw for prospects who otherwise must walk the floor to talk business with the various contractors. After the prospect reaches the floor, each vendor has equal access. But the Pavilion gets them there.

"To accomplish all this, you have to separate exhibits from egos. Get past what some call the 'edifice complex' and the costly contest of who owns the glitzy exhibit of the year. What you want is the use of exhibit tools. Flexible tools. What's more, you really need flexible arrangements and usage. If you own a custom exhibit and later see the need to add a new show for a new product line, you could find yourself with a round hole/square peg exhibit problem.

"Instead, gain access to a flexible exhibiting capability that can meld to your needs. Seek out a vendor with light weight, modular components. If you have an international focus, make sure that vendor has dealers or associates who know how to handle your exhibit needs in Europe and the Asia/Pacific convention centers. These markets are changing and you need expertise familiar with changing laws."

Exhibit graphics should cite benefits but keep text to a minimum. If something doesn't grab attendees' sense of self-interest quickly, they will move on. Focusing on features and exotic product names is an easy fallback, but forgets the fact that attendees are rushing through many exhibits. So don't force people to do lots of reading to figure out what you can do for them. All the creativity in the world means little if it doesn't strike the "benefits control center" of the prospect's psyche.

Once your plans for designing your show theme and objective into the exhibit graphics are in place, it's time to review your literature program to make sure it is ready for the show.

Although collateral sales literature is covered in more detail in the "Tips for Integrating Your Program" portion of this chapter and in Chapter 9, one item is worth mentioning in the context of exhibit design and traffic flow. Any exhibit larger than 1,500 square feet or featuring more than one product line for different audiences should provide an exhibit guide for walk-ins when they approach the reception station. It will keep them busy as your receptionists enter their names and call the field reps to the station.

The exhibit guide should have a clear layout of the exhibit indicating where prospects can find specific products. Large exhibits should color-code various product stations with the layout in the guide. The guide should include the telephone numbers of the exhibit and your hospitality suite in case prospects decide later in the show that they need a second visit. To increase the guide's retention rate, add the names and phone numbers of several restaurants in various cuisines. The exhibit theme should be on the front panel of this piece (a pocket size 6-page gatefold works best). A space should be left open for the field rep to write in his name and business line or attach a business card.

The "main idea" message of an exhibit can be enhanced by the type of exhibit approach you take. The most common is the simple display of the various products. Another approach is the theatrical exhibit that catches aisle traffic by portraying "slices of life" meaningful to attendees. The attendees' curiosity brings them into the theatrical presentation and motivates them to sign up for demos or further discussion.

The environmental exhibit attempts to replicate the surroundings of the attendees' day-to-day work space. The environmental exhibit is expensive but can create the perception that the exhibitor intimately understands the attendees' daily dilemma.

REORIENTING THE SALES STAFF

Believe it or not, field sales reps are not inherently good at handling the sales environment of a trade show. Technical people from your research and development staff can surely be important to overcoming some prospects' objections, but technical people are often more attentive to the beauty of their product engineering than to customer needs and wants. Product managers suffer from feature focus, and by the time the show opens for a product introduction they are focused on the next product.

That's why it is important to orient your show staff to the objectives for the show and the essential priority of each customer's individual focus. As for the field sales staff, they need to be oriented to selling in an environment quite unlike the field.

Field Reps' Responsibilities

Let's discuss field reps first. Even in the context of cold calling, a field sales rep can concentrate on one prospect at a time. Each prospect site may have a variety of interested individuals each asking questions germane to personal needs, but it is still one prospect site. The field rep can assess the situation and the time needed for each visit, set appointments, decide who requires the fuller attention of lunch or dinner, follow up accordingly . . . and tomorrow is another day.

Not so at a trade show, especially if it truly is a show that attracts the target audience desired. At the next show you attend, take the time to see how people are received, processed, directed, and attended to. If the exhibitor is a hot one with a high-interest product, the reception counter (and please, make sure you have at least a small one) will be deep with prospects.

The people crowding your reception counter will range across a spectrum of interest. There are the "booth groupies" who got permission to take a day off for a show they told the boss was essential. Then there are the "casually curious," wanting one or two quick questions answered, but not intending to buy right now. Then come those "blessed innocents" who are seriously interested but not budgeted for 12 months or more. There are the "live ones" seriously interested with approved budgets, often carrying a list of questions from colleagues back home. Lastly, there are the "gurus and disciples"—a key executive and an evaluation team—who arrive at the counter fully budgeted and looking for a "here-and-now" solution.

What is the reception manager to do? His job is a tense one: keep everyone at the counter content until each is assigned to the correct territorial rep, track down the rep, and reserve demo time if appropriate.

Is the rep taking a break or is the rep with another prospect? Or is the rep back at the suite talking seriously with a guru and his disciples? Alas, it is discovered the rep is with another prospect. The rep is hesitant to abandon the current group, yet has another prospect ripe for qualifying. The rep knows little about the waiting prospect because the usual logical progression of things done on a field sales call is not happening.

Qualifying Prospects at Trade Shows

To make the change from field selling to exhibit selling, both the reception personnel and the field sales reps must be politely efficient about the main qualifying questions. After the introduction at the reception counter, the rep should make liberal use of the attendee's badge to find out her title and function:

- "Do you know Mr. Jones, my customer there in Des Moines?
- "So, who else is attending the show with you?

- "What product are you reviewing at the show?
- "Do you have a deadline for making a decision about that product or do you have some luxury of time?"
- Are you budgeted for it now?"
- As the meeting progresses toward qualified status: "Would it be helpful if your team could meet with our team to further the conversation?"

Admittedly, it's a rapid progression of questions and takes a graceful but commanding manner that cuts to the quick. But you don't have the luxury of a casual visit at the prospect's home office.

This is why field sales reps have a love/hate attitude about shows. Psychologists call it approach/avoidance—i.e., they know the show is important and they know they must attend, yet they hate the disorder and disruption often commonplace at shows. But cut a trade show from the budget and watch them scream. It isn't much different with the non-sales staffers you bring to a show. Those with more introspective jobs (e.g., R&D) may be uncomfortable talking with prospects. Worse yet, they can become argumentative.

Trade Show Staff Handbook

You can begin working out these problems by distributing to all exhibit staff a show participants' orientation handbook. At the very least, this handbook should clearly indicate your objectives for each kind of exhibit visitor (i.e., current customers, prospects, press). It should summarize the state of the company and its products at that point in time. It should brief staff on the show theme or slogan and how that will be used in the exhibit graphics and literature.

The show handbook should list the attendees and their specific show roles, where each is staying, and the dates of each staffer's arrival and departure. If several staffers are taking the same flight, arrange shuttles from your office to the airport. Keep in mind, travel and overnights are uncomfortable for some people and their families. Do you want these people stressed out or impressed with the conveniences you provide?

The main show roles should also be specified so there is no confusion about who is in charge of what:

- Show management relations
- Press relations
- Dealer relations
- Technical set-up
- Exhibit installation and dismantle

The list will vary with industry and product line.

Exhibit rules are essential, and they should be in the employee hand-book. Specify the appropriate attire for men and women in the exhibit. It is essential that you address the issue of smoking, eating, and drinking in the exhibit. We recommend prohibition. Aside from the health issue of smoking, you don't want to pay for burned carpeting or furniture. You can't very well tell customers to put out their cigarettes, but you surely can tell staffers. The same goes for eating or drinking in the exhibit. It looks awful, and customers don't want to interrupt someone who is eating a sandwich. Another issue is chairs. Although demonstrators may need stools, and the-ater areas obviously need chairs, no exhibit staff people should be sitting down.

Remember that not all staffers are used to overnights and finding places to eat in strange cities. They will want to know what facilities their hotel has, e.g., pool, exercise room, fax numbers, shops, and in-house breakfast and dinner facilities. Have the hotel send a property layout and multiple copies of their facilities description. Get a list of restaurants according to each cuisine (including vegetarian) with reservation numbers and address-es. Include a map of the city specifying where the hotel is from the con-vention center and what public transportation is available. The hotel or local convention and visitors bureau will gladly send these.

Why include all this in the show handbook? Your show handbook assures staffers that everything has been thought out with authority and experience. It enhances the perception that there is no need to worry about personal logistics, so staffers can concentrate on their assigned task. You want your staffers to be comfortable with this often involuntary assignment to a trade show. You want them to communicate their comfort level with prospects and customers. You want them to be as relaxed and attentive as possible. You want them to be fully tuned in to the show theme and com-pany message. As we point out in the chapter on employee relations, you want to create a sense of job ownership that customers notice.

Unique Opportunities at Trade Shows

While trade show selling can be a disorienting baptism by fire, its con-trolled environment affords an opportunity not quite available in field sales. For one, an exhibit staffed top-to-bottom with the right people from your company can handle far more objections than a field sales rep can. Secondly, the exhibit theme and staff can raise the comfort level of a seri-ous prospect and build positive mindshare for those prospects budgeted for later years.

As mentioned earlier, the idea of "exhibit as message" is a real tool—a macro concept—at your disposal. Listening attentively to customer prob-lems, probing the source of those problems, answering questions, building mindshare, establishing comfort level—this is the stuff of a productive

BREAKING MURPHY'S LAW

When you pack your bags for your first trade show, remember Murphy's Law. With unionized workers and a queue of exhibitors looking for service on installation day, anything can get lost or go wrong. The following tips will help you avoid some pitfalls.

First, make copies of every service form and contract and the checks your company sent. These records will be useful if any misunderstandings arise.

You can avoid lots of waiting by hiring your own labor crew. Avoid using show labor. Show labor views the show management as their client. Hiring your own crew makes you the client. But you must send a letter of intent to show management that you want to use outside labor, citing the name of the installation and dismantle company. Bring a copy of that letter.

Bring a list of all the important home office and show site phone numbers and fax lines. Your independent show labor crew will likely have its trailer office outside the hall. Include those voice and fax lines, as well as the cellular phone the labor crew supervisor carries with him. The list should include every vendor involved, the local sales rep's home phone, the hotel voice and fax line, and the voice and fax lines you will install in your exhibit. Include your public relations agency's numbers as well as the office and home phones of your exhibit management firm. Make several copies of this list and place them where you can reach them.

Bring a copy of the shipper's summary or exhibit shipment sheet so you know what is arriving on which trucks. Bring an inventory of crate contents.

Make several copies of the exhibit set-up drawings. Put one inside the exhibit crates (what if you get sick and can't leave the hotel), one in your briefcase, and leave one with your secretary. But even the drawings aren't enough. Bring photographs of your installed exhibit from all relevant angles.

Take a camera. Labor crews can get nasty in some cities. You want to take a picture of your exhibit when it is installed and take pictures of any obvious damage. Report damages immediately.

Keep a supply of regular company letterhead and news release letterhead in your trade show briefcase.

Always have your company phone directory, plus the home phone numbers of important people in the office you may need to contact at odd hours.

Buy a multi-function tool (Swiss army knife) and a first aid kit that includes lip balm, bandages, aspirin, antacid tablets, and hand cream. You will need all these things.

Lastly, bring a good book for escape. The first time you find yourself waiting until 2:00 a.m. for your freight to arrive on the floor, you will wish you had it. A deck of cards or other portable game can also spell relief.

---

exchange that can greatly shorten the sales cycle. That's why exhibit marketing is relationship marketing at its best.

But be aware that the comfort level, the relationship, exists only in the prospect's perception. For the customer to feel good about a vendor, he must visualize a long-term relationship. If that isn't perceived, you have no relationship. What many companies forget is that most of the relationship occurs after the sale—customer support and service. Closing the deal may be uppermost in your mind, but the customer's concerns about service and support are uppermost in his mind. In the modern era of commodity markets and industry standards, customer service and support are the feathers on the arrows of target marketing.

Your exhibit must clearly embrace this reality. Include your customer service manager in the exhibit. Make sure graphics convey a credible image of what your support system is like. If necessary, include in the exhibit whatever technology is necessary so your existing customers can remotely tap into your support system should they need to from the show. What a great display of customer service!

As customer budgets shrink and their review committees add more decision makers, the sales cycle lengthens. This trend is killing many companies in the business-to-business arena, especially in high-end capital equipment sales. Therefore, anchoring your exhibit marketing to the issue of the sales cycle is critical.

Find the right trade show to attract the prospect company's entire buying team, i.e., the evaluation team plus the key executive, or what we call the guru and his disciples. Match them with your complete team. Listen. Probe. Be curious about the source of their problems. They perceive their differences as unique—they are right. Learn that uniqueness from them. A credible perception that your company and its team can be trusted for the long haul is the overall goal of a business trade show exhibit. The sales follow thereafter.

DEMONSTRATION MANAGEMENT

A product demo is a form of marketing communication. As with any other form of marketing communication, you must select your target audience carefully. In this case, has the walk-in been qualified sufficiently to justify the expense of a demo?

Product demonstrations are very expensive. The demonstrator is typically a knowledgeable person, often someone taken away from her usual duties and brought to a strange environment called a trade show. Therefore, it is important to use demonstrators' time wisely to avoid burnout. Equally important is the need to orient the demo team to the show goals as well as the do's and don'ts of effective product demonstrating.

A good product demo done for a qualified prospect starts with careful listening. What are the problems the prospect is having with the current product or service in use? But listening is an acquired skill. Product managers easily lapse into features. After all, they spend considerable time trying to build products with more features in them.

So what is the profile of a good product demonstrator? Aside from listening, empathy goes a long way. Being able to control a group so you can complete a scheduled demo on time is also important, and that takes gentle firmness. Good eye contact is essential to pick up those faces of confusion or disbelief. In essence, we are talking about a good classroom teacher. If your company has a product training department, make friends with them well before your big trade show. You may need them.

Product Demonstration Checklist

If a product demo is another form of marketing communication, you need a good generic description of the medium:

1. Length of demo—This depends on the product. But no product really needs to have anyone's attention for more than 30 minutes, especially at a show full of distractions and ambient noise.

2. Major points—Limit a demo to no more than two key points. Make sure they are benefits, not features, e.g., increases productivity because . . . , or reduces operating costs by . . . , etc.

3. Product differentiation—If the average person can't readily see that your product is better, rewrite the script to make it so.

4. Tease—Don't drag something on and on. Brief glimpses and previews heighten curiosity. Leave it to your direct marketing efforts to keep the prospects in the loop of a relationship.

5. Focus on solution—If the prospect isn't readily seeing the solution, something is wrong with the script, the demonstrator— or the product.

Public Speaking Checklist

In addition to these generic tips, remember the old tried and true classics of public speaking and personal influence:

1. Ask who they are. Get a sense for the crowd. Quickly glance over the rep's lead qualifying sheet. Develop a general qualifying question that gives you a sense for the group's product awareness, such as "What other products have you seen at the show?"

2. Basically, tell them what you are going to show them, show them, and then summarize it at the end. Focus on the major points and benefit statements.

3. Think in terms of benefits and simplicity, not features and jargon.

4. Every group has one—the guy who needs to impress his group (or his boss). Don't let one question blow away the objectives of the demo. Bring it back to home base.

5. After your summary, ask "Now, have you seen anything better than this today?" The worst thing the group can do is say yes. If so, then

probe. You might discover something of interest to both the field rep and the product manager.

MANAGING EXHIBIT TRAFFIC: THE ROLE OF PRESHOW PROMOTION AND SHOW LITERATURE

In developing a production schedule for your show, make sure you recognize the three critical periods of a show's management: preshow, show site, and post-show.

Attending a trade show without priming the marketplace with a preshow promotion is akin to opening a store and expecting people to just show up. Lots of former retailers thought that way.

Preshow mailers, done well, can capitalize on two human emotions: "I don't want to miss something important" (What will I tell the folks back home if they know and I don't?), and "What can I get for free" (to give to the kids, put on my desk, etc.).

To begin with, people basically like opening their mail. They are already preparing for the show and building a file of notes, literature, and other mailers. A mailer that arrives with the show name used in the envelope teaser copy is bound to get attention. The preshow mailer should have some call to action. It could be an 800 number or business reply card (BRC) to reserve a demo. It could be a contest coupon that motivates the recipient to come to the exhibit and match a number or enter his coupon. At show site, literature should really be used sparingly. After all, you are there to qualify walk-ins and move them through the sales cycle, not pass out literature. But as mentioned under the heading "The Exhibit as Message," you need to provide walk-ins with a map and layout of the exhibit. That is done with a simple show guide. A show guide distributed by the exhibit receptionist aids attendees to find what they want.

Post-show literature is an important part of managing exhibit traffic, too. In large capital equipment markets, a prospect may remain active through next year's show. The manner in which post-show literature fulfillment and follow-up is handled can positively enhance the prospect's perception of your company. If you develop a mailing program, the call to action in each piece can be instrumental in keeping prospects' curiosity high.

This also points to another reality of business-to-business exhibit marketing—a show must be evaluated for the long-term purchase stream it may generate from a group of prospects, rather than the sales it generates in just the next twelve months.

MANAGING INQUIRIES FROM THE SHOW

Inquiry management is still an evolving art form. It embraces such diverse factors as mechanics and the human instinct of territoriality. But aside from that, inquiry management has two primary goals: tracking leads to convert them to closed sales, and quantifying the cost of a trade show's return on investment (ROI).

As new technologies develop, faster and more complete inquiry/lead handling is now possible. Many shows now offer a plastic data-encrypted attendee name badge on which the attendee's professional and purchasing profile are stored based on preregistration information. When the exhibit receptionist runs the card through the electronic imprinter, a lead form is printed out detailing valuable information about that prospect.

Some companies enter inquiries and their qualification status on-line from the exhibit and transmit the data directly to a fulfillment operation back home. When the prospect returns from the show, she receives a packet with the teaser "information you requested."

If you can focus your inquiry management with the following five basic guidelines, you will at least start off on the right foundation:

1. An inquiry or walk-in isn't a lead. Big difference—as big as the difference between a lead and a qualified lead.

2. Be quick with post-show fulfillment before the prospect forgets what was requested. Yours isn't the only exhibit she visited.

3. In demos or literature, don't provide all the information. Leave room for simple human curiosity to motivate further communication from and with the prospect.

4. For inquiry/lead management purposes and to measure show results, you must sit down with management to gain their support for a controlled inquiry-fulfillment program under your direction.

5. You must convince sales management that the sales staff needs a special briefing on your inquiry-fulfillment system. In particular, you need the cooperation of field reps regarding follow-up and qualification reporting. Reps can't be permitted to hoard the inquiries away from you.

Focusing on Qualified Prospects

As ideal as these guidelines are, your company must put its long-term focus on qualified prospects who are ready to buy. How do you do that?

Some call it discovering the purchasing points or thresholds of credibility, but what you are really doing with walk-ins is isolating perceptions. They may not be accurate perceptions, but knowing the prospect's "top-of-mind" attitudes is important, nonetheless.

1. How does the prospect perceive your company? After all, wouldn't it be good to know early on if he perceives you as overpriced? Top quality? Questionable customer support? Unstable future? Try to

isolate perceptions, regardless of whether they are correct or erroneous.

2. As psychologists say, what is the prospect's approach/avoidance? What does the prospect like about your product and what bothers him? What is pushing the prospect to buy, yet what is holding him back?

3. What is the pattern of purchase decision making at the prospect's company? You might start here by asking if they purchased other items recently (of comparable price range), and who got involved, i.e., committee, the prospect and her boss, a consultant?

4. What are the prospect's expectations for the product of interest and the company behind it? What does he perceive as standard features in either respect? (Wouldn't it be helpful to know this before you write your demo scripts, do fulfillment and field rep follow-up?)

5. Where else is the prospect shopping and what perceptions does she have of those products and companies?

6. What are the prospect's perceptions of the product and company?

By now you can see that the inquiry process is becoming more of an interview and survey-taking activity instead of pitching features. The reason is fairly simple. You cannot shorten the sales cycle without knowing certain critical information about the prospect's needs and perceptions.

In the business-to-business arena, the old wine, dine, and close approach to selling is being replaced by *creme de la creme* teamwork. The team members are perceived by prospects as consultative and flexible in both their interpersonal skills and product knowledge. If you assemble the right team at a trade show attended by the right prospect, the sales cycle can be greatly shortened.

That is why people who think the purpose of trade shows is to demo and pitch products have a fundamental misunderstanding of the increasingly tough business-to-business environment.

Unfortunately, many field sales reps fall into this category. Some of them suffer from a sense of misplaced territoriality—i.e., if he is in my territory, the prospect is mine. Companies cannot build database marketing capabilities with this kind of insularity. If necessary, offer a large prize to the rep with the most complete, returned lead form. Another incentive for people motivated by incentives is a small price to pay for good lead forms.

Designing the Lead Form

Rather than provide a static example of a lead form, we prefer to guide you with a sense for the concepts and pitfalls and let you design the form appropriately. The lead form itself should be simple to use and retrieve information from. Keep in mind the field reps may be filling in information while standing and using a clip board. The form should be a three-part one with copies for you, sales management, and the field rep.

Aside from such vital information as name, address, phone number, etc., the form should focus on four areas of critical lead qualifying points:

1. When is the prospect budgeted to buy and at what volume?

2. With whom must the prospect consult in order to buy?

3. What is the prospect currently using and what is she currently considering?

4. What are the prospect's perception of your company and product going into this show?

When you complete the first draft, brief your sales management on it to gain his or her absolute support for your efforts. After all, you are trying to manage costs by evaluating the show's ROI. Should your company ever need to cut costs, trade show costs suddenly become conspicuous numbers. Getting sales management to see the worth of the endeavor is critical. Getting management to write the memo to field sales introducing the inquiry/lead management program and show forms is just as important. Delegate upward!

Post show follow-up is the great killer of inquiry management dreams. Either the information is allowed to become stale and forgotten, or the field reps never report back on the status of each inquiry. In short, you don't know who the qualified leads are.

One way to solve this problem is to use in-house telemarketing to requalify prospects who visited your exhibit. In the rush and press of bodies on the floor, both receptionists and field reps can miss vital pieces of information. What's more, you don't know what has happened to the prospect's perceptions since he left your exhibit. What has your competition said? What have the prospect's colleagues learned?

TIPS FOR INTEGRATING YOUR PROGRAM

Exhibit marketing is the most direct form of marketing communication because it brings the seller and buyer face to face. Instant feedback is available. Or, to apply the term developed by Stan Rapp and Tom Collins, trade shows are where "maximarketing" should reach the state of an engine purring like a kitten.

Shows shouldn't operate in a marcom vacuum. Shows are perhaps the marcom component that most benefits from an integrated strategy.

Shows are planned long in advance; use the same time frame for planning preshow promotions. An essential tool in preshow promotion is targeting your prospects through a database of direct response opportunities.

Direct response results built from show to show and mailing to mailing are critical database marketing ingredients. Ingredients can also include highly specific industry lists you rent. As we cover in the chapter on database marketing and direct response, you should seek to build records of prospects' behavior"—i.e., buying patterns, attendance patterns, trade publication subscriptions. Such records of action or initiative make for better database marketing than mere compilations of names and addresses.

Your database files reflect such information by updating them through relational database systems that permit the addition of call reports from field reps or telemarketing reps. The new walk-ins to your exhibit have taken an action. As you qualify the walk-ins and their inquiries you create a profile that helps build a long-term purchase stream. It also helps you evaluate that show.

The prospects who respond to the call to action on your preshow promotional mailers have taken an obvious action. Did they indicate they plan to attend the show and visit your booth? Did they show interest in all products or only a couple of related products? Did they plan attending with colleagues? That's an indicator of a possible review committee about to take action.

Exhibit marketing is also an opportunity to practice press relations. Trade press editors will be there. It's a chance to meet them, learn their preferences and prejudices, and learn from them.

But don't make the same mistakes your naive competitors will make. Announcements at shows are a dime a dozen. Trade shows are not great places for routine interviews or "get acquainted" meetings between editors and management. The typical editor is exhausted after one day and still has to file copy for the week's deadline. As significant, every editor comes to a show with a checklist of news opportunities he wants to tap. Unless you are the biggest player at the show or you are certain to have the biggest news, make your announcement before the show. That will help give you at least a running chance to make the editor's "must see" checklist.

Aside from that, make sure you know what the editors' deadlines are, especially for preshow, on-site, and post-show issues. They are likely to be different from the regular monthly or weekly deadlines.

Find out far ahead of time if any trade publication is publishing a show daily. This is becoming a popular way for publications to develop a "quick-to-market" news reputation. Also, show daily publishers are offering their services in many key industries and convention cities.

Remember, mindshare with editors is as important as mindshare with prospects. Both go to shows with some sense of priorities of what they want to see or learn, and only those exhibitors who have something new will make the "must see" list.

However, there are ways of gaining editorial breakthroughs if you have no substantial news: booth traffic contests, hospitality suites, and program sessions.

Contests draw attention, and editors are as intrigued as anyone else by clever promotional contests. Make sure the contest ties in with the exhibit theme or some special feature or benefit of the main product displayed. After all, why go to the expense of running an exhibit traffic contest if it isn't integrated with your other efforts.

Hospitality suites should be used as a respite for selected, qualified prospects and the press. Depending on your product, it may be the preferable place to offer a private demo to an editor away from the noise and conspicuousness of the exhibit. If the suite adjoins your top management's rooms, a quiet breakfast meeting in the parlor may well be appreciated by an editor otherwise forced to push through show masses for a donut and coffee. However, be mindful that some publications prohibit their journalists from accepting entertainment. Suggest a suite breakfast but don't be pushy if you get resistance. Depending where your product is in its life cycle, a slot for an editor could be more valuable than a slot for a prospect. As exhibit manager, work closely with your colleagues to make sure time slots at the suite are available for the press.

If your company wants to be perceived as a leader in an area critical to your product strategy, then develop the trade show or association relationships necessary to get someone on the program. Propose new sessions on topics not already overdone in pervious programs. This must be done at least one year in advance of the show, so use your time at the show to define the program needs and how your organization can serve them next year.

When you get scheduled for a session, make sure you use color slides or overheads loaded with graphics. Graphics, color, and humor are essential ingredients to keeping a jaded and tired trade show audience awake.

Develop a sense for the politics of the association or trade show. Find out what key influences will be on the show's board of advisors. If necessary, put together a road show presentation you and your management can take to each key influence so that your company and product strategy are placed in the right context. Demonstrate that your company is a leader, a vendor to be recognized for the long term. Visit with association management at their headquarters during the off-year. Keep them briefed. Make sure their perception is that you and your organization are worth their time. The last thing you want is for a show or association to see you as the exhibitor who complains every year about space location and show hours. Convince management and the sales staff of that, too.

Press kits are necessary for trade shows, but be careful how you use them. If you identify beforehand which editors and other key influences you want to reach, you can send them kits ahead of time. If you have meetings with these people, you can review the important contents with them, annotate important pieces according to the editor's specific interests, and mail them to their offices. Editors dislike having to carry heavy press kits around an exhibit hall, and will often toss them.

Believe it or not, there is no law of marketing that demands you place piles of press kits in the show's press room. Any smart competitor knows he can go into the press room and cause many kits to fall accidentally into a briefcase or show bag. Is that where you want your press kit? Don't rely on the show's press room to distribute information about your company. You are not in charge there, and the press room manager doesn't care about your company. You alone must manage the distribution of information about your company.

Important to the success of trade show press relations is to understand what writers and editors are there to do. Aside from looking for news, they also must fill an inventory of space assigned to them. You must be aware of the angle each publication has for the show or the particular viewpoint and perspective that runs that publication.

As important is the need to think objectively. Ask yourself prior to the show if you really have any news. What is the attraction for an editor? What new twist do we offer the trade press this year? Don't waste editors' time with retread announcements because they have long memories for such things.

Preshow promotion involves more than just direct response techniques such as mailers. If the show is the first public showing of a new product announced prior to the show, advertising in the appropriate publications can develop mindshare and thus enhance traffic. Remember, you are not the only exhibit the attendees plan to visit.

But advertising also builds preshow credibility and legitimacy for a new product. Advertising that features a product should include photography rather than line art to convey product completeness. Testimonial reactions are also important.

Some firms need to build on corporate awareness rather than product awareness prior to a trade show. Others needs to drive home the overall benefit or solution they provide that industry. These considerations should be discussed and identified at least six months prior to the show, ideally around the time the exhibit house is briefed. You want everything to work together. Rushing an ad agency to do last minute creative to meet special show issue deadlines can be costly and lead to mistakes.

We've discussed specific pieces of exhibit collateral and literature such as the attendee show guide and the employee show participation handbook. But it doesn't end there. At least three months prior to the show, you need to update the following essential pieces of literature:

1. Corporate history and backgrounder.
2. Product data sheet.
3. Quick summary of company facts, customer quotes, and press commentary. Editors love this handy reference.
4. New product promotional pieces.
5. Pocketed folder with logo (press kits).

6. A 1- to 2-page product overview for those who need a quick glance only. Very handy to the press and a good reception desk giveaway.

7. Reprints of ads (not for press kit).

A final IMC note: A communications strategy meeting with your ad agency, exhibit house, collateral designers, and public relations counsel is an ideal way to make sure each strategic vendor understands the message that the show should convey.

MEASUREMENT AND EVALUATION

Ultimately, you must be able to intelligently report a show's long-term revenue potential. Start by collecting the following information:

- All show costs: Space fee, exhibit house fee, construction, shipping, drayage, labor, electrical, graphics, hospitality, specific show literature, air travel, per diem, hotel, etc. Don't include field reps' travel and entertainment (T&E) since that isn't in your budget and you have no discretionary control there.
- Total show attendance: This is a bogus number but one you need to know. It includes all exhibitors and all attendees and it will be the only number you ever see unless you dig further.
- Audited net show attendance: This is the number of nonexhibitor attendees, or the universe of all potential visitors (qualified and unqualified) who might walk into your exhibit. Make sure this number excludes nonqualified spouses. Unless you ask, they will be thrown into this number.
- Number of walk-ins: Simply the total body count in your exhibit. Qualified or not, they took up staff time and square footage, plus it gives you a ratio to qualified leads you can compare annually.
- Number of demonstrations given: Regardless of how many people in a party attended a demo, this shows how active the demo program was or wasn't.
- Number of companies represented in your exhibit: Regardless of the number of people who came from that company.
- Number of qualified leads: This will not likely be known until after the telemarketing-based requalifying calls are made. This is the number that nets out of the number of walk-ins above.
- Number of leads closed as sales: The killer number that really tells you the ROI for each show. But as we said elsewhere, in large capital equipment markets a prospect may go through two shows before being budgeted. That is why you need to think long-term and not label one year's show as unproductive. You were still establishing a relationship.

From these numbers you can make some evaluations on:

1. Cost per exhibit walk-in (cost per show attendee is meaningless)
2. Cost per demo (helps evaluate hidden costs of demos)
3. Cost per qualified lead (the big enchilada of numbers)

All these figures help you to measure and evaluate a show. You might discover that the ratio of walk-ins to qualified leads is too large to justify the show against, say, direct mail.

RESOURCES

1. Appendix D includes the Trade Show/Exhibit Marketing Checklist and the Trade Show Participation Plan Outline.
2. You also need the resources of the American Marketing Association. The AMA's conferences, library research services, and local chapter programs make this a must organization for someone charged with integrated marketing communications. Two AMA publications are particularly helpful. *Marketing News,* a biweekly, and *Marketing Executive,* a monthly review of abstracts, book reviews, and articles. Contact AMA International at 250 South Wacker Drive, Chicago, Illinois 60606. Ask for the name of your local chapter president.
3. Dr. Allen Konopacki and his InComm International provide clients with on-site training and training materials aimed at successful trade show selling. Incomm is located at 1005 North LaSalle Drive, Chicago, Illinois 60610.
4. Active exhibit managers should subscribe to the monthly *Exhibitor: The Magazine of Trade Show Marketing and Exhibit Management.* Lee Knight is publisher and editor. Headquarters: 745 Marquette Bank Building, P.O. Box 368, Rochester, Minnesota 55903-9990. Also, every February Knight and the magazine sponsor The Exhibitor Show in Las Vegas. This is a five-day program of practical seminars by hands-on experts on specific exhibit marketing problems and processes. The exhibits are all about exhibit marketing, thus connecting you with the leading vendors. The Exhibit Show, in partnership with San Francisco State University, provides continuing education credits toward a Certified Trade Show Marketer credential. Attend the show, get the magazine, and put CTSM next to your name on those business cards.
5. Diane K. Weintraub is president of Communique Exhibitor Education, Inc. She and her organization specialize in trade show training for exhibitors, especially in the area of exhibit selling and communicating. Aside from being a dynamic and convincing presenter at many marketing communications forums and conferences, her organization does on-site training for companies tailored to their specific needs. Her organization also does self-study courses and customized training courses. Don't ever miss an opportunity to hear Diane. She is a mover and shaker and knows where business-to-business exhibit marketing is heading. Contact her at 995 North Collier Boulevard, Marco Island, Florida 33937.
6. Join the International Exhibitors Association (IEA). It's an association of exhibit managers—you and your colleagues. Each year IEA runs TS2—the Exhibit Industry Conference and Exposition. IEA seminars can earn you continuing edu-

cation credits toward the status of Certified Manager of Exhibits (CME), offered exclusively from IEA. IEA also has a relationship with Drexel University of Philadelphia to give you university credits and a concentration in Exhibit Marketing, a sequence of four courses tailored to your job as exhibit manager. IEA's *IDEAS* newsletter, its annual budget guide, its annual salary survey, plus its many publications make it a must-join. IEA is located at 5501 Backlick Road, Suite 200, Springfield, Virginia 22151.

7. The Trade Show Bureau is a nationally recognized source of research information, publications, exhibit marketing consulting, and customized reports. Membership is offered to businesses and individuals. Contact them at 1660 Lincoln Street, Suite 2080, Denver, Colorado 80264.

8. For more in-depth reading on exhibit marketing, get Edward A. Chapman's *Exhibit Marketing: A Survival Guide for Managers* (320 pages with 52 illustrations).

9. *Tradeshow Week* is a newsletter filled with practical information on what is happening in the industry. Contact them at 12233 W. Olympic Blvd, Suite 236, Los Angeles, CA 90064-9956.

10. Exhibit Designers and Producers Association (EDPA) in Milwaukee is a good source of information on installation and dismantle vendors that operate in certain convention centers.

11. *Exhibitor* magazine publishes an annual *Buyers Guide to Trade Show Exhibits: A Comprehensive Directory of Portable, Modular and Custom Trade Show Exhibits.*

12. *Exhibitor Times* is a monthly trade magazine published by Virgo Publishing, 4141 N. Scottsdale Road, Suite 316, Scottsdale, Arizona 85251.

13. *Managing Sales Leads: How to Turn Every Prospect into a Customer* (1995), by Donath, Obermayer, Crocker, and Dixon. Lincolnwood, Illinois, NTC Business Books.

CHAPTER 13

Event and Seminar Marketing: There's No Business Like Show Business

> "Experience is awareness of encompassing the totality of things."
>
> —Sidney Hook

A tough year finds you looking at a reduced budget for promotion. Media costs went up another 8 percent as expected. You may have to cut the public relations agency and go in house with media relations. What's more frustrating is the result of an anonymous telephone survey you had done that indicates your company is not viewed as a leader in product development or customer service. You wonder, "What can I do that will gain substantial media attention and help establish us as a leader within the next 12 months?"

You don't have to play by the rules all the time. You don't have to play with the cards you're dealt. Sometimes you can actually create your own rules—or your own game. In this chapter, we will show you how to create solutions to problems not easily solved by other marketing communications tools. In a sense, this chapter is about creating your own medium, and blending your medium into an integrated marcom mix.

Whether by adopting an existing event and sponsoring it, or creating your own event, event marketing can be as effective for business marketers as it has been for consumer marketers such as beer, tobacco, and sports shoe companies. You can learn how to apply what the big guys have done while minimizing the unfortunate surprises.

THE DIFFERENCE BETWEEN EVENT AND EXHIBIT MARKETING

In several ways, event marketing is similar to exhibit marketing. But one critical difference defines them. A trade show is a periodic event sponsored by an association or promoter. You play the game their way. So long as the trade show delivers the correct audience and you do a good job of preshow traffic promotion, that trade show will continue to deliver.

Event marketing works differently. The reason is control. In short, you have more of it. Nonetheless, the control you exercise is gained by first being very clear about your marketing objectives and communications strategy.

Without such clarity, it will be frustrating to differentiate among the many event choices that come your way. That's especially true if your firm is visible and thus an easy mark for every association, cause, and festivity in town. After all, you can't sponsor everything. Rather, the event sponsorship should have a clear thematic tie to a specific product, product line, or promotion or it should reflect a definite customer lifestyle connection.

For example, is the purpose of the event solely to entertain dealers or clients? That's an acceptable and reasonable goal, but mixing in other objectives could defuse the success of all the objectives. For example, a weekend for dealers and spouses at a destination resort would surely build rapport. But would you want to use the evening banquet for a series of product introductions, dry speeches on sales, and a question-and-answer period on customer support? If dealer issues are the main focus, then you should have a spousal program built into the weekend so the dealers can attend to business—and save the banquet dinner for entertainment.

Another consideration is the lifespan you want for the desired effect or message the event is intended to create. If the desired effect is for the duration of this event only, the promotional and collateral support needed is very different than an event intended to kick off a long-term campaign. If your objective is to corral a special target audience using exclusivity and status as the promotional hooks, event marketing can be a useful tool.

Emotional appeals such as exclusivity are hard to quantify and measure. But used in the right context, appealing to lifestyle perceptions your target audience has of themselves, such hooks can be very effective.

Psychologist Abraham Maslow wrote extensively about the human hierarchy of needs and how those needs are ranked in order of their importance for fulfillment. The base needs are for physical sustenance and personal safety. Slightly higher in the hierarchy are social needs, such as the need to belong and be accepted. At the top of the hierarchy needs relating to self-actualization are paramount.

Maslow's hierarchy provides a convenient metaphor for relationship marketing. You might call it a target audience hierarchy of needs. It begins with the customer's search to fill a business need. Then he and you discover each other. At this point it's still an untested, by-the-numbers business deal rather than a long-term relationship of trust and partnership.

But next on the customer's hierarchy of needs are various levels of nonquantifiable comfort. These levels are beyond the logical and cognitive and nestled in the warm and fuzzy domain of emotions and subjectivity. This isn't achieved by coding invoices to read "We appreciate your business." In the competitive business-to-business arena, it's a matter of seeking out customer opinion with the goal of long-term mutual benefit. If your dealers do well, if you seek them out for advice on how to improve the product line, if you recognize their expertise, if you maintain an open line with them, they will attain the upper levels of comfort you want.

Thus, in event marketing, be it a sponsorship or a workshop, it is important to recognize the potential role exclusivity can play. You don't have this relationship with everybody, and if you did it would turn a special event into something not so special after all.

CHECKLIST OF DO'S AND DON'TS

- Do's:
  1. If you're planning it correctly, your event is tied to the overall marketing plan. Thus, an event used for tactical marketing support isn't just another party or meeting. You must plan for something value-added and execute it.
  2. Events should be special. Therefore, your event must be one that meets the minimal expectations customers have of your company or, better yet, exceeds those expectations. Otherwise, how can it be special?
  3. Do make sure the appropriate local, regional, business, and trade press know about the event. If you don't think they might take interest in it, then reevaluate why you're doing the event and how special it really is. After all, publicity is one of the major goals you must have.
  4. In planning the event, think as your target audience might think. Use that perspective in planning the invitations, the roster, the signage, the airport arrivals, the venue, and even the spousal program.

5. If management is reacting ambivalently to your event plans, this should raise a red flag. Get enthusiastic endorsement, or you will have trouble getting employees in other departments to cooperate.

6. Perception is reality. Expectations often drive perceptions. Make sure you all agree about what's expected and what look and feel the event will have. Supporting vendors will need to be briefed on the desired look and feel before their design efforts can begin.

7. Do thoroughly research event sponsorship opportunities presented to you before adopting. Find out why the current sponsor wants to give it up.

- Don'ts:

    1. Event marketing isn't a matter of simply arranging accommodations. Therefore, don't delegate event planning to the department secretary unless he knows event marketing. You wouldn't do that with your ad campaign. Event marketing is no different.

    2. Don't "me too" your industry. If you feel pressure to have an event because a competitor's doing it, make sure you read the rest of this chapter. Your event must stand out. It should serve your special needs, which may be totally different than a competitor's needs.

    3. Don't dream up something your staff can't take some measure of pride in. There must be an aura of excitement or "specialness" among the employees involved, or they will betray the event.

    4. Don't try to serve too many masters with your event. Isolate one or maybe two objectives. If you have more than that, rethink the entire plan and go back to the root problem you're trying to solve. You may not have fully defined it.

    5. Never accept the verbal word of hotel or resort management. Get the agreement in writing or summarize your understanding of the agreement in a follow-up letter. Remember, the salesperson may have to depend on three shifts of clerks and set-up crews. Can you recall a time when a large hotel didn't get something mixed up?

THE CARDS YOU WANT VERSUS THE CARDS YOU ARE DEALT

At your last trade show, you were told to set up a cocktail party with mounds of fresh shrimp carried in by servers in formal attire. Your competition did the same thing last year, said your boss, and it's expected. And your dealers seem to need help with generic skills, such as telemarketing and doing demos. So your boss told you to find some book that looks helpful and send a copy to each dealer.

This is the kind of thinking that misses the mark and often spends money unwisely. The bigger the pile of marketing dollars spent, the more likely your CFO will want to have an impromptu lunch with your CEO.

You must start at the right place—problem definition. The problem isn't that your competitor has a party and thus you must do so. That's reaction, or living at the effect of cause. In fact, the problem may have nothing to do with your competitor.

Let's return to the chapter opening scenario. As a business-to-business marketer, you need a regular flow of information about how your marketplace perceives your company. Basically, marketing communications management might better be called external perceptions management because perceptions are the problems you face. It takes integrated communications tools and gestation time to change perceptions. Everything else—your marketplace, technology, financial conditions—changes underneath your feet. It's how you handle perceptions that determines your latitude and skill in solving problems.

If you're considering some form of event marketing to solve a particular problem, it is essential to start with a project worksheet such as the one in Serena Leisner's checklist in Appendix I. Think of that worksheet as an algorithm to logically think through the problem at hand. It's far less expensive to conceptualize a problem at this level than to finance and stage an event you only hope will hit the mark.

Use the worksheet to ask questions from all angles.

- Does the competition really have the same problem?
- How have they, in the past, solved the same problem perplexing you? Or is the problem truly unique to you?
- What are the current expectations of your target audience given the problem that exists? What do they want? What do they expect of you? More importantly, are you sure this special event—with all its expense and distraction—is the real answer?

Think for a moment: how do you want to be perceived? What would be the ideal turnaround for your firm, i.e., a 180 degree switch in perceptions? This may seem like a silly exercise. After all, you're in a competitive swamp up to your baseline in alligators. The problem seems beyond your firm's ability to control.

But dream on anyhow. Treat this as a chapter exercise—what is the ideal external perception you would really like to have? Let's even give this pie-in-the-sky thinking a serious sounding name: *ideal market position.*

Can the ideal market position be attained using available media and the communications tools familiar to your company? A public relations campaign? A new flight of direct mailers? A different trade show exhibit, or perhaps a different trade show?

Do you have a knot in your stomach? If your marketer's intuition tells you this isn't enough, you've just discovered you're at the game table with an inadequate hand of cards—or perhaps inadequate experience. You need new cards, or you need to abandon this game and learn to play another. The alternative may well be event marketing. Event marketing can be divided into two types: sponsorship events and company events. Let's analyze each now.

ADOPTING AN EVENT: SPONSORSHIPS AND SPECIAL EVENTS

Sponsorships are more common in the business-to-consumer arena than in business-to-business. Since this book concentrates on the latter, we will borrow from the experience of the packaged goods/consumer products industries and tailor some advice for you.

The most common form of sponsorships have been in the tobacco, beer, and soft drink industries, where sports marketing and sports events sponsorship are serious business. These industries clearly identify their target audience in demographic and psychographic terms. They use events such as tournaments or races to build an identity and a relationship between their brand and the people who attend the event.

Sponsoring an event means you get the baby and the inheritance as well—both good and bad. You inherit all the liabilities as well as the established pay-back. Just because the previous business marketer abandoned the sponsorship doesn't mean it can't work for your firm. Whatever tweaking is needed can be handled quickly, especially with the assistance of the vendors your predecessor used.

Sponsorships have chalked up both failures and successes. Thus, event marketers have come to choose sponsored events with the same serious deliberation by which they evaluate advertising media. In fact, one of the attractions of such events is that their demographic reach and frequency can surpass that of traditional media, often at a fraction of the cost.

So how can you learn from the big-budget guys in our business-to-business markets? A considerable amount can be learned, especially from their basic mistakes. That's why we began this chapter with the pitfalls of event marketing.

One of the classic mistakes business marketers can make is to choose a sponsorship based on the CEO's personal affinity for the sport or event. This is where a disciplined marketing communications professional can diplomatically come to the rescue.

Special events are intended to create publicity or to improve public relations in the belief that the bottom line will eventually be affected. A major mistake is not having a clear understanding of which outcome is the objective and how it will affect the business buyer.

As you develop your Marketing Information Platform (MIP), you will seek the acknowledgment and sign-off of all executives. Part of that document is a review of communications tools and how your company can use them appropriately to reach your communications objectives. One of those sections should be event marketing. In that section, you remind yourself and your colleagues (including top management) who the target audience is.

It is particularly important that you analyze event marketing right after you outline public relations/media relations in your MIP. If you sell direct to businesses, it should be relatively easy to isolate the one or two market issues most on these decision makers' minds. If your firm sells through a distributor or dealer channel, that adds another layer of complexity to the picture.

If you market direct to businesses, an event would have to directly support and be related to the *unique selling proposition (USP)* of your position in the market place. That could be superior customer service, technical leadership, industry knowledge and expertise, or a superior research and development effort that makes your customer base feel comfortable about the future.

Right now it should be clear that sponsoring a sporting event in such a framework would be a very expensive proposition. The tie-in to your USP would have to be fully engaged throughout your IMC program, and the cost implications due to the geography of your marketplace could be awesome.

If a dealer or distributor channel takes your business product to other businesses, the event must address either the resellers or the end users. An event that addresses both is unrealistic due to cost and the different issues involved. A dealer is concerned with quantity discounts, fast order processing, marketing support, cooperative selling, and promotion. The end user is interested in customer support, dealer support, training, warranties, product quality, and price.

Checklist for Screening Event Sponsorship Opportunities

Screening event sponsorship opportunities is an important process in itself. Bud Frankel is president of Frankel and Company of Chicago, an event marketing consultancy to consumer sponsors. He recommends several screens for his type of customers. We have adapted them slightly for the business-to-business environment:[1]

1. Exclusivity: Are the event and the promotion opportunities solely yours?

2. Organization: Do you have an organization and structure in place to help you execute a successful sponsorship? If not, what will it cost to build such a structure? What are the liabilities and insurance implications?

3. Facilities: Can they handle what you have in mind for audiovisual, break-out rooms, conference halls, traffic flow, and traffic management?

4. Signage and identification: Can you be sure your corporate identity will be prominent in the facility and the promotions?

5. Hospitality: Are there adequate services and accommodations available, e.g., catering, transportation, restaurants for private meetings.

6. Press/communications facilities: Are photocopying, facsimile, and secretarial services available?

7. Celebrities: Are they willing to make personal appearances and televised appearances and at what cost?

8. Public relations: What media relations, government relations, or community relations needs do you have that can be served by this event?

9. Approvals and limitations: Will your promotions off the sponsorship need legal or other approvals from the event management? What restrictions must you observe?

10. Before/After: How far ahead and how long after the event may you promote your sponsorship?

11. Extensions: Could you use your sponsorship to promote your firm in markets other than the one for which this event serves?

12. Logos and other identifiers: How well will the event's logos, taglines, themes, music, and promotions blend with yours, and what restrictions are there for cooperative marketing?

13. International: Can the event sponsorship be taken international, and at what cost?

14. Event organization and structure: What field organization does the event have that you can tap for assistance and cooperative management?

15. Awards: Are you permitted to present special awards publicly at the event?

16. Ceiling on costs: Is the event's management willing to accept a ceiling on your financial support?

Sponsorships in Business-to-Business Marketing

Creating an event of your own makes it tailor-made to your market position and your particular problems. You don't have to pick up the baggage that comes with adopting a sponsorship event.

A company-generated event is clearly one where you make up the game, the rules, the promotion, and the participants. You are in charge, but you and your management shouldn't expect to accomplish your goals the first time out. Unlike a sponsored event, which is often well established, the time-line for success is understandably longer when you start from scratch.

A good example of business-to-business marketers using sponsorship is the area of office automation and computers. Sponsorships are often sports oriented, and for largely the same reason a consumer/packaged goods marketer would use: lifestyle marketing. If the profile of the prime decision maker for a new private phone system is an upper-income male, age 35 to 55, sports event sponsorship may well provide you good exposure for your market area.

The budgets are much smaller on the business marketing side. Where Anheuser Busch might spend $200 million on sports sponsorships, the highest budget you might see among business marketers would be under $20 million. Even that figure could be spent only by such firms as IBM, 3M, or the like. That is why some experts believe business marketers should use sports sponsorships solely as sales incentives and entertainment.[2]

But sponsorships don't have to stop with sporting events. Keep in mind, the goal is to associate your firm or product with lifestyle values that might mean something to your target audience. Special concert performances, a dinner theater series, a motivational speaker, a famous lifestyle lecturer or author—it's a matter of understanding your customers' profile and how they want their employees to be rewarded or motivated.

SEMINARS AND TUTORIALS

As mentioned, event marketing can take different forms. It's not all sports sponsorship. If the question of industry leadership is a critical one to refocusing perceptions of your firm, hosting a seminar or tutorial on a key market issue can be influential.

As with all forms of communication, you must first identify three important facts: what is the specific perception problem you're up against, who is the exact audience you have this problem with, and what is the objective you need to correct it? You simply cannot devote the time, logistical planning, and expense to a seminar program or tutorial without first being quite clear on these points.

PARTY TIME LIABILITIES

If you serve liquor at an event, be aware of legislation on the books in many states that can hold a sponsor liable in case of injury related to the alcohol consumption. Taking certain precautions can avoid injuries and culpability, e.g., serving food before drinks are served, limiting content of each drink, limiting cocktail time to one hour, and using a ticket-per-drink system that helps monitor people's consumption.

Next, for the same reasons cited above, you must be sure your other communications tools are working in tandem with the seminar idea. For example, are those tools already adequately addressing this perception problem with this audience? Given reasonable time, will those tools do the job?

The specificity of the issue or topic is important. You can't cover everything and expect to be credible. Ask your sales representatives about topics, and invite them to pick apart the one you're considering. It's far better to get this advice ahead of time than in hindsight.

A specific audience within your industry may deal with the issue at a totally different level than their subordinates or superiors. For example, a purchasing manager looks at computer purchases in terms of quantity pricing and bid proposal. The CFO is concerned with depreciation and return-on-investment (ROI). The information manager is concerned with connectivity and ease of upgrade. The president may be more concerned with long-term planning and how a computer system can accommodate his or her plans for expansion and acquisition. But they each have a keen interest in a computer system. No one seminar is going to draw all four people. Thus you must narrow the focus to strike a responsive cord with the specific key influence you seek to reach.

If leadership is a key perception goal, identify a major issue in your industry that your research indicates is void of leadership. If confusion over choices is a major hindrance in the buying decisions of your customers, a tutorial on the selection process can be helpful. If the industry you sell to lacks a common direction for future planning, hosting a panel discussion composed of industry experts, consultants, and the trade press could lead to important insights for your guests. It could also garner publicity for your firm. Basically, use a seminar to focus on a problem your audience needs to solve.

After the topic and audience are identified, your next task is to compose an agenda that serves the purpose. A series of speakers or a panel, as mentioned before, provides a credible range of viewpoints. Break-out sessions that allow attendees to ask questions provide you with valuable insight into their hot buttons and decision path.

The selection of time and place is very important. Avoid Mondays and Fridays because they are used for extended weekends. Avoid the end of the month because of accounting closing. Avoid August because of vacation plans, but avoid all summer months unless you are sure it will not affect attendance. This is especially true in European countries, where July and August suffer from a mass exodus to vacation spots.

Mornings tend to be better than afternoons because people can be distracted and corralled in their offices once they get to work. But never underestimate the need for a morning wake-up or get-acquainted session with lots of coffee before you hit attendees with the seminar. Given the investment you make in developing a seminar, one good insurance plan is to offer two sessions: the afternoon of one day and the morning of the next day. This may also cut set-up charges from the hotel.

Location is important and clearly a function of the geographical area you are servicing with the seminar. If you are holding a seminar for a nationwide audience, selecting a city that's a major airport hub is important. A local audience needs quick access to and from the downtown business district, and parking should be ample. Hotels offer a good venue for all these reasons.

For a seminar or tutorial that spans several days, consider the local university facilities. The atmosphere and feel of the sessions will be quite different, often setting a tone that cannot be had in a hotel or convention center. If you are trying to establish a leadership role in research and development, for example, an agenda of several experts fits well in a university environment.

In our busy professional lives, few of us get the chance to go back to campus. Leaving time in the agenda for visiting the campus library, for example, or visiting the local campus watering holes, would be like stepping into the past. Even eating in the campus cafeteria and sleeping in the dorms can fit the program if an educational objective in an isolated setting is part of your plan. A campus meeting is not one people will forget quickly. However, don't make any assumptions about conference services or even air conditioning. Check everything out and summarize your assumptions in writing with a campus administrator rather than a student employee.

The question of a registration fee is a difficult one. You do have expenses with a seminar, and charging a small fee helps cover costs. A fee also lends value to the overall perception of the event, plus it helps weed out the less serious attendees. In the end, the question of charging a fee is one you consider with your sales manager. There are distinct advantages if you are confident it won't deter the right people from attending.

You need the right staff at the seminar. Administrative people are needed at the reception table. Depending on the topic, technical people from your firm may need to be ready to answer questions. The sales staff will want to attend, but keep in mind your original objective: a tutorial or seminar to help establish a leadership perception (or whatever other goal you had). You cannot turn such an event into a sales pitch or your objectivity will be tarnished. People are coming to get enlightenment, not to be closed. If you do the event correctly, the sales cycle will be shortened for closing later on.

AGENDA ESSENTIALS

The agenda helps sell your event to the right audience. So it's worth spending time on its preparation. Make sure you cover these essentials:

- Why: Specifically, what's it all about. What is the objective, theme, and purpose of the meeting or event? (Of course, the theme, objective, and purpose as you want to portray it to the attendees).
- When: Date, beginning time, ending time.
- Who: Who else is being invited. Folks want to know with whom they will rub shoulders.
- Where: City, meeting location, hotel arrangements, and directions for those who drive.
- What: Profiles of speakers and what they will confine their remarks to, plus time for each speaker.
- Break times: Busy people will leave your meeting to make important phone calls, so you need to build break time into the meeting just to control the group.
- Expectations: Do attendees need to bring anything or prepare in some way?
- Spouses: Some will bring them. You might as well find out ahead of time if people will do so, because planning a spousal program may be necessary—and a nice touch.

ROAD SHOWS

A series of seminars or presentations can be used to reach target audiences in various strategic locations. This type of event marketing, oftentimes called a road show, may be the only course of action if you know you can't get these key influences to attend one seminar in one location.

Road shows have special logistical considerations regarding scheduling, trafficking, and location. The planning of such a series will require almost full-time attention by a staffer for weeks before commencement. The itinerary should be checked carefully to make sure no local events will hurt attendance in each locale. Rescheduling can involve lost airfare and possible cancellation fees from hotels. If equipment is involved, everyone along the way needs to be mindful of the packing and trafficking requirements. One lost box or a carelessly executed shipping form could kill an entire day on the schedule.

If you have local offices or show rooms, costs can be contained by holding the road show there. But of course that depends on the communication objective of the road show. If it is a topic dealing with an industry issue or perception problem you seek to solve, attendees may not perceive the objectivity you wish if it's held in a company sales office. After all, you want the attendees to be the right people to meet the objective you set for yourself. It may be the road show is best held at an airport hotel.

SALES MEETINGS: YOUR PRIMARY EVENT MARKET

A marketing department often takes for granted the first target audience it should address—the sales staff. For some odd reason, many salespeople suffer in silence when they disagree with their marketing department. It is far preferable to know their misgivings about your strategy and plans than to live the fiction that those smiling, polite faces represent endorsement. An unenthusiastic sales staff can compromise your game plan just as much as an uncommitted management staff. Worse, they can communicate their attitude to customers.

In many companies, sales meetings are run by marketing management rather than sales management. That doesn't mean marketing should handle territorial reviews with individual reps, but marketing is in charge of defining products, message, and strategy. Those are reasons enough for marketing to run sales meetings. The alternative is that aggressive sales reps or sales management will try to fill the marketing void with nonmarketing people such as the research and development team or manufacturing or someone else.

What we suggest is that you convince management and sales that your marketing group start out by being the cohost of each sales meeting. That makes the initial change less threatening. Sales reps are always looking for tools to close sales, so turn your portion of this critical event into a showcase of tools: slide presentations they can use on the road, trade show plans, upcoming collateral and direct mail campaigns, and reviews of marketing research you've conducted.

Use your first sales meeting to introduce an informal weekly newsletter for the sales staff. The newsletter can be a combination of company and industry news, competitive information, closing "war stories," as well as a digest of industry trade press articles and publicity your efforts have produced. This weekly newsletter will give you instant credibility and will showcase the importance of your involvement in sales meetings. The four or five hours you spend each week on the newsletter will be a constant reminder of marketing's importance to the sales effort.

TIPS FOR INTEGRATING YOUR PROGRAM

Events and seminars, like trade shows, also require an integrated marcom strategy to make them successful. This requires the support of the database and direct response specialists, the public relations people, the advertising department, telemarketing, customer service, and the sales force. Not only are these departments involved in the strategic planning for these events, but they are essential to generating turnout, hosting the event or presenting the seminar, and doing the follow-up to assure that the appropriate relationship objective or objectives were achieved.

Fujitsu's SPARClite Seminar Series

Anderson Solone, Inc. of Sacramento, California has a specialty: integrated market-ing communications, primarily in the business-to-business arena. One of their clients is Fujitsu Microelectronics of San Jose, California. In early 1993, Fujitsu identified an awareness problem and asked Anderson Solone for help.

Fujitsu discovered that design engineers had very little awareness of its new SPARClite embedded microprocessor. Without awareness at the design level, their sales reps were getting nowhere selling it. Also, unlike other microprocessors with discrete, specific applications, such as computers, the SPARClite embedded micro-processor was for a controlling function with applications as varied as photocopiers, digital switches, and traffic lights. With all the possible applications, advertising in trade journals wasn't the answer. That made the marketing communications task more difficult.

Anderson Solone was chartered with taking the SPARClite story on the road. The idea was to get a highly qualified list of design engineers, identify their job site locations, and do technical seminars in those cities.

Twelve cities were identified as having the largest concentrations of the qualified engineers. The zip codes of the design engineers were plotted on maps of the cities to identify locations for seminars.

A multi-gate mailer with a nonstandard trim size was used to make it stand out in the mass of mail these prospects get. The teaser on the mailing surface said "Attend a SPARClite seminar and win a free PoqetPC or HP95LX palm top comput-er!" The mailer described the processor and its applications, the agenda for the sem-inar, and the complete schedule of seminar sites and dates. An 800 number, spe-cially set up for managing responses to the mailer, was prominently featured. The registration reply card asked respondents to check off appropriate job functions, their company business niche, and design application areas.

The response rate to the mailer was 2 to 3 percent. Calls were made to regis-trants a week before the event to remind them and determine their intention to attend. This was important because Anderson Solone knew from past road show experience that actual attendance would be only 50 percent of those who registered. All this points to how important the quality of the list is—more important than aiming for a large list. The end result of the promotion was that attendance, including walk-ins, was 1 percent of the number of mailers sent. But it was the right 1 percent.

Ray Solone's guidelines for a road show are important to know:

1. If your company thinks it needs some form of event marketing or road show, build that into your budget early on. This allows you to plan ahead.

2. Planning ahead is essential. Most conference facilities in large cities are booked a year in advance.

3. Define your marketing objective early on, ideally before you bring in a con-sultant or marketing firm. But once they are involved, allow them to prod your assumptions. Listen to their advice.

4. Identify the prospects' hot buttons—what makes them tick? What is their thinking process and how does that affect the way you set up a seminar to build awareness. For example, should the seminar be in the morning or the afternoon or all day? Is it worth their while?

5. Choose a marketing firm carefully. Aim for an event marketing firm or a marketing communications generalist. This is a specialty involving nearly all forms of communications, and integrated marketing communication is the route to take.

6. Road show logistics are very time consuming. The Fujitsu project was twelve cities. That's twelve times the details and management task of a one-site event. Do you really want to have a staff person otherwise engaged drop everything to handle that?

7. The logistics themselves are in four periods:

   • Planning: identifying the cities, locking up facilities, developing the promotions

   • Preconference: content development; 35mm slide production; assembling materials, equipment, etc. and shipping them to the site

   • On-site: place directional signage, position back-up slides for emergency use, test A/V equipment and power line, set up product demo tables, set up computers and printers at registration table for sign-ins and home office reporting

   • Follow-up: fulfillment, database updates, getting sales reps out

8. Give yourself time for adjustments of materials. Run one week, skip the next, run again, and so on.

9. Have PC and printer on site to handle walk-ins' badges and to do daily reports for the home office.

10. The person who assembles materials for a site should also do the shipping. You don't want materials for a business application discussed in Chicago sent to the group in Atlanta that deals with some other application.

Principal Mike Anderson said, "The results of these efforts were highly qualified sales leads that the Fujitsu reps could work to close." But Anderson cautioned "Don't divide up the tasks among several agencies and consultants. You need to put control, accountability, and unity with one vendor. Make sure they have a track record of handling all the separate generic elements of what it takes to do a road show. Asking an ad agency to handle this kind of promotion is like asking a divorce lawyer to handle a corporate merger."

Whatever form of event marketing you use, clearly you are trying to make a statement or convey some specific point about your firm and the audience the event is targeted to hit. If that message or point is not one you think the trade or business press would be interested in, do yourself a favor: ask yourself whether event marketing is the right communication tool after all.

Passing that test, make sure the trade press and local business press are invited. Their presence can be in two forms: as participants or as observers.

If your event is a seminar or topical program, the trade press editors may be eager to participate in a panel discussion with consultants or industry experts. That would give them a forum for their publication that raises mindshare for the important role they play in your industry. The downside of a participant role by the press is that they will find it difficult to write about your event if they are part of the story and the news.

The obvious alternative is the traditional one of the press attending all sessions and reporting as they see fit. They should be included in the social time as well. If the press participants are numerous, you may need to set up a special press room with phone lines.

The trade press and business press should be notified early of the event using a press release with program or a press advisory. For local business press, follow up on the advisory about one week prior to the event because they may well need to be reminded of the event's significance.

The use of paid advertising, either in the broadcast media or print media, is a decision based almost entirely on the scope of the event you are hosting. For business marketers, using print ads in the trade press or local business press might well spotlight the event as special and credible. But it should never be used as a substitute for a direct campaign using your database profiles of key influences.

If your event is a series of seminars aimed at a horizontal group of decision makers, e.g., executive secretaries put in charge of buying or leasing a new copier, you may want to consider a teaser ad campaign comprising both direct mail and radio spots aimed at this demographic.

If your event is a series of seminars aimed at a vertical group of decision makers, e.g., all insurance agents who have not purchased notebook computer–based insurance management systems, you might consider backing your direct marketing with ads in the regional insurance industry newsletter or local business journal.

Advertising collateral, in the form of specialty advertising, signage, and literature, can build positive mindshare prior to the event, make the event run smoothly, and add staying power to the impressions you create.

If the budget permits, attendees should leave the event with some useful memento that connects your company with their special business or lifestyle profile.

In sports sponsorships, the popularity of imprinted t-shirts and caps still remains high. For special events such as a grand opening or announcement, make sure the specialty items match the "feel" of the event. For example, a black tie event for dealers and spouses might be better served by imprinted wine glasses rather than an imprinted fanny pack. A seminar series will be remembered if the carefully chosen attendees walk away with a folder, mouse pad, or clip board with an imprinted decision-making algorithm related to the seminar topic. A tutorial focused on how to make a purchase selection for a widget can make good use of a custom made slide or wheel chart.

You can never have enough signage at the event. You cannot assume that prospects know where to go and when to be there. This is especially true of events held at your company facility. Such events can be disruptive to employees. You also don't want guests wandering into development areas or mingling with the wrong employees. If broadcast media will be present, make sure the company logo and event theme are prominently displayed in the designated interview area or on the rostrum. Too often companies sponsor a major event at a hotel only to have the hotel name prominent across the podium instead of the sponsoring firm's name.

The program agenda, mailers, speakers' biographies, and other literature should all be designed using a common format. The press releases and advisories should announce the event theme and carry any logo or logotype to be used at the event. The company backgrounder should also carry the event logo and be amended to explain the event in the context of company market and history.

If the event is a seminar, tutorial, or road show, your most effective tool is computer-generated 35 mm color slides or color overhead transparencies. Software programs for both the IBM and Macintosh environment are available that put maximum control in your hands. Multimedia programs give you the flexibility to integrate video and special effects into text. For the impact these programs provide, the investment is minor. One client we know attended a high-tech conference that was put on in a very low-tech manner. Most of the presentations were lectures that relied on dense overheads. There was little evidence of multimedia technology or Internet connections for the attendees. Needless to say, the client's comment was, "They won't see me again."

MEASUREMENT AND EVALUATION

Event marketing is one of the most difficult forms of communications to measure and quantify. Even the big players in consumer-oriented sports marketing admit it's difficult.

The most basic measurement done in the consumer arena is counting: number of stories run in the trade press, the inches of copy those stories ran, the number of times your firm and the event are cited in speeches, on-air broadcast coverage, camera shots of signage, letters and calls received from customers (for and against the event), follow-up calls from trade press editors, and so on.

Such measures give you some baseline, especially if you made the same counts for one or two months preceding the event. But how do you measure affective, emotional results, such as employee pride, company esteem among customers, and general comfort level? These are relationship factors. As with much of marketing, event marketing is designed to solidify relationships that will ease the sales cycle.

One way is to regularly survey your marketplace using an independent survey research team that polls a sampling of your customers. This should be a series of surveys with the calls made anonymously. The questions should be related to those qualitative factors event marketing can enhance:

- Who is the leader in this industry?
- Who has the best management?
- Who has the best R&D?
- Who has the best customer service?
- Which company is the most stable?
- Which company has the best direction and fix on the future?

What you are seeking with such questions is perceptions. You are trying to assess "top-of-mind" reactions to questions. If your firm comes out well on the survey, so much the better. But if you hit some significant negatives, even if they are inaccurate, you quickly realize how your communications program must be adjusted. Remember, perceptions are reality.

RESOURCES

1. The American Marketing Association is the omnibus organization for all marketing professionals regardless of profession. For example, its biweekly *Marketing News* carries regular articles on sports marketing.
2. Promotion Marketing Association of America. 257 Park Ave. South 11th Floor, New York City, NY 10001.
3. The International Special Events Society (ISES) can offer assistance and expertise regarding the use of audiovisual "accents" and attention-grabbers such as laser lights. Their address is 8335 Alison Pointe Trail, Suite 100, Indianapolis, IN 46250.
4. Independent meeting planners belong to Meeting Planners International. MPI has a special interest group on computer software, called CSIG, that compiles a software resource guide with short descriptions of more than 100 programs.
5. *Meeting News* is a monthly published by Miller Freeman/United Newspapers, 1515 Broadway, New York, NY 10036. MN covers news, but also special fea-

tures and destination reviews, plus a regular "MN Job Bank" and classified ad section.

6. *IEG Sponsorship Report: The Newsletter of Sports, Arts, Event and Cause Marketing.* This is a biweekly newsletter of marketers who actively use event marketing and sponsorships in their business. Published by the International Events Group, Inc., which also publishes the IEG Directory of Sponsorship Marketing and the IEG Legal Guide to Sponsorship, plus IEG produces the Event Marketing Seminar Series and IEG Consulting. 213 W. Institute Place, Suite 303, Chicago, Illinois 60610.

7. *Meeting Planners Alert* is a monthly newsletter written by and for meeting planners. Topics include news, trends, and how-to articles on planning and meeting management. Published by MPA Communications, Inc., which also publishes the *MPA State-by-State Sales Tax Survey.* Joan Mather, CCM, is Editor/Publisher. P.O. Box 24, Prudential Station, Boston, Massachusetts 02199.

8. The 3M Meeting Management Institute produces a free newsletter on making meetings more productive. Contact Virginia Johnson, Manager, 3M Meeting Management Institute, 3M Austin Center, 6801 River Place Boulevard, Austin, Texas 78726-9000.

9. For anyone who plans lots of meetings, especially across the country and beyond, become a subscriber of *Successful Meetings: The Authority on Meetings and Incentive Travel Management.* This is a thick, resourceful, splashy, and practical monthly published by Bill Publications, 633 3rd Avenue, New York, NY 10017. There are regular updates on locations, meeting management software, legalities, issues, news, and more.

10. *Meeting Software Review* is a publication that reviews meeting management software. Douglas Fox, publisher.

11. *A Guide to Campus and Non-Profit Meeting Facilities,* 2150 West 29th Avenue, Suite 500, Denver, Colorado 80211. Surveys US and Canadian campuses. Some campus facilities may be members of the International Association of Conference Centers.

12. *Making Meetings Work,* by Dr. Gayle Carson, is an audiotape tutorial published by CareerTrack Publications, 3085 Center Green Drive, P.O. Box 18778, Boulder, Colorado 80308-9930.

13. *Creating Special Events: The Ultimate Guide to Promoting Successful Events* (1991). Linda Surbeck, Master Publications, 10323 Linn Station Road, Louisville, KY 40223. Linda Surbeck is the founder and president of a firm called Master of Ceremonies. This book is her guide to promotional event planning. Linda provides do's and don'ts, plus specific chapters on specific types of events, e.g., sales meetings, grand openings, etc.

14. Levasseur, R. E. (1994). *Breakthrough Business Meetings.* Holbrook, MA: Bob Adams Inc.

15. Lippincott, S. N. (1994). *Meetings: Do's, Don'ts and Donuts: The Complete Handbook for Successful Meetings.* Pittsburgh: Lighthouse Point Press.

16. Planning meetings and events in foreign countries isn't complicated just because of travel, time, and language concerns. The issue of local habits, sensitivities, protocol, business practices, and introductions is also important to the success of your event. Here are sources of help:

    Snowdon's Protocol Database is a software program containing country-specific information on local peculiarities that can affect your event's success. The software isn't inexpensive, but includes quarterly updates and even access to author Sondra Snowdon. Snowdon also has a 900 line service that provides a menu of countries and topics for quick fax turnaround: 1-900-PROTOCOL. Snowdon International Protocol Inc., One World Trade Center, Suite 7967, New York, NY 10048.

International Cultural Enterprises, Inc. publishes an audiotape cassette series on business customs in 20 countries, including the new Russia. Negotiation realities are also covered. 1241 Dartmouth Lane, Deerfield, Illinois 60015.

Translating materials is always a problem, especially with technical terms. Both European and Asian language translations are available from Adams Translations, 12885 Research Boulevard, Suite 206, Austin, Texas 78750. Telephone 800-880-0667.

17. Travel planning can be a headache—which hotel, what are the facilities, is a map available with mileage easy to calculate? Software is available to make it easier:

Personal Travel Guide is published by Personal Travel Technologies, 166 East Jericho Turnpike, Mineola, New York 11501. Telephone 800-345-8501. Also available in some retail software stores. DOS, Windows, or Macintosh versions.

Zagat-Axxis City Guide is published by famed travel/restaurant guide publisher Zagat Survey. Microsoft Windows 3.0 or Macintosh. Address: 4 Columbus Circle, New York, NY 10019. Telephone 800-333-3421.

Easy Sabre is the travel portion of Prodigy Interactive Personal Service, an online service that provides access to other Prodigy customers. PC or Macintosh with modem required. Prodigy is at 445 Hamilton Avenue, White Plains, New York 10601. Telephone 800-PRODIGY. It is also available through America On-Line at 1-800-827-6364.

Local Expert is a program providing local maps and corresponding information on the areas. Microsoft Windows or Macintosh 6.07 or higher. Contact Strategic Mapping, 3135 Kifer Road, Santa Clara, CA 95051.

NOTES

1. Adaptation of article by Bud Frankel, Frankel and Company, Chicago (December 1988). "Event Marketing: Panacea or Problems?" *Marketing News,* page 12. Revised with author's permission.
2. Eisenhart, T. (January 1988). "Sporting Chances Zap Competitors." *Business Marketing,* p. 92. Copyright, Crain Communications, Inc.

CHAPTER 14

Telemarketing: Creating a Second Sales Staff

"Mr. Watson, come here! I want you!"

—Alexander Graham Bell, Boston, March 10, 1876

Your company has opted to establish a telemarketing function. This entails establishing specific, measurable objectives for the telemarketing function. Appropriate resources, including a budget for facilities, hardware and software, personnel and compensation, have to be provided. The telemarketing staff has to be hired and trained. Lists have to be secured. Calls have to be made. And all phases of the telemarketing operation should be monitored, tracked, analyzed, and evaluated.

What are the critical elements of a telemarketing program and your overall marcom program that should be addressed?

There is almost an unconscious bias in many organizations that telemarketing is inferior to personal sales, that it is perceived by the marketplace as a hard-sell, high-pressure boiler room selling strategy. As a result, telemarketing efforts are frequently doomed by a self-fulfilling prophecy; it fails because it is expected to fail, so it is not used or supported vigorously.

More enlightened organizations have adopted the perspective that, in sales, the telephone isn't the next best thing to being there, but better! It succeeds, because it is given a mission, is supported and expected to succeed.

Personal selling has some nonproductive elements. The buyer may be put off by first impressions. The telephone allows an image to be projected, but the perception is solely in the mind of the listener. One of the authors, who worked his way through college as a radio disk jockey, was always bemused when meeting fans for the first time. Their invariable reaction? "Gee, you don't look anything like your voice."

Face-to-face sales is a more naked negotiating circumstance. With the phone, response can focus on the denotative message. Personal sales requires an etiquette of politeness, which means less bottom-line probing. The telephone permits a more blunt interrogation style. Closing in personal sales is frequently too ritualistic and, hence, risky; the ritual reinforces the risk. By nature, telephone closes are less ritualistic. Appropriate techniques can overcome the weaknesses and capitalize on the strengths of the telephone. The telephone is successfully utilized as a sales medium when

- People or companies with a need for your product or service are
- Contacted by highly trained telephone salespeople using
- A carefully designed sales dialogue supported by
- Efficient work flow, fulfillment, and measurement systems via
- Telecommunications equipment
- To achieve specific marketing objectives.

CHECKLIST OF DO'S AND DON'TS

- Do's:

  1. Do start new telemarketers on easier calls that have a higher success rate. This reinforces success, rather than failure, and reduces the new employee turnover rate.
  2. Do train callers and provide the means for them to regularly tape, play back, and evaluate calls.
  3. Do have more successful telemarketers mentor less successful workers, including sharing successful phone call tapes.

- Don'ts:

  1. New telemarketers should master one type of call before moving on to a more difficult call objective. Don't rush them. Let them crawl before they walk.
  2. Don't randomly modify the payment and incentive structure. Telemarketers should be able to have set expectations about the monetary benefits.

3. Don't alter factors that are directly related to the ability of tele-marketers to be successful, e.g., implementing unreasonable dial and completion quotas during off-peak periods.
4. Don't focus on success or failure during training and the proba-tionary period; focus on learning and skill development. The tele-marketers should feel they have an opportunity to succeed, not just a chance to fail.

WHERE DOES TELEMARKETING FIT IN THE OVERALL MARKETING PLAN?

Basic strategic decisions about the role of telemarketing in the overall mar-com strategy will to a large extent define telemarketing tactics. The concept is that telemarketing isn't a stand-alone marcom activity, but is integrated with other marcom tools. A product or service roll-out, for example, might be preceded by a mass media campaign, followed by a lead generation and qualification phone call which results in additional printed materials being sent to the potential buyer. A second phone call verifies the receipt of the materials, answers any questions that may have arisen, and either makes a sales appointment or attempts to close on the sale.

One major strategic area is how the telemarketing operation fits with sales. Are the two groups in competition with one another? How is man-agement going to allocate inquiries between the two? Or is telemarketing playing a support role by prequalifying prospects and establishing sales appointments? Does telemarketing handle the less productive accounts? Occasionally field sales reps and telemarketers are the same people, though this should be the exception, rather than the rule. One successful strategy for integrating the two sales functions is to have the groups share or swap jobs for a brief period of time.

Telephone sales and direct mail used in concert represent a powerful sales combination. The simplest utilization would be a mail offer followed by a phone call or a phone call followed by a mail fulfillment piece. Most marketing strategies involve expanded permutations of this basic framework.

The mail-phone combination is most effective when

- There is a new, relatively complicated product or service to introduce.
- There is no prior relationship between your organization and the prospect.
- The visual elements of the product are important to the purchase decision.

The phone-mail combination is most effective when

- The target is relatively small in number.
- The target consists of prequalified prospects or current customers.
- The product represents the opportunity for large profits from a skimming sales strategy.
- A prior relationship exists between your organization and the buyer.

Inbound Telemarketing

Another strategic decision is whether to use inbound or outbound telemarketing, or both, and what the specific objectives of each will be.

Inbound telemarketing calls can be classified by three major functions: lead response, order taking, and customer service. Each is briefly described below.

Lead-Response Function.   Operators are handling leads that have typically been generated through a mass marcom campaign, either mass media or direct response. Their objectives:

- Lead qualification: for follow-up by outside sales or outbound telemarketing department
- Fulfillment response: determining which fulfillment materials will satisfy the caller's needs and initiating the mailing, faxing, or other distribution of the materials
- Consultative selling: answering questions about the product or service, being prepared to overcome objections
- Taking the order: being prepared to accept the order when the lead makes a purchase decision
- Closing on the sale: knowing how to listen to identify when the inquirer is close to a purchase decision
- Follow-up function: checking back with the caller to make sure that the requested fulfillment information was received and was sufficient.

Order-Taking Function.   The buyer initiates the purchase; telemarketers take and verify orders. Their objectives:

- Taking the order: being prepared to accept the order when the lead makes a purchase decision, accurately accumulating correct order, payment, and delivery information
- Consultative selling: answering additional questions the caller may have about the product or service, being prepared to overcome objections
- Closing on the sale: knowing how to listen to identify when the inquirer is close to a purchase decision.
- Follow-up function: checking back with the caller to make sure that the product was received

Customer Service Function. Responding to customer concerns and needs is the major objective of the telemarketing center. Among the operators' responsibilities:

- Information gathering: getting to the real problem, e.g., the order was correct, but this shipment was specified for overnight delivery, not by second-day air
- Resolution function: being empowered to take action and make decisions that are important to maintaining a customer relationship
- Follow-up function: checking back with the caller whether or not the complaint was resolved

Outbound Telemarketing

Outbound telemarketers are salespeople who are usually the initiator of the call. As a general rule of thumb, outside salespeople don't convert readily to outbound telemarketing and outbound telemarketers are not, by nature, automatically successful outside salespeople. The strategies may be similar, but the media are very dissimilar.

Outbound calls can also be classified by their three major functions: sales support, soliciting new accounts, and account management. Each of these functions is described below.

Sales Support. Providing a supplemental tool for the field sales force. Among the objectives:

- Scheduling function: time and territory management; the objective is a cold-call phone appointment, a call appointment at a later time and date, or an appointment for an outside sales call. It is imperative that, if the latter is the objective, the caller have the ability to make an appointment commitment without additional calls.
- Marginal account sales function: the outbound telemarketer can sell to accounts that don't justify the time and expense of the personal sales call.
- Inventory control function: maintaining inventory control and reorder points for existing customers. The caller initiates the contact to verify the need for a reorder, and can also upgrade sell or cross-sell.

Soliciting New Accounts. This is cold-calling on the phone to carefully screened lists in narrowly targeted market segments, the only way outbound sales can be successful. Objectives include:

- Intelligence function: the caller's objective is to identify and get through to the decision-maker

- Consultative function: probing to identify product or service questions the prospect or customer may have about the product or service, being prepared to overcome objections
- Sales function: make a telephone sale

Account Management. This is bringing the account management function inside by using the telemarketing center for selling and servicing existing customers. The major objectives are:

- Relationship management function: servicing the account in the same manner an outside sales rep would. Regular relevant communications with the account, anticipation of purchasing needs, responding to customer emergencies, etc.
- Notification function: keeping the account informed of product or service changes, price or delivery changes, or other relevant information that maintains the efficiency of the customer's buying function
- Sales function: make a telephone sale, including cross-selling and upgrade selling
- Inventory control function: maintaining inventory control and reorder points for existing customers. The caller initiates the contact to verify the need for a reorder, and can also upgrade sell or cross-sell.
- Reactivation function: calling on inactive accounts to reestablish the buying relationship
- Information function: providing product or service intelligence for the buyer, information which can be leveraged to make them more efficient as a customer

A typical problem for organizations that sell through a combination of field sales, telemarketing sales, trade shows, and direct response is identifying the source of the sales lead, primarily for commissions and bonuses. One strategy is to eliminate commissions in favor of better compensation, and make the incentives available to all of the departments and personnel who contributed. This can also reduce internal competition for territory and budget dollars.

The easiest solution is to ask the customer the source of the sales lead. Six additional strategies are, for each sales channel, to create price differentials; use a different response address or phone number; offer unique product or service bundles; reconcile field rep and telemarketing call sheets with orders; assign them separate accounts; and use staggered cut-off dates.

HIRING FROM THE INSIDE OR THE OUTSIDE

There are always two options for hiring telemarketers: hire from within the organization or from the outside. For internal purposes, the key term is "hire." Current employees should voluntarily apply for and be screened for telemarketing; this isn't a function which just anyone can move into. Just as some people are not meant to be outside salespeople, some people are not meant to be telemarketers.

An advantage of hiring internally is that the current employee knows the company, its products or services, its marketing objectives and the customer profiles. This knowledge could also be a disadvantage. The employee may believe there is no reason for training or may be biased so strongly for a product line that she will never adapt to rejection, will never be able to understand why the customer didn't buy. In either situation, the current employee brings some emotional and psychological baggage to the new job.

A disadvantage to hiring someone outside the organization is that she doesn't know the company and its products, which requires additional training. On the plus side, the new hire will likely bring telemarketing skills and an objective perspective that allows her to sell from the customer's perspective.

Current employees should be able to apply with the understanding that their status doesn't necessarily mean bonus points in the hiring process. But they should also be given the opportunity to succeed with the understanding that, if they fail any of the training or probationary period, they can return to their previous position without a loss of seniority, status, or pay.

This is especially important if the organization is shifting from an inbound-only to an inbound-outbound center. Outbound callers typically make significantly more than inbound telemarketers, so there is an incentive for the latter to want to switch to the outbound center. Inbound and outbound telemarketing have different and unique requirements; being successful at inbound telemarketing isn't a significant predicator of outbound success.

Where Are the Qualified Applicants?

Telemarketing does offer job benefits that are particularly desirable to certain workers: schedule flexibility and the availability of nighttime or weekend shifts, if appropriate for the organization's target markets. This flexibility is a plus for single parents or two-parent families where one parent has a fixed work schedule, retirees, and college students. Salary and commissions are attractive to parents, college students, and homemakers.

Specific characteristics to screen or listen for would include

1. Do the applicants like to talk on the telephone?
2. Do they have telemarketing experience? Inbound or outbound? Selling what?

3. Do they have previous sales or other customer-related experience?
4. What is their employment objective? If it's money, what happens when that need has been resolved?
5. Do they have stable employment histories?

The most effective and least expensive way of recruiting high-quality, long-term employees is the recruit-a-friend campaign in which the referring employee receives a bonus for each referral who successfully completes the training program and probationary period.

Voice Characteristics of Successful Telemarketers

Control of a telemarketing sales presentation is a key to successful telephone sales. Control is established by the caller who establishes her- or himself as an intelligent authority figure. This is accomplished largely by the voice. People assign specific personality traits to individuals based on their voices. The voice is used to assess the speaker's honesty and believability, integrity, likability, energy level and interest, and self-confidence, all of which are important to making a telephone sale.

Initial screening of potential telemarketers—including present employees who may apply for a telemarketing position—should be done over the phone. The checklist that follows provides a list of desirable voice characteristics; it can also be used as a guide for developing improved voice skills during training. These characteristics create the impression of intelligence, education, and authority, all of which translate into control.

1. Does the voice have authority, is it commanding? Does the person have a deliberate speaking style and little hesitation when responding?

The speech should be nonrhythmic, well-modulated with varying inflections, and loud enough to be heard without being overbearing.

The speaker's rate of delivery should be slightly faster than the listener's. The voice should be well-modulated and loud enough that all words are clearly projected. Enunciation (articulation of the words) should be clear without being exaggerated.

2. How well does the speaker use language? Do they enjoy words and do you enjoy listening to them?

The words the speaker uses also contribute to—or detract from—the ability to control the conversation. Is the speaker's vocabulary appropriate for the speaker and for the purpose of the conversation? Erudite verbiage is onerous and vitiates the derivational purport of the missive. Is there a clear thought structure in the responses? Are separate points related or disjointed? Do the words create visual mental images? Can you see the speaker's body language in his speaking? Physical movement while speaking does translate through the phone during a conversation; the recipient can "see" the added emphasis, which adds to the control.

Effective telecommunicators are people of few words. They use short, declarative sentences. They avoid jargon with prospects, but are comfortable using jargon with customers. They avoid "weasel" words—words that sound as though the telemarketer is hedging her commitments, words like might, maybe, possible, if, or perhaps.

3. Is he or she articulate, well-spoken, and easy to understand?

4. What sort of energy level and self-confidence did he project? Was it real or forced?

5. To what level of the business world do you perceive this person belonging? How much do you think she could earn a year in telemarketing?

6. How honest is the individual? Were the responses believable?

7. Is your initial reaction to the individual favorable? Is he likable? Did the speaker personalize the conversation?

8. How well did the person listen? Did she interrupt? Or was the fact that the person was listening reflected in her comments, questions, and phrases that acknowledged what you said?

The second interview should be a group interview in which additional tests are administered, as needed or required by personnel. A powerful technique is to have them place mock phone calls using a script in small groups of fellow applicants; use the applicants to provide peer ratings, which are surprisingly valid as an indicator of potential success as a telemarketer.

TRAINING

The cost of the initial and ongoing training is relatively low in comparison to the potential net lifetime value (NLTV) of relationships that are established by competent, well-trained telemarketers. These individuals represent the company as assuredly as any outside sales force.

Training as a permanent, ongoing activity is a relatively inexpensive way to counteract the fact that telemarketing can become routine and tedious. This results in loss of interest by telemarketers, who lapse into shoddy phone habits and become less productive or quit.

The initial training should have the following structure.

1. Well-planned, specific objectives
   Phase 1: orientation, which includes

   - Company history
   - Corporate image

- Presentation of overall marketing objectives and marcom goals. Discussion of where telemarketing fits.

3. Phase 2: training on hardware and software, including
   - Systems and programs
   - Headphones
   - Transfer calls, calls on hold
   - Taping and monitoring systems

4. Phase 3: product or service training, which includes
   - Learning company and product or service literature
   - Sales presentations by the sales department
   - Marketing presentations by the marketing department

5. Phase 4: Observation of successful telemarketers, a powerful modeling technique

6. Phase 5: Training in selling by phone, including
   - General sales techniques
   - Telephone sales techniques
   - Learning the sales call sequence
     How to get through to the decision maker
     Call introduction and set-up
     Probing questions
     Making the offer
     Overcoming objections
     Closing the sale
   - Establishing the call agenda
   - How to make the phone call
   - Overcoming objections
   - Time management and productivity

7. Phase 6: Mock telemarketing using
   - Verbatim scripts: actual call transcripts of successful and unsuccessful calls; used to analyze and critique the call sequences
   - Outline scripts: key areas of a sales call highlighted, used in early role playing
   - Role play and evaluation

8. Phase 7: Graduating tests and on-line evaluations

9. Probationary period. The general strategy is to
   - Start new callers with the easiest calls which have the highest success rate. Most organizations throw people into the lowest success-rate arena, which guarantees failure and a high turnover rate
   - Fewer hours initially, followed up with group and individual assessments and constructive critiques
   - Weekly support group activities

Managing the Four Basic Telemarketing Fears

A major outcome of any telemarketing training program should be teaching people how to recognize and deal with the four basic fears shared by all telemarketing professionals: the fear of being disliked, the fear of rejection, the fear of loss of control and the fear of objections.

The fear of being disliked by the caller is human nature. The key to dealing with this fear is to work to be respected by the people you are calling, not to be liked by them. This is accomplished by having objective goals that can be met, and by both self-reinforcement and reinforcement from the work environment. Telemarketers shouldn't have to use an alter ego to make the calls. If she is, that person probably doesn't belong in sales.

The fear of rejection is the single most consistent fear in any sales situation. It is axiomatic in outside sales that it takes 10 calls to make a single sale. One ambitious salesperson thrived on rejection; each one put him closer, in his mind, to that one sale. An outbound telemarketer who makes 15 contacts per hour is likely to make eight sales presentations from those contacts; she will experience a 20 percent success rate. That means 6.4 "yes's" and 25.6 "no's" during a four-hour shift, which is a lot of rejection. To handle rejection, you should be a realist, not a perfectionist; count the successes, not the rejections; and understand that it is not the telemarketer who is being rejected, it's the offer.

Losing control of the presentation is a fear that can be overcome with thorough preparation. The caller has control as the initiator of the call. Control is maintained by knowing what the objectives are and understanding the call agenda.

Objections are not something to be feared; they are challenges that the buyer is presenting for you to overcome.

Handling and Overcoming Objections

Perhaps the most basic sales principle is that the sale doesn't begin until the objection is raised. If the telemarketer calls and says, "We have fluorescent widgets for sale" and the customer says, "Ship me 40 gross," the telemarketer is an order-taker. When the customer says, "Well, I don't think we need widgets because we're currently using tuits," that's an objection.

The first step is to distinguish between a legitimate objection and a phony one. A legitimate objection can be overcome; a phony one can't. The difference? When an objection is countered with a rational response and the prospect doesn't react rationally, then the objection is probably phony. "You're concerned, Mr. Justice, that our price is five percent more than the Byrd company's tuit. I'll match their price. So, how many should I ship?" If Mr. Justice replies, "No, it's still too expensive" or raises another objection without responding, the original objection was a phony one.

Other tips for identifying phony objections include those that are too vague, objections that are raised before the customer has asked any questions or if the customer doesn't seem to be attentive and subsequently raises objections.

Why would a customer raise a phony objection? Because an objection doesn't exist, the customer doesn't want to state the objections, she doesn't think the objection is strong enough, or for expediency—to get the salesperson to go away.

The goal in countering a legitimate objection is to get the customer to understand that the objection isn't a real reason for not making the purchase decision. Several techniques are available for effectively accomplishing this.

One is to acknowledge the objection, agree that it seems to be a problem, but provide an explanation. For example, "Our product is more expensive, but that's because we have a patented alloy process that we use in manufacturing this part. As a result, we have a failure rate that is 95 percent less than the industry standard and 98 percent less than the Byrd Company's product. That sounds like a fair trade-off, doesn't it? Better quality for a slightly higher price?"

Another way of handling this same objection is to rephrase it so that the answer is set up. "What you're asking, Mr. Justice, is why would I pay 5 percent more per gross for these tuits when I can get the fixintoos at a lower price? The reason is . . . ."

You can also agree, but offer terms or benefits that counteract or negate the objection. "I hear your concern about the costs. What we're prepared to offer is our own financing program at one percent over prime for 15 years." There are myriad ways of overcoming objections, each of which can be effective in specific situations with certain customers.

Overcoming objections is almost a game of one-upmanship. The most effective way to prepare for the game is to collect or anticipate all of the objections that have been or could be raised and pre-script a dozen potential responses for each. We also suggest that every new objection be collected, along with the responses that were made and which response overcame the objection. These should be added to the script, and discussed and evaluated at the weekly training sessions. This could be another incentive bonus category: the most unique, the most unusual, the phoniest objection of the week and the most creative or the most productive response of the week.

QUALITY CONTROL

The monitoring area should be physically separate from the main phone operation. Supervisors should be able to access each phone and computer for review and immediate critique, if necessary. A monitoring frequency should be established and met. A good rule of thumb is to have each telemarketer monitored at least three times per week by different supervisors. The rating criteria should be objective and each employee should be aware of what they are. Call evaluations should be discussed with the employee within 24 hours.

Absenteeism can be a problem; flexibility of hours may be perceived as flexibility in showing up. The company's policy should be fair, but firm. Employees should understand that an unstable staffing situation reduces productivity and results in unfair workload demands on the employees who are on the phones. Two ways to combat this problem are to provide long-term scheduling and a shift-trading option.

Performance files provide an opportunity to give commendations for consistently high ratings or assistance in performance improvement for low ratings. It s important that employees who deserve commendation receive it and that those who deserve criticism are appropriately reprimanded, perhaps placed on a probationary status. Failure to take either action encourages substandard performance both individually and for the group.

These records can also alert the organization to potential problem areas, which provides topics for the ongoing training sessions.

MOTIVATION

Telemarketing is a sales function that requires constant motivation due to its relatively low success rate. The most effective motivation is monetary bonuses given on the basis of meeting or exceeding lead, appointment, sales or profit quotas, depending upon what the telemarketing objectives are.

Some motivational strategies are:

1. Hold weekly group meetings to share war stories: successes and failures, the best objection of the week, and how the telemarketer didn't, did, or could have overcome the objection.

2. Vary the basis for incentives. For example, a random daily bonus for the first person to reach a certain sales level that day. A bonus for the highest dollar average per sale should be supported by a wide range of products or services to sell. A bonus could be established for the lowest 30-day return rate or for the most sales of high-profit products.

3. Distribute inbound calls and outbound leads objectively and fairly. There will be top producers who should be rewarded for their success, but not at the expense of the old reliables.

4. Incentives should be for short-term results. If they're long-term, they lose motivational value and may be perceived as being unreachable. This leads to a "So why even try?" attitude.

5. Don't base incentives on unproven call objectives. Make sure that the objectives are attainable.

6. Incentives shouldn't be designed so that only a small percentage of the telemarketers will ever earn them. Be creative in devising ways that the old reliables can earn bonuses, etc.

Discussing and setting group goals can also be a motivator, and sets the group up to participate in helping to motivate less productive employees, either subtly or overtly.

Recognition is also a strong motivator, as it is in most management situations. Being told that you are doing a good job is a reminder that management is aware of your existence and your contributions.

Recognition can take the form of

- Letters that are placed in the employee's permanent employment file
- Acknowledgments added to commendations from a prospect or customer, which are also placed in the personnel file
- Employee of the week, month, quarter, and year contests with appropriate bonus awards
- Other awards: gift certificates, free lunches, comp time

Motivation shouldn't be simply a bottom-down process. Periodic job satisfaction surveys afford the employees the opportunity to provide management with their assessments of working conditions, management policies and procedures, equipment strengths and deficiencies, and company marketing objectives. To be effective, the results should be shared with employees, and legitimate concerns and issues acted on by management. This responsiveness is important in any management situation in maintaining employee morale.

A final comment: it is common to overlook the employees who aren't superstars or problem employees. These are the steady producers without whom an organization can't survive. Motivational programs should be devised so that each of these reliable performers has an opportunity to participate in earning bonuses and other recognition.

Compensation

A graduated compensation plan should be established through the probationary period. For example, the first two weeks should be at full salary equivalent to that of medium- to well-paid secretary. The main objective is two hours of calling a day; the balance of the day is review and training. The next eight weeks should be at full salary with weekly objectives to be met; no draw against commission. The next 12 weeks would be a diminishing base salary and increased commission draw. Commissions are computed at each pay period. Ultimately, the base salary should be about 15 percent of annual gross sales, unless the telemarketer is on straight commission.

To keep overhead costs down, most telemarketing operations— whether in-house or an outside agency—offer low wages and use a high percentage of part-timers on the telephones. The result is a high employee turnover rate, low productivity, and a lack of commitment to the organization and its marketing and marcom goals.

These issues also apply to customer service operations, which is frequently treated as an entry-level position. This is an inappropriate strategy. Customer service represents one of the organization's most critical touch points with customers or potential customers. These people should be educated, articulate, well-paid, well-trained, highly motivated, and fully empowered employees. Anything less defeats the basic premise of customer service: maintaining and extending the lifetime relationship of customers.

MAKING SUCCESSFUL TELEMARKETING CALLS

The objective of any telemarketing call is to be successful on that first call, which reduces the need for additional calls. Successful is defined by the call objective, which is always a sale. Not necessarily the sale of a product—sometimes all that's being sold is an informational response. Selling is a negotiation process; telemarketing sales training should include training in negotiating strategies and techniques. The following are techniques successful telemarketers use to make the sale.

1. Successful telemarketers sell to or negotiate with the people who are in a position to make the purchase decision or direct the purchase decision to be made.

2. Effective phone salespeople are tenacious without being obstinate. Their goal is to meet the call objective and they will do everything they can to successfully negotiate that objective. But they also need to know when the other party is saying "stop."

3. The most successful salespeople approach a sale with a "win-win" mentality. Successful telemarketing is based on relationships— mutual cooperation for mutual benefit—not warfare. They also use positive reinforcing terminology to continually reinforce the idea that the sale can be concluded as a "win-win" proposition for both.

4. A principal negotiation strategy is being willing to give ground. This can be achieved by opening with less realistic expectations and then allowing yourself to be negotiated down to a more realistic, but acceptable, fall-back position.

5. Another negotiating strategy is to start with the easier purchase decisions and then move the buyer to the more important, riskier ones. Success breeds success. Being able to point out that you and the buyer have already reached agreement in several areas sets up further sales negotiations.

6. Information is a major part of a negotiation. The successful negotiator uses both one- and two-sided information, which was discussed in the direct mail section of the direct response chapter. This means being willing to openly discuss the potentially negative sales points. What would you be prepared to say if you were a Chevy truck salesperson making sales calls to prospective fleet truck buyers about sidesaddle gas tanks and the perception that they have a tendency to explode in accidents?

7. Continued success in telemarketing means constantly analyzing and evaluating your performance, seeking critiques from objective and skilled third parties, and constantly seeking new strategies and techniques to enhance the phone relationships with prospects and customers.

There are five major mistakes which telemarketers routinely make. These can be used to develop checklists for self- or group evaluation or training purposes.

1. Not being prepared to make the call. If you're not prepared, don't make the call. An outside sales rep wouldn't. Preparation means understanding the call objective(s); have an agenda and list of probing questions prepared, supported by a formal or semiformal script; have the objections list at hand; and anticipate which closing techniques is most likely to be successful.

2. Forming an early assessment of how the sale is going. We've heard telemarketers give up on a sale when the customer was willing to continue negotiating simply because the telemarketer didn't believe he or she was going to be able to close. Don't form perceptions too quickly. As in opera, "It isn't over until the fat lady sings."

3. Losing sight of the overall telemarketing objective. Any sale represents the acquisition of a relationship, not the completion of a transaction. This holds true for telemarketing as well. The most successful phone salespeople understand the fast nickel versus the slow dime dilemma and work toward achieving the latter.

4. Being distracted by note-taking during the conversation. The major responsibility of the telemarketer is to listen and respond, neither of which will occur if note-taking is the primary objective.

5. Being a poor listener. Like the salesperson who didn't hear the buyer say "I'd like 100 gross of these widgets," and proceeded to make a full-blown sales presentation to someone who was already sold.

BECOMING A BETTER LISTENER

There are eight simple techniques to help you become a better listener.

1. Study yourself, your listening techniques, even in personal communications. How often does someone ask, "Did you hear what I said?" Or do they feel you are focused on them?

2. Concentrate on the conversation. The individual should know that you're focused on this conversation, not other thoughts, external problems or situations.

3. Be prepared, which requires less thinking and allows for more listening. Telemarketing calls aren't extemporaneous communications. The best telecommunicators sound spontaneous, not scripted.

4. Keep note-taking to a minimum. Most conversations can be recalled in the short term. Use the time immediately after the conversation to make notes.

5. Don't interrupt. Let the other person have his or her say, even if you "know" what it's going to be. Interrupting is a barrier to effective communications, and is frequently perceived as rude and even arrogant.

6. Don't allow yourself to be interrupted. Ask for the same courtesy you have extended to the other party.

7. Don't argue mentally with what the person is saying. Keep track of his most important points and then use a reflective listening technique to provide time to shape a rebuttal.

8. Use a reflective listening style. This means paraphrasing back to the speaker what she just said to you. This does several things. It gives you time to think about a response. It demonstrates your attentiveness; you couldn't have reflected the speaker's message if you hadn't been paying attention. And it allows the speaker to "hear" what she said filtered through your perceptual framework. This permits immediate feedback and clarification so that the communication is accurately received.

Preparation and Time Management

Telemarketing calls require planning to be successful. Preparation means understanding

1. The target profile, identified by the column headings in Figure 14.1;

2. The recipient's level of involvement or experience with the product or service being offered, which results in different information needs, depicted by the row headings in figure 14.1; and

3. Call structures—the type of call, call subject, and call objective, as defined in the overlay in Figure 14.1.

Each call objective has three dimensions:

1. Behavioral: what is it you want the receiver to do?
2. Observable: the behavior should be something that is observable.
3. Measurable: the behavior should be stated in measurable terms.

A call is successful when these objectives are satisfied.

It should be understood that the customer also has expectations that a series of basic questions will be answered when she accepts a telemarketing call. These include

- Who is calling and from what organization?
- Why are you calling me?
- How long is the call going to be?
- What is it you want me to do?
- How will I benefit if I say "yes?"
- What is my liability if I say "yes?"
- If I say "yes," what happens next?

A precall planning guide would include not only the contact information, but the information included in the previous list and an agenda. The

FIGURE 14.1   *Checklist for Analyzing Telemarketing Calls*

	Business: small, medium, large; at-home	Professional	Institutional	Governmental	Consumer
Unqualified Prospect (UP)	Type, Subject, Objective	Type, Subject, Objective	Type, Subject, Objective	Type, Subject, Objective	Type, Subject Objective
Suspect: Qualified UP	Type, Subject, Objective	Type, Subject, Objective	Type, Subject,	Type, Subject,	Type, Subject
Prospect: Highly Qualified Suspect	Type, Subject, Objective	Type, Subject, Objective			
Inquirer	Type, Subject, Objective	Type, Subject, Objective			
Previous/Current Customer	Type, Subject, Objective	Type, Subject, Objective			
Influencer	Type, Subject, Objective	Type, Subject, Objective			

Call Type	Call Subject	Call Objective
• inbound	• product	• lead generation
• outbound	• service	• qualify lead
• live	• information	• application
semiautomated	• fulfillment	• fulfillment
• automated	• qualification	• take order
• interactive	• membership	• appointment
• conference		• sale
		• post-purchase follow-up
Call Structure		• upgrade
for Each Cell		• cross-sell
		• test
		• survey
		• service

For each category of call, defined as a cell, there are three structural call elements that need to be defined and analyzed. For example, an at-home business suspect phone contact can be planned by the type of call it is, the subject of the call, and the call objective.

agenda would include the opening lead-in statement or theme; the basic informational message that needs to be given; probing questions to identify the target's information needs; a list of key features, primary benefits for each, and sales aids; and closing statements.

As a rule of thumb, business buyers respond most favorably to phone sales from 10 a.m. to 12 noon and from 2 p.m. to 4 p.m. Upper-level managers can successfully be contacted before or after their organizations' normal business hours; they arrive early and stay later, and the screeners aren't running interference.

The number of hours each telemarketer spends on the phone per day and the types of calls she is making are relevant to preventing burnout and reducing turnover. A telemarketer who spends less than four hours a day making calls is underutilized; one who spends more than six hours is subject to burnout. The optimum time frame is between four to six hours with hourly breaks.

Varying the type of call is also important to successful direct marketing. Four hours of cold calls to unqualified prospects is stressful for even the most successful telemarketer.

A better strategy is represented by the clock in Figure 14.2. Each hour starts with a type of sales call that has a fairly high success rate, followed by a more difficult call, and ending with the least successful type of call. This provides positive reinforcement at the start of each hour, rather than scheduling an hour's worth of calls that have a very low success rate. Each block

FIGURE 14.2 *Sample Telemarketing Production Clock*

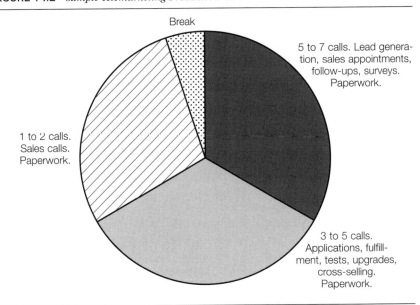

allows for basic record keeping, and the hour ends with a break. A six-hour shift can be preceded or followed by training, or more in-depth paperwork.

TELEMARKETING COSTS CHECKLIST

Budgeting is a consideration for any marcom activity. Ideally, a budget should be established using an objective and task strategy that identifies the objectives of the telemarketing center and then lists all of the tasks that are necessary to accomplish those objectives. Costs are assigned to the tasks and then are totaled to represent the projected budget.

Costs are fixed or variable. Fixed costs include those that won't change with program variations. For example, equipment hardware costs don't vary with the number of calls or sales made. Variable costs are those that will vary due to workload. Telephone access and toll charges will be affected by inbound and outbound volume, for example. Cost categories include personnel costs, telephone costs, and physical plant costs.

Personnel Costs: salaries, commissions, overtime, and incentives; supervisory salaries, commissions, overtime, and incentives; secretarial support; recruiting and hiring costs; training costs; payroll and bookkeeping costs; and taxes.

Telephone Costs: equipment costs, including hardware lease, purchase, installation, maintenance, and connect/disconnect charges; monthly service, leased or private line and access costs and toll charges; maintenance and repairs; and taxes.

Telemarketers should have binaural headsets with pencil mikes that leave the hands free. Traditional handsets and speaker phones should be banned. There should be sufficient cord to allow the person to stand and move comfortably around in the work area, rather than being shackled to the desk or computer during a call.

Physical Plant Costs: rent, utilities, maintenance, renovations; office furniture, equipment, and supplies.

The ideal telemarketing workstation is in a quiet, nondistractive area. There should be adequate desktop space, a comfortable chair, and neutral walls unadorned with any personal pictures or posters or other non-sales-related materials as distractors. A mirror should be provided so the telemarketer can observe facial expressions and body language. Subdued lighting seems to also produce a more productive environment. Dress codes are important to psychologically reinforce the idea that these are sales calls; the customer can't see how the caller is dressed, but the caller can. Casual or sloppy dress diminishes the importance of the calling activity.

Weekly, monthly, quarterly, and annual estimates of telemarketing costs in relationship to sales are helpful in scheduling workload and identifying seasonal cycles of sales offers. The overall objective of continually analyzing estimated versus actual costs against sales is to quickly detect and correct variations that could affect profit goals.

FUTURE TECHNOLOGIES: TELEMARKETING IN THE 21ST CENTURY

Technology will dramatically change the marcom environment in the next decade, especially in telemarketing. Callers will be able to communicate visually as well as verbally and not just over traditional telephone systems, but through cable, direct broadcast, and information superhighway linkups. Sales calls will eventually move into a virtual reality environment.

There is always some discussion about the need for a face-to-face, eyeball-to-eyeball, handshake-to-handshake sales meeting. For the computer literate, especially among the younger generation of decision makers, computer contact provides all of these in a trusted, time-efficient manner.

Much has been written about the March 1993 snowstorm and how a snowbound East Coast ad agency closed a major deal with a Chicago client via an interactive video linkup. Both the client and the agency agreed that the technology provided a more efficient sales relationship. Travel and socialization time was eliminated. The two have agreed to extend and enhance this long-distance sales relationship. This type of experience is the harbinger of the ultimate "death of a salesman."

TIPS FOR INTEGRATING YOUR PROGRAM

Telemarketing is too often relegated to the role of transaction generator and not integrated into the overall marcom strategy.

The integrated marcom concept is probably no less important in telemarketing than it is in any other marcom activity. The telemarketers not only have direct contact with the business buyer, but represent an important and immediate feedback loop in the communications process. So it is imperative that the telephone reps be fully aware of not only their role in the marketing process, but that their communications are supportive of and consistent with the overall marcom strategy.

Integrated marcom depends on communications to establish, support, and maintain the customer relationship, and understands that each touch point is critical to that communications process. Being able to provide immediate, accurate, and responsive feedback to the customer's information needs is fundamental and indispensable in relationship marcom.

This implies that the telemarketing reps must be constantly trained and updated in the overall marketing and marcom strategies, and should understand the messages that are being communicated through the various marcom channels. One company of which we're aware, for example, had launched a massive ad and publicity campaign for a new product roll-out, complete with an 800 number for further information. Unfortunately, when potential customers called, the response they received was, "Sorry, but we haven't been given that information."

It is also imperative that the telephone reps be well trained in the collection of marketing intelligence. Customer concerns and information needs must be immediately channeled to the appropriate department. One of us recently tried to call a membership club's 800 number, but was frustrated for more than three days by a busy signal. This was despite the fact that the calls were auto-dialed for more than 30 minutes at four different times of the day. The company apparently doesn't have the capability to roll calls into a waiting mode, but instead simply turns customers away.

While that's a "no-no," the real issue is that the customer service rep was asked whether she had a formal way of filing a customer's suggestion or complaint. She didn't, but said that she would note the concern in our file. And there the information will sit, when it should be forwarded and matched with other customers' complaints, providing a clear indication of how the level of customer service could be improved.

MEASUREMENT AND EVALUATION

Yogi Berra once said, "If it isn't broke, don't fix it." Our qualifier: "Unless you are going to make it substantially better." There's no way to know if the system is functioning or if it's broken if it is not monitored, analyzed, and evaluated.

This is a relatively simple process if specific telemarketing goals are established. If they are not, it is difficult to tell what's working or not. The specific data collected and the analysis call sheets that are designed to collect this information will be determined by your organization's telemarketing objectives.

Having specific objectives establishes directly measurable telemarketing results, *e.g.,* the ratio of sales calls to dials; the number of calls handled by the telemarketing center and specific operators; the number of sales and average dollar amount; the average revenue per sale; the distribution of sales within and across product lines; the sales conversion rate for lead generation programs, and NLTV to expense ratios, to name a few.

Qualitative measurements can also be made; indirect measures of productivity and promotion effectiveness, *e.g.,* the ability of the telemarketing specialist to do consultative, cross- or upgrade selling; the telemarketing center's overall productivity; the efficiency of inbound versus outbound programs; the effectiveness of target market selection, and so on.

We also recommend that these measures be expended to include the customer base. Customers should be surveyed or interviewed at least once a year about not only the level of service, but the nature of the interaction. Were the reps knowledgeable, helpful, efficient, responsive, personable? Did they establish a sense of relationship with the customer or did it seem they were more interested in getting on to the next phone call? Does the customer know or remember the name of the telephone rep? We would recommend a random sample of the top customers—those who buy the most often; a sample of mid-range customers—those who buy at the median frequency; and a sample of inactives—those who haven't made a purchase in the last 12 months. Benchmarking this customer data provides an important standard, since marcom is a customer-driven activity.

RESOURCES

1. Goodman, G. S. (1984). *You Can Sell Anything by Telephone!* New York: Prentice Hall Press.
2. Harlan, R., and W. M. Woolfsen (1991). *Telemarketing That Works: How to Create a Winning Program for Your Company.* Chicago: Probus Publishing.
3. Linchitz, J. (1990). *The Complete Guide to Telemarketing Management.* New York: AMACOM (American Management Association).
4. McCafferty, T. (1994). *In-house Telemarketing: The Masterplan for Starting and Managing a Profitable Telemarketing Program.* Chicago: Probus Publishing.
5. *Start Your Own Telemarketing Business* (1990). Glenview, IL: Scott, Foresman.
6. *Telemarketing: The Magazine of Electronic Marketing and Communications.* Published monthly by Technology Marketing Corporation, 17 Park St., Norwalk, Connecticut 06851. Telephone 800-243-6002.
7. *Inbound/Outbound.* Published monthly by Telecom Library, 12 West 21st Street, New York, New York 10010.

PART 4

Managing Important Relationships

Marcom is about relationships, which continue to be the focus in Part 4, again, we hope, without getting academic or burying you in production details.

Marcom isn't solely an external function. Marcom also has an internal component, charged with communicating the organization's marketing message to its internal stakeholders, as we discussed in Chapter 1. If there is not an internal buy-in to the marcom message, it will be difficult to sustain that message to the external marketplace. These stakeholders include not only the employees, but stockholders and the community or communities in which your business operates. In many cases, getting messages to these groups is a function of something traditionally called "public relations," usually relegated in the organization to a "media relations" function. We'd like to suggest that the public relations aspect is much broader and more proactive.

Finally, handling crises has become a complex communication problem in the era of strict laws regarding safety, the environment, and health. You need to mesh crisis management plans into your overall marcom plans, which is the theme of the final chapter in Part 4.

CHAPTER 15

Public Relations: The Best Defense Is a Good Offense

> "I never thought of [public relations] as power. I never treated it as power. People want to go where they want to be led."
>
> —Edward Bernays,
> the father of public relations,
> in a 1984 PBS interview

Your organization was recently publicly embarrassed by the revelation that some of its salespeople were providing kickbacks to local and county officials for awarding large contracts to your company. The result was a shakeup not only in the sales department, but in the top executive ranks as well. There are those in the organization who feel that the public relations department didn't do its job in quelling the news stories about the illegal activities and that the damage control was too little, too late. The new CEO has put you in charge of reviewing the public relations functions within the organization.

What are your objectives and how do you plan to achieve them?

Perhaps the three most prevalent myths about public relations are that public relations 1) means churning out press releases and tracking the number of insertions achieved, 2) is nothing more than media relations, and 3) is only responsible for external marcom.

Press releases and staged events are products of a public relations strategy. Using a template, press releases can be constructed and mailed by an external agency; media events can be coordinated by a special events planner. If placement of press releases, stories, and quotes from company sources is the sole objective of the public relations function, then media relations are indeed of primary importance. If the public relations function is defined more broadly, however, then managing the media relations becomes a means to an end, not the end itself.

Managing relations only with the organization's external audiences isn't only myopic, but foolish. The internal audiences—management, employees, and stockholders—are perhaps even more critical to the overall success of the company. Allowing employees to learn about major company changes or decisions from external media sources, for example, is one way to very quickly destabilize and demoralize the workforce.

CHECKLIST OF DO'S AND DON'TS

- Do's:
  1. Do define expected public relations outcomes in observable and measurable terms.
  2. Do assign responsibility for both internal and external marcom activities to the public relations area.
  3. Do keep up-to-date and accurate media contact information, including who the appropriate contact is, his or her name, title, phone number, address, and fax number. Reciprocate by keeping your company's public relations contact and phone numbers updated with the relevant media outlets.

- Don'ts:
  1. Don't relegate public relations to the primary role of firefighter, spin doctor, or damage control specialist. Public relations is primarily a proactive marcom function.
  2. Press releases should be newsworthy and relevant for the media to which it is submitted. Cranking out a dozen press releases a week isn't PR. What it does create is a "crying wolf" mentality among the media gatekeepers; when a legitimate story does come from you, they have learned to ignore it.
  3. Don't measure the success of each promotional tactic or tool. Measure success as the result of the marcom mix.

PUBLIC RELATIONS OBJECTIVES

Over 50 years ago, E. L. Bernays wrote the first "how to" book of public relations called *Crystallizing Public Opinion* and forever changed the profession. Public relations, he said, means ideas, not mechanics. This is especially true in integrated marcom. How public relations is to be integrated into the overall marcom strategy is something that has to be strategically defined within the organization. The "mechanical" part of public relations—producing press releases, managing media relations, handling special events, etc.—can be outsourced. The strategic component can't be.

Bernays perceived public relations as *information* that is given to the public, *persuasion* directed at the public to modify its attitudes and actions, and the *efforts to integrate* an organization's policies and actions with the attitudes and reactions of its publics.

Until the Public Relations Society of America (PRSA) began to wrestle with the issue in 1980, there was no consensus about what public relations is. Some saw public relations as the engineering of public consent. Many public relations professionals still believe that public relations means doing something good and telling people about it so that your company gets credit for it.

In 1982, the PRSA Assembly adopted its "Official Statement on Public Relations," which defined public relations as a management function which

- *Anticipates, analyzes, and interprets* public issues, opinion, and attitudes which might positively or negatively impact the objectives and operations of the organization.
- *Counsels management* at all levels in the organization about the potential public ramifications of policy decisions, proposed courses of action, and marcom activities, and whether or not they conform to the organization's social or corporate citizenship responsibilities
- Continually *researches, conducts, and evaluates* action programs and marcom to ensure that the public is informed about, understands, accepts, and trusts the company's objectives
- *Plans and implements* the organization's efforts to influence or change public policy
- *Manages* the personnel and resources to achieve the above responsibilities

Clearly, the most desirable outcome of a public relations strategy is developing and maintaining a hospitable, friendly public environment for the organization. This implies that management must buy in to the belief that acceptance by an organization's publics is the highest priority if it is to function successfully today and in the future. This buy-in is reflected in ensuring that the publics are considered in setting corporate strategies, which allows the public relations practitioner to communicate that the company is acting for the collective good of its publics and society in general, and not for its own short-term advantage. Building mutual understanding and acceptance between the company and its publics through effective marcom is a fundamental marketing strategy.[1]

PUBLIC RELATIONS IS MORE THAN "FIREFIGHTING"

Reactive, emergency, or damage control public relations has the highest public profile both within and outside the organization. These are the activities that occur, for example, when there is an emergency situation, such as product tampering, a disgruntled ex-employee who wounds or kills a former supervisor on-site, or a private plane that hits a fast-food restaurant during lunch hour following an abortive take-off from a nearby community airport. The company may also be under attack by the competition, consumer activist groups, employee unions, or regulatory agencies; or when it is entering a new product or market area, or has merged with, been bought out by, or has bought out another company.

Chapter 19 deals more at length with crisis management, but there are some major points which should be made here. Implementation of reactive public relations measures is dictated by external forces that are beyond anyone's control, even with extensive "what if" preplanning and anticipations. The immediate public relations objectives are damage control and restoring the company image to its *status quo.*

The public relations strategy is typically a defensive one, and frequently entails attempts to hush up or quell media reports, to play down the seriousness of the incident, and to deny media access to the pertinent information. Problem-solving also becomes part of the strategy; a company announces the hiring of additional security personnel to prevent similar random acts of violence from occurring in the future.

The public relations tactics are generally *ad hoc,* focused on the current emergency with little consideration for the long-term marketing or marcom implications. This may be in spite of the fact that the company has a public relations handbook on what to do in a major emergency, including who to contact, who has responsibility for media relations, what should and can be said to the media or other parties, etc. Emergencies, unfortunately, rarely go according to scripted scenario; perhaps the best preparation is for everyone in the organization to understand the company's overall image and to react accordingly.

The two quintessential reactive cases that provide an important contrast in how to and how not to handle an emergency situation are the Johnson & Johnson Tylenol tampering cases in late 1982 and the Exxon Valdez oil spill in early 1989. The lessons from both have been case-studied to death, but they do provide an important blueprint on how an emergency should be handled.

First, there needs to be a clear indication from the outset that the company's top officials, especially the CEO, have not only been fully apprised of the situation, but are directing the company's response. Unless exceptional circumstances warrant, the CEO is usually the organization's best spokesperson and should be prepared to step into that role. Exxon CEO Lawrence G. Rawl elected to remain at the company's New York head-quarters rather than going to the scene, a responsibility assigned to lower-level officials. The decision was interpreted as indifference by the general public and by companies that purchased petroleum products.

The CEO and other top officials should be available to and openly frank with not only investigating officials, but media representatives. Regulatory and investigative agencies, the media, and ultimately the public should not be treated as adversaries. The old axiom of refusing to release information because of a lack of "a need to know" fails to fly in today's post-Watergate environment. Internal and external audiences all have a need to know.

The damage control response needs to be immediate, decisive, and well-publicized. Johnson & Johnson halted production, stopped distribution, and initiated a widespread recall campaign. It also cooperated fully and openly with all local, state, and federal agencies, which fostered public confidence in the company and its product. And it offered a $100,000 reward for the capture of the individual(s) responsible for the tampering.

Communication needs to be not only open, but two-way. Johnson & Johnson provided additional access for consumer lines to handle the increase in consumer inquiries. Reporters on-site in Alaska had trouble filing dispatches and reports from that remote location, and Exxon officials in New York refused to comment on the crisis for more than a week.

The results of the two approaches speak for themselves. Exxon continues to deal with the Valdez stigma in the minds of the public. However, within six months after the Tylenol poisoning story broke, the product had recaptured 32 percent of the 37 percent of market it had previously held after falling off to a 6 percent market share within days of the first story.

THE BEST DEFENSE: PROACTIVE PUBLIC RELATIONS

While it would be interesting to develop an entire chapter on reactive PR, it should be stressed that reactive PR is only one aspect of the public relations strategy.

We would like to suggest that only 20 percent of an organization's public relations effort be focused on anticipating, planning for, and conducting mock exercises in reactive PR, and that 80 percent of the public relations commitment and budget be allocated to proactive public relations.

A proactive public relations program is dictated by long-term company marketing objectives and is strategically intended to support, supplement, and enhance the company's overall marketing and marcom strategies. This function is especially relevant when the company plans to initiate new products or services, enter new markets, or change its status.

This should once again dovetail with the ongoing theme of integrated marcom. Since public relations is one element of the marcom process, it has specific strategic objectives that augment or supplement, not duplicate, other marcom. Consider the public relations department head who learns from a trade advertisement that the company is rolling out a new product line in three weeks. Checking with management, he discovers that it is expected an appropriate public relations campaign should be designed and in place to coincide with the rollout. The public relations manager subsequently learns that the advertising director had been working on the ad campaign for more than six months and the new product rollout had been planned for more than 18 months. This isn't only an example of a management that doesn't understand PR's functions and subsequently mismanages that marcom tool, but a public relations department that fails to take the initiative and proactively respond to the internal grapevine.

Proactive public relations objectives include publicizing the company and its products or services, ultimately contributing to the company's bottom line. Rather than being responsible for damage control restoring *status quo,* the goal of proactive public relations is to enhance the organization's image, creating a bankable corporate citizen identification that defines for both internal and external audiences what the organization is. It's this citizen image that can be drawn upon in times of crisis.

The proactive strategy is typically an offensive one. It anticipates, researches, analyzes, and interprets issues, and internal and external public opinion. It advises management about the potential impact and consequences of policy decisions, actions, and communications. It seeks every opportunity to demonstrate good character and responsible performance by the organization. It constantly monitors and evaluates company marketing and public relations programs, as well as internal and external marcom, to assess impact.

The public relations tactics are defined by the marketing and public relations objectives, rather than by external circumstances. The tools are selected based on their ability either by themselves or when used in conjunction with other marcom to achieve the desired objective with the appropriate audience. Public relations tools include print or video or audio press releases, speeches and interviews, management by walking around or small-group luncheons, plant tours and special events, brochures and handbooks, newsletters and magazines, annual reports, videotapes or CDs, sponsorships and foundations, press kits, posters, and employee incentive programs. The company boilerplate, i.e., the standardized company profile that should be inculcated into all of the company's formal and informal communications, is also an important proactive public relations tool.

THE 4 A'S OF PR: A PUBLIC RELATIONS CHECKLIST

This chapter is intended to establish a strategic framework for PR, not to be a public relations primer. However, there are certain strategic and tactical aspects of the public relations process that need careful management, whether the activities are in-house or outsourced.

There are innumerable models of public relations processes, including John Marston's RACE (Research, Action and Planning, Communication, and Evaluation) acronym and Jordan Goldman's ROPE (Research, Objectives, Program, and Evaluation).

Our acronym is the 4 A's:

- Appraise: preliminary market research.
- Arrange: coordinate the strategies and tactics, integrating with other marcom activities.
- Administer: execute the program.
- Assess: the post-campaign research activity to assess effectiveness and other factors. Bernays said that successful research was based on three things: research, research, research.

The marketing objective, strategy, and tactic shape the public relations campaign. For this example, Peterbon, Inc., produces a windshield treatment chemical that has been used for almost 20 years by the military on the windscreens of jet fighters. To counteract declining domestic military sales, Peterbon has developed a commercial version of the product. The marketing objective is to have a national rollout of the product completed in 18 months.

The initial marketing strategy is to target companies with a fleet of vehicles starting with the Southeastern U.S. region.

One marketing tactic is to initiate an integrated marcom campaign, including a proactive regional public relations campaign to create awareness of this product and its potential applications. The primary objective of the public relations campaign is to create an awareness of the product among 75 percent of the Southeastern U.S. target market by the time the company is ready to ship commercial version of the product.

The public relations campaign centers on the 4 As.

Appraisal Phase

This is the preliminary research, which is intended to determine the size of the potential market; the need for a product that improves driver visibility in the rain and prevents windshield dirt build-up; and what the benefits could be in terms of reduced operations costs for washing windshields, reduced costs for accident repairs, reduced sick-time for diver recuperation, and/or reduced insurance costs. It is determined that less than

5 percent of the fleet managers in the Southeast are aware of the military product.

Arrangement Phase

The strategy is to develop a high-profile campaign that will generate awareness of the product's benefits. The tactics include conducting product tests for police departments in three Southeastern markets: Atlanta, Birmingham, and Ft. Lauderdale. Departments will be provided with free samples. The controlled test will assess the safety and operations costs of police cars in the three fleets that used the product and those that didn't. This field test will be supported by appropriate press releases, interviews, media kits, etc.

Administration Phase

The six-month tests are conducted, along with other special events, trade show attendance, trade ads, etc.

Assessment Phase

Follow-up research among Southeastern fleet managers shows that awareness is up to 80 percent and presales levels are 30 percent ahead of projection. Frequently, public relations assessment focuses on the number of print news clips or broadcast reports generated or how many people attended a special event. By establishing specific, measurable objectives, the evaluation process can be accomplished by the right research mix: pre- and post-campaign attitude and opinion surveys conducted via mail or phone, news report content analyses, focus groups, and syndicated or secondary data, to suggest a few primary methodologies.

It should be stressed again, however, that an integrated marcom strategy acknowledges that none of the marcom functions operates in a vacuum. Marcom is a synergistic process. Since any of these outcomes would have been the objective of an integrated marcom strategy, the success of the campaign should be attributed to the marcom mix, not to just one of the individual marcom elements. (See Appendix J.)

This information also provides relevant baseline data for future programs, which prevents the organization from getting trapped into a "formula" mentality. Formula marcom is what it implies; using the same public relations or marcom programs repeatedly because they worked once, without testing or follow-up to see if they are still functional.

OTHER TACTICAL CONSIDERATIONS

The statement was made earlier that public relations tools are selected because of their ability to achieve the desired objective with the appropriate audience. That ability should be defined by the audience, not by the public relations practitioner. For example, the Peterbon public relations department wouldn't approach a police department in the desert Southwest, for example, where rain is a minimal problem for drivers.

Back in the mid-1980s, a public relations specialist for the U.S. Forest Service told us at a seminar that he had discovered a way to get more of his press releases published in some major Northwest newspapers—he downloaded his press release file to the newspaper's computer via phone line. This put his release in front of the section editor electronically, which meant the material didn't have to be re-typeset in the composing room. The efficiency of the delivery and the fact that it was well-written in the newspaper's journalistic style made it a win-win public relations tool for both parties.

The credibility of a message's source is also relevant to the audience, as Exxon found out; lower officials didn't have the same credibility as the CEO. The higher the credibility, the higher the message acceptance. Which has more credibility? A canned press release or a live, on-camera interview?

Credibility is based on two broad parameters: perceived level of expertise and the source's perceived trustworthiness or honesty. Expertise is defined as the ability of the source to make valid statements. What happened to the credibility of Secretary of State Alexander Haig when he informed the press he was in charge following the assassination attempt on President Reagan? What happens to the credibility of a spokesperson who can only comment "No comment" or "I don't know the answer to that question"? Trustworthiness means that the source generates a perception that a valid statement has been made.

Source credibility is also a function of source attractiveness: is the source likable and is the source perceived as being similar to the audience? How effective is Bill Gates when pitching Microsoft products to the business world?

OBJECTIVES AND STRATEGIES FOR MEDIA RELATIONS

The objective of media relations is to create a positive relationship with critical media that will improve the chances of your news releases being placed. This placement was the initial purpose for public relations.

It should be kept in mind, however, that the media are simply intermediaries in the communications link between you and your prospects and customers. The objective of media relations isn't simply to create relationships with the media; it's to create working relationships with media that are used by and relevant to your target audiences.

If one of the marcom objectives is to attract investors and one of the targets established by your marcom strategy is investment counselors, you'd better know which trade publications, business newspapers and magazines, TV business reports, and specialized newsletters they read or watch. Those media outlets become primary targets for at least one phase of the public relations campaign. This concept is discussed in depth in the infographics section of the advertising chapter.

The strategy to achieve the media relations objective is twofold: making you and your organization an important information source for the media, and learning how to create relationships with the gatekeepers who control access to the media that reach your desired target.

It has been said that every news story is either a public relations department's triumph or a public relations department's worst nightmare come true. That's not meant to imply that the relationship is an adversarial one. Quite the contrary; the relationship is symbiotic. The media rely to a great degree on the activities of public relations people to provide them with stories or story ideas, leads and referrals, background or additional information. A professional working relationship between a public relations department and a medium is to their mutual benefit. This is especially true of the broadcast media during sweeps periods in which ratings are accumulated. Providing a network or a station with "sexy" story leads prior to the sweeps months is also beneficial for that medium.

A professional working relationship implies an understanding of each other's roles and expectations. Editors and producers and writers understand that your public relations function is to generate news and information about your company that increases its profile and credibility, and to create or reinforce or perhaps attempt to shift attitudes.

You should understand that editors, producers, and writers are targets of a gazillion public relations efforts. Their responsibility is to decide which stories are relevant to their audiences and how much of each story is relevant. You should respect that function by pitching stories that are of interest to their readers or viewers or listeners, and by accepting the editorial decisions they make.

While most media relations strategies and efforts focus on the editorial gatekeepers, there are several other relevant departments that shouldn't be ignored. Production is one such department. These people can help provide some of the answers discussed in the tactical discussion that follows, for example. The advertising sales department should also be contacted; there will be corporate advertising and advocacy advertising campaigns that will be placed with this department, as well as classified and display classified for hiring, for example. If a medium has an editorial and/or marketing research department, your public relations group may be able to provide some value-added information or sources for their research activities.

Media Relations Tactics

Once the relevant media outlets have been identified, there are some simple basic tactics that can help create the appropriate relations.

The most obvious is to put together a traditional media kit for each medium which includes relevant background information about the organization, its history, basic product information, etc. Ideally, this is delivered to an appropriate editor during a face-to-face appointment, which provides the opportunity for selling your company's personnel as a resource for information relating to your company's industry, its markets, the regulatory environment, technological or other developments, or other information that the editor or the reporters would need. If not presented in person, the kit should contain a well-written cover or sales letter that achieves this purpose.

There are at least two obvious benefits to be gained from this contact. One is the ability to determine who at that magazine or newspaper or TV station will be responsible for screening the newsworthiness of your press releases and to make a personal contact with that individual or committee. It also provides the people at the medium an opportunity to gain an important personal contact within your organization.

The second is intelligence: you can determine how best to satisfy the gatekeepers' needs and expectations. For example:

- What are the news deadlines for the medium? It is shorter for broadcast media than for local or national papers; most magazines have longer deadlines.
- What is the medium's writing style for hard news versus features or soft news or human interest? The less editing and rewriting that has to be done, the more likely the newsworthy story will make it past the editor.
- For print media, do they accept photos? If so, what is the preferred medium—print or negative—and what composition is the most likely to be selected?
- If you are providing video news releases, what format is preferred?
- Referring to our story about the Forest Service employee, how would the medium prefer to have the press releases delivered? Hard copy, on disk, modem, or via fax?
- Does the TV station or network bureau want the story prewritten or preproduced, or does the producer prefer simply to have a story idea with a list of suggested contacts so that the reporters can develop their own story or stories?
- If sound bites are being provided for broadcast, what is the most appropriate length?

TWO OTHER PUBLIC RELATIONS FUNCTIONS

Corporate or institutional advertising and advocacy advertising campaigns are also the responsibility of the public relations department. These involve buying space or time to deliver a specific message through targeted media.

Corporate advertising is nonproduct advertising whose message is specifically intended to enhance public perception of the company, or to create, modify, or change that perception. These ads, for which the company pays, may supplement nonpaid publicity about the company and its products or services generated by traditional public relations techniques or may be necessary because the traditional public relations efforts have failed to generate the desired publicity.

Corporate ads are relevant to three broad areas of image management. The first is when the corporation lacks public perception, perhaps because its name hasn't been in front of the public or perhaps even due to a name change. Examples include the campaign in the early 1990s by Intel to let the public know what chip was inside their computers. The campaign resulted in the "Intel Inside" becoming a value-added feature for a broad range of computer manufacturers. The Burroughs and Sperry-Rand merger in the late 1980s which resulted in Unisys is another example of this corporate advertising function. One successful tactic here would be to associate the company with a credible source, something AT&T accomplished with Cliff Robertson in the business market in the mid-1980s following divestiture.

The second function of corporate ads is when there is confusion about who the company is or what products or services it provides. The classic example is the B. F. Goodrich campaign that differentiated itself in both the business and consumer markets from Goodyear by positioning the company as the one "without the blimp." Redesigning corporate symbols or logos or slogans has been a successful tactic in this area.

A third function of corporate advertising is to create congruence between corporate image and marketing reality or to reduce the dissonance between the two. An example of the former is the 1993 campaign "Be There Now" launched by Sprint to bring the public perception of the company into line with the reality; at that time it was the only one of the top three telecommunications companies to offer local, long distance, and cellular services.

Another opportunity for using corporate advertising is to reinforce a positive image that already exists, as a supplement to other public relations activities.

In contrast, advocacy advertising is intended to advance a company's position as a corporate citizen on an issue or issues in which it or its publics have a vested interest. The classic example is the long-running ads sponsored by the Mobil Corporation which deal with issues ranging from legislation that would affect the petroleum industry and ultimately the consumer to the use of alternative fuels. Recent ads by RJR Reynolds Tobacco encouraging the American public to call or write their representatives in Congress about proposed tobacco regulations is another example.

Advocacy advertising may be necessary to counteract inadequate access to publics through the media via traditional public relations efforts. It may be necessary to counteract inaccurate or misleading information. Or it may simply be a way for the company to make sure its position on issues is heard clearly and fairly and by the appropriate audiences, as exemplified by the 1994 Pfizer Pharmaceutical ads that discussed possible solutions to the health care crisis.

INTERNAL PUBLIC RELATIONS

Today's employees are much different than they were 20 years ago. They are more educated, more interested in the organization's objectives, more empowered, and more participative. They are concerned and vocal about their rights and personal as well as career development. They expect an employee-friendly environment. Many of these issues are discussed in Chapter 17, which deals with employee relations.

It is important to note here that frequent, open, and honest communications are critical to satisfying these employee expectations. While internal communications have traditionally been the responsibility of human resources, a case can be made for public relations being integrally involved in those activities and the production of internal marcom materials such as newsletters to assure that the company's "one voice, one message" strategy is also being applied to the internal communications process.

There is nothing more demoralizing than employees being exposed to two conflicting messages, one internal and the other gleaned from external sources. Consider the sales rep trying to assure a customer that parts will be available for delivery without interruption for the next six months, only to learn that one of his own company's vice presidents has been quoted in one of the trade publications the buyer reads as saying that there will be some slowdown, but that back orders will be filled on a first ordered, first filled priority.

Returning to the definition of public relations that opened the chapter, the public relations department should be responsible for anticipating, analyzing, and interpreting issues that concern employees, as well as employees' opinions and attitudes that might positively or negatively impact the objectives and operations of the organization. Based on this activity, public relations should discuss the potential ramifications of proposed personnel policy decisions, proposed courses of action and communications activities, and whether or not they conform to the employees' expectations. Public relations should be involved in the planning and implementation of efforts to create, modify, or change employee attitudes and perceptions, and be involved in research evaluating internal marcom and management programs to ensure that the internal stakeholders are informed about, understand, accept, and trust the company's objectives.

TIPS FOR INTEGRATING YOUR PROGRAM

Public relations is a marcom activity that can set the public stage for other internal and external marcom mix elements, run concurrently with those communications, provide a follow-up for marcom, or do all three.

In the early days of public relations study, PR was defined as "doing something and telling somebody about it." That is not a bad general strategy for anyone involved in marcom to follow. But in order to tell somebody about what's going on, the public relations people have to be in the loop, and not just for the firefighting activities. Don't you wonder what the Benetton public relations people told management and the company's advertising agency about its advertising campaigns? Or what the impact will be on small- and medium-sized businesses that bank with the Chicago bank that is charging $3 for a customer to walk up and use a teller? Were the bank's PR people contacted about the possible effect of the customer service charge?

The public relations function must be a major element of any marketing strategy, and the public relations specialists be involved as consultants, if not a participant, in all marcom planning and execution. That's an ideal world recommendation. As we frequently tell clients, "Don't give reasons why this can't be done, provide justifications why it is essential to the desired marcom outcomes."

MEASUREMENT AND EVALUATION

Evaluation of public relations outcomes was discussed earlier in the chapter, but it wouldn't hurt to review the major premise. Public relations has traditionally been difficult to defend due to the inability to provide evidence of direct results from the efforts.

However, by clearly establishing observable and measurable objectives for the public relations elements of any marcom mix, this validation becomes much easier. As has been said several times, outcome-based marcom assessment isn't dependent upon the success of one or more elements of the mix; it is dependent on analyzing the total effort without affixing responsibility for failure or giving all the credit for successes to any one element.

RESOURCES

1. Bernays, E. L. (1923). *Crystallizing Public Opinion*. New York: Boni and Liveright. An interesting read, still in print and available in many libraries.
2. Goldman, J. (1984). *Public Relations in the Marketing Mix*. Lincolnwood, IL: NTC Publishing Group.
3. *Directory of U.S. Trade Journals*. Low Associates, Box 149, Pittstown, NJ 08867.
4. *Bacon's Publicity Checker: Magazines and Newspapers* and *Bacon's Radio/TV Directory*. Bacon Publishing Co., 332 South Michigan Ave., Chicago, IL 60604.
5. *National Directory of Magazines* and *Directory of Newsletters*. Oxbridge Communications, 150 Fifth Ave., New York, NY 10011.
6. *National Radio Publicity Outlets*. Resource Media, Box 307, Kent, CT 06766.
7. *TV Contacts and TV News Contacts*. BPI Media Services, Box 2015, Lakewood, NJ 08701.
8. *PR Reporter*. Box 600, Didley House, Exeter, NH 03833.

NOTE

1. One of the authors has practiced and taught public relations for a number of years. Many of the ideas in this chapter are shaped by these experiences, including a classroom appearance by Edward Bernays in the late 1980s. He has also been influenced by the writings of Jordan Goldman in his 1984 book, *Public Relations in the Marketing Mix: Introducing Vulnerability Relations* (Chicago: Crain Books), which has been used as both a textbook and as a guide for practicing public relations.

CHAPTER 16

Financial Relations: Of Stockholders and Stakeholders

> "Let Wall Street have a nightmare and the whole country has to help get them back in bed again."
>
> —Will Rogers

It has been determined that a statement you made to a financial reporter was based on erroneous information given you by the vice president of sales. The information was reported the next day. You have just received a letter from the SEC indicating you may have violated the law. "But I got the information from someone else! I'm not at fault," you say.

Guess what? You are at fault and you may have violated federal security laws—and you could go to jail.

In this chapter we will discuss financial relations. We use the term to include more than just investor relations. It also includes financial relations problems that arise, such as Chapter 11 filings or fighting a takeover.

Financial and investor relations, whether in normal times or crisis conditions, should involve the marketing and communications professionals in your organization. But, alas, it is frequently the exclusive domain of the CFO and chairman. It's up to you to drive the importance of marketing involvement, and to show the added value such participation yields.

But you must know what you are doing and what the consequences can be for making a mistake. To play a role in this vital area, you will need to earn the confidence of the chairman and the CFO, and you will also have the anxious collaboration of your CPA firm and company attorneys.

Financial relations involves the same strategies and tactics other areas of communication involve: targeting the right audience, carefully defining the message and the media used to distribute that message, and making sure both the financial and marketing communications are working together. Increasingly, it also involves using as many communications tools as possible so that your company and its stock rises above the others.

There are some qualifiers. There are strict laws about disclosing information regarding a publicly traded company. Some people have been indicted for passing information that was untrue or just premature. Therefore, it is important to read this chapter and its cases and resources with the goal of understanding where you can fit into the picture.

CHECKLIST OF DO'S AND DON'TS

- Do's:
    1. Do become familiar with the concept of material disclosure and make sure you and your colleagues understand what you may and may not say, and when.
    2. Do develop a manual of policy and consensus regarding such things as predicting or forecasting financial performance, handling rumors, and making references to your competition.
    3. If someone asks you why they should buy your stock and all you can answer is "it's a good investment," recognize that you have a serious investor relations problem.
    4. Investor relations programs must be cognizant of all audiences, not just stockholders and the business media.
    5. Your annual report is a potentially powerful document. Agonize over questions such as primary audience, secondary audience, objective, look and feel, and message.
    6. Do build a time chart for periodic financial announcements and their preparation. This will help guide your peers and superiors to plan ahead about what will be said and how it will be explained.
    7. Do keep a personal investor relations logbook in which you record the substance and participants in any telephone call or conversation you have regarding the SEC, important company information and secrets, requests made of you by management, and press requests to confirm or deny rumors or forecasts. Lock up that log every night, and keep cumulative copies in a separate place. Someday this log could keep you out of trouble.

- Don'ts:
    1. Never presume that investment analysts, money managers, and the rest of Wall Street will automatically follow your stock just because

your firm is in a "hot industry." Stocks that are not properly pitched and communicated are no more successful than products that aren't promoted.

2. If management was out front during good quarters providing interviews and commentary, don't let them hide during the bad quarters. Be consistently available and up front.

3. Don't try to bury or sugar-coat bad news. Get it over with quickly and early and elaborate on the corrective actions management will take.

4. Don't provide data to the investment community or financial media if you know the data is wrong. You could be indicted.

5. Don't tell secrets. If you haven't learned how to keep a secret, handling investor relations will teach you fast. A premature slip of the tongue could lead to premature disclosure of material information. Use project names for products in development, and code names for activities or transactions in all conversations regarding them.

THE SEC AND ITS AGENDA

Always remember: The Securities and Exchange Commission (SEC) is concerned that the average investor have the same opportunity to make an investment decision as the major stockholders have. The matter of disclosure centers around this point, and the SEC has been very zealous in protecting the smaller investors from what is called insider trading.

Basically, insider trading means that a company's management has bought or sold the company's stock for personal gain using nonpublic information that gives them a head start advantage on the rest of the investor community. Not fair, says the SEC.

That was one of the main purposes of the Securities Exchange Act of 1934 that created the SEC: to prevent corporate officers, major stockholders, or outside acquaintances from making big gains in the stock market by trading shares as a result of management's knowledge of important undisclosed information. For that matter, making stock trades as a result of insider information gained in just about any professional capacity can be illegal, as a journalist for the *Wall Street Journal* found out in 1987. Important or material information is information that would motivate a reasonable and prudent investor to buy or sell the same stock if the information were disclosed.

Insider trading can be costly. Liability can extend to the financial gain of those informed of the inside information. Those outsiders informed of the material information can be held liable if that information resulted from an insider's breach of duty.

However, trading on rumors or information gained inadvertently wouldn't be a breach. This lends new value to the notion of hanging around bars and delis on Wall Street to pick up the cocktail napkins scribbled on by well-heeled customers!

Checklist for Staying within SEC Guidelines

If the chapter opener did its job of catching your attention, let's elaborate on why your attention to SEC rules is important. In short, a company's communications manager can be held liable for disseminating incorrect information even if that information came directly from the chairman or CFO. It's up to you to check out the information on your own to determine if it is correct.

Here are some ways to stay within both the letter and spirit of the SEC regulations:

1. Establish a regular schedule for announcing financial results. This will help discipline your colleagues up and down the line about the importance of full disclosure, and will help you with media planning.

2. File the required financial forms (10-Q and 10-K) at the same time you release news of financial results.

3. Avoid making earnings projections. This is a tough one, because everyone from the national sales manager to the CFO wants to keep expectations positive. The problem is that unmet projections can result in litigation. Any projections you make must be based on solid data and not mere wishes.

4. If you or someone within your company issued some material information to the public, and changes have occurred that outdated that information, you are obligated to publicly update the information. However, if an outside analyst publishes comments or information that didn't come from your company, you aren't obligated to comment on it or revise it. But you had better be sure it didn't come from inside your organization.

5. Avoid commenting on rumors or information that you or your colleagues didn't release. Update and comment on your own information, but avoid commenting on anything outside your domain.

6. Release the announcement first to your stock exchange representative or surveillance committee before releasing the news to Dow Jones.

7. Confirm that the information has been distributed on the wire services before management acts on the news. This is especially important for smaller companies that aren't as recognizable. Some companies' management allow a full day to pass before taking personal buy/sell action on disclosed news.

8. To avoid even a hint of insider advantage, tell stockholders that the management, board members, and other knowledgeable people promise to wait three working days before trading stock after news of material importance is released.

9. Always carefully check the Dow Jones run on your release to see if you were accurately covered. If there's a mistake, waste no time in getting it corrected even if the error in interpretation is a result of how you wrote the announcement. Again, the correctness and veracity of the announcement is your job.

10. Designate one spokesperson (you, preferably) or a limited few who will talk with the business media and the analyst community. Keep a careful record of what is being disclosed and make sure the company is kept informed of what's said publicly. There should be a written policy about all this. Accessible employees or those vulnerable to outside questions should sign the policy.

11. Initiate your investor relations program several quarters prior to the start of public equity financing. If the two activities start at the same time, the SEC could conclude that you are intentionally "hyping" the stock. If investor relations starts well before the initial public offering (IPO), the SEC may well permit you to continue the program during the financing.

MANAGEMENT AS MESSAGE—
AND THE CHAIRMAN'S AGENDA

As with any product or service, competitive differentiation is essential. If you think of your company and its publicly traded stock as a product, you must consider how to differentiate it. Traditional methods don't differentiate securities and public offerings any more than traditional ways differentiate products and services.

Your underwriter and the minimum periodic financial statements can't do the job alone because the commodity mentality had overcome investing just as it has everything from pork bellies to PCs. Discount securities retailers now handle a sizeable portion of the daily volume. The analyst community has declined in number because of budget cutbacks, thus leaving fewer analysts to report on more securities. As if that were not enough, the growth of non-stock investment (NSI) opportunities makes the equity market even more difficult.

These factors influence publicly-held companies to direct more attention to the short-term perspective of money managers while trying to build long-term investor commitment through relationship marketing. So this is both your challenge and your opportunity.

How do you differentiate your stock from all the others? Making use of all communications vehicles is essential, as is integrating the message. That includes integrating the company's marketing message with the story on your company's stock. But it also includes positioning your management as a unique selling proposition (USP)—and unique educators.

Investors, fund managers, and analysts alike all share an interest in the quality, background, and vision of a company's management. One need only note the turnover of CEOs at large, visible corporations to understand how management is scrutinized when times are bad for a company.

Your job includes positioning your company's stock as a sound long-term hold because your management has a finger on the pulse of what's happening in your industry. Here's where both traditional and modern communications tools can act to elevate investor awareness of a unique investment opportunity.

The usual tools are still important: annual and quarterly reports, media relations, road trips to see the analysts, employee communications, toll-free message lines, corporate image advertising, videos, cable and teleconferencing links, fax response services and "fax-casting," audiotapes aimed at freeway commuters, and mailings to brokers. But tie them together with a message that says "this is a unique management team."

When Lee Iaccoca became one of the first chairmen to put himself in his own advertising, he did more than sell cars. He sold an image of true grit. He sold a perception of confident determination. He also sold many Americans on the notion that it was entirely possible that American cars could be better than Japanese cars—a tough sell in the early 1980s. In the process, he sold investors, brokers, and analysts confidence in a new Chrysler Corporation and its securities. He may have used a "them versus us" appeal, but he also sold many on an "I want to believe" appeal.

Selling a new car is definitely a "buy and hold" selling strategy, and most of us who buy cars are definitely thinking of holding that investment for at least five years. Why not stocks too? With the right management appeal woven into an integrated communications campaign, it is possible to do that.

For companies heavily involved in research and development, showcasing the top technology executive is especially important. Both analysts and trade publication editors can gain insights to the company's direction from personal visits by management.

The annual report is a popular place to showcase management, including the directors and the division and group executives. Executive historical profiles tell an investor or analyst a great deal more than simply listing the executives' names. A section on investment opportunity of buying and holding your company's stock may be as important as the explanation for the year's performance.

But it would be unfair to you to end this section without addressing the matter of the chairman's agenda. As mentioned elsewhere in this chapter, you must gain the confidence of the chairman and determine his or her goals for the stock. Such an agenda is tied to the chairman's contract and/or his personal stock holdings. Obviously, capital appreciation, revenue growth and increased profits are uppermost in any chairman's mind.

The problem is that there may be a hidden agenda. The hidden agenda may have to do with divisions or subsidiaries of the company or individual product lines. Depending on your position in the company, you may not be privy to such information. Being out of the loop on such plans will make the job of investor relations difficult. Thus, it is important to gain the ear of the chairman early on to explain how important it is for you to know about all plans.

INFORMATION MANAGEMENT: UNDERSTANDING VERSUS FACTS

A publicly held company might meet the minimum reporting requirements by simply listing financial results in the annual and quarterly reports and issuing minimum disclosure releases. Just the facts. However, throwing columns of numbers at the contemporary, turbo-charged investment community is both presumptuous and wasteful.

It is presumptuous to think your financial reports need no elaboration or marketing, regardless of whether the results are positive or negative. It is wasteful not to elaborate because a) you just might get lucky and get someone's attention, and b) educating your financial audiences by packaging financial information with your marketing message adds value to both stories.

That blend of information produces a whole that is larger than the sum of its parts. And with nearly 20,000 publicly traded companies screaming for attention, a company needs a communication program that symbiotic.

Educating the investment community and the other stakeholders is essential in an era of exploding information that budget-strapped analyst firms are trying to handle. An example is the annual report. It can be more than just a financial wrap on the year. It can also be a marketing tool for gaining the right response among those other stakeholders as well. The trade press and your local business reporters are keenly interested in both the financial and marketing successes you have. The annual report should take their needs into consideration.

Analysts seek a quick, quantitatively oriented summary of a company's stock. It's the job of the broadly based information manager to lead analysts to the nonquantitative factors on capital growth.

Irrespective of the quantitative view analysts and the rest of the investment community have of individual stocks or particular industries, the reality is that raw perception plays a big role on the market as a whole. It always has. The best recent example is the stock market crash of 1987. There were no obvious logical reasons for the drop in prices. The economy was in fair shape as reflected in the GNP and the decline in inflation. But apparently there was a perception that prices had reached the maximum and that a correction was imminent. The perception became a self-fulfilling prophecy.

Tom Peters says perception is all there is in marketing. Investor relations that focuses narrowly on facts ignores the role of perception. Investor relations is best packaged when the financial facts are combined with the overall promise of corporate direction, corporate values, and management vision.

But this value-added approach cannot be achieved if investor relations is treated as a quarantined function behind a closed door in the back offices. Many investor relations (IR) professionals have perpetuated an aura of selectness and mystery to their specialty, thus cloaking themselves with an appeal of status. Unfortunately, such a barrier makes it difficult for the overall corporate strategy and marketing communication function to blend together neatly with IR.

Here are some elements to use in crafting your message to the varied financial audiences:

What Business You Are In.   Both your current business and the businesses you have left are relevant. Many computer companies used to manufacture hardware and develop software. Many have given up the hardware and focused on software and systems for specific vertical markets. That's a big change. A bank once heavily involved in off-shore investments may now want the investment community to know its focus is regional business.

Product Research, Development, and Future Direction.   What percentage of revenue and company resources is devoted to R&D? What is the R&D road map? What are the new vertical markets that road map might take the company? Where are the beta sites (test sites) for some of the products? Are there any joint ventures with a major customer on some future product direction? What trends in the marketplace play into your R&D effort and thus confirm the wisdom of management's choices?

Corporate Values

The broader media are attracted to statements and policies concerning a variety of nonbusiness concerns. Among these are minority training programs on site, time off to employees to teach in local schools, the "greening" topics ranging from waste treatment to environmental planning, accelerated programs for female and minority managers, flexible scheduling programs for employees, on-site services such as child care, and health maintenance programs such as on-site exercise facilities. A broad-based integration of both financial and public relations can wisely cite such values to help the reader and investment consumer further differentiate your company and its stock. These kind of programs also play well as photo essays in annual reports.

THE INVESTOR RELATIONS MESSAGE MANAGEMENT TASK FORCE

A designated team should be involved in formulating investor relations strategy and tactics. In any publicly traded company, the chairman is the main figure, followed by the chief financial officer (CFO).

However, modern companies hoping to compete in a crowded securities marketplace must build a more diverse team. The ideal composition of IR task force should include the top marketing and sales officers. Each of these two conduits of external communications has valuable market insight and considerable opportunities to leverage you IR message. Wiser yet, the task force should include those responsible for government relations and human resources.

Once assembled, the team must do a communication audit on the company's position in the securities marketplace:

- Identify factors, good and bad, peculiar to your stock's trading zone.
- Identify the specific problem your stock must overcome.
- Identify specific audiences that need to be reached.
- Identify specific message each audience must get.
- Develop a message checklist or grid to see which audiences need the same message or messages (this is an important tool in collateral and literature development).
- Initiate benchmark studies of the various audiences to establish the depth of the program and the timeline needed to execute it.
- Determine the specific communication media needed for each audience or message group.
- Inventory current tools, collateral, campaigns, etc. to diagnose their current effectiveness for the new task.
- Initiate the development of new collateral, literature, or media to make up for gaps in the inventory.
- Develop a production schedule for the identified new tools.
- Develop a time schedule of media opportunities and deadlines by which these audiences should get the message.
- Determine the extent and regularity of your analyst presentation tour.
- Lay out a periodic meeting schedule of the task force to monitor progress on all actions items.

TESTING THE TASK FORCE CONSENSUS AND CONTINGENCY

Are your investor relations task force members in agreement about their relative roles? Given the monetary and legal issues involved, it may be good insurance to find out. Retaining a consultant to conduct interviews of task force members is a good way to see if their perceptions are in line with the IR program. The interviews will help uncover what conflicts exist and what pitfalls could happen.

The next stage of task force preparedness is to stage a simulated crisis involving the team members. This helps isolate various contingency plans and guidelines for handling a variety of typical crises. The crisis doesn't necessarily have to be a financial crisis, since many events can have an adverse affect on the stock price.

RELATIONSHIP INVESTING: INVESTOR RELATIONS OR SPECULATOR RELATIONS?

A great change has occurred in the investment marketplace. In the 1960s, the average stock remained in one owner's hands for up to seven years. Trading volume per year was under one billion shares. In the 1990s, over 50 percent of shares owned are changing hands each year with annual volume rising to 40 billion shares.

This volatility in ownership makes many observers wonder if the term *investor relations* should be dropped for a more accurate term—*speculator relations.* Whatever the name, the task is all the more difficult and all the more important: to position your company and its stock so that they are noticed, understood, recognized, and fairly valued.

Stocks are like products. You wouldn't want your products to be thrown into a commodity marketplace where price is the only criterion. The same is true of your stock. It needs to be positioned as unique and it needs to be perceived as a value that serves its purpose for the long term. Like any other sale, it is easier to sell to an existing customer than to find new ones. In short, you want stockholders to remain stockholders. It's called "buy and hold."

American business is criticized for focusing on short-term financial results. But if stockholders, be they individual investors or institutional portfolio managers, held securities for the long term, think of how much longer management's focus could become! That ideal is driving an important concept called relationship investing. It's the investor relations version of relationship marketing.

Relationship investing is all about making capital investors knowledgeable, comfortable, and patient about their investments. Companies need patient capital investors in order to make long-term plans—in other words, to get the space to think beyond the next quarter's financials. This requires an active relationship marketing program that puts your management face-to-face with the primary investors and key influences. The purpose is to team up management with the primary stockholders on a regular basis rather than just the forced, often adversarial context of the annual stockholders meeting. Enter you—with an integrated investor relations program flowing in concert with the overall strategic goals of the company and its product or service.

Nonetheless, you shouldn't leave this section thinking a relationship investing program will keep your stock price safe. Anyone who was hurt during the market crash of 1987 knows that sound fundamentals soundly communicated don't protect stocks. The reality of market forces, fueled by the self-fulfilling prophecies of crowd mentalities, can sweep away all your good plans and programs.

But would you rather take the risk of not even trying?

INVESTOR RELATIONS: TWO APPROACHES

Although aspects of this section are touched on elsewhere in this chapter, let's describe two approaches to investor relations and spotlight their relative differences: The first approach entails facts only, no interpretation, no

WHAT IS A STOCK WORTH? THE DEBATE ON EQUITY VALUATION

Investor relations professionals often must educate the analysts and the investment community about their stock's intrinsic value when the price is too low. The task isn't simple: how to get the outside world to believe that the stock is underpriced. The task involves showing the market new information or pointing out errors in their perceptions. Sometimes the market responds and the stock price climbs upward. Other times the IR message isn't received or believed, and the stock sits there.

But this raises a question of economic theory applied to stock prices. Let's use a metaphor—selling a house. During the recent real estate price decline, how many times did you hear someone say, "We got an offer for $110,000 on our house, but it's worth $120,000. We won't accept anything below its true worth!"

Ideals are great in politics and religion, but the marketplace just told this homeowner what her house was worth: $110,000. Higher offers would confirm a higher valuation. As most commissioned real estate agents will admit, a house is worth what it sells for, the new Italian tile and custom barbecue pit notwithstanding. The same may well be true of investment securities. If the book value of a company isn't reflected in the stock price (a dangerous situation in the era of takeover fever), then the job of investor relations is to explain the disparity. That explanation should include a healthy dose of management's vision and the overall strategic road map the company is taking.

But in the meanwhile, the stock is priced as it is perceived, just like your friend's house in the example.

elaboration on marketplace niche. The annual report that makes no attempt at marketing the company or fostering confidence in the directors and their expertise. Minimum required distribution is initiated in the least effective media times, e.g., on Friday at 5:01 p.m. so that little time is left to report it, or releasing it late Thursday of a three-day weekend. Target audiences are restricted to investment audiences only. No explanation of the long-term value of buying the stock is given. There is an unstated presumption that the stock's value is apparent. No attempt is made to leverage the investor relations message off the marketing message and vice versa.

The second approach to investor relations entails a proactive explanation of the financial figures regardless if the results are good or bad. An effort is made to educate the reader about internal and marketplace factors that are responsible for those results. There is no attempt to bury the bad news by releasing it at non-peak media times. There is clear delineation of the various stockholder, analyst, brokerage house, and key opinion leader audiences, with tailored message matched to each group's particular investment hot buttons. A clear rationale is presented to each audience as to why the stock is a long-term "buy and hold." A concentrated effort is made at using relationship marketing for all investors and institutional buyers. Management regularly visits with influential investment opinion makers. An integrated program exists between the chairman, CFO, and investor relations staff working with the company's marketing department to make sure product announcements, marketing messages, financial reporting periods, and investment messages are coordinated.

ANALYSTS: HIGH-STAKES POKER

Stock analysts play a very important role in stock valuation and the flow of information. They have considerable power because brokers and money managers follow what they say. Basically, analysts want to scoop your quarterly forecasts and other news just as a journalist does. As with journalists and their newspapers or trade journals, analysts and their organizations vary in focus, scope, and audiences.

You must build a working rapport with analysts. Being credible and helpful in routine matters and in good times goes a long way toward establishing credibility when times get tough. There is, however, one big difference in dealing with analysts: you must avoid disclosing material information prematurely, and that includes unwisely confirming information the analyst has that might then be published and result in material disclosure.

Controlling an interview is probably more important with a stock analyst than with other observers and reporters of information. Jerry Kalman of Kalman Communications (Santa Monica, California) isolated nine key kinds of questions and how to control them:[1]

The Closed-End Yes or No Trap: It's in your face. For example, "Are you going to make my estimate on your third-quarter numbers?" Kalman suggests even showing mild displeasure with such a question, then reframe the question with an answer that would be appropriate as a response to an open-ended question.

Keep in mind, the analyst's stock-in-trade is information. By reframing the question with factors that could lead your quarterly numbers one way or the other, you help the analyst without violating your disclosure policy. Start your answer by drawing a backdrop to the issue that shows how complicated the issue really is: "In the current business environment affecting our industry, competitive pressures and the current buying patterns could have such and such impact on our margins. But if we were to have X sales, we might reach Y revenues for the quarter." So, with this recasting, you give him some events to follow and a scenario to watch, but you haven't made a projection or a disclosure.

Of course, if an analyst abandons all pretext and asks outright for a forecast, Kallen recommends you wince and politely answer "As you know from earlier meetings with us, our policy is to avoid making forecasts. Sorry."

The Open-Ended Bait.   "What's going on around here anyhow?" You can view this question as evidence that the analyst knows about something you want to hide, or view it as an opportunity to reframe the picture of your company in his or her mind. In short, don't presume it's a plant. You can provide an overview of some key sale or some new techniques put into use or new personnel hired. If that isn't what the analyst had in mind, you will find out soon enough!

Speculating on the Competition.   Some companies have a policy of avoiding any comments or questions concerning the competition. The reason is such discourse can come back at you, especially from the competitor. If you engage in a conversation that's based on incorrect facts, your firm could be sued for unfair practices. While you have the analyst's attention, keep the focus on your company. Your competitor will take care of his or her company.

The Rolling Why.   "Oh, is that so? Why would you do that—can you elaborate?" The problem is that once you complete your elaboration on your previous comment, the analyst will hit you with another request, e.g., "But won't that affect the quarter?" Basically, this rolling technique is designed to get you off center and to say something you shouldn't have said just to get rid of the analyst. Remember, you need to control the interview. So stop the rolling elaboration by indicating that the questioning is leading to unproductive and relatively unimportant speculation.

Stay on the Record. As with journalists, it is best to conduct interviews with the presumption that everything is on the record and could be reported. If you don't want it repeated, don't say it. Even doing backgrounders with analysts, where the understanding is clear that it is not for reporting, can lead to revelations later on in another context that could be traced back to you. If that's rumor or involves material information, you could be in trouble.

What If. Cause and effect kinds of questions can prove fruitful for both you and the analyst. You are not likely to make a forecast in such a situation. However, as with the "rolling why" discussed previously, the "what if" can go on and on until you lose control of the discussion. You could also come close to endorsing some contingency that may need far more thought than the momentary interview. Take control by adding more conditional factors and situations (in other words, options) so that the discussion doesn't lead to a narrow cast of events.

Black and White Simplicity. You don't want to reveal your greatest source of concern, or imply your focus is locked on only one area of the business. So when the analyst is pursuing a line of questions that appears to be aimed at revealing your major concern, divert the discussion (again, take control) by elaborating on other issues that any business could reasonably concern itself with: inventory control, trade policies, legislative actions, etc.

Presumed Guilt. Instead of a question, this analyst hits you with an accusation that presumes you're guilty and now wants you to prove your company's innocence. The task is easier than the execution needed: you must defuse the adversarial tone and lay out the facts.

Again, nonverbal control is as important as the words you speak. You must look the analyst in the eyes (better yet, between the eyes) and stare her down as you explain the facts. In short, let her blink first.

Stay serious no matter how frivolous the implication of the question is. Try shifting the direction of the discussion to more pertinent matters. If the question or accusation is totally wrong, say so at the outset of your rebuttal but tell why. At the end of your comments, ask if the charge has been adequately answered. If not, probe to find out what's still on her mind and summarize your information again. If she's still not satisfied, ask if you can get back to her with additional information (presuming you have it) that will support your story.

Kalman's general advice is to start interviews by outlining the main points you would like to cover. It may be the best way to control the conversation, especially if time is limited—and by the way, always ask how much time the analyst has.

GETTING INVESTOR RELATIONS ON-LINE

Keeping track of institutional investment criteria and following the right analysts is easier in the information age. On-line database services can provide match-maker services tailored to your company's industry and market position.

The SEC requires institutions that manage portfolios in excess of $100 million to file statements of all the stocks bought and sold during the previous quarter. This is valuable information to any publicly held company wanting to position its securities for big volume sales.

You can buy reports on institutional holdings of your competitors. Or you can use the services to identify money managers who select stocks with the same generic characteristics as your stock. You can also scan institutional money managers based on criteria that could lead to the purchase of your stock.

OF STOCKHOLDERS AND STAKEHOLDERS: IR'S INTEGRATED AUDIENCES

To rise above the shouting masses of stocks seeking attention, integrated marketing communications is necessary. As with other forms of public and media relations, you must first reach the key influences who lead and mold opinion about a product. In this case, the product is your company's stock. That means going beyond the annual report and formal stockholders meetings.

Added to the communication problem is the decline in the number of security analysts trying to cover an increasing number of publicly traded stocks. The landscape has also been clouded by an era of leveraged buy-outs, restructured companies, and acquiring companies. Keeping track of them and keeping them all straight became a big problem in the 1980s and 1990s.

On the "buy side" (e.g., fund managers, pension funds, university endowment funds), cuts in research staffs mean that money managers must do more of their own leg work. Nonetheless, institutions have become increasingly influential. But that presents an opportunity for a company: it can market the stock's uniqueness to the needs of a portfolio manager's investment goals.

On the "sell side" (e.g., stockbrokers) publicly traded companies must get the attention of the analysts whom brokers trust and quote to potential clients. Since your management can do much to inspire or deflate confidence in company direction and long-term equity growth, well-rehearsed presentations to these key influences are essential.

The spectrum of target audiences is diverse and specialized. Each audience or group has different needs and thus requires a different mix of communication media.

Distinct Audiences

Sherwood Lee Wallace of The Investor Relations Company of Northbrook, Illinois identifies 26 distinct audiences:[2]

1. Shareholders: they are interested in your announcements for an obvious reason—they already own stock. You don't want them to sell it. This group includes brokers and portfolio managers who advise clients to buy your stock.

2. Small float artists: These brokers specialize in small floats of 200,000 to 800,000 shares. If your firm is offering fits in this range, you need to communicate with these specialists.

3. Low-price specialists: These traders may not restrict themselves to low-priced stocks, but they like to have an interesting one handy should a client nix a high-range offering. If you fit the picture, you need to find these brokers and attract their attention with the right message.

4. Lower-to-middle-price specialists: Same disclaimer as above, but for new offerings or anyone seeking investment novices, these brokers can come in handy if they know your stock and niche.

5. Management backers: Forget price of stock, these folks focus on management teams. The message they want to hear is one of a strong CEO who understands the fundamentals of the market niche and has a clear vision of its direction.

6. Contrarians: When your stock is being hammered downward, these folks will notice you if you communicate effectively—and they may be your saving grace.

7. Chartists/technicians: This is an arcane and mysterious lot, steeped in some sort of esoteric shroud. But they follow trends and if your stock starts to fit a fundamental trend, these people are important targets. You will need help from your underwriter in understanding and matching your stock with trend chartists.

8. Turnaround buyers: If you have a true turnaround situation going for your firm, with multiple quarters to show for it, this is an important target audience.

9. Asset players: Undervalued assets, in whatever combination of current, fixed, and/or intangible assets, attract attention. What's tricky here is that this group includes those who go after firms they consider easy acquisition or merger candidates. If your firm falls into this category, you need a special plan of attack.

10. Below-book-value buyers: Should your company's stock price go down to 50 percent of book value, certain investors might consider it a very good investment opportunity—if they know about it. That's your job. Below-book stock prices can also attract takeovers, so be mindful of that as well.

11. Industry followers: Regardless of what vertical marketplace your company is in, its stock fits into some collection that has its own special followers. Getting information to these people on a regular basis is important, advice that could prove fruitful should your stock fall out of favor. Should that happen it could prove helpful to go horizontal—look for analysts who might group your stock into a generic rather than vertical category, e.g., future technology, service award winners, or low cost-of-sale leaders.

12. Home-town loyalists: These are investors and analysts who focus on regional or local buys regardless of vertical market niches.

13. Exchange-listed loyalists: Some investment portfolios are based solely on New York Stock Exchange and/or American Stock Exchange listed securities.

14. OTC rebels: Unlike the previous group, these observers don't restrict themselves to listed stocks and find the smaller base prices of over-the-counter stocks attractive opportunities.

15. Current income: This group of investors focuses on current income and the expectations of continuance.

16. Aggressive acquirers: If your firm has had success with acquisitions and is planning on expanding market share through acquisitions, this group of investors needs to know about your firm and its niche.

17. Investment advisers: There are scores and scores of investment newsletters and gurus out there, and each has a following of trusting clients.

18. Computer oracles: In spite of the 1987 crash, often attributed to computer-generated sell programs, many investment houses and serious small investors use software to keep track of the swarm of numbers on potential buys and sells. Unfortunately, as a manager of investor relations you cannot influence the programs, per se. You must focus on the decision makers who are in a position to amend the data on your firm.

19. Bottom fishers: These are the folks who look for opportunities among companies that are in the worst possible shape and the stock price reflects it. (Of course, knowing which ones will rise again is the trick).

20. Return-ratio buyers: What is the overall return on investment that someone gets by buying your company's stock? How does that ratio compare to other firms in your marketplace? If your return ratio is only so-so, what are the reasons you can enunciate to reassure this type of investor?

21. Margin-elasticity elitists: Somewhat similar to both bottom fishers and return-ratio devotees, these investors look for companies with problems and clearly enunciated recovery plans.

22. Internationalists: If your company has a clear global opportunity and you have global sales and marketing to back it up, your stock could be very attractive to investors and mutual fund managers who focus on the fast-changing international business environment.

23. Low price/earnings hawks: Some investors are attracted to stocks with low price-to-earnings (P/E) ratios, i.e., price of a share of stock divided by the company's earnings per share over a 12-month period. For example, the stock of company A sells for $25 per share with earnings of $5 per share, a P/E of 5. But the stocks of other companies in the same industry have a higher P/E ratio. This group of investors finds company A's stock very conspicuous and a possible opportunity because the stock's price may be undervalued.

24. Five year planners: American publicly traded companies are often criticized for their focus on short-term results rather than long-term planning to grow the company as a whole. Some investors are sensitive to this and look favorably on companies with sound five-year plans.

25. Emerging growth investors: These investors score gains by staying ahead of trends that could spell growth in particular industries. If your company fits this profile, mutual funds of emerging growth company stocks may be interested in your stock.

COMMUNICATING ABOUT PRICE/EARNINGS RATIOS

The subject of price-to-earnings ratio is a very subjective one. Before you get into it, be prepared to discuss these factors as well:

- Where is your stock relative to peer companies in the same industry? How are they performing? What is their P/E?
- What big contracts or products help explain your P/E ratio?
- What fundamental event affected the P/E ratio, for example, a one time write-off.
- Is yours a new company (initial public offering, or IPO) or a mature company in your industry? A mature company is focused more on maintaining its hard-earned market share against a horde of competitors.

Low P/E ratios are common among utilities, railroads, and other older technologies. But remember: many people consider utilities to be good investments anyhow. High P/E ratios are common among companies that some might regard as stingy with dividends because that money is reinvested in R&D. That fits the profile of companies engaged in newer technologies, and such companies have their fans as well.

26. Fundamentalists: No, these are not investors who make decisions based on Biblical revelation. These folks focus on the more traditional and fundamental characteristics of a company: its management, its product lines, its marketing and distribution, its specialist niche, its trademarks and patents, and its cash condition.

There are several specific audiences beyond Wallace's thorough summation. They may or may not be investment-driven audiences, but the message of your investor relations program could well be important to them. These are the other stakeholders referred to in the section title: employees, key customers, suppliers, dealers, and distributors.

Employee stock ownership programs can substantially increase how closely the stock is held within the company's extended family. If the employees are kept informed about company direction, they will feel more comfortable about buying and holding company stock for the long-term investment potential.

Suppliers are critical to any business. Making sure they are well informed about a company's direction and plans will come in handy during the tough times when payments are slower than usual.

Major customers and customer user groups are key stakeholders in your company's future. It is more difficult and costly to acquire a new customer than to get the long-term purchase stream coming from an existing customer. Customers who have made a sizeable capital investment in a company care very much that the company will be there to support their future needs. Being sensitive to that emotion is the job of both investor relations as well as marketing communications. It's good business to show a customer the value of investing in both your stock and your products or services.

Dealers and distributors are very sensitive to company health and longevity. Your dealer relations program can and should blend with your investor relations program. Any marked increase or decrease in your dealer network could have a substantial impact on revenue. Product plans can be material information to dealers as well as investors, as early PC guru Adam Osborne found out when he prematurely announced the Osborne II.

THE BASICS: FACTORS, PROBLEM DEFINITION, OBJECTIVES SETTING

Developing any investor relations campaign, event, or program involves the same basics as any other communication task:

- Isolate the immutable factors and situations you have to deal with, good and bad.
- Define the problem that needs to be solved.
- State the objective and by when you want to meet the objective.

- Define the precise audience.
- State the strategy of the IR program.
- Determine the tactics to be used in this strategy.
- Set up benchmark studies for pre- and posttest measurement.
- Build the project management schedule and allocation of resources.

Michael Rosenbaum of the Financial Relations Board of Chicago, the nation's largest investor relations firm, posed some basic guidelines for the IR task.[3]

- *Why should anyone buy your stock?* Rosenbaum says this question is so basic it's often overlooked. You shouldn't do so. As with any product, a stock must be differentiated from all the others available to investors.

- *Who wants your company?* After determining why your stock is a good buy, now determine for what kind of investor it is a good buy. Determine which analysts already follow your competitors' stocks. What analysts have investment parameters that fit your stock?

- *Can they find you?* They will be able to if they are added to your investor relations database. The database should be divided into the main categories: stockholders, brokers, analysts, trade press, business press, key influences, and others who have requested annual reports. Make sure you use database management software with extra fields for interests, action taken, reviews and commentaries, and so on.

- *Avoid missed opportunities.* As indicated earlier in the section about understanding versus facts, help readers of your financial reports to understand the significance of the information. Educate. This is especially important if the news is bad. While you have their attention, describe the pending corrective action.

- *Reinforce the message.* If a strategy is announced in the annual report, update readers on the progress of that strategy in subsequent quarterlies. Remind them of tactics taken in concert with the strategy, because most won't remember back to the last report.

- *Take it to the street.* An integrated investor communications program must include an important element: the face-to-face meeting. Engage the key influences in your investor marketplace at least annually.

- *Don't be a fair-weather friend.* Don't let investors become distant. It's all part of building an investment relationship. Keep in touch with investors during the down times as well as the up times.

Management has a bad habit of disappearing when the numbers are in brackets, and then wonders why some investors go elsewhere.

- *Meet the press.* Keep in touch with local business writers who have a keen interest in home-town public companies. Keeping them informed will pay dividends in the future when you need a sympathetic ear.

- *Avoid the traps.* In an era of "vulture capitalists" and quick-action money managers, it's tough to keep the company operations geared to long-term building and development. The pressures for short-term quarterly results are heavy. This is one reason why companies often go private after a period of frustrating public exposure. Only the chairman and the management can resist this pressure. Whatever resources and information you can muster to aid in this conditioning could have long-term advantage.

- *Who's in charge?* Get yourself put in charge of investor relations. If that is not successful, help make sure the IR person reports to the same executive who is responsible for the marketing communications program. If outside counsel handles the investor communications, urge that there be a close integration between the strategy and the messages of both domains.

WHAT IS NEWS AND HOW TO REPORT IT

With all the publicly traded companies clamoring for attention, news must be just that—news. To get information carried by Dow Jones it must have some significance to it.

The key criteria for getting attention is "will it affect the market or will analysts likely act on this information in some way?" Minor management changes don't make it; CEO changes do. Acquiring a new plant site is only significant if you can show its acquisition will have a quick affect on capacity or efficiency. The same holds with product announcements.

Chapter 15 deals more in depth with public relations, but some points are relevant here. The basic rules of preparing and handling news releases apply to financial news as they do to nonfinancial news. In addition, here are some specific guidelines:

1. Tables should start with the latest quarter, then the previous or last year's quarter.

2. Don't abbreviate the company name or it could be interpreted as your stock symbol. Spell out the name in full, followed by the appropriate exchange and symbol in parentheses, e.g., (NYSE, HP). Then list where the company headquarters is, e.g., with headquarters in Palo Alto, California.

3. List the spokesperson(s) and make sure they will be available following the release. It is easy to forget to check this when using a template news release on your computer.

4. Make sure your stock exchange representative or surveillance committee is sent the release before you send it to Dow Jones.

5. Keep a file of all press announcements and the resulting coverage. Simultaneously, note the concerns, qualifiers, or patterns of analysis made by each reporter or commentator. This will help you to tailor one-on-one meetings and spot who needs extra "attention" in the event of changing news.

THE INITIAL PUBLIC OFFERING CHECKLIST

An initial public offering (IPO) of stock is often compared to a product launch. That's a useful comparison, except that product launches aren't regulated much by federal law and an aggressive federal agency.

If your company is planning to go public, you need to begin the investor relations program well ahead of time, i.e., ideally one year prior to the time you plan to issue. As with a product launch, you have to build corporate identity and awareness to hope for any action on this very important product—your stock.

Because of SEC filing benchmarks, an IPO requires unusual attention to the calendar. The SEC is very concerned about equal access to information so that a level playing field exists for all potential investors and not just management. Here's a partial schedule of basic IPO events:

1 Year Prior to Planned IPO. Begin an investor relations program. This includes setting up the internal team and the external advisors. An internal investor relations person should be identified, ideally reporting to the same executive as the marketing communications manager.

150 Days Prior. Underwriters are chosen, as are attorneys and a substantial accounting firm knowledgeable about securities law.

120 Days Prior. Choose a financial printer for the IPO prospectus. Not any printer will do. Confidentiality and awareness of SEC rules are essential. This should be a printer who understands that the schedule is dictated by a powerful arm of the federal government. Typography must be checked and rechecked because "typos" of financials will be costly. Also chosen at this time is a transfer agent to keep stockholder records.

90 Days Prior. Begin preparation of the registration statement. This document consists of two parts: Part I is the prospectus. Part II is supplemental data available for review at the SEC.

The prospectus is the legal offering document, which means it is the sole piece of sales literature on the stock and its issuing company. The prospectus will need considerable marketplace information and thus marketing communications involvement.

The first-draft of the prospectus is prepared in-house and has a disclaimer in red ink stating that the registration hasn't yet been approved (i.e., "become effective") by the SEC. That is why this draft is also called the "red herring" statement. It is reviewed and revised by the underwriter. It eventually becomes the official prospectus once the price and size of the offering is established, typically the day before the IPO. This addition to the preliminary prospectus is called the "pricing amendment" and makes the document final.

The prospectus requires a copywriting balancing act. Since it is the official sales piece for the offering, you must write about the company in the best possible light. At the same time, this isn't like writing a promotional brochure or a direct mailer with teasers on the envelope. In fact, because the fair disclosure of information is essential, you must cover the negatives and weaknesses about the company and its marketplace along with the positives and strengths.

45 Days Prior.　Filing of preliminary registration and prospectus (red herring). The SEC can take 4 to 6 weeks before approving the preliminary prospectus. During this 45-day period, the official "waiting period" prohibits management from saying anything that is not in the red herring statement. This is critical because the prospectus is supposed to stand on its own. Any additional comments could be construed as promotional.

30 Days Prior.　Management roadshow begins. This is required by the SEC to give equal access to all concerned. This is how the underwriter introduces the client IPO to the investment community. These meetings are also called "due diligence" meetings.

1 Day Prior.　The SEC says "go effective" within a specified period of time. At 4:00 p.m. EST of that same day, there is a pricing meeting to establish the price of the stock and the number of shares to be offered. This important information is then added to the preliminary (red herring) prospectus to create the complete and official prospectus.

Day of the Offering.　Your company runs a tombstone ad in the investment/financial print media.

Offering Day Plus 90 days.　The SEC's mandated "quiet period" begins. During this period your company may not say anything that violates the rules prohibiting the "public offering of a security," i.e., any publicity release that could be construed as part of promotion of the stock itself, even if the publicity says nothing about the IPO.

7 Days following the Offering. Your company gets the cash from the investment banker.

91 Days after IPO. Brokers are no longer required to provide the prospectus to clients. The quiet period ends and you begin the main part of your regular stockholder/investor relations program.

As observant and aggressive as the SEC is, remember their primary concerns: 1) equal access to information officially presented in the prospectus and roadshow, b) prohibition of any public offering of a security, either orally or in writing, prior to the filing of the registration statement. The term public offering is broadly (and wisely) construed as any publicity effort that seems designed to promote the stock and thus stimulate the market for it. So any press release or other promotion could be construed as a violation of the public offering.

Nonetheless, the SEC doesn't discourage normal product advertising, new product announcements or announcements of factual business and financial developments. But be careful not to make forecasts of revenue or income or stock valuation.

All this points to the need to execute an investor relations program early on so that its elements are part of the regular process of building awareness of your company and its position in the marketplace.

HANDLING A TAKEOVER BID

Corporate takeover activity in the 1980s raised the value of strategic investor relations to a new high. Suddenly, having a undervalued stock price could lead to a very difficult and often nasty situation. Added to that is the enormous power of institutional investors (mutual funds, insurance companies, bank trust departments, pension funds) that own the majority of all common stock. These fund managers are, by and large, more interested in the short-term return on profit-taking than the long-term payback of "buy and hold."

Let's look at three fictitious publicly-held companies—ACME Inc., Bravo Inc., and Charles Inc.:

ACME Inc. has no investor relations program. Only minimum filing requirements are made. There is little awareness of the company and its stock among institutional investors, and only analysts specializing in ACME's business are even slightly aware of its quantitative assets, let along qualitative assets. ACME stock is at $15.00, but its book value is $21.50.

MAINTAINING CREDIBILITY

By Lance Ignon, Vice President, Sitrick Krantz and Company

In the end, the argument hinged on one word: "some."

The fast-growing entertainment company was facing its first major earnings disappointment, and the prospect of losing luster on Wall Street was causing a collective migraine for senior management. The average analysts' expectation was 25 cents a share for the quarter. The CFO reluctantly conceded that the company would be lucky to hit 20 cents.

Like so many others faced with similar earnings disappointments, the company at first opted to obfuscate the results by drafting a press release with the earnings on the second page and the claim that results were below "some" expectations. In fact, they were below all expectations—well below.

This may seem like a minor point, but it underscores how companies end up doing themselves additional harm by trying to pull a fast one on Wall Street—a tactic that merely erodes the credibility that every company must assiduously develop if it expects to be rewarded with a higher valuation during good times and forgiven during short-term setbacks.

As the company's investor relations counsel, Sitrick Krantz & Company began by scratching the word "some" from the statement that "earnings were below some analysts' expectation." The firm then added to the press release an explanation of what caused the shortfall *and* a description of what the company was doing to avoid another disappointment. It also moved the earnings to the first page where they belonged.

With the press release finally wrestled into its final draft, a detailed plan for its dissemination was put in place. The earnings announcement would be released after the close of trading. That would give investors a chance to fully digest the news and reduce the chances of a panic sell-off triggered by an out-of-context news-wire headline such as "XYZ Corp.'s Earnings Below Expectations."

The following morning, the company's CFO, chairman, and a Sitrick Krantz investor relations executive hosted a conference call with major institutional investors and analysts. With a detailed explanation of what caused the disappointment and a plan to improve future results already included in the press release, most of the tough questions already had been answered. The CFO and the Sitrick Krantz executive then followed up with personal phone calls to the most influential conference call participants to give them an added degree of comfort. The executive also contacted daily financial reporters who were most likely to cover the earnings release to encourage a balanced portrayal of the results. Trade magazines with longer lead times, as well as shareholders, were sent a copy of the release and a brief letter.

The result? The company's stock lost about 5 percent the morning after the release, but then recovered most of the loss before the end of the session as those who had participated in the conference call began to snap up what they realized had become a bargain. More importantly, the company retained its credibility by addressing its problem head on and avoiding the temptation to hide the bad news in an unlocked closet.

Nice catch for a skilled bottom fisher. Most investors in the company are amenable to a takeover given that they have little or no relationship with management and its plans.

Bravo Inc. has a public relations staff that also handles investor relations, although the latter is primarily handled by the chairman and his corporate counsel. Undervalued and conspicuous in its industry, a takeover bid becomes apparent. The chairman and his counsel begin a program of defensive operations. These include the purchase of assets that muddy the regulatory waters and by-law revisions that require that mergers must be approved by the majority stockholders. Press releases start flying about the environmental problems of the suitor, and the local press is briefed on the jobs that will be lost should the suitor successfully bid. The staff is also pressed into a major effort to get shareholders to grant proxy to management. Shareholders are balking and want more information about Bravo's assets and direction.

Charles Inc. has had an ongoing investor relations program tied strategically with its marketing communications program. An aggressive corporate image campaign in the business press keeps the Charles name and image recognizable. There is an active program for using the disclosure of new products and product research successes to the maximum benefit. Meetings with analysts and the business trade press provide a variety of written and verbal summaries of successes and plans. The annual report is used as a broad-based selling tool that takes the reader into Charles' corporate strategy, values, and financials. Quarterly reports provide sound information for investors to project earnings and return. The corporation has a high recognition factor in benchmark studies, and is regarded as a credible company with credible visionary management. Its stock is trading $6 below book value. Then, a suitor raises its head. But management is successful in communicating that, all things considered, the bid is wholly inadequate. The bid fails.

Idealized, antiseptic cases? Probably so. But they provide the contrast needed to make some general points about fighting takeovers. Management must have an ongoing relationship with the investment community to build the comfort level and credibility needed when takeover bids are presented. An ongoing program that communicates the totality of valuation of a company is a proactive and offensive strategy that is inherently more credible than a last-minute, defensive, and reactionary strategy.

Other precautions can also be implemented. As part of your contingency planning, write a takeover scenario for your IR team to play out. Evaluate the roles played by each team member and rehearse tactics each should take to better handle the situation should it ever go "live."

Although it's not always easy to find out, try to identify key institutional holders. They should definitely be included in any management one-on-ones, just as key trade press and analysts should be.

Brief employees on any merger/acquisition situation, since long-term employees have accumulated considerable stock holdings. Such employees' knowledge of the company is better kept in confidence rather than distributed through the rumor mill or outside the organization.

Make sure brokers and other "sell side" analysts are fully briefed on your side of the question. Be observant of local or national interests that may be adversely affected by a merger or acquisition of your company. It may be necessary to gain their vocal assistance to help your case.

HANDLING CHAPTER 11 RESTRUCTURING

Filing for protection under Chapter 11 of the U.S. Bankruptcy Code is a crisis, but it's recoverable. Many big-name companies have successfully emerged from this action in much better financial shape and often with a clearer sense of purpose and direction.

Filing under Chapter 11 is used to gain time to restructure finances. It is not insolvency or liquidation, which is the essence of a Chapter 7 filing. It should be noted that the United States is virtually the only country with this type of restructuring protection. That's why your non-U.S. markets will need special attention in understanding what Chapter 11 is all about. In most countries, a company simply liquidates.

Bankruptcy communications is a form of crisis communication. As such, you should also read our chapter on crisis communications to gain further perspective.

As a crisis, bankruptcy communication involves careful preparation by a well-organized task force whose members clearly know which person handles which responsibility. The two main goals of your Chapter 11 team are to stabilize the employee base and to control the flow of information and rumors.

Filing for protection under Chapter 11 doesn't happen overnight. The signs appear long before filing. Therefore, there is no excuse for not positioning the action and preparing support materials well ahead of the filing time.

Such a filing should be seen as a proactive tool used when negotiations with creditors or the banks fail. This will help you position the action to employees and the outside world in offensive rather than defensive terms, i.e., "We did this to protect our customer base and our employees while we try again to work things out with the creditors."

Your Chapter 11 task force should initially include top management and operational department heads, including human resources, marketing, legal, sales management, and accounts payable management. Closer to the actual planned filing date, the team will need to include those responsible for third-party suppliers and prime vendor relationships.

The reason for such a broad team is that your company will be deluged by questions from all sources. In preparation, you must help your communication team develop and initiate a timeline of actions and supporting materials. But as with any communication plan, you first must identify all the target audiences:

- Employees on site at headquarters
- Employees at branch offices, designated by time zones
- Employees at divisions and subsidiaries, designated by time zones
- Largest, key customers
- Customer leadership or user group officials
- Main customer list
- Dealers and distributors
- Prospects
- Top 20 unsecured vendors (for legal documents)
- Local business media
- Trade industry media, designated by deadline and time zone
- Industry analysts
- Banks
- Landlords
- Local political leaders

Each of these audiences is interested in slightly different information. Thus, you and the task force must prepare by developing three important documents for each group:

1. List of likely questions and best answers (Q&A)

2. "Talking points" or script guidelines

3. Customized letter for distribution or mailing

The Q&A is particularly important because it will guide you in writing both the script and the letter. You must be honest enough to list every tough question you could get, because the tough one you omit will surely be the one that comes up. The full Q&A isn't necessarily for distribution, but to help you be prepared. A separate, shorter Q&A for distribution to each audience, including one for the press, can help you control the story and keep fires from starting.

The script is a device to help management stay on track when they talk with employees. Even with advance preparation, this will be a difficult announcement. All the more reason to make sure it's carefully delivered and the points made in logical order. Scripts will be handy for all those who must talk with key audiences: vendors, landlords, prospects, customers, accounts payable, and so on.

Any employee who is regularly in a position to answer questions from the outside world should be given a script for guidance. That includes the receptionists and employees who get customer service calls. It is vitally important that these highly exposed employees know to whom certain calls must be directed. They need to be calmed and assured that all is well so that they sound confident and relaxed on the telephone. They and all task force members must have an important document: an inquiry referral guide. This guide is a two-column list of various types of inquiries and to whom they should be forwarded. Include the responsible person's office extension and home phone number.

In addition to the news release, several special information pieces regarding Chapter 11 filings will be useful to management as they brief employees:

- Common Chapter 11 terms and definitions
- Typical sequence of events in a filing
- Procedure for handling vendor reclamation attempts
- Procedure for paycheck cashing problems at banks.

Most of these items can be reviewed by management in the announcement meeting with employees. But it is also essential that presentations to employees and other groups be followed by a written summary of the same points. They won't mind the repetition; in fact, they will want to hear the message again.

Likewise, management should keep the doors open for informal talks with employees. Be visible, accessible, and reassuring without being Pollyannaish or misleading. And listen! Employees may well have good ideas for productivity improvement that they never felt like sharing before. They probably will have sound operational insights.

As mentioned earlier, positioning your reorganization decision is critically important. Although both Chapter 7 and 11 filings are within the U.S. Bankruptcy Code, one of the first rules to follow in handling a Chapter 11 filing is to banish the "b" word—bankruptcy. You are restructuring and reorganizing, not going bankrupt. Secondly, it is imperative that you convey to all audiences your intention to conduct business as usual. With few exceptions, that's what Chapter 11 protection is all about.

To help you craft the message, consider how your restructured "new" company will eventually be able to do things you cannot do right now: office or branch expansion? International marketing? Research and development? New product offerings? Production advances or plant expansion? Will relief from creditors permit you to add employees? These are all potential positives that can be juxtaposed with the negative of the filing.

The 48-hour period prior to your anticipated filing time should be divided into hourly segments listing the actions to be taken by respective task force members. The time periods should reflect the concurrent times in your international offices so no notification mistakes are made from misreading time zones.

As you near the filing time, you must carefully alert people according to their "need-to-know" and their time zone relative to your announcement time. Several news services, primarily the Bloomberg news service, monitor such court filings. You wouldn't want the news of your filing to reach a subsidiary or key customer or major vendor before you had a chance to make contact.

Key among the early calls would be influential industry analysts or trade press journalists who need and will appreciate having the full story early on. Because the local business press will often call industry analysts for their assessment of the situation, you want the resulting local stories to carry knowledgeable third-party quotes.

The news media will need a quick summary of the history of your company and your marketplace. This can be done in a 5-to-10-page media fact sheet that covers contact names and numbers, company overview, major operations worldwide, facility offices, revenues in a two-to-three-year comparison, key management, CEO biography, and company history divided into key dates. This is a good overview to have for the media regardless of the news.

In preparation for the many calls that will come in, consider setting up a special 800 telephone line as a "crisis hot line." This should be managed by a knowledgeable person who can route the calls appropriately. The 800 number can be added to all written communications so that people clearly see you are open to discussing the filing.

A final point: stay current with the invoices from your marketing consultants and strategic agencies. Pay bills on time and make sure you are billed promptly for the work you engage. The last thing you want in marketing communications is to have the invoice of a communications agency caught in a Chapter 11 filing. The reason is that any invoice for work done "pre-petition" may not be paid until the court approves. You don't want that to happen to a strategic vendor. You can engage them for more work after the petition filing and pay them for it, but paying a pre-petition invoice would be in violation of a court order.

TIPS FOR INTEGRATING YOUR PROGRAM

Monte Gordon, vice president of research for the Dreyfus Corporation, once said that buy-side institutions such as Dreyfus are influenced and their decisions affected by what they see, hear, and read. That being the case, an integration of communication tools in your financial and investor relations can be a very good investment indeed.

Investor relations has historically used direct mail to great advantage, targeting the right analysts and institutional "buy-sider" portfolio managers with the right message. The fulfillment system for such a program

SERVICE AMERICA CORPORATION'S SUCCESSFUL CHAPTER 11

On average, restructuring under Chapter 11 of the U.S. Bankruptcy Code usually takes 12 to 18 months from date of filing to completion. But one of the largest privately held food service providers in America, with nearly $1 billion in sales, completed the process in 9 months—thanks in part to the help of Los Angeles/New York based financial relations specialist Sitrick Krantz & Company.

It wasn't without its difficulties. Service America Corporation, at the time of the filing in October 1992, had considerable debt due to a merger many years prior. As with many companies in the late 1980s, the recession compromised some strategic growth plans. Debt was restructured twice, which left bondholders with less each time.

Several months prior to filing for Chapter 11, Service America judiciously retained Wilbur Ross of Rothschild Inc. as financial advisor. Ross was well-known and liked by the bondholders. His reassuring comments in the initial Service America news releases announcing another restructuring did much to facilitate communication to that important audience.

Part of the communication plan was to thoroughly brief bondholders through a group meeting and national teleconference, follow-up letters, and direct one-on-one phone calls—all this to prepare them for another restructuring.

Once the company recognized that neither an out-of-court restructuring nor a prenegotiated Chapter 11 filing (in which a plan of reorganization is already prepared) was possible, the company moved swiftly to prepare for the impact of a voluntary filing. Service America had nearly 20,000 employees servicing institutional and commercial accounts through 4,000 field managers. Thus, the careful planning of internal communications was a huge task. It was essential that the employees be on the job in the food service lines the day of and after the filing.

Sitrick's Rivian Bell worked with the company's marketing, operations, and human resource executives to supervise communications for all the Service America audiences, including a substantial number of vendors and bondholders. A full day "Bankruptcy 101" course was held several days before filing with 45 key vice presidents, supervisors, and managers to inform them of the process, the company's

---

should be especially efficient, and should ideally include a fax response capability.

It is very important to maintain contact and relations with analysts once you have gotten them to a roadshow presentation. An 800 line just for analysts supervised by a knowledgeable investor relations professional is an ideal tool for providing these professionals tied into your company. A sophisticated database system should be used to manage both mail and telephone inquiries and responses.

There are also various media materials that will need to be planned and produced in financial and investor relations:

expectations, and provide a walk-through of all communications documents. The day-long program also gave managers a chance to work through personal concerns, relieve anxiety, and effectively buy into the need for the filing.

Despite bright sunshine the morning of the filing, the lights and power suddenly failed due to an electrical malfunction at Service America's Stamford, CT headquarters. Employees were already nervous, and people wondered if power had been cut off because the bill hadn't been paid. As administrative personnel scrambled to get the one-line emergency telephone operating so executives could conduct their final telephone briefing with attorney Sitrick, colleagues transferred data to their laptop computers and set up an emergency "comm center" in the refrigerated confines of the MIS department where auxiliary power was available. Bell and associate Ross Palmer stood for several hours generating the final 25 communications documents that would be distributed throughout the country that day.

Company executives, including the new president and CEO, personally called or visited key vendors to make sure they were comfortable. Managers were well briefed on all aspects of the filing issue, with Q&A's tailored for each concerned group. Every evening, wrap-up sessions were held at headquarters to review the latest activities and solve new problems that had arisen during the day.

Current and prospective clients were also targeted for written, telephone, and face-to-face communications. As testimony to the company's efforts in reassuring clients that the filing wouldn't affect its operations, Service America succeeded in closing twice the amount of business in the days immediately following its Chapter 11 filing as it normally closed in the same period of time.

Negotiations proceeded with bondholders, vendors, and secured lenders, with the course changing late in the game. Agreements came and went, and amendments to the company's reorganization plan were made through the company's final court hearing. But Service America completed its restructuring and successfully emerged from Chapter 11. While the court recognized the legal team of Paul, Weiss for its efforts, the board of directors recognized the communications team for a job well done.

Media Fact Sheet. The fact sheet should contain basic bulleted copy points—headquarters, subsidiary, division, and branch office addresses and phone numbers; benchmarks years in the company's history; marketplace niche; number of employees (professional, nonprofessional, international, customer service, R&D, sales and marketing); revenue for last two years; management biographies.

Company Profile. Aim for three descriptions, one of 10 to 20 words, one of 100 words, one of 400. This permits the journalists to pick and choose descriptions that you have written.

Corporate Backgrounder. This is the classic, multipage description of the company, its marketplace, its customers, products, and management.

We won't claim that tombstone ads for a new stock offering are a strategic communications device. They are merely part of the IPO process.

Corporate image advertising, discussed in Chapter 15, is influential. A 1984 Erdos and Morgan study found that 93 percent of institutional investors surveyed thought a company's corporate image was important and that 78 percent of them read corporate advertising to get current information on a company's products and markets, while 77 percent said corporate advertising encouraged them to investigate a company's investment potential.

In the section on IPO, we mentioned the necessity to allow yourself a one-year marketing effort before the targeted date of the offering. The SEC is suspicious of corporate or product advertising that magically appears during the IPO waiting period. However, they are not bothered by a company's pre-IPO advertising continuing through the offering period. The SEC doesn't interpret a continuing campaign as a promotion of the new stock, per se.

As we said earlier, a company needs to be marketed and positioned to gain any kind of mindshare and recognition. You can do that with an ad campaign designed to promote your corporate identity. This doesn't mean that you initiate a campaign aimed squarely at the investment community. That's too transparent and could prompt SEC action during the IPO process. But a broadly based, business media campaign including local, regional, or national broadcast or cable programming sponsorship could definitely make it easier to brief analysts during later roadshows.

Annual reports can be misused, overwritten, deceptive, and even egotistical. Some investors look suspiciously at every annual report that lands on their desks. But annual reports can also be informative, educational, targeted, and confidence building.

So how do you maximize the potential while minimizing the hazards? The answer is to plan the document the same way you would a brochure or direct mail campaign. Use the project platform in Appendix B to isolate the major communication elements:

- What is the problem we are trying to solve with the annual report?
- Given that problem, what shall be our objective for this annual report?
- Which of our many audiences are we trying to reach with this annual report, i.e., to whom should it be written?
- What attitude change are we trying to effect with the annual report?
- What is the look and feel we want this document to convey?

Based on your completed annual report project worksheet, submit to management a positioning statement tied to the five questions listed above. This shows you are taking charge and clearly concerned about key issues, but it will also give you quick feedback—either they will agree or disagree. Better in the beginning than a month later! The key point is to get management to think long and hard about the primary audience for this year's report. It may be different than last year's audience, and it could be different again next year.

Once you have identified the audience, the tone, and the goal, you will have an easier task directing the copywriting and design of the report. For example, if the audience is really the stone wall of the analyst world, you need to present market and competition information as well as your financials in a variety of graphs and charts that make it easy to extract information—a quick read for busy eyes.

Many of the answers to these questions hinge on the chairman's agenda—or should we say the chairman's hidden agenda. Unless you're fairly well informed on this point, you will likely be doing your first annual report by trial and error. For example, if your company has many divisions and subsidiaries, it is important to know if anything will be sold during the current reporting period.

Therefore, throughout the early planning process, engage management (particularly the chairman) in a discussion about the real purpose they see for the annual report. Try to get them to be as specific as possible. You can't do much with an answer such as "We want the annual report to boost the stock price another $4." The annual report is unlikely to do that and you would find it difficult to measure anyhow. But an answer such as "We want the annual report to convey a new conservative, mature management confidence in our place in the market so that analysts forget past mistakes." Now you have a firmer platform for copywriting and design.

Given the sensitivity of the annual report, production planning must be built around contingencies. Regardless of how much you identify objectives and audiences, anxious management minds will see a need to make lots of changes in the copy. Agree to a schedule by getting your designer and management together for the first major briefing for the report. Allow for trips, planned and unexpected, that the chairman may take, In general, you will need at least 60 days to do the report but plan for more if you can. If you initiate the first planning meeting on your own, it will be much easier to remain in control.

A theme should be developed for each year's report. The theme ties the elements together and works with the design to present both the financial and the marketing copy. The theme is distilled from the overall marketing message your company decides it wants for the annual report. The theme and marketing message drive the copywriting. The copy, theme, and message are then enhanced by the design.

Credibility is more important in an annual report than any other piece of corporate literature. If there's bad news to report, deal with it in the beginning of the annual report followed by management's intended corrective action. The worst thing to do is to bury the bad news in some footnote or encrust it inside language that could make some top ten list of Wall Street obfuscation.

Seek to educate in your annual report. Not everyone will be familiar with your overall industry and your niche within it. So take some time in the beginning of the report to explain your marketplace and overall business environment. Define key terms and explain the distribution or OEM channel you're in. Media kits from your trade publications may include overviews of your marketplace and thus provide ideas to help you educate readers of your annual report. These things will also be helpful to brokers who get lots of questions from individual investors who may never have heard of your firm.

Don't overlook the opportunity to showcase your corporate objectives, mission, and civic values. This is important to a market that has seen so many mergers and acquisitions in the last fifteen years. Stories about incompatible corporate cultures are legendary. For new readers to this year's annual report, be they analysts, money managers, brokers, or investors, such elaboration goes far in developing the relationships that will be remembered.

In summary, this is called an annual report for more than just financial reasons. Done correctly, you have a multipurpose selling tool that lasts a year: for shareholders and stakeholders, analysts and brokers, customers and prospects, vendors and employees.

The section above on news/media relations includes other pieces of printed information you will need.

Financial relations, whether to report good news or bad, traditionally makes use of roadshows, briefings, presentations, and speeches to large audiences. If you control the event and the facility, you can control the message and its memorability. The main point you should get from this section is simple: control the event. As mentioned before, remember that your company is trying to be heard above the noise of the crowd. The only time you will likely have the luxury of total attention is when some crisis occurs.

The event must be packaged for the particular audience regarding type of information, focus, and time of day:

Stockbrokers live according to market hours—10:00 a.m. to 4:00 p.m. Eastern Standard Time. Breakfast, brunch, or a brief presentation at close of market, rather than lunch, best fit their schedule. Remember that stockbrokers are on the "sell side" of the investor world, i.e., they're salespeople. Therefore, craft your message to help them sell your stock over the telephone. Provide them with a script listing the 3 to 5 main reasons why their clients should buy your stock. Keep in mind that brokers get about one or two minutes to catch their clients and make a pitch. Your script should also provide shorter pitches for the frequent voice mail messages brokers must have to leave with clients.

Money manager and analysts are more likely to accept luncheon invitations. The large New York-based analyst community gets many invitations to lunch presentations, so be prepared to do morning or afternoon sessions with light snacks. This audience wants the facts: charts, graphs, ratios, and so on. Packages need to be complete, and you need to go beyond the minimum financials and cover market overviews, management strategies, plans, corrective actions to be taken, and so on. Remember, brokers and many individual investors follow what analysts say.

Presentations should seek to highlight the main points in 15 to 30 minutes with time allowed afterwards for questions and answers. During the crisp highlight of points provide listeners with directions for finding in-depth information in their packets.

Prepare well ahead of time by listing all the possible questions you are likely to get and the appropriate answers. Where bad news is the topic, the answer should include management's corrective action. This roadshow requires a variety of communications tools and communication specialists, from speech writing for the CEO and CFO, to four-color slides, overheads, video, and information packets.

Premeeting invitation packets should reach prospective attendees 2 to 3 weeks in advance. Include the kind of information that will likely draw attendance, e.g., reprints of articles in the trade press, previous quarterly and annual reports, fact sheets about the company and its place in the market. Include a business reply card (BRC) to get a commitment on attendance and to ask what they want out of the meeting.

These meetings must involve top management, especially when analysts and fund managers are the audience. But you cannot cover the whole country each quarter. Instead, break the meetings into regionals that require less time. Make sure quarterly results are released in sufficient time for the news to hit the financial and investor press before your meeting.

Following these meetings, remember to do two things: sample their reactions and maintain communication. You may find a consistent item missed in one region that can be corrected next quarter in another region. And once you have gone to the expense of getting them into the room, don't drop the ball. Remember, relationship marketing works far better than ephemeral marketing.

MEASUREMENT AND EVALUATION

How do you know if an investor relations program is working? What kind of budget is needed to affect a particular stock price? How do you measure the effectiveness of an investor relations program? The CFO and chairman are as concerned about costs in this area as they are in others.

Benchmark studies are very important for evaluating a long-term investor relations program. Such studies can tell you not only what recognition mindshare your company has, but also what perceptions your IR program must overcome. For example, if a publisher of books branched into software for elementary school classrooms two years ago, a benchmark study that revealed a lack of awareness of such diversification would provide real direction to the IR staff.

Let's suppose your chairman wants to increase the value of the stock by 50 percent in three years. Let's assume the board approves the chairman's allocation of $25,000 per year for the investor program. There are two million shares outstanding, with a current value of $10 per share. In other words, $75,000 is to be used to get the stock to $15 per share within three years. Let's see what might happen:

Regrettably, the price of the stock may climb only to $14 in the third year. Earnings remain stable at $2 per share as it was in the beginning of the program. That translates to an increase in the P/E ratio (i.e., the price/earnings ratio, an indicator of value) from 5 to 7 (i.e., 10/2 versus 14/2).

What is significant here is that the stock went up even though earnings per share did not. The increase in stock value of $4, albeit below goal, translates to an increase in total equity value of $8,000,000 (i.e., $4 × 2 million shares). Such an increase in stock value helps bolster employee morale, at least for those with stock options. It can attract more investors and help guard against unwanted takeovers.

Now let's say the board is feeling really good and decides to issue an additional one million shares of stock. That's another $4,000,000 in market value and considerable capital after the underwriter has received its fee.

All things considered, the chairman says your efforts were only 50 percent responsible for the increase in value: 50 percent of $12,000,000 in increased equity, or $6,000,000 in value for $75,000 in program expenses. Not a bad return.

Now use a similar set of calculations to judge the impact of your product promotions and ask to be put on a bonus program!

RESOURCES

1. Several court cases have affected how publicly traded firms and their management and staff must function in order to be in step with the intent of the Securities Exchange Act of 1934:

    Pig 'n Whistle v. Financial Relations Board, 1971. This was the important case in which the SEC warned that investor relations practitioners must take steps to verify the accuracy of information given them by employers or clients for public dissemination. Because of this case, a public relations firm must disclose in its press releases that it is being compensated to act on behalf of the issuer. *Securities and Exchange Commission v. Texas Gulf Sulphur Company,* 401 F.2d 833 (2d Cir. 1968). This is a classic insider trading case because a major implication of the case is that investor relations counselors should consider themselves "insiders," not mere communicators.

Securities and Exchange Commission v. Switzer, 590 F. Supp. 756 (Oklahoma, 1984). The classic case of someone making a huge gain by benefit of inadvertent disclosure.

Howard Bronson Case: The SEC published a report on July 12, 1984 rebuking the Bronson public relations firm for disseminating false and misleading statements of material facts made in connection with the offer and sale of unregistered securities.

Carpenter v. U.S., 108 S.Ct. 316 (1987). This is the famous case of *Wall Street Journal* columnist R. Foster Winans, who was found to have leaked information to colleagues regarding information on companies he was covering for the daily.

2. The National Investor Relations Institute (NIRI) is an association of 3,000 investor relations professionals. Louis M. Thompson, Jr. is NIRI's president/CEO. NIRI publishes a monthly magazine entitled *Investor Relations Update.* It also publishes a newsletter entitled *Executive Alert* that covers "issues vital to the practice of investor relations." *Washington Alert* is an NIRI newsletter aimed at keeping members abreast of government actions that can affect equity value and investor relations. In addition, NIRI has a very active nationwide seminar program including a fundamentals of investor relations course. A must membership for an investor relations professional. Headquarters: 2000 L Street NW, Suite 701, Washington, DC 20036.

3. *Investor Relations Newsletter* is a monthly publication in its third decade of service to IR professionals. The editor is Gerald Murray, general manager of Ruder Finn and Rotman Public Relations in Chicago. Managing editor is Elizabeth Hintch of Remy Publishing Company, 350 West Hubbard Street, Suite 440, Chicago, Illinois 60610. Call 800-542-6670 for a sample copy and subscription information. Fax 312-464-0166.

4. The New York Society of Security Analysts represents over 30 different industries.

5. The National Association of Securities Dealers, Inc., 1735 K Street NW, Washington, DC 20006.

6. The National Association of Investment Clubs serves members who are relatively sophisticated individual investors. Direct mail campaigns to NAIC members is important for this target.

7. *Going Public* (1983). New York: Technimetrics, Inc., 21 pages. Profiles the IR programs of nine companies that went public in the early 1980s.

8. Graves J. J., Jr. (1982). *Managing Investor Relations: Strategies and Techniques.* Homewood, IL: Dow Jones-Irwin Publishing, 392 pages.

9. *Investor Relations: A Practical Guide for NASDAQ Companies* (1982). Washington, DC: National Association of Securities Dealers, Inc..

10. Budd, J. F., Jr. (1983). *How Video Can Vitalize Financial Reporting.* New York: Corporate Shareholder Press.

11. DiNapoli, D., S. Sigoloff, and R. Cushman (1990). *Workouts and Turnarounds: The Handbook of Restructuring and Investing in Distressed Companies,* 1990. Homewood, IL: Business One Irwin, 520 pages. This is a must guide for anyone professionally interested in the essence of the book's subtitle. The chapters cover the latest strategies, tactics, and procedures.

12. Media relations and news release distribution vendors that provide special services for investor relations:

    Business Wire has offices in 17 U.S. cities. Its *Analyst Wire* goes to hundreds of stock market analyst firms throughout the country. Their Minimum Disclosure circuit goes to 16 wire and print media. Headquarters: 44 Montgomery Street, 39th Floor, San Francisco, CA 94104. Telephone 800-227-0845.

    PR Newswire has offices in 17 U.S. cities. Services include Investors Research Wire, InvestorFax, and InvestorGram. The IRW accesses 2,000 locations in North America. Headquarters: 150 E. 58th Street, 31st Floor, New York, NY 10155. Telephone 800-832-5522.

NOTES

1. Kalman, J. L. (August 1987). "Mano a Mano with Wall Street." *Business Marketing,* pages 81–83. Adapted with permission. Copyright by Crain Communications, Inc.
2. Wallace, S. W. (April 1983). "Plumbing the Investor Market." *Public Relations Journal,* pages 28–30. Reprinted with permission.
3. Rosenbaum, M. (January 1988). "Launching an IR Program." *Business Marketing,* page 60. Adapted with permission. Copyright by Crain Communications, Inc.

CHAPTER 17

Employee Relations: Creating Company Loyalty That Customers Notice

> "He who considers his work beneath him will be above doing it well."
>
> —Alexander Chase

One Friday the advertising department employees at a major American newspaper were having a problem with a commonly used software program. These folks prided themselves on their computer literacy, but were increasingly baffled by their inability to get the program to do a common but important task for their classified pages. Panic started setting in with deadlines approaching. They finally called the customer support line at the software company back East. The response was, "Oh, sorry. We close shop at 5 p.m."

Perhaps the most ignored audience in marcom strategic thinking is the employees. The impact they can have not only with the customers, but internally, is often misunderstood or ignored. We have said it before, but it bears repeating. Everything you do in marketing says something, explicitly or implicitly, about your company. And employees say it the loudest, by word and by action.

But how often do you form an unfavorable attitude toward a company because the switchboard operator is not helpful or is too curt? What about the customer service representative whose insensitivity to a customer's concerns damages a relationship with a high NLTV (net lifetime value)? Or a company recruiter whose formality and aloofness insult a prime employment candidate?

Positive employee relations should be a major cornerstone in the foundation of any marketing structure. If your employees aren't knowledgeable about your unique selling proposition (USP), or don't understand the value you bring to the marketplace, or simply don't trust the company, how long do you think it will take for customers to find out?

Not long, actually. So if your intuitions are telling you that something is wrong with employees' attitudes, employees' company knowledge or, worst yet, employee agreement with your marketing plan, we suggest you read this chapter right now.

CHECKLIST OF DO'S AND DON'TS

- Do's:
    1. Do make sure employees have all been oriented into the company with the same game plan. We'll call it the company mission.
    2. Do alert all employees when customers are visiting and remind them how important the visitors are.
    3. Do choose receptionists carefully. First impressions last, especially those gained over the telephone.
    4. Do survey employee attitudes frequently to make sure no hidden suspicions or rumors are eating away at them.
    5. Do introduce employees to the ad campaign and make sure they understand what it all means.
    6. Do provide employees incentives to find new employees and customers, even if they aren't in human resources and sales.
    7. Do involve employees in an ongoing charity or "cause" that's fun and gives them prideful visibility.
    8. Do make sure customer service employees understand the customer/revenue cycle, and how customer problems relate to employees' jobs.

- Don'ts:
    1. Don't relegate employee suggestions to a box. Actively seek them out. Reward the ones that work.
    2. Don't let salespeople be the only view of your company that customers ever see.

OWNERSHIP AND MOTIVATION

We started this chapter with a stage setter you probably found amusing. It wasn't for the metro daily that experienced it. Yes, it is a true story, and one still told in the newspaper industry. Obviously the staffer at the software company didn't stop to think that an influential newspaper might just run a story about their unfruitful support call.

Employee relations, when related to your overall marketing engine, touches on concepts such as employee communications and job ownership. If employees don't "own" their jobs or act and talk in harmony with the company message, customers are likely to notice inconsistencies across the organization. It can make the difference between a company reputation of being difficult to deal with or one perceived as cooperative and solutions-oriented.

Abraham Maslow, the prominent American psychologist, wrote about various layers of motivation he called a human hierarchy of needs.[1] First, people seek satisfaction of obvious physiological needs such as food and shelter. After they are satisfied at that level, they seek a sense of personal safety and security. Once they get that, they move on to seek a sense of belonging and acceptance. And once they feel accepted they move on to seek the high self-esteem that comes from a sense of approval and recognition.

Employees, like anyone else, fit into this hierarchy. But if an employer's management style is one of intimidation and keeping employees in the dark, where will employees' attitudes be? Clearly, they will still be seeking a sense of employment safety and security. Until they are satisfied that they are safe in their jobs, an employer can hardly expect them to feel a part of the organizational family. And if employees feel like outsiders, how much attention do you think they will give to satisfying customer needs?

Psychologist David McClelland[2] specifically studied high achievers and found that employees who seek excellence really enjoy being in charge. They want to have their own circle of responsibility. They want to *own their jobs*. They like challenges, said McClelland, and they also like feedback about how they are doing.

If what McClelland says is true about high achievers, then employers should seek them out as employees and then let them perform. If customer satisfaction is among the goals for high achievers, regardless of their departmental affiliation, they will go out of their way to satisfy the customers because they want to excel in all their goals. Everyone wins: the customers, the employees, and the employer.

The Ritz Carlton Hotel chain, one of the first service organizations to win the Baldridge Award, has a customer service philosophy which says an employee owns a problem until it is resolved. A maintenance person stopped by a guest who wants additional towels doesn't tell the guest to call the front desk or housekeeping. He or she gets the towels and then determines if there's anything else the guest needs.

Are you beginning to see why marketing should initiate a program that brings employees into the loop of the marketing plan? Employees want to belong, they want recognition, and they want the responsibility and challenges implicit in any good marketing plan. While we are not suggesting that all employees approve of your marketing plan or that it be put up for vote by employees, they should be sufficiently familiar with how it affects their interplay with customers and order fulfillment.

DEPARTMENTAL MARKETING

Many companies have a formal evaluation structure that includes performance reviews of specific objectives set for each employee. That way, an employee knows what is expected of him or her within each review period. Often times these performance evaluations include objectives established with the employee.

We will not get into a lengthy discussion of performance evaluation in a book on business marketing communications. However, you and your colleagues in the marketing department should meet with other managers and your human resources manager to identify objectives in each operational department that tie back to the marketing plan. The following discussions will provide some examples.

The Receptionist

There is a bad joke running around corporate life that a person cannot qualify for a receptionist position unless he or she has a heavy accent, a hearing problem, and speaks faster than Joe Moschitta in the old Federal Express commercial.

Being a receptionist is a tough position. Even with PBX phone systems, automated call processing, and voice mail, it's not for the faint of heart. If a company has over 25 employees, there will be lots of incoming calls. And at that size, you can be sure the receptionist is also handling clerical overload for other departments.

Marketing must provide the receptionist with sufficient information to adequately describe the company in seven words or less. With three lights blinking on the terminal, that's all the time the receptionist has.

When marketing issues a news release, the receptionist should be informed to heighten awareness of incoming calls from editors and reporters. Each receptionist station should have a list of reporters who most frequently call, citing their publications or station affiliations. Likewise, a copy of the news release should be at all receptionist stations.

Company literature placed in the main lobby should be maintained by the receptionist. The literature should include the company capabilities brochure, a company backgrounder, a short company overview, and general product catalog. When revisions come due, ask the receptionist if visitors are asking for something not covered by the current array of literature.

The Customer Service Department

In markets increasingly saturated with the commodity mentality, the post-sale service function performed in large part by the customer service reps (CSRs) may be the only differentiating way to keep customers.

Unfortunately, for most organizations this is treated as an entry-level position; the wages and the benefits are low, the workload high. More enlightened organizations have learned how critical this touch point is to customers' net lifetime values (NLTVs) and have started staffing the CS centers with well-paid, well-trained, experienced, and highly motivated people who are not only empowered to maintain the relationship, but also taught how to communicate with the customer.

If customer support is a 7/24 operation (i.e., seven-days-per-week, 24-hour-per-day), you must recognize how different the swing and grave shifts are. Unless those people are rotated periodically, they never really see the rest of the company in full operation. Also, not everyone likes working rotating shifts. This makes it difficult to find enough of the right support "personalities" able to function at the level you need.

Which is a major reason why marketing information must be put in the hands of customer support people. This information goes well beyond product information sheets, catalogs, and technical support manuals. Like the receptionist, these employees need to know the mission statement and how their support affects both customer buying cycles and your market share.

Likewise, customer service people can be a great source of market information. With proper briefing from sales and marketing, customer service employees can record product complaints, wish lists, and trend information that can be valuable in product development. Really proficient customer service employees develop strong rapport with customers and thus are capable of getting lots of information out of them. In these competitive times, it's all relationships, and relationship marketing is the tool to counteract commodity thinking.

However, there is also a danger in the close relationship between a customer and the customer service rep. In smaller, high-ticket capital equipment markets involving considerable post-sale support and substantial repeat business, some customers have become suspicious and nervous. They can't afford to lose a large vendor if that vendor is a single source. Such markets are lousy with rumors about financially troubled vendors or management turnover or product snags. Savvy customers have learned to pump customer service personnel for inside information and gossip. All the more reason to make sure all employees, on all shifts, are working with the correct information instead of rumors. You might read the chapter on crisis and contingency planning for more detail on this point.

Accounting/Finance

Every marketing person quickly learns that the accounting department can be a source of conflict. Although more broadly educated people are entering the finance and accounting area, the problem resides with those in the field whose education is narrowly focused. In short, they don't understand marketing. All they see are the big expenses the marketing department incurs. In some firms, marketing spends as much money as manufacturing or production. In a sense, the difference is that accounting people can see what production buys, but they can't see what marketing buys.

Nonetheless, your marketing department needs to take responsibility for briefing the accounting/finance area:

Invite the CFO to participate in the communication audit process so that the logic of your work is center stage. CFOs often see marketing as a black hole for unaccountable expenses. Showcase the process of arriving at your marketing information platform (MIP) so that the expenditures are perceived as a sensible support to the company's overall plan.

Submit a detailed calendar of expenses by month so that the CFO and your accounts payable manager can manage the cash to pay for your advertising, exhibiting, and research—on time.

Invite the CFO and accounts payable manager to social functions where they can meet agency account executives. This provides an opportunity for your folks to ask questions about marketing that they may be hesitant to ask you.

Clearly differentiate for your finance and accounting managers which vendors are strategic vendors, which are single-source, and which ones are casual vendors. If times get tough, they won't all get paid on time so you need to put them in priority order. A strategic vendor is one you brief using the MIP. Advertising and public relations agencies and your exhibit/trade show house are strategic vendors. A single-source vendor might be a specialty film processor or a talented free-lancer you use for overflow project management. Casual vendors are those you can change easily because they provide commodity products or services—and haven't read this book yet.

Field Sales

Nearly everything that applies to customer service applies also to your field sales staff. This is command central for relationship marketing, and with it come opportunities as well as the liabilities.

There are several areas in which quality employee relations impacts upon field sales: marketing plan, pricing, field information, and rumors:

If sales management doesn't understand the marketing plan, don't expect the sales plan to mesh well with it. Although the marketing plan should be developed by the marketing department, surely the views of field sales should be heard in the drafting of the plan.

When the sales manager participates in the communication audit and signs off on the MIP, you have done much to reach consensus between the two functions. But without consensus, you may suffer the consequences of salespeople making negative comments to customers about anything marketing does that is visible, such as the new ad campaign or your last trade show. After all, is the relationship with the customer improved if the customer senses dissension in the troops? Not in an era of relationship marketing it isn't.

Your pricing is a form of communications. Many companies successfully sell their products or services at far higher prices than their competitors using the basic tactic of "you get what you pay for." And if the product truly is superior, so much the better for the supplier and the customer.

But the job of field sales is to close deals. In the case of large volume purchases where customers sense price softness, many salespeople are quick to discount. Therefore, if pricing is a form of communication, what does knee-jerk discounting convey about quality or value-added? The solution here is to make certain that the sales organization understands your pricing policy and has had an opportunity to review it. Without that opportunity, you again suffer the consequences of another disenfranchised employee—except this one is in the field talking to prospects and customers. Unless your customers all lack intuition, they will perceive a problem here.

Salespeople are quick to criticize an existing product when they experience resistance to it in the field. It is marketing's job to define product strategy and product development, and good salespeople can provide valuable contributions to defining product content. If you leave them out of the process you once again expose the company to discernable dissension.

A good salesperson looks for any opportunity possible to get in front of a prospect or customer. Many customers become fascinated with the politics of their industry and the developments within it. Obviously, a good source of information to such customers is a sales representative. But along with the politics of an industry come the rumors and horror stories. That's why salespeople must be kept sufficiently informed of company developments to counteract rumors that customers pick up—especially from competing companies. Marketing wins no friends in sales when several salespeople find out something negative about their company from a customer instead of their sales or marketing manager.

The marketing communications department should play a major role in communicating with field sales to overcome the foregoing problems. E-mail can be used for quick, vital news. A broadcast or multiple-site fax can also be used.

Another tool that will be highly valued by field sales is a weekly newsletter. This newsletter has two parts: The first part is a summary of important information field sales can use immediately: product information, product strategy, competitive information, success stories sent by individual sales reps, and confirmed news or developments within the industry. The second part is photocopies of news articles on the company. Field salespeople want to know when the company hits the news, be it good or bad, and they want to know it before a prospect brings it up. Your weekly newsletter thus serves the purpose of being the company's official clipping service.

Keep the focus of this newsletter on important information regularly distributed, not elaborate production colorfully printed. Go from computer output to photocopy and get it out on time each week. You will be a hero.

INTERNAL MERCHANDISING OF COMMUNICATION PROGRAMS

Marketing must seize every opportunity it can to describe its marketing and communications plans to employees. This section gives you some tips to follow to accomplish this.

1. Initiate with human resources a periodic survey of employee attitudes and awareness of the company's markets and mission. As with any marketing project, you must start with some knowledge of existing perceptions. Such a survey should be done at least twice per year. Make sure some of the questions yield information about what employees *really* know about the company's market niche.

If the issues employees raise differ from management concerns—and that is likely—use the survey results to form a task force made up of employees, supervisors, and management to refine and isolate key differences. Consider videotaping the task force meetings or the final meeting when conclusions are isolated.

2. If you don't have an employee newsletter, start one with the human resources department. If production resources and time are an issue, produce an informal videotape every two weeks and place it in a video player kiosk in the lunchroom. With both departments involved, work is shared and human resources is closer to the needs of your marketing communications plan. That benefits all employees.

3. Before new ad campaigns break, make a presentation to employees about the campaign, its objectives, and its creative rationale. Distribute copies of the ads to the bulletin boards. Use employees as much as possible in the photo shoots (getting signed permission, of course).

4. Develop an incentive program to reward employees for beneficial suggestions to improve operations. "Benny suggs" incentives can be bonus points toward items in a special awards catalog, or the actual items themselves. A weekend for the family in a nearby leisure destination brings the spouse into the incentive program. Cite the contributors and winners in the newsletter.

5. With the recruitment manager in human resources, develop an incentive program for finding new employees. Good employees can be good salespeople for your company. In the process of selling a friend or colleague on joining your company, the employee resells himself or herself on being an employee. The incentives can be points toward items in the special awards catalog cited above or a cash payment. Cite the referring employee and the new hire in the company newsletter.

6. With sales management, develop an incentive program for finding new customers. After all, employees travel and have contacts, too. Make it worth their while to bring a possible lead to the company. The incentives can be two-part: points toward the awards catalog for a lead, more points for a qualified lead, and a bigger cash prize for a closed customer whose order gets processed. Cite referring employees in the newsletter.

7. The company mission statement should include two elements: a conversational description of what your company does, and an enthusiastic call-to-action that clearly shows company movement and direction. The former is the "noun" statement, while the latter is the "verb" statement. You need both for a mission statement.

8. Prior to customer visits, use a display sign in the lobby to advertise the visitors' names and company. Use a memo or e-mail to alert employees to the visit and what the customers bought from you. Alerting everyone to customer visits also helps cut down idle conversation that customers—or *that* customer—shouldn't overhear.

9. Good community relations helps build employee pride and vendor loyalty, and aids your recruitment effort. Ideally, choose a cause or charity that relates to your market niche. In any event, give employees the opportunity to share the project by being volunteers or contributors.

10. Keep in mind Maslow's hierarchy. Salary buys the first-level needs of food and shelter. However, salary doesn't buy a sense of personal safety and security, nor a sense of belonging and acceptance, nor the higher-level need for recognition. Remember that last word: recognition. Monetary, physical compensation is great, but being recognized and admired for something you did is compensation to the ego.

11. Use e-mail to broadcast weekly or even daily calls-to-action, reminders on sales contests, and reminders of incentives to recruit or offer beneficial suggestions.

12. Encourage management to hold quarterly or even monthly meetings to brief employees on major developments and to take employee questions. Also, encourage management to hold departmental meetings that permit them to focus on the mission of each department and its employees' goals.

13. Develop a special message in your telephone system "mailbox" so employees can quickly access basic facts about the company or hear new developments. Use the message capability of your PBX to burst important messages or pep talks from your CEO to all employees.

14. The typical excuse for not having regular meetings with employees is that the brass is always traveling. Fine. Then produce a videotape of the CEO being interviewed by the human resources manager, using questions that come from the latest employee survey. It doesn't have to be a Hollywood production. Create a simple kiosk in the main employee lounge with a videocassette player so employees can watch the interview at their leisure.

15. Many large firms produce an annual report to employees. This isn't the same as the financial annual report for stockholders. Rather, this report summarizes the year for employees while briefing them on the operations of remote divisions or subsidiaries. Such a report is especially helpful for organizations that have been affected by mergers and acquisitions.

16. Join with the human resources manager to organize a monthly "brown bag" lunch for all department managers. The human resources person should be the group leader or facilitator. Use these luncheons to isolate common or generic manager problems. Take an active lead so that communications issues are well known to your colleagues.

TIPS FOR INTEGRATING YOUR PROGRAM

Employees must understand your advertising campaign and how it is supported and integrated with direct mailers and telephone-based sales. This knowledge gives them a more complete understanding of how orders are closed and how fulfillment is handled.

Earlier in the chapter we offered suggestions for distributing the ad campaign amongst employees. Reprints of ads are popular among employees, especially if some of them were used as the "talent" in photo shoots. Keep in mind that customers often see the company through its advertising and other promotions. If a customer refers to an ad or its call-to-action, employees need to know what the customer is referring to—especially if the customer is accidentally misrouted to someone outside marketing.

But there is another side to the question of advertising and employee relations: recruitment advertising. Less glamorous than product or corporate advertising, it is rarely used to its potential. Here are some suggestions:

1. When you run ads to fill open positions, especially professional exempt positions, your ad gives readers a first impression of your company. Don't run ugly ads! Resist the temptation to crowd lots of technical, meaty details into a cramped ad with no graphics or personality. Have the ad typeset and use the company logo.

2. Indicate your value-added feature to your marketplace. Sell them on it. They may not know your firm, so tell them what you're all about. It doesn't have to add more than one sentence to the opening paragraph of the ad.

3. Work with human resources to develop your own recruitment advertising tag line. It may be totally different from your product advertising tag line, but it sets your company and its ad apart from all other advertisers in help-wanted. The tag line should imply some aspect of career building or job futures at your company. Keep it to seven words or less.

4. In crowded metro areas, commuter conditions are serious factors for some people. Briefly indicate where you are and how easy it is to get to your site from the interstate.

5. If advertising outside your area, sell your region's major cultural and recreational features. The extra words are well worth the cost.

Marcom managers should also work with human resources to assemble a new employees brochure or a simple packet of information. It should include a description of the company's market niche and the company's mission statement. Corporate culture and corporate values can be included, as well as a calendar of yearly events that could have an impact on the new employee's job, e.g., a large trade show.

Develop for employees a laminated card of basic company information. One side should be your company mission statement and the unique selling proposition that sets your firm apart from the pack. On the other side are basic telephone numbers: customer 800 line, customer service 800 line, the marcom manager's phone number, and any other important numbers.

All company building lobbies should provide visitors, be they customers, prospects, employees, or the media, with a complete profile of what you are, your marketplace, and how you're different. This means more than just being careful in hiring receptionists, as we outlined earlier. It means more than a supply of literature for visitors. Decor and furnishings should make visitors feel comfortable. Signage shouldn't be overbearing. A video kiosk is a good way of keeping visitors informed without the need to interrupt the receptionist. That way you add further control to how your firm is described to the outside world.

We mentioned earlier the idea of an employee annual report. You don't have to make the employee annual report look like General Motors stockholders' report. The key here is to brief employees on the state of the company and its past year, and tie their jobs and divisions into the broader picture, especially if the company has acquired other firms or has many remote operations. Thus, the emphasis should be on completeness rather than splash.

Employee annual reports should tell staff enough about the marketing plan so they can adequately relate it to their own divisional goals. An assessment of the competition is a good addition, as well as a layperson's guide to company finances. How will anticipated economic developments affect the company in the year ahead, or how will NAFTA or GATT changes relate to company plans.

Format can be used to show how special the employee annual report is. A larger, tabloid size or smaller 3 × 8 inch booklet size gets away from the triteness from which the more typical 8½ × 11 inch format suffers.

Employee relations is an area where special event planning can be productively used. Think of three types of events:

- Product rollout/marketing briefing
- End-of-quarter/end-of-year celebration
- Awards presentations

If a new product or target market or customer is a big deal for you, you should not only tell employees, but build excitement. In doing so, make sure they understand the role this new product will play in the company's future and their careers.

Some companies take this type of event seriously—and with serious fun. Intel hires Dick Clark Productions to put on product extravaganzas. You may not have Intel's budget, but you can still spotlight the product. If you can't hire a video/sound system service, pull a group of staffers together who can improvise using special effects lighting and noncopyrighted music. Imprinted specialty advertising items that tie the product to a promotional theme can be a big hit, especially if that theme solidly hits on the product's unique selling proposition (USP).

An event with staged and controlled lighting and music can also be used to introduce employees to the overall marketing communications plan, focusing especially on the visible advertising and exhibit components.

End of quarter/year celebrations is another way to demonstrate to your employees how valuable they are to the customer relationships and the marcom activities. This isn't the same as your annual Christmas/New Year's dinner and party. If you have that tradition and it has been positioned as a holiday thank-you gift, you obviously don't want to leaden it with presentations on financial performance that will prompt spouses to tug impatiently on employees' sleeves.

Rather, consider the importance of celebrating with all employees their efforts toward producing a good quarter or superior year. It should be during working hours, with videotapes made available to shift employees.

As for those presentations on financial performance, provide the information in the context departmental employees can appreciate. That means going beyond the usual praises to field sales for increased revenue. How about the fulfillment/shipping department that worked overtime the last five days of the quarter? Most employees don't understand how physically draining it is to meet a deadline to ship all orders before the 31st. Recognize other departments that jumped through hoops to make the numbers the company is celebrating. Bonus points toward an awards catalog can be issued to the individuals in the department, but also provide something for the department as a whole. It could be a daily delivery of fresh pastries for one month, or a plaque citing the effort and the quarter it covers. The idea is to build departmental esprit de corps and an interdepartmental competition to make goals.

Recognizing employees with an "award ceremony" makes the function sound too formal—you want it to be fun. Hold the event during the day so you can hire a local news anchor as the MC, a tactic that could lead to later coverage of the company's good employee relations practices. Do you really want to build incentives for employees to find customers, recruit new employees, and offer beneficial suggestions for improving operations? Then get their spouses involved—send the awards catalog to employees' homes. Your awards catalog should include weekend trips for two to nearby resorts, as well as tickets for two to concerts and other evening entertainment. Buy a box seat at the local stadium and use evening games as an incentive to employees.

MEASUREMENT AND EVALUATION

Earlier in the chapter we talked about the importance of doing some benchmarking through employee surveys. Periodic employee surveys, at least every six months, can be used to mark progress on key evaluation points that management wants to monitor.

Marketing should work with the human resources department to develop such a survey. As spotlighted throughout the chapter, employee relations and its impact on external perceptions isn't a job exclusively for either marketing or human resources.

Decisions will be made from the survey information gathered, so you must be certain you're phrasing questions for the type of information you seek. Good survey questionnaires aren't easily constructed. This is a specialty of its own, so don't hesitate to have your questionnaire reviewed by someone familiar with survey research methodology. If necessary, call your local college or university and find out who teaches survey research methods in political science or sociology, two disciplines that use survey research extensively. We suggest employee surveys seek attitudes and information in the areas described below.

"Top-of-Mind" Attitudes. By this we mean the first thing that comes to mind when certain questions are posed to people. Right or wrong, such attitudes have much to do with what employees might say about your company and products to neighbors, vendors and professional colleagues.

Employment Environment. Are employees happy with the environmental surroundings of the company? This gets down to such basic factors as climate control, availability of food vendors or cafeteria conditions, lighting, potentially injurious repetitive movement, flexible work hours, and training and educational benefits.

Career Possibilities. Do they feel they can grow in their trade or profession at your company? Or is the company culture one that doesn't even permit someone to do the job they know has to be done? For exempt professional people, this is a critical area and the source of much turnover.

Supervisorial Conditions. Knowing how employees generally think of supervisors can tell you much about the supervisors' need for managerial training.

Benefits. In an era of "cafeteria benefits," taxable benefits, and the rising cost of medical insurance, it's time to be as creative as possible about the range of benefits your firm offers. There may well be an inexpensive but valued benefit you have overlooked. Many high-tech companies completely close down for Christmas week to save on plant costs. Employees are given one free day and can use accrued vacation or comp time for the remaining days. It's considered a big attraction to employees with children.

Product Direction Knowledge. Here is where you and your colleagues in marketing can learn a great deal. Do employees have a clear notion of what the company's product direction is? If they don't, you are highly exposed at trade shows to a mixed bag of answers that muddy the waters. Do employees understand the key value-added feature your firm brings to your marketplace? If they don't, how can they possibly apply that knowledge to the work they do? How can they relate their work and the task they perform to anything meaningful? In short, how do they know they are making a difference?

Once you reach a baseline of information from the first survey, you can identify areas for concentration in your employee relations program. Identified problems can then be matched with reasonable objectives. The objectives will precisely cite what improvement is to be made and by what date.

For example, let's suppose the survey indicated that only 10 percent of your employees understand the ad campaign and that employees often joke about it even with customers. Your objective would be to develop a program that explains the marketing communications plan and its advertising component to employees such that 80 percent will understand the campaign within 30 days. To test the objective, you obviously must measure employee understanding with another survey that focuses on your advertising.

RESOURCES

1. Since the 1950s, the Opinion Research Corporation has done an annual national survey of employee attitudes. The survey is of four groups: managers, professionals, clerical, and hourly nonexempt employees. ORC surveys worker opinion and offers changes management can make. ORC, a subsidiary of Arthur D. Little, Inc., is located in Princeton, New Jersey.
2. Deal, T. and A. Kennedy (1982). *Corporate Cultures: The Rites and Rituals of Corporate Life*. Reading, MA: Addison-Wesley Publishing Co. What are the networks and customs that really communicate to employees and, through them, to the outside world? These and other less visible phenomena are discussed in this highly readable book. Published in 1982, your best bet to find it is a business library.
3. Beveridge, D., and J. Davidson (1988). *The Achievement Challenge: How to Be a 10 in Business*. Homewood, IL: Dow Jones-Irwin.
4. Garfield, C. (1986). *Peak Performers: The New Heroes of American Business*. New York: Avon Books.
5. *How to Prepare and Write Your Employee Handbook* (1984). New York: ANACOM.
6. D'Aprix, R. (1982). *Communicating for Productivity*. New York: Harper & Row.

NOTES

1. Maslow, A. (1970). *Motivation and Personality*. 2nd ed. New York: Harper & Row.
2. McClelland, D. C. (1961). *The Achieving Society*. Princeton, NJ: Van Nostrand.

CHAPTER 18

Community and Government Relations: Don't Forget to Call Home

> "Those who don't use local guides are unable to obtain the advantages of the ground."
>
> —Sun Tzu,
> Chinese general (500 B.C.)

You're in charge of marketing communications at a growing firm located in a city of 120,000 people. The orders for your product, and the planned product extensions, paint a favorable picture for revenue and jobs.

But you're running out of production space. When the price was a steal, your board bought undeveloped land closer to the airport. You want to use that land to build a new headquarters with larger production and fulfillment capabilities. Then you find out there's a snag in your plans. The county board is cool toward rezoning, due in part to an active environmentalist network in town. You face a real decision: rezone and build, or move elsewhere. How to proceed?

You might ask—or more likely your CEO might ask—"Why should we make community relations a high priority when we have so many important and competitive business issues surrounding us?"

Obviously, it's not priority one. But long-term survival for either growth companies or mass employers will often depend on maneuverability and support from various local publics.

Even if your marketplace is beyond your headquarters locale, you still must draw upon the local community for vendors, employees, and other support. It should take little persuasion to see that all such audiences should perceive you favorably. And long ago General Sun Tzu clearly recognized the strength of locals. These factors suggest a need for a strong community relations program. Other factors argue likewise.

If your firm is the least bit conspicuous, local civic associations and charities will single you out for support. They have learned how to push the right buttons, too. A common approach is to say, "We're sure your firm would want to be known as a supporter of our cause." Some causes will be worth pursuing. Others, unfortunately, won't be a good fit. But how will you know? Obviously, you can't contribute to everything, and employees can do only so much volunteering. What do you tell the rejected charities and causes? A community relations plan tackles this dilemma and provides direction.

As the chapter opener sets the stage, you may someday have to plead your case for some action with a government board or agency. In many cities, political officials are unsympathetic to the concerns of business. Municipal bureaucrats are usually worse. County boards of supervisors are more sympathetic to business development issues. In any event, with environmental laws enacted in the last two decades, it's no longer simply a matter of walking into the courthouse and saying "We want to build more buildings and employ more people—aren't you glad!" Guess again.

Suppose you did get that rezoning and build a massive plant. Suddenly, the concerns of local officials become very real during the morning and afternoon commute times. Just as suddenly, the local residents' association is parked in your lobby demanding you stagger work hours to relieve the traffic.

What if an outside corporation launches a hostile takeover of your firm's stock? The fear of the unknown and what it might bring can mobilize a community—but you will have to do the mobilizing.

All these situations call for a marketing communications plan that includes policies and programs aimed at managing relations with the local community and its government agencies. Thus, community relations should be viewed as part of the overall process of developing a marketing plan.

We quickly add that this isn't a chapter on community organizational skills. Nor is it a chapter on lobbying techniques. Our focus here is on community relations and public advocacy using the same integrated marketing communications tools you find elsewhere in this book. We have placed community and government relations together because the decision makers and opinion leaders you face in one camp are closely aligned with people in the other camp. We also urge you to read the chapters on media relations and event marketing.

CHECKLIST OF DO'S AND DON'TS

- Do's:
  1. Do make sure your CEO gets to know the other CEOs in the area, including those managing much smaller companies. A group of CEOs, standing as one on some point, can get the attention of just about anyone.
  2. Do clearly delineate what monetary and time donations you will make to local charities and causes. Without a thematic definition to your giving, you will need either an unlimited budget or your flat refusals will do more harm than the yes's do good.
  3. Do be a pro-worker, benevolent employer—and that doesn't mean you're pro-union. In fact, it could mean keeping a union out.
  4. Do something conspicuously good each year for the local community—conspicuous to the average resident in town. It doesn't have to be a big budget item, and may cost little compared to the recognition received.
  5. In any town, there are several individuals in the private sector whose influence on local government is swift, certain, and self-assured. Get to know who these people are, and make sure they understand your needs.

- Don'ts:
  1. Don't be a hermit in your town just because your firm is a national business-to-business concern. Hermits are not very good communicators.
  2. Don't assume the most familiar groups have the leaders you need to reach. For example, the Chamber of Commerce may not be the most important group to know your story.
  3. Delineate well ahead of time the broad direction you want government agencies to take as it affects your business. Don't wait for the issue to surface only to find you dumbstruck and unorganized.
  4. Don't hide your company light under the proverbial basket. Make known your benefits to the local community. Make it easy for local agencies and civic groups to point proudly to your firm as a local success story.
  5. Don't fail to include your legislative and city council representatives on your mailing list for major announcements and updates. Make sure they understand what helps and hurts your business.

SETTING THE OBJECTIVES

What are your marketing objectives? What is your overall marketing communications plan? These are the base questions to ask before formulating community relations plans. To do otherwise is to ignore the plans you have already made.

If your new fiscal plan calls for substantial increases in research and development investments, that will likely mean hiring talented specialists. Thus, professional recruitment will be more important in the new year. If you're lucky, you can draw those people from the local area and avoid relocation expenses. Some may have to be recruited outside your local area.

But if you're relatively invisible locally, you and the human resources department will need to develop a plan for building corporate awareness as an employer. Thus, you can see how setting objectives at the corporate level can trickle down to various departments, such as human resources and marketing, each playing a special supportive role.

In short, what are your community relations goals for the next five years? Where do you want to be in public awareness or perception by that time? Likewise, what are your goals for the next 12 months? What reasonable accomplishment do you want to achieve and evaluate by that time?

Likewise, what specific publics do you want to influence? The preciseness of your answer(s) directly impacts the success of your program. Any community has a variety of audiences your firm may want to reach: these include local media, public officials, educators, business groups, bankers, environmentalists, venture capitalists, unions, charitable foundations, religious groups, ethnic groups, commissions and boards, citizen advisory groups, bureaucrats, political action committees (PACS), and employee prospects. And the list goes on, almost *ad infinitum.*

The operative word is *reasonable;* what can you reasonably accomplish in this time-frame with this group of people?

Upper management is quick to confuse ideal "dream lists" with reasonable, specific goals outlined in sequence over time, e.g., one year, five years. For example, a CEO might say, "Of course, in one year I want you in community relations to take us from zero awareness to on-the-street familiarity!" Guess again, especially if you have the typically small budget that community relations gets.

The determination of success in community relations problems rests on measurable, reasonable goals adequately funded to execution. If your particular awareness problems can't be solved by the budget you have, then the timelines need to be stretched out. If the CEO insists on the timelines, then it's your task to show where funding is the issue.

All this is made much easier by having the information or data that shows a baseline of perceptions you seek to move away from. That should involve the objectivity of a professional survey research expert who polls your target publics to find out just how your firm is viewed. Otherwise, you are dealing with impressions and intuitions. If you don't have the funds for a survey of the outside publics, ask employees to fill out anonymously a survey that unveils what they know public impressions to be. At least then you are getting reactions beyond just executives' impressions.

As we have said elsewhere in this book, survey research isn't for the uninitiated. It is a body of knowledge few people have. If small budgets are a problem, check out your local college or university. Find out who teaches survey research methodology in the departments of political science or sociology. These instructors are experts at survey research and may well have a graduate student eager to handle a corporate project for credit.

YOUR ACCOUNTS PAYABLE DEPARTMENT

One of the authors once dealt with a chief financial officer (CFO) who adopted a scorched-earth policy when the company had a lean quarter. He insisted on personally calling all vendors with outstanding payables to demand that they would just have to endure the 120 days wait or "we'll just take our business elsewhere." This included small vendors, such as the janitorial service, and strategic vendors, such as the exhibit house and advertising agency. All were treated alike. Some stayed with the company, some walked—and all still have a bitter taste in their mouths.

Accounting and financial people have a different perspective from yours. And they are especially suspicious of vendors who deal in intangible services. Although you will face this situation sometime in your career, it is another reason why you must brief your CFO on your marketing communications plan, the rationale behind it, and the budget needed to execute it. The CFO should be a signatory to your marketing information platform (MIP); the logic of it will position you favorably.

All this preparation will make it easier for the CFO to understand that a strategic vendor, unlike a casual vendor such as a printer or courier service, isn't a relationship that can easily be changed. The authors hasten to add, however, that newly trained accounting/finance professionals come to work with a much broader education. Some "big eight" accounting firms are actively demanding such depth.

What does this have to do with community relations? Simply put, you want your vendors to perceive your firm favorably. If words gets around about scorched-earth tactics by your accounts payable—and we assure you word will get around—you will lose considerable favor in the community. It will take just one mixer of the Chamber of Commerce to pass the word that your firm is one to avoid.

LOCAL GOVERNMENT OFFICIALS

In times of crisis, any delays or lapses in communication can really back-fire with local officials. Don't put them in an embarrassing situation if you think reporters will ask for official comment on your crisis.

The crisis communications chapter goes into more depth on this point. Here we can simply state that if an accident or serious problem develops within your company, you should brief the appropriate officials so they're comfortable you have the situation under control. For example, if financial conditions require a reduction in your employee count, explain the situation to the mayor or your city council representative so they can be more authoritative should reporters ask for comment.

QUESTIONS ALL COMMUNITY RELATIONS MANAGERS SHOULD ASK THEMSELVES

By Joe Williams, President/CEO of Joe Williams Communications of Bartlesville, Oklahoma, and publisher/editor of the monthly newsletter *The Community Relations Report*[1]

- Do you have a community relations strategy and a plan that mirrors your company's strategy and business plan? Does it involve more than just contributions?

- Is your community relations effective? Have you conducted a valid survey or audit in the last year?

- Does top management see community relations as "social work," or as a valued business function?

- What are the major issues facing your company? Facing your communities? Have you conducted a recent community needs assessment audit? Have you done an internal assessment audit of your top management? Do you use these audits to determine your community relations plans?

- Can you justify your community relations efforts as contributing to bottom-line business issues?

- In what ways is your company changing? Has it restructured recently? Do you think it will in the next year?

- In what ways have you changed your community relations over the last few years? Were these changes initiated by you, or as a result of other forces, such as budget cuts?

- If you were starting from scratch, what should community relations do in the company?

TRUE POWER: FINDING THE KEY INFLUENCES IN TOWN

Ask someone where community leaders meet and the answer often given is the local Chamber of Commerce chapter. Surely, this is a place with many civic and business leaders. But we urge you to look beyond the Chamber, too. For one thing, chambers of commerce tend to be dominated by retailers. Other groups or associations may be populated by industrial leaders from firms such as yours.

Some cities seeking new business have organized promotional groups that travel widely to pitch the advantages of relocation to companies in other states. Here is where you can find some very influential people. If your business is located in a zone prime for new business, it may well be to your advantage to become visibly active in such a group.

Other business groups are composed of company CEOs and entrepreneurs who want to encourage local start-ups. Such groups tend to attract developers, venture capitalists, and leaders in higher education. Such a group is valuable to anyone in the business-to-business arena, and it's highly likely they have the ear of government officials.

All this is merely to say that if you are tired of mixers where you talk aimlessly with small shop owners, you might need to search around for another business group.

CORPORATE SUPPORT: "WE'RE SURE YOUR FIRM WOULD WANT TO . . ."

With the role of government declining, businesses are constantly asked to supplement the difference. Business-to-business firms are less conspicuous, but you will be found and solicited nonetheless. And as a good corporate neighbor and member of the community, you need to step up and be counted.

But while contributing to charities or supporting community activities, there's no harm in making it work for your firm too. The community relations portion of your marketing communications plan should outline the kinds of charities or public causes that most closely relate to your business. The deeds themselves can spotlight your firm in a memorable way. In short, linking your generosity in a thematic manner adds value to both the contribution and the theme.

Here are some examples of thematic harmony:

✔ If your firm is a manufacturer of something related to health or fitness, you have a vast selection of charities, events, fundraisers, and programs to choose from—or even initiate yourself. The event marketing and sponsorship opportunities abound. This book's chapter on event marketing can help you further.

✔ If your firm is engaged in some aspect of the computer industry, you might want to tie your company to technology education. This could be something as simple as volunteering employees to advise a local "adopted" elementary or secondary school. A software company can link itself to the vertical market it services and take advantage of its calendar of activities.

✔ A clothing manufacturer could assist a local Salvation Army unit or make donations of clothing available at holidays or during a natural disaster.

✔ As a commercial trucking company, your firm can regularly donate the use of trucks and drivers to food banks, second-hand shops, charity recyclers, and boy/girl scout donation drives. Imagine the good will created by your truck parked at a busy shopping mall with a banner indicating the donor.

✔ A medical engineering firm specializing in diagnostic technology could team with a disease-related foundation and possibly sponsor its local fund-raising event. The media will cover the event and thus its sponsor. Now contrast this example, say, with a mechanical engineering firm that makes a monetary donation to a disease-related foundation. Nice, but who will remember other than the foundation and the CEO? The donation is there and appreciated, but the thematic linkage is lost.

If you find it difficult to make such a thematic link-up, persuade one of your top officers to sit on the annual fund-raising committee for a local charity. The exposure to the local media and officials will last a long time because the charity will go out of its way to include the volunteer board members' names on everything they send out.

If a top executive can't volunteer for board-level volunteering, encourage one or two employees to get involved in the coordination of the fund drive in your local corporate neighborhood.

There are some interesting business benefits from such encouragement. For one thing, your firm becomes visible where it once was not. But you could discover a diamond in the rough this way. The donated employee may have a latent talent for management that surfaces in the volunteer project. Managing people and money is not easy for everyone, especially when dealing with volunteer workers and donated money! Your employee may come back quite ready for a job previously outside her reach—simply because you didn't know how good she was.

There is yet another way of contributing to the community even without a direct thematic link. Supposing your location is near a proposed park site or undeveloped city lot. Ask the city if you can develop the lot into a noon-time lunch area—with your plaque visible as the donor. Or perhaps you could develop a history exhibit showcasing great moments in the city's past. This is permanent, memorable, and the city maintains it.

INFLUENCING GOVERNMENTAL CHANGES

We mentioned earlier that this chapter does not provide guidance on legislative lobbying techniques. That is a skill set for someone else's book. However, if an aggressive effort is needed to get something your firm needs and it involves a local referendum, make sure you are prepared for a big-budget task.

Here are some of the essentials you may need to execute:

- Fact sheets
- Position statement or rationale
- Press tours/editorial board visits
- Video or color overhead presentations
- Advocacy advertising ("advertorials")
- Exhibits at public gatherings
- Standard media Q&A
- Internal worst-case Q&A
- Assembling a citizen advisory task-force
- 800 line information source
- Fax-back information service
- Direct mail
- Organizing speakers bureau for community groups
- Short bulletins
- Testimonial advertising
- Event marketing

TRADE SCHOOLS AND UNIVERSITIES

Suppose Acme Engineering specializes in hazardous waste management. Think of how long they will be remembered if they partially endow a position for an instructor in waste management at the local technical school or help pay for the classroom lab equipment.

Education-related corporate activities and donations are often a strategic necessity for most firms that embrace them. Unless a company is located in a large metropolitan area with many technical trade schools, finding the right employees can be a costly problem. Likewise, local trade schools suffering from government budget cuts often use outdated equipment or suffer from constant turnover in the teaching staff. The result is a pool of job applicants trained on yesterday's technology.

If strategic business planning starts early and is thorough enough, marketing and human resources departments can develop a long-range plan to assist lagging schools. The result is an up-to-date recruitment pool and improved community relations.

Specifically, business can contribute to the community's educational effort in several distinct ways:

✔ Becoming members of a school's industrial technology curriculum development team
✔ Contributing materials and equipment to those courses specifically aimed at producing competent and modern technicians
✔ Helping to recruit contemporary instructors and matching school funding through a challenge campaign
✔ Developing an internship program at your local plant site for course credit
✔ Developing a mentor program at your plant site
✔ Lending managers to schools for night courses or other part-time teaching

LOCAL REPORTERS AND EDITORS

The local media are always eager to cover human interest stories, and not just at Christmas. The criticism that they only search for stories about murders and accidents isn't lost on them.

Community relations, like overall public relations, is a two-part effort—doing public good and getting recognized for it. That requires coverage from the news media as much as it involves acknowledgment from community leaders.

Treat the local media with the same respect you would have for regular corporate announcements. Reporters have a job, they have deadlines, they operate with an unstated quota of sorts, and they need to work quickly. So make it easy for them to cover you and the organization benefiting from your contribution. Have the pictures and data they need to do a story *that day.* An incomplete package could be pushed aside and thus forgotten.

As we point out in the media relations chapter and elsewhere, remember the inherent differences in print, television, and radio. Your new announcement should be written in a matter-of-fact manner devoid of promotional or self-righteous adjectives and come-ons. Ideally, you want the newspaper reporter to use your copy as much as possible. If she has to correct lots of back-patting, she may go on to another, simpler story and discard yours. Television needs a quick, interesting "sound bite," which you should craft and rehearse with your CEO so the station keeps that part of the video footage. And radio needs an appealing audio segment. This is why three ads for the same consumer product have slightly different compositions when you read it, see it on television, and hear it on the radio.

Don't play favorites. Be careful of exclusives. Releasing a story about your project for newspaper coverage on the 15th is likely to be seen first on televised news the evening of the 14th. If you don't want that, then change the release date.

A word of caution. We already spoke of the danger of overly promotional language in press releases. Reporters have very good intuitions. If they do not see the benefit in what you are doing, they are likely to forgo the story or, worse, raise questions about your intentions and plans. (We cover examples of this in the crisis communications chapter.) All the more reason to strive for thematic linkage between your overall marketing plan and the community relations projects your firm provides. If there is real value, you will be recognized, but do not drag a pedestal around with you everywhere you go.

Community relation projects will not, in and of themselves, make your firm profitable or even successful. After all, this is a book that asserts the need for full integrated marketing communications, of which community relations is but one element. Nor will your community endeavors buy you perpetual favorable press. But real, recognized, value-added community relations might someday prompt a reporter or editor to give you extra time to explain some unfavorable news knowing that your firm has otherwise been a good corporate neighbor.

BIG IDEAS FOR LITTLE BUDGETS

If we have not given you some ideas, perhaps the following list will light a bulb:

1. If you do not have Junior Achievement in your area, work with other businesses to start a program in the adjoining high schools. These programs often lead to products that the news media are fascinated with.

2. Your business is doing so well, truck deliveries in and out of the plant are increasing. So is the noise and the traffic. Volunteer to place signage asking drivers to slow down. Volunteer to pay for a stop light to slow traffic further.

3. In the beginning of the chapter, we suggested you do something each year that is highly noticeable by everyone in the community. Given that business-to-business firms are often relatively invisible to residents, this is important. Did you know that a half-hour fireworks show can cost under $5,000? It doesn't have to be Independence Day either. How about the first day of school in September to salute students everywhere? Or on the anniversary of your incorporation to say thanks to the community. (Make sure you get a permit!)

4. If your business is international and growing, think what a sight it would be for commuters to pass your offices and be dazzled by a display of the flags of every nation in which you operate. At $500 per flag and pole, it's a relatively inexpensive way to show your pride to the community. Every time someone asks "why are all those flags there?" their colleagues can say "Oh, that's Acme Inc., a growing firm in our town." (The flag center should have a kiosk and a small pavilion or speaker's platform for company meetings or announcements.)

5. Organize a 5K race for the community's runners. These are big events that get news coverage, especially if the race is through the downtown area on a weekend. (Make sure you get a permit!) The prize can be a cash award to a charity presented by the winning runner—and you.

6. Organize a tongue-in-cheek talent show for everyone who thinks a karaoke machine will bring stardom or at least the promised Andy Warhol 15 minutes of fame. Tie it to a charity involved with speech disabilities or a fundraiser for the music department at the high school or college. Encourage your employees to participate as "lost-leader talent" or volunteers. It should get broadcast coverage as well as print.

7. If your firm is located in a small town far from metro centers, work with local officials to develop a town festival and crafts fair. Many small communities have developed highly successful annual events based on such things as pumpkins, squash, mushrooms, chili, straw flowers, and even garlic. Your employees will get involved as residents and help spread the word of your good deed.

8. Sponsor a candidates' forum for a small municipal election and offer your meeting facility and parking.

9. If your city holds a seasonal festival or carnival, get a top executive on the planning committee. Alternatives include contributing promotional advertising with on-air credit, or hosting one of the festival's newsworthy events in your parking lot.

10. Sometime a community might not realize what you do for them. This happened once in a small Oregon town where the college felt unappreciated because town officials were complaining about students, traffic, and noise on weekends. The college responded with an inexpensive campaign: it printed stickers with the college name that fit on pennies, dimes, and quarters. After about a month of that, the merchants and city fathers got the message.

TIPS FOR INTEGRATING YOUR PROGRAM

Community relations programs can make very good use of numerous coordinated marcom efforts to benefit the community and win favorable community reaction.

If your new manufacturing site could potentially raise concerns about pollution, toxic wastes, or increased traffic, you would be well advised to hold an open house and plant tour on a Saturday prior to opening. Invite the local media and the adjoining neighborhood using a direct mail campaign. Make it easy for your residential neighbors to attend by asking employees to volunteer to operate games for children. Ask the recruitment coordinator in human resources to have a table or small exhibit ready for job inquiries. Have job listings handy. You may very well find the executive secretary or inventory clerk you were seeking.

Should a new facility prompt negative reactions, companies are usually quick to rent an auditorium for a public forum. But you have probably seen how public forums at council meetings or board meetings go—one speaker after another standing at the microphone and rattling accusations and blame. Instead, try one-on-one communications. The open house idea discussed above could prove a better route so long as you have key employees leading tours for small groups of people who can easily ask questions of the knowledgeable guides. Thus, you stay away from unintentionally corralling individuals into a herd mentality.

Civic organizations and regional trade and industry groups are eager to promote the business climate in their area. They want outside companies to consider relocating plants or headquarters, but this usually involves "on the road" promotional tours. Such tours are sophisticated marketing endeavors involving video presentations, exhibits, literature production, and direct response tools—expensive. Helping to produce such promotions is rewarding activity that helps your own employees learn new skills.

Regional industrial trade shows often include exhibits to promote specific areas for business development. Your trade show managers and your exhibit vendors can lend expertise to such shows and gain considerable loyalty for your company in the process. Trade show exhibiting is a body of knowledge most business people don't have. Your expertise can truly make a difference for the community.

Does your city have a promotional brochure that parades the area's educational and cultural assets, its tax base, and its housing profile? If not, volunteer to produce and print such a document for the city. Having your name as a sponsor on the literature is an entirely acceptable request even if shared with other firms in the area.

It may be advisable for you to produce a monthly or quarterly newsletter just for government officials and key business leaders in your area. The letter should be no more than two pages with short summaries of your market, your successes, your employee count, your new products—and your community involvement. That latter item should also detail the community activities of your employees.

If your firm decides to help with charitable fundraisers, advertising in local print and broadcast is an essential ingredient. To help the charity save money, coproduce the advertising campaign with your ad agency. The disclaimers on the ads can cite your contributions and win considerable good will for both organizations—plus raise money for the charity. Ad agencies are often eager to be involved in such promotions because of the access it gives them to other community leaders.

All business-to-business operations need to develop in-house database marketing and direct response programs just to stay even with the competition, especially in commodity-minded markets. Your staff's knowledge in database marketing, direct mail, telemarketing, and fulfillment can be very handy to charities, educational agencies, and other nonprofit causes.

MEASUREMENT AND EVALUATION

The evaluation and measurement of a community relations program isn't as easy as counting leads from a direct response campaign or inquiries at a trade show. But you can measure results over the long term. As we mentioned earlier in this chapter, an ideal first step is to survey the outside publics you wish to influence. That survey gives you the essential comparison and baseline. An important goal of such a survey is to gather and assess "top of mind" perceptions of your firm.

Here are other measures:

1. Survey employee prospects when they complete application forms. Do this for a year. What perceptions do potential employees have of your company and how has the perception changed, if at all, in one year? Obviously, the number of applicants has to be sufficiently large to acquire a statistically significant set of measures.

2. As indicated earlier, survey employees. Do so at the beginning of the evaluation period and at each one-year anniversary. Keep in mind this isn't a survey of their own feelings about the company; rather, this is a survey of what they believe outside perceptions to be. Of course, personal feelings will influence their answers, but it does give you some indicator of movement.

3. Analyze the news coverage you have received during the evaluation period. Are newspaper articles moving from negative coverage to neutral coverage, or from neutral coverage to positive comments? Is there an increase in the length of stories about your company?

4. If your firm is actively engaged in influencing some government agency or board, there is a very real measure of how you're doing: the vote of the board. What would the vote have been one year ago? If the answer is unfavorable, you probably made progress as a result of community relations planning.

RESOURCES

1. The Center for Corporate Community Relations is located at Boston College, Boston, Massachusetts. The center offers a certification program in corporate community relations. It also runs a resource library and does consulting and custom research, and publishes a bimonthly newsletter entitled *Corporate Community Relations Letter*. Edmund Burke is its director. Address: c/o Boston College, 36 College Road, Boston, Massachusetts 02167.
2. *The Community Relations Report* is a monthly newsletter published and edited by Joe Williams Communications, Inc. Address: 300 S.E. 4th Street, P.O. Box 924, Bartlesville, Oklahoma 74005.
3. *Great Ideas—Award Winning Strategic Community Relations* (1994). Bartlesville, OK: Joe Williams Communications Books.
4. Kipps, H. C. (1984). *Community Resources Directory*. Detroit: Gale Research Publishing.
5. Yarrington, R. (1983). *Community Relations Handbook*. New York: Longman Publishing.
6. Kruckeberg, D., and K. Starck (1988). *Public Relations and the Community: A Reconstructed Theory*. New York: Praeger Publishing.
7. Aiken, M., and P. Mott (1970). *The Structure of Community Power*. New York: Random House.
8. Berry, J. M. (1985). *The Interest Group Society*. Boston: Little, Brown and Company.
9. Dominguez, G. (1982). *Government Relations: a Handbook for Developing and Conducting the Company Program*. New York: Wiley and Sons.
10. Nagelschmidt, J. (1982). *The Public Affairs Handbook*. New York: AMACOM.
11. Pedersen, W. (1989). *Winning at the Grassroots: How to Succeed in the Legislative Arena by Mobilizing Employees and Other Allies*. Public Affairs Council, Washington, DC.
12. Clutterbuck, D. (1981). *How to Be a Good Corporate Citizen: A Manager's Guide to Making Social Responsibility Work—And Pay*. Maidenhead, Berkshire, U.K.: McGraw-Hill.
13. You never know when things could get downright unpleasant. When it does, you may need to do more than glad-hand public officials and give tours to boy scouts. Read Saul Alinsky's *Rules for Radicals,* published in 1972 by Random House. Alinsky was the Prince Machiavelli for the proletariat in the 1960s, helping the dispossessed and under-franchised get their way with the powers that be.

NOTE

1. Reprinted with permission of Joe Williams, Joe Williams Communications.

CHAPTER 19

Crises and Contingencies: Communicating During Times of Trouble

> "We learn geology the morning after the earthquake, on ghastly diagrams of cloven mountains, upheaved plains, and the dry bed of the sea."
>
> —Ralph Waldo Emerson

It's 6 a.m. and the phone rings. Shaking yourself into consciousness, you hear the breaking voice of one of your most experienced sales reps calling from his car. He's just received word from an operating room physician that the pulse monitor your company manufactures failed in the middle of an operation. The patient died. The physician and his colleagues are scrambling for excuses.

So, too, is your sales rep. He sold them a solid, tested product—or so he thought.

Your job is customer service, which is part of the marketing department. What are the first three things you should do?

E merson was not a marketer, but his comments about learning geology
the hard way can apply to corporate crisis management just as well.
Crises can be turning points in an organization's life cycle. John F. Kennedy
once said "When written in Chinese, the word *crisis* is composed of two
characters. One represents danger and the other represents opportunity."
We can't claim this chapter will help you turn every crisis into an opportunity, but it will help you manage crises.

The scenario described above happened to a real company, although
we've changed the details. Some crisis will befall you, in one form or
another, even if death isn't a factor. It may be a crisis with customers, a crisis with the general public, or one with a government agency. If it becomes
known outside your company, you must handle it carefully. If it is known
only inside your company, consider yourself slightly blessed—you at least
have time to prepare.

Crisis communication is primarily a reactive endeavor. But what you
will learn in this chapter is that crisis communication planning is very much
a proactive endeavor, and one that lends itself well to integrated marketing
communications. As you develop your marketing information platform
(MIP) and refine it with regular communication audits, you should include
a separate crisis management section tailored to the specifics of your firm's
possible problem areas. In this chapter, we will help you to prepare for
crises and to handle them with minimal damage.

CHECKLIST OF DO'S AND DON'TS

- Do's:
    1. Do get the story out before the media or other outsiders define it
       for you.
    2. You can acknowledge a problem without admitting culpability.
    3. Do put the crisis in the context of your overall marketing story.
    4. Do give the same attention to media questions you would give to
       stockholder or employee questions—this is a crisis.
    5. Do have one company spokesperson and make sure employees
       understand why.
    6. Printed explanations may be more enduring than the verbal
       explanations, but prepare carefully nonetheless for broadcast
       interviews.

- Don'ts:
    1. Don't let attorneys determine your firm's response all by them-
       selves. A crisis is a public relations issue as well as a potential
       legal issue.

2. Don't lie. Things are bad enough when crisis hits, and you will be found out.

3. Don't speculate on what might be facts. Release facts that you have confirmed are facts.

4. Don't appear to be aloof and robotic. Show genuine concern.

5. Don't confuse a business problem with a marketing problem. A business problem that produces a crisis may be too big to lend itself to a marketing department fix.

PREPARING AND PLANNING AHEAD: TAKING THE GRIM INVENTORY

What is the worst thing that could happen to your company? What exposures or problems could you have with dealers, end users, or suppliers that could make for a really bad Monday—all week long? Major areas of exposure or potential crises are all around you:

- Manufacturing: mass injuries, product tampering, product recall, product quality collapse, ground water contamination, illegal toxic disposal, or hazardous materials poisoning
- Research and development: major programming code errors (bugs) or virus infections, product contamination, an unfinished product portrayed and promoted as completed
- Customer service: an errant or intentionally destructive employee, a misdiagnosed customer problem that erupts at several sites, network failure, premature product release
- Operations and administration: illegal employee treatment or harassment, financial irregularities, stock manipulation, insider trading
- Dealer or distributor revolt or lawsuit
- Financial: lay-offs due to declining revenue, Chapter 11 bankruptcy protection, or Chapter 7 liquidation.

You can think of other problems that fit your firm. Also, get suggestions from colleagues. As negative as it sounds, this is really the first place to start in preparing for crises: list them!

Your firm must face the reality that someday a crisis could strangle it. The difficulty, however, is that new companies and older ones that have "right sized" have fewer people doing more work for less money at lower revenues. Thus, crisis management sounds like something everyone would prefer to do next month or after the trade show or after the first of the year. Sound familiar?

A better solution is to seize the right opportunity. Barely a week goes by that some business hasn't faced some crisis. Be alert to such news and keep a crisis folder on your desk with clippings from trade publications.

Pay particular attention to other business-to-business firms that experience a problem generically possible in your firm. For example, supposing you read about a company having a revolt within its dealer network or user group. The trade press is paying the controversy lots of attention. That's because it's out of the ordinary, i.e., it's news.

Have your crisis management "call to action" memo ready to staple to the tear sheet of the story on this unlucky company's week of woes. Distribute the two items to the internal group you're seeking to motivate. Now you've made the point! Suddenly, preparing for a crisis makes some sense. In your cover memo, you should propose a date and time that is convenient. Schedule it after the big distractions being used as excuses, and make it easy for them by suggesting a working lunch in a conference room. Give the committee a working title that stands out from the other committees these people have to attend. Call this precautionary team the "crisis busters" or something else with an almost entertaining spin on it. Remember you're lucky to get them this far. Make it either educational or fun or both.

ASSEMBLING THE CRISIS TEAM

The working members of your crisis planning team shouldn't be just the top executives, but you will never get cooperation unless you first convince management of the need for crisis precautionary planning. That's why you should encourage the chief executive to issue an early memo that endorses the effort and the need for all to participate.

Your crisis study team should have a representative from each "exposure area" within your company. In your first meeting, or preferably in the agenda prepared for the first meeting, ask them to begin listing the worst things that could happen in their departments. Encourage them to wax verbal and consider every plausible error or problem that could occur. The few suggestions that might be implausible could prompt ideas with other departments.

Ask your managers to identify times or seasons for periodic reoccurring exposure to mishaps within their work areas. In subsequent meetings, persuade each member of the crisis study team to report on recent critical incidents. Companies such as Control Data Corporation have used such reporting to great advantage.[1] After all, these internal events are the best case studies your group can use to prepare for that one situation that slips through the cracks. This exercise will also help make company managers more attuned to crisis management, and less inclined to cover up events that almost exploded on them. Thus, your crisis team is both an exercise in prevention as well as a managerial support group.

REMEMBERING CRISIS CONTEXT: A COMPANY CRISIS AND YOUR MARKETING PLAN

You must maintain the positioning of your company the way it was before the crisis. After all, isn't that the ideal goal? If that's the ideal goal, then go for it. Always describe the crisis in the macro context of the larger company identity rather than the micro details of the incident itself. By doing so you ask your marketplace to judge your firm as a whole rather than to judge you by this crisis. You're saying this incident isn't characteristic of your company; rather, its characteristics and reputation endure in spite of this event.

For example, you might say "our customer service grades have always been high in all customer surveys, so we really regret that this problem blemishes an otherwise zero defects program. We fully expect our service operation henceforth will be as good as our past reputation." In short, focus on the larger context of who your firm is and what you have been. To elaborate on the idea of the larger context, here is an inventory of perceptions that you and your crisis study team need to audit:

- What factors have inspired trust in your company and/or its product(s)? What has been the unique selling proposition (USP) of your overall company up to now irrespective of the current trouble?
- What has been the historical driving "soul" of your company? Outstanding post-sale support? Highest quality products in the category? Whatever it is, identify it and don't lose sight of it.
- Has management always inspired credibility and trust in employees, vendors, customers, dealers, and stockholders? When and when not?
- How have past problems been resolved with each of your internal and external audiences, even if it was a different problem with each group? Was the solution satisfactorily perceived?

But let's turn things around slightly. Go through the preceding list for each of your major competitors. Why? The cold reality is that one or more of your competitors may well try to take advantage of your crisis situation. Going through this exercise may enable you to anticipate their individual moves and plan accordingly. In fact, go to the trouble of putting you and your competitors on a grid, with columns listing potential strength and weaknesses. It's worth doing and probably fun, too.

Identifying Internal and External Audiences

How will the crisis or rumor affect your employees, customer, and other publics and their attitude toward you? What are the short-term and long-term effects you will have to endure? Employees are greatly affected by crises. Their worries center, understandably, on their jobs. But remember, too, that employees also have business acquaintances, professional associations, vendor relationships, and neighbors. Employees are capable of communicating either facts or rumors. The choice is largely up to you. It is imperative that you keep employees fully informed on the facts of the crisis so that rumors are stifled before they reach the outside world. In times of crisis, the trade press is very good at digging up business cards from your employees and calling them to get the "inside story." If a reporter reaches a talkative employee or one who resents management for some reason, the message about your crisis can get very garbled. You can tell employees not to discuss the crisis with outsiders, but a) that won't keep them from doing so, and b) if they have the facts and you've dispelled the rumors, you needn't be so secretive.

Sales representatives, in particular, need special attention in a crisis. Although modern sales training focuses on the need for salespeople to listen more and talk less, you must understand the sales imperative: give the customer the space to become increasingly comfortable with the product and service so that closing the sale takes as little time as possible. If a customer is in shock over some event that might well compromise the sale, the sales rep is under great pressure to say whatever will comfort the customer. Some customers are gossips who love to visit with competing salespeople to get the latest industry politics. Likewise, some salespeople latch on to such customers to ingratiate themselves with the prospect. A word to the wise: keep sales reps informed and aware of the importance for them to stick with the company message and plan.

Even though vendors and suppliers are physically outside your organization, they can be a very important "internal" audience when kept informed. This is especially so if the trade press is aware of a primary, strategic supplier of components for your product line. Your advertising agency and public relations firm must be kept informed, too. Agencies have been financially victimized by many client crises. The last thing you need is trade press reporters finding out from their publications' ad reps that your ad campaign has been suspended for some reason. The reporters will find out the reason, and then they will control the direction of the story.

Think of your employees, suppliers, and customers as your best possible communication network. Keep them all informed and you will be more successful in managing the message and the correctness of the information about your problem. If you're in a publicly traded company, you have a board of directors. Whether you consider them an internal or external audience, they need to be informed of any problems that could affect the value of your firm. In the business-to-business environment, your external audiences include your dealers or distributors, your end users and their organized users' groups in each city, your stockholders, and the financial analysts who cover your industry and stock. Regarding the latter two audiences, you should read the chapter on investor relations/financial public relations (Chapter 16).

We don't want to repeat that information here, but be aware how important a crisis is to stockholders and the investment community. A distribution network can be composed of value-added resellers (VARs) or value-added dealers (VADs). Likewise, your product may be a component added to a fuller system by an original equipment manufacturer (OEM). In a business-to-business environment, your dealers or distributors are your customers. End users are primarily the customers of your dealers. However, in a crisis that may appear to affect service or product development or survival, end users might become very concerned and raise that concern with their dealers. Thus, it is imperative you keep the distribution network informed and calm. If the crisis you have is a local one with no particular impact on your image in the industry, don't minimize the impact. The local community is a pool of vendors and employees, but public officials can read, too. Reporters may well ask the mayor or county supervisors for comment. If you've been seeking permit changes or development concessions, the last thing you want is to embarrass the people who have a vote on such matters. Take the time to place a courtesy call to them.

Lawrence R. Werner of Ketchum Public Relations/Pittsburgh uses an audience spreadsheet to isolate different publics and the message and materials needed to keep them informed.[2] He calls it his Message Action Plan (MAP). We believe this is the kind of organizational tool that fits right into a marketing information plan (MIP) and an integrated communication strategy. We include the Message Action Plan spreadsheet in Appendix H.

Mapping Out Contingencies: Frameworks for Recovery

After your crisis team has listed the possible crises or areas of mishap that could befall the organization, it is important to outline a contingency plan for handling each type of crisis event.

A crisis contingency plan should have the following elements:

1. A title citing the type of crisis event.
2. All relevant team members' extensions and home phone numbers so that everyone is accessible at all times.
3. Someone designated as the internal plan monitor to make sure the plan is being implemented. This isn't necessarily the company spokesperson, but rather someone who acts as a crisis plan auditor of sorts.

CRISIS MANAGEMENT RULES OF THUMB

1. Prepare for the worst. Don't pretend it will never happen or couldn't happen. You're a marketing professional, not an ostrich. This is your livelihood, not a fairy tale. Not convinced? Then call your insurance agent and cancel your house fire coverage.

2. Be open, accessible, and factual. If you are close-lipped and decline interviews during a crisis, you're inviting suspicion. Not convinced? On your return from your next trip, when your spouse asks what you did during your free time, try answering with "no comment."

3. Recognize human tragedy and empathize with it. Whether it's a layoff, accident, product failure, customer revolt, recall, or whatever, someone has at least been inconvenienced. You don't have to claim culpability just to recognize someone's dilemma. Not convinced? Remember Exxon's responses to the Valdez spill, including the announcement in early winter that they did a lot but prefer to return next spring to clean up the remaining oil?

---

4. An assistant monitor for backup.

5. A description of how that department or location or building fits into the company's overall mission.

6. A general description of how the crisis team decided this type of crisis should be handled, the options for handling it, the special procedures to take and the tactics to avoid.

7. Confidential Q&A—a preliminary list of questions and answers focusing on the worst possible questions the media might ask. This is the internal Q&A to be kept handy just in case. This isn't the general Q&A you will need to develop around a specific crisis and that becomes part of a press kit.

The baseline for a crisis contingency plan is the same baseline for a general marketing plan:

1. What do we know about this marketplace and how and where do we fit in the picture?

2. Where do we want to be in this marketplace?

3. What should be our strategy and tactics to get to our goal?

4. How do we evaluate our success in reaching our goal?

This all starts with some market research. It is relatively difficult to plan communications management in times of crisis without first assessing the baseline attitudes and perceptions your marketplace already has of you in normal times. Even if research spotlights an attitude that is erroneous, that is the perception nonetheless and you need to know it. Only then can you build a contingency plan that is observant of the "art of the possible."

Remember the words of ad man David Ogilvy, equally applicable to crisis management as they are to advertising: "Advertising people who ignore research are as dangerous as generals who ignore decodes of enemy signals."

As with any kind of marketing plan, a crisis contingency plan should have its own objective, strategy, and tactics, all in the context of your marketing plan, yet observant of the "art of the possible" just mentioned.

Some would advise that you rehearse your contingency plan so that your staff is comfortable with the assigned roles, but a crisis contingency plan should be a conceptual guideline for handling an emergency. An overly detailed plan could be difficult for colleagues to remember and activate. What's more, each crisis will have some peculiarities that will require thoughtful adaptation of the plan. So keep your people focused on the macro concepts behind the recovery plan rather than memorizing specifics.

Flexibility is important. This is a plan, not a play.

Once It Hits the Fan: The "Situation Room" and Information Central

One of those crises your group talked about so academically has happened! At this point all the work of the crisis team must be put into practice by a designated crisis management task force. This crisis management team must quickly assess the extent of the damage to the company. Specifically, what is the short-term and long-term impact this event has had or is likely to have with each specific internal and external group.

The members of this crisis task force are those directly involved with the department or operation where the crisis has arisen. With the right contingency plan in hand, it's time to put the plan into operation.

The crisis management task force will need to have a special, secured headquarters to discuss events. Call it the "situation room" or command central. A voice line and a dedicated fax line should be set up for the team's use as well as a dedicated printer. The company's external 800 line, the one most known to your external audience, should temporarily terminate in the situation room.

The task force should meet late each day, following most of the media deadlines, to discuss the day's events and new developments. The contingency plan monitor can discuss how the plan is working and where the problems are. The team should delegate certain roles within the group, including the facts czar, company spokesperson, and audience auditor.

Facts Czar.   The facts czar gathers all facts and information about the crisis, thoroughly checking out rumors and suspected misinformation sources.

Management should make sure the facts czar gets the full cooperation of all managers.

Company Spokesperson.   One person should speak for the company during the crisis. If you don't assign one person to the task, answers to questions will vary in length, specificity, exposure, consistency, and credibility. Employees, in particular, need to be briefed on this necessity because many of them will be approached by reporters. If reporters insist on talking with the CEO, then the spokesperson can arrange that quickly. But if you are one company, you must speak with one voice.

Ordinarily the spokesperson would be your media relations manager or marketing communications manager. But this role might properly go to another person depending on the nature of the crisis and the knowledge needed to discuss it intelligently and credibly. In either case, this should be someone capable of handling the media properly and comfortably. If not, the marketing communications manager should thoroughly rehearse the task with the spokesperson, and management should make sure the spokesperson accepts the request to rehearse.

Audience Auditor.   This team member will evaluate the effectiveness of your crisis management with each internal and external audience. Therefore, this team member will need the cooperation of the human resources manager, your shareholder relations manager, your VAR or OEM relations manager, and so on. If the message isn't getting through to one or another important market or audience, it is this person's job to bring it to the attention of the crisis team at the afternoon "situation room" meeting.

CRISIS CONTEXT: AN INDUSTRY-WIDE CRISIS

Suppose the crisis is industry wide. Here's a perfect application of the Chinese symbol example mentioned by John Kennedy that we mentioned earlier. As a crisis, there is obvious danger. But an industry-wide crisis could provide potential opportunity for the firm that stands out as well-prepared and decisive—your firm. The opportunity exists in the context of your overall marketing plan, i.e., to reinforce how different you are, the micro, from the mass of competitors caught in the same storm, the macro.

Such a situation provides the chance to reiterate your overall position in the market and how certain factors isolate you from the pack—e.g., better customer support, "no questions asked" overnight replacement parts shipping, better quality control standards, and so on. These are the very factors you must inventory ahead of time in your crisis team, with competitor-by-competitor comparisons. Making your executives available for interviews is another way of portraying your firm as more organized and forthcoming. The focus of these interviews should be on educating the public about the industry crisis, bringing into the discussion how fortunate your firm is that its staff is larger, its programs more responsive, and so on. "We've been able to minimize the impact of this situation on us and our customers because . . ." The net perception you create could be, "This is a bad situation, but this is the company to ride it out with."

The Blame Game

The pressure of a crisis, with a reporter on the line or in your face, can produce a chain reaction that leads to uncontrollable heat.

Keep the contingency plan in mind. Stay at the macro level and remember your company's overall context, avoiding the micro details that can suck you into saying something you shouldn't, like blaming someone else for your problem.

Freud and other psychologists since him have called it *projection:* ascribing to others faults or mistakes you make. This can be a fine line, to be sure. But you should avoid claiming others have done it when the focus is on your incident. Such tactics are too defensive and don't win much ground. Instead, focus attention on company value-added strengths or product strengths, depending on the nature of the crisis. Put another way, avoid burying your message in defensiveness because messages can't develop limbs to crawl out of quagmires.

A MARKETING PROBLEM—OR SOMETHING ELSE?

Marketing people like to think that all business problems lend themselves to a marketing fix. That may not be so in some crises. A marketing department is responsible for all elements of the business and its success, but it cannot be responsible for all actions of upper management. This is especially true if management does something illegal or obviously stupid. If management manipulates the stock price, tries to fix prices with competitors, engages in unethical employment practices, or tries to bribe public officials, they should not expect marketing to magically fix the problem. Adding sugar and spices to rancid garbage doesn't transform the garbage into haute cuisine. If the matter is one of criminal charges, your only route is a containment strategy—e.g., "the management of the company will continue while the matter is resolved, and we will cooperate with the authorities in their investigation." This is definitely a situation where a defense attorney will have a considerable voice in what is said, and admissions of guilt are not likely to be among the answers. If the matter is one of poor business judgement, you escape the perception of possible criminality. However, another cloud appears—the perception of incompetence. We're not referring to an acquisition that failed or a product that didn't sell. Any business is entitled to make some mistakes. What we're referring to is a mistake that, to the typical outside observer, looks just plain stupid.

In marketing, and business in general, don't be overly proud of never having made a mistake. First, no one will believe you. Second, a business or a marketer who has made no mistakes may not be a very good business person, too concerned with avoiding failure and not taking enough intuitive risks and chances. After all, that's what business is all about.

DE BONIS & PETERSON'S BUSINESS MARCOM RULE #10:
"Never making a mistake is a bad sign."

For example, let's say you produce security systems for commercial buildings. One product line is security doors that you promote as impenetrable. You produce a short demo video showing how two guys using a battering ram can't break in your door. But a leak to the press, perhaps within your organization, suggests it was a specially reinforced door made for the video. That would be perceived as rather dumb, especially if anybody could go out and test one of your doors. Likewise, if your door could be smashed open by two guys and a battering ram, you should have found another focus for your dealer video. This could be a crisis, especially for dealers who have been promoting your doors as ram-proof. It will be a bigger crisis for end users who have installed your doors and are now rushing to cover up your logo. The solution may well be to offer replacement with the most secure door in your line. You may also have to hint about the new features you are working on to make industry doors impenetrable to sudden shock. Better yet, don't make a claim you can't prove.

ADMISSIONS AND PRECAUTIONS: "I'M THE CORPORATE ATTORNEY AND I'M HERE TO HELP YOU."

In a crisis, you will be working closely with your corporate counsel or company attorney. Although you are both working for the same organization and both want it to survive the crisis at hand, there's a difference in perspective within this relationship.

The attorney wants to minimize legal exposure. He will want to avoid admissions of responsibility or culpability. His counsel will be to stay away from any discussion of the causes of the crisis. His concern is with lawsuits, not public relations.

Your perspective is to get the company past this crisis while retaining the firm's credibility and good will with all your audiences, not the few who are angry enough to sue.

Both points of view have validity. It's your responsibility to sharpen this difference for management because it is unlikely the lawyer will think that broadly. Management needs to realize that public relations as well as legal interests are important to the long-term survival of the organization. Your company's standing in a courtroom is important, but so is your standing in the court of marketplace opinion.

Your job is to release known facts (the who, what, where, and how) and to squelch rumors that can aggravate the crisis. What you should avoid is speculation on causality, i.e., the why.

The lawyer mantra of "no comment," roughly translated, means "We're guilty and our lawyer told us to shut up." Silence or refusing to take reporters' phone calls are not the tactics that will work. Rather, it is reasonable and value-free to say "We are still looking into all aspects of this situation, all developments. We are cooperating with everyone involved. We will continue to collect data, but commenting on causes is premature until we have all the facts."

MEDIA RELATIONS DURING A CRISIS

Stonewalling reporters isn't productive. It's like telling them, "go dig for the smoking gun." The same goes for using that favorite line of all attorneys, "no comment." You might as well put your head in the sand and hope your corporate feathers don't get ruffled. Likewise, telling reporters that "management is unavailable for comment" will probably lead to headlines implying your management is too aloof to talk.

Rumor control is critical. If you want to avoid rumors, get the facts out instead. Simple. The press will seek information through unapproved channels in spite of all your plans and precautions. But if you actively seek out the rumors floating about, you will do much to contain the flow of incorrect information.

If it is apparent (to you and the press) that only scattered information is available on the problem, acknowledge what is being done to gather a more complete picture and to prevent a reoccurrence. Otherwise, strive to issue all the facts in one statement, because a series of facts issued at consecutive times will likely result in a series of headlines.

You don't want a series of headlines about your crisis. You want the coverage of the crisis to end as quickly as possible with the news media confident that your firm has the situation under control. Keep in mind the maxim of former newspaper reporter Mark Twain: "Get your facts first, and then you can distort them as much as you please."

Sometimes, however, a series of announcements will be necessary. Try to limit them to these generic messages:

- Initial discovery or announcement of the problem
- First damage assessment or impact report
- Fixes in place, action taken or in progress

CHECKLIST OF CRISIS MANAGEMENT MARCOM MATERIALS

Media Fact Sheet.   The first thing the local press will ask is, "Who are these people and what is their business?" You need to prepare answers to such basic questions in a variety of lengths including one-sentence versions for broadcast. If you don't do this, reporters and editors will develop their own description and you won't like it.

Brief Crisis Description.   It is essential that you define what happened. Don't let the media or other external audience define it for you. To do so, put it in writing. Describe it in several variations of length so that the media can easily fall back on your descriptions: Use 10 to 20 words for broadcast headlines, 25 to 50 words for newspaper briefs, and 75 to 100 words for in-depth details. Keep in mind that the written word tends to carry more credibility. The discipline of doing this will also help you when you have a reporter and microphone in your face.

Crisis Location Description.   This will vary depending on the type of crisis and if it was in one locale, one office, one customer site, etc. In the case of injuries, information should include plant layout, number of employees on each shift, location of first aid stations and showers, location of lunch rooms, summary of fire sprinkler status, and so on.

List of Distributors or Dealers.   This may or may not be appropriate to every crisis situation, but such a list is a staple element for non-crisis communications as well.

Financial Summary.   Unless you're a publicly traded company, this is a voluntary disclosure. You don't have to reveal finances. But stating that revenues in FY 96, for example, were in excess of $20 million may be a route that doesn't give away too much.

Photos.   Color and black-and-white photos of your executive staff, and black-and-white photos of the buildings in each location. If the crisis involves a building, someone in the print media is likely to ask for a picture of the building.

- Closure: it is now under control or over; precautions and preventions for the future

The other basic element of productive media relations is to respect the special competitive nature of reporters' environment. Whether newsroom managers want to admit it or not, a quota system of sorts operates with their reporting staff. Each reporter, over the long term, has to justify the expense of keeping him in the field. To do so, each reporter must deliver a certain amount of news that is ready for publication or airing.

If a crisis hits, this pressure to produce is severe. Such a time is probably not one in which you can expect friends in the media to return favors.

Similarly, don't preface your comments with the disclaimer "off the record" and expect it will gain you protection. Acknowledge their pressure and deal with the media fairly and equitably. And quickly. Reporters' calls should be returned immediately or they may write the story with the unfortunate line "Acme Inc. wasn't returning our calls as of deadline time."

Keep a media log book to list reporter calls and check them off when completed. Press handouts should include a media fact sheet that answers all the rudimentary questions about your organization. But avoid bulking out press kits just to hand reporters something that just looks substantive. Reporters are under deadline; they don't want to flip through 100 pages to find the five pages they need to write or tell a story. You should prepare informative graphics that help tell your story, but don't delay responding to media calls just because you haven't finished producing some charts or diagrams or schematics. Remember, they are all competing and working with inflexible deadlines.

Some reporters will want to talk with industry experts outside your company. In your crisis team, develop a list of knowledgeable experts whom you believe could help the media interpret your story. Such an expert won't be the company's voice or spokesperson, per se, but they could substantially help calm the waters for you. It is far more preferable for you to offer such names to the press than for reporters to dig up someone whose knowledge is old or limited. Which do you prefer?

Access to the crisis site is important to the news media. However, as with any nonemployee, you have the right to regulate where people go and how they are supervised. The news media understand that and the potential liabilities involved. Thus, you may well have to designate a member of the crisis management task force as the media tour guide. It should be your marketing communications manager or other person capable of answering detailed questions about the facility.

It may be necessary to set up a temporary media/press room for journalists. It shouldn't be near your situation room. You will need to provide some temporary phone lines, output devices, and a fax machine. Make sure the room is easy to find, is in a low-exposure place in your building, and is close to ample parking.

AFTER THE CRISIS: REFINING PLANS FOR THE FUTURE

It's over and you would like to get back to life as it was. Before you do, however, gather the task force together for one last meeting in the situation room. This last meeting has a two-part goal: critique the crisis management against the original contingency plan and then update the plan accordingly.

Other fixes may be in order. If the crisis involved something in the public interest, you may want to work with a community group involved in that interest. For example, ground or stream contamination from a plant wastewater outlet will surely irritate the local community. After the problem is corrected, you might offer a scholarship in environmental testing at the local community college, and host the program students for a field trip to show what precautions your plant management is now taking.

However, wait for the crisis to be resolved first. Attaching yourself to a cause before crisis resolution can be perceived as contrived, manipulative, and insincere.

TIPS FOR INTEGRATING YOUR PROGRAM

There's a good argument that product advertising and direct mail should continue as is during a time of crisis, unless of course the crisis hits firmly on the credibility of your product line.

But a crisis is no time to hide, especially if your crisis is handled within the macro context of your overall marketing plan. One tactic you should consider, depending on the crisis, is a new corporate image or corporate awareness advertising campaign. Special fulfillment pieces providing in-depth analysis of the crisis could be the call to action at the end of the ad copy.

In a more severe situation, you may need to ensure wide distribution of your message and crisis action using paid advertising called corporate advertising. This is the ultimate way of controlling the content and spin of the message desired when the media are not providing fair coverage of your crisis.

Earlier in this chapter we advised you to produce a media fact sheet. This is a good item to have regardless of circumstances, but it will save you considerable time during a crisis. Here are some important elements:

1. Main addresses, voice and fax lines
2. Name, titles, office telephones for: marketing communication manager, human resources manager, CFO, attorney, public relations firm, president
3. List of building locations and subsidiary locations
4. Short company history.
5. Senior management list with short biographies for each
6. Short revenue summary for last two years
7. Number of employees by exempt and nonexempt categories, and by whatever departments or functions are important to your industry, e.g., R&D, manufacturing, etc.

Another important piece that you should prepare for the press is a crisis Q&A. It should anticipate the most likely questions they will ask and provide your answers to them. For any outside inquirer, this summary of the most likely questions and your answers to them can often quell the storm before it grows worse.

However, this shouldn't be confused with the internal Q&A that lists the most damning questions and your answers. That's a document you keep to yourselves—just in case someone asks the tough ones. Other advertising collateral and literature that could be useful in a time of crisis include a company backgrounder, product information sheets, and the annual report.

Company Backgrounder and History. This is usually a 5- to 10-page document printed on letterhead to facilitate changes and updates. It should cover how the company started, its ownership, history of product lines, description of distribution, background of management and board of directors, and an analysis of the competition.

Product Information Sheets or Data Sheets. If the crisis involves some failure of a product, there will be a need for extra copies of the relevant product information (PI) sheet.

Annual Report. The annual report can be a handy piece in a crisis because it usually is designed to showcase successes and new products and key corporate messages. Note: embargo 100 copies of each year's annual report in a locked file cabinet for emergency use only.

With all this printed material, you inherit a fulfillment problem during the pressure of the crisis. It may be too much for the receptionist or your secretary, and too risky for a temporary employee.

Scout now before the storm. Identify a local database/fulfillment firm that can maintain your database and handle order fulfillment from advertising, the 800 telephone line, and other sources. Remember, the speed of fulfillment is worth the cost of the service, and many such firms can really do it less expensively than you can.

If you have developed a precise database of target audiences, you can use direct response to get the crisis explanation in the hands of the right people. But their responses will tell you how well the explanation is working. If they choose to call the 800 crisis line, it's because of curiosity and concern. If callers are still unsatisfied, notations should be made of what additional information they need. Such calls from customers should be logged electronically so field reps know who needs a personal visit.

The respondents should have a number of options available on the mailers, including a personal return call from management—an option you would likely reserve for the largest customers only.

Exhibit marketing is an effective sales and marketing tool in good times. Its role increases in times of crisis. The last thing you should do after a crisis, especially a product crisis, is to cancel a planned show. An exhibit provides a complete sensory assurance that you have moved on and that you are here to talk about it. Bring to the show the key players in the crisis management task force. Dealers and customers will be eager to hear about the fix from those who were in the action. The net message effect of such forthright accessibility is simple: "It was bad, yes, but we fixed it and here's how. We've moved on. But we're still the same good guys."

This provides the opportunity to showcase recovery, solution, and the future. Whether at a trade show or back home, even formalize the opportunity with a breakfast meeting and a speaker tackling the subject head on.

Companies that are respected in the local community are often given more benefit of the doubt in crisis situations. Sponsoring an annual charity event, as a part of your overall community relations program, gives you the visible perception of being a good corporate citizen.

Such a local perception might prompt an editor or reporter to pause before he pounces, or at least listen more patiently to your explanation of the crisis. Such sponsorships also improve employee perceptions of the company as well as the perceptions held by potential job applicants in the community. Ideally, choose a charity or cause that can be tied thematically with what your company does. We urge, however, that you not initiate a sponsorship in the midst of a crisis or it is likely to be perceived as contrived and insincere.

MEASUREMENT AND EVALUATION

The obvious element you want to measure in a crisis is audience satisfaction that your firm has handled the crisis and business has returned to normal. But you need to measure several audiences. Employees should be surveyed early to determine their comfort level. They may well have suggestions that can be incorporated into the revised crisis management plan. But it is essential that employees who are in regular contact with customers be satisfied that the firm has closure on the dilemma. If they are not satisfied, customers will easily sense it.

The media are relatively easy to assess since their broadcast and editorial comments will indicate their satisfaction level. If suspicion is apparent in the coverage, then calls to the reporters should be made to see what additional information, interviews, or reassurance they need. Media coverage that largely uses your press statements or runs management interviews fairly are a good indication that your story is believed. Negative editorials and requests for on-site follow-up interviews are largely a sign that the media sense a deeper story or perhaps a cover-up of important informa-

THE INTEL PENTIUM CHIP ERROR

Many marketers were very surprised how the Pentium calculation error problem unfolded in 1994. The issue was a blemish on the record of a company that stands for high quality and "high output management," as Intel president Andy Grove calls it. What's more, it is difficult to find a business-to-business company anywhere in the world that values marketing and public relations higher than Intel. Silicon Valley PR guru Regis McKenna was for many years a member of Intel's board of directors.

To review, certain professionals who used precise mathematical calculations in their work noticed that Pentium-based computers would miscalculate divisions in minute decimal point values. A Virginia professor posted an inquiry on the Internet to see if others noticed the same problem. Many did. Intel initially responded by asserting that the problem was highly remote and, therefore, it would replace chips for only those who could prove they used such division calculations.

But IBM suddenly stopped shipping PCs with Pentium chips, and the influential Gartner Group urged clients to postpone purchases. In the end, Intel agreed to replace all Pentium chips free and took a $475 million charge against their fourth quarter earning in 1994.

Again, keep overall goals in mind. Remember the overall context of the messages you are sending to your target audiences. If Intel's main message was the speed and quality of its chips, then perhaps they should have offered to replace all Pentium chips immediately, because what Pentium PC user wasn't just a little bit worried that his next spreadsheet calculation for the annual budget might have a similar problem? Remember, according to Tom Peters, perception is all there is.

Intel was probably correct in its assertion that most PC users wouldn't have to worry about this small flaw. What's more, nearly all chips and software have bugs, which is why Intel's competitors crafted their response promotions very carefully.

You can do everything we recommend in this chapter and have award-winning crisis management plans, but we cannot guarantee for you that something unfortunate won't happen. It happened to Intel, but the company recovered quickly.

---

tion. Field sales reps always look for excuses to call on a customer, and a crisis is surely not a time to hide from a customer who is likely to find out elsewhere. Reps can make a quick telephone field survey to determine who needs more attention.

Another measure of how successfully you've handled the crisis is the stock market. (In this regard, be sure to read the chapter on financial relations in this book.) The price of your stock may be adversely affected by a crisis, and can be badly hit if the perception is that the crisis was mishandled. Compare your pre-crisis stock value and your post-crisis stock value. How do these prices compare to the year's high and the year's low? How are analysts commenting, and have they changed their recommendations? If they are recommending that clients drop your stock, then you have more work to do.

RESOURCES

Note: Many of the resources in Chapter 16 on financial public relations are also appropriate to this chapter.

1. *Crisis Management Report* is a newsletter published by Remy Publishing Company, 350 West Hubbard Street, Suite 350, Chicago IL 60610. Telephone 312-464-0300. Fax 312-464-0166.
2. Crisis Communication and Media Interview Training Workshop. Produced by Charles Graves Associates, 258 Ensign Vista Drive, Salt Lake City, UT 84103. Two-day workshop that makes its way around the country. Cost in 1994: $595. Call 801-532-6688.
3. Marconi J. (1992). *Crisis Marketing: When Bad Things Happen to Good Companies.* Chicago: Probus Publishing Company and the American Marketing Association. This 216-page book is the one to get if you want more depth beyond our chapter on the subject. Marconi, a Chicago advertising executive, delivers the goods with a conversational and common sense approach. He also takes time to discuss crisis marketing in the context of pre- and post-crisis and the overall marketing plan you should have in place.
4. Mitroff, I. and T. Pauchant (1990). *We're so Big and Powerful Nothing Bad Can Happen to Us: An Investigation of America's Crisis Prone Corporations.* Secaucus, NJ: Birch Lane Press/Carol Publishing.
5. Dilenschneider, R. L. (1990). *Power and Influence: Mastering the Art of Persuasion.* Englewood Cliffs, NJ: Prentice Hall Press. Hill and Knowlton's former president/CEO discusses many aspects of influence, both personal and professional. His coverage of financial public relations and crisis management is insightful.
6. Gershman, M. (1990). *Getting It Right the Second Time.* Reading, MA: Addison Wesley Publishing Co. Gershman's book discusses crisis situations, but also market misjudgments, and how some marketers turned from failure to success in a second attempt.

NOTES

1. Boschee, J. A. (July 1987). "Control Data's Crisis Control Team." *Management Review,* pages 14–15.
2. Werner, L. R. (August 1990). "When Crisis Strikes Use a Message Action Plan." *Public Relations Journal,* pages 30–31.

Marketing Information Platform (MIP)™ Sample Template

The Marketing Information Platform (MIP)™ is the outcome of the first four steps of the marcom timetable discussed in Chapter 3. It can be created annually or for each project.

The MIP helps you define what the real core problem is and determine what the real marketplace perceptions are right now. Unless those are identified and precisely stated, it doesn't much matter how many awards your brochures, ads or exhibits win.

It is also a consensus builder. The MIP helps identify differing views within the organization. Once consensus is attained, it is important that everyone sign off on the MIP so that it can do the job as its name implies, i.e., function as a platform for all marketing communications. In that role, it also becomes a tool to help maintain marcom discipline and achieve seamless communications.

The template should be adapted for your own organization's use. Ask each of the people involved with developing the marketing plan to submit an MIP, filling out those sections which are applicable to them. There are other pieces of information which are unique to your organization or industry which should also be included; make sure to add them. Compile a composite MIP formulated from all of the responses and re-circulate for evaluation and feedback. Draft a final document to take to the summit meeting.

The first time your company compiles an MIP, it may seem like a long, involved and somewhat tedious process. Each time the MIP is reworked, the process becomes simpler, the result more detailed.

1. **Problem Statement.** What's the marketing problem to be solved?
   a. What type of problem is it?
      (1) Is it an "above-the-ground" surface problem?
      (2) Is it a "below-the-ground" surface problem?
   b. Fully and precisely state the problem.
      (1) What's known
      (2) What's unknown

(3) What needs to be known?

c. What's the reality of the marketplace?

2. Situational Analysis

a. Company Background

(1) What is it that we sell? This should be stated in generic terms rather than traditional marketing "hype."

(a) Differentiate attributes, advantages and benefits by targets, e.g., prospects, customers, influencers, decision makers, users, etc.

(2) What is our "value-added"?

(3) What's our current mission statement?

(4) What are the specific markets or niches our company or product occupies?

(a) Primary markets, domestic and international, e.g., North American, South American, Pacific, European

(b) Secondary markets, domestic and international, e.g., North American, South American, Pacific, European

(c) Provide a marketplace overview and analysis of respective market shares in these markets.

b. Product/Service or Market Positioning

(1) How are we positioned today from the outside perspective? How does the marketplace currently perceive our company, products?

(a) Describe the market need and how our product/service or market promotion meets this need. What is it we do for a customer, i.e., from his or her point of view?

(b) Describe the attributes, advantages, and benefits that we want our customers to most readily identify with the product/service or market promotion.

(c) Differentiate attributes, advantages, and benefits by targets, e.g., prospects, customers, influencers, decision makers, users, etc.

(2) How are we positioned today from our internal perspective? How do we currently perceive our company, products? (Use the same elements as in the previous section.)

(3) Where do we want to be positioned in the future?

(a) How do we want the company and products to be perceived? What are the perceptual targets?

(b) What is needed to get there, i.e., what changes must be made in the current corporate plan, current marketing program, current sales plan?

(4) Where is the market for our products/services heading? Are we heading in the same direction?

    c. Who is the competition in each major market or for each major target segment?
      (1) Rank the top five companies.
      (2) What are the strengths and weaknesses of each?
    d. What are major historical benchmarks in our company that have had impact on market perceptions or confusion, product loyalty, or customer decisions?
    e. Product/Service Marketing Calendar
      (1) List all rollouts, upgrades, events, announcements, etc., foreseen for the next 12 months. Use a 12-month planning calendar.

3. Marcom Objective(s). How does marcom fit into the overall marketing strategy?
    a. What are the specific, measurable marcom goals that will have to be achieved in order for the Marketing Objective(s) to be reached? Example of a measurable marcom objective: To achieve 60 percent awareness of new product/service offerings among the target audience within six months of introduction.
      (1) For an annual MIP, what are the marketing objectives for next year? Three years from now? Five years from now? Ten years from now?
    b. What are the short- and long-term objectives for each customer segment? Differentiate between targets, e.g., prospects, customers, influencers, decision-makers, users, etc.
      (1) What should the marketing plan be for each market or target segment?
      (2) What should the product direction/product development plan be for each market or target segment?
      (3) What should the sales plan be for each market or target segment?
      (4) What should the marcom plan to support these base plans be for each market or target segment?
    c. What are the internal marcom objectives?

4. Target Market Profile. Who are the customers?
    a. Identify and describe the target(s), including typical types and sizes of business, and product/service usage patterns.
      (1) What's the discounted net lifetime value for each?
    b. Identify the specific buying center(s) or individual(s) who should be targeted. This could include the buyer, the end user or local executives as well as corporate decision makers who have to make a purchase decision.
      (1) Are these buyers or buying centers; decision-makers; influencers; end users?
      (2) Describe the target, including demographics, psychographics, and infographics of these individuals or buying centers.

(3) What are the "hot buttons" for these individuals or buying centers that help them make their purchase decision?

(4) What is the average sales cycle for these individuals or buying centers?

(5) What trade shows do they attend? What trade publications do they read?

c. Survey research results: Have you done any mail or phone surveys of prospects or customers to determine their "top of mind" perceptions of your company and your competition? If so, what are the perceptions that can be leveraged or must be overcome?

d. Media & Media Relations.

(1) Which media, materials have traditionally worked best with target audiences?

(2) How would you characterize your relationship with the key reporters/editors covering your industry?

(3) How do they describe your company?

5. Marcom Strategy(ies). Strategies are the "how to" meet the Marcom Objectives.

a. What is the current marcom strategy?

b. What should the strategy be? Be specific.

Example of a marcom strategy: Coordinate a regional product launch utilizing a special event utilizing a direct mail invitation-only campaign and supported by public relations and sales promotions.

c. Which marcom tools would be most appropriate for the audience? For example,

(1) Sales collaterals, e.g., Generic overview brochure; Rate sheets; User's guide; Technical report; Sales brief; Testimonial brochure

(2) Sales promotions

(3) Advertising, e.g., TV ad; Radio spot; Trade print ad; Print media

(4) Direct response, e.g., Prospect mailing; Fulfillment; Customer referral

(5) Public relations, e.g., Press releases; Press kit; Press conference

(6) In-bound Customer Service Center contacts; provide CSRs with company alerts via FAXes, e-mail, newsletters, sales briefings, training sessions, etc.

(7) Trade shows

(8) Special Events

(9) Other marcom activities

d. Prioritize based on research, market knowledge and revenue potential.

6. Creative Message Strategy(ies)

a. Why should buyers purchase our company's product(s)/service(s)?

(1) Describe the specific competitive advantages we have over our competitors.

b. Why should buyers purchase our company's product/service solution?

(1) Provide an honest, straightforward statement about the most important reasons our company is the best choice to meet the customer's needs.

(2) Provide a bullet list of key features and benefits.

    (a) Provide quantitative data, facts where possible, not simply subjective impressions.

    (b) Provide specific competitive advantages, if applicable, or indicate that the company's base positioning statement is the best message.

    (c) Features: a characteristic or quality of a product or service. Practice writing features as descriptive nouns, e.g., 24-hour toll-free customer service line.

- Primary features: those desired by most of the buyers
- Secondary features: desired by smaller segments of the target

    (d) Are any features unique to our product(s)/service(s), i.e., not currently duplicated?

- How do these unique features help the customer do the job that your competitors cannot claim? Do prospects know this?
- How is the buyer able to leverage these features to make them more efficient, effective?

    (e) Benefits: what the user derives from the feature. Practice writing features using verbs, e.g., provides immediate response to customer needs.

- Primary benefits: desired by most of the buyers. The rule of thumb is to develop a half-dozen primary benefits for each feature.
- Secondary benefits: desired by smaller segments of the target. For each feature, at least three secondary benefits should be listed.

    (f) Are any benefits unique to our product(s)/service(s), i.e., not currently duplicated?

- How do these unique benefits help the customer do the job that your competitors cannot claim? Do prospects know this?
- How is the buyer able to leverage these benefits to make them more efficient, effective?

(3) Here is how the product(s)/service(s) work(s).

    (a) Provide a simple explanation about how the product(s)/service(s) actually work(s).

(b) Provide diagrams, when applicable.
  c. "Here is how our product(s)/service(s) can help your business."
    (1) Answer the age-old question the customer will ask: "What's in it for me if I buy your product(s)/service(s)?" Focus on the benefits that will solve the customer's business problems or help the customer become more competitive in its industry.
  d. Provide a brief description of how a current customer benefited from our product(s)/service(s). If possible, use the customer name and/or testimonial.
  e. What are the limitations of our product(s)/service(s)? Be honest, be candid.
    (1) Do competitors exploit this weakness in (a) their marketing communications and (b) on sales calls?
    (2) Are prospects and customers aware of this weakness?
  f. Creative guidelines.
    (1) General design considerations
      (a) Are there any design or creative mandates that your audience is sensitive to?
      (b) What taglines, slogans or logos could we use for marcom materials? Is the logo registered and unchangeable?
      (c) Do you have an 800 number for ads, for media calls or other outside audiences?
      (d) What trademarks, service marks, copyrights should be used?
      (e) Do you currently have a company or product tag line used in advertising?
      (f) Do you have a show theme for trade shows that dictates exhibit design? Do you own an exhibit and, if so, how modular is it?
    (2) Graphics: Are there any "hard" preferences? i.e., what should be used and what, on the contrary, should be avoided vis-a-vis photography, illustrations, colors, design formats, etc.?
      (a) Should the content generally be verbally oriented, visually or a combination?
      (b) Should the style and design be traditional or contemporary, technical or conversational?
      (c) What's the customer's preferred graphics style: do photos have more impact or illustrations?
      (d) What color(s) best support the creative message?
    (3) Copywriting: Are there any recommendations on copy styles, e.g., conversational, confrontational, formal, technical, non-technical, interview style or other approaches to copy? Are there legal constraints, especially in international advertising or sales materials?

7. **Company boilerplate descriptions.** Helps develop consistent, seamless messages for ads, press releases, trade shows, directories, etc.
   a. Provide a boilerplate description of the company, its product(s)/ service(s). E.g., "Widget Manufacturing, Inc. is. . . ."
      (1) In 25 words or less
      (2) In 50 words or less
      (3) In 100 words or less
   b. Provide "one-voice" statements relating to the company's marketing strategy(ies).
      (1) In 25 words or less
      (2) In 50 words or less
      (3) In 100 words or less
   c. Provide the official company profile statement.
      (1) In 400 words or less.

8. **Marcom tactics for internal strategy(ies).**
   a. Determine applicable internal marcom audiences.
   b. Employee relations
      (1) Have you surveyed employees about their understanding of your product direction, market niche, USP, and goals?
      (2) What is their perception of your firm as an employer, i.e., are they nervous about the industry, or about your future?
      (3) If a trade editor got the typical employee aside and assured confidentiality, what would that employee likely say about the firm?
      (4) Internal communications; e.g., daily, weekly news bulletins or e-mail; newsletters; on-demand on-line bulletin boards; grapevine, etc.
      (5) Corporate communications; e.g., company magazine; company newsletter; on-demand on-line bulletin boards; broadcast FAX. etc.

9. **Marcom Project management checklist**
   See Appendix B

Project Platform
Worksheet

Marcom task: To precisely define the cited problem this project will correct. To think through the proposed solution and suggested medium (e.g., slides, brochure, mailing, meeting, specialty advertising, etc.), and to get consensus on the final plan. On the form that is circulated to the appropriate parties, leave appropriate space for their responses.

PART 1: PROBLEM DEFINITION AND PROJECT RATIONALE

A. What is the basic problem we are trying to correct? What are we really trying to accomplish or solve here?

B. Who is the intended primary audience for this project?

C. Any secondary audience? Can both audiences be served by this project?

D. Objective, i.e., what attitude or behavioral change do we want from this target audience using this project? What do you want the customer to remember or do as a result of seeing this?

E. Why does the requestor think this project will correct the problem?

F. Project's requestor or originator:
Date requested: ⎯⎯⎯⎯⎯⎯⎯⎯⎯⎯⎯⎯⎯⎯⎯⎯⎯
Date request received by Marketing: ⎯⎯⎯⎯⎯⎯⎯⎯⎯⎯

G. Medium or format requested (e.g., slides, printed piece, video, brochure, etc.): ⎯⎯⎯⎯⎯⎯⎯⎯⎯⎯⎯⎯⎯⎯⎯⎯

H. Requested look and feel (e.g., factual versus marketing hype; glossy, established look or young up-start look, data sheet style, etc.):

PART 2: PROJECT EXECUTION

A. Medium or tactic recommended to solve problem: ⎯⎯⎯⎯⎯⎯⎯

B. Format and execution (check as relevant):
   1. Number of pages/slides/units? ⸻
   2. Number of colors ⸻
   3. Price labeled? ⸻
   4. Perforated business reply card? ⸻
   5. Paper stock ⸻ weight desired ⸻
   6. Trim size ⸻
   7. Quantity likely ⸻
   8. How often revised? ⸻
C. What are the critical paths and dependencies affecting completion?
D. Schedule for completion, working backwards:
   1. Requested delivery date: ⸻
      Delivered to: ⸻
   2. To printer or other vendor by: ⸻
   3. Paste-up/mechanical approved by: ⸻
   4. Complete copy/graphics for paste-up by: ⸻
   5. Photography/illustrations completed by: ⸻
   6. Changes/approval of galley type: ⸻
   7. Final copy to typography by: ⸻
   8. Review comp by: ⸻
   9. Revised copy to reviewers by: ⸻
   10. Revised copy due to marcom by: ⸻
   11. Marcom makes copy changes by: ⸻
   12. Design ideas for new comp (if new design requested) to vendor by: ⸻
   13. First-draft copy comp due to marcom by: ⸻
E. What in-house resources are needed for completion?
F. What outside vendors will be needed to complete the project?
G. Copywriting style needed, (i.e., straightforward/formal, conversational/chatty, etc.)
H. Benefits to be spotlighted in project:
I. Types of illustrations needed, i.e., environmental shots, box shots, screen close-ups, boxes with people, simple line art, graphs/charts, lifestyle shots, cartoon?
J. Customer action desired:
   1. What are they going to get from reading/seeing this?
   2. What do we want the audience to do upon reading/seeing this?
K. Primary selling surface (if printed collateral)?
L. Legal considerations, (i.e., copyright citations, offices to be listed, tag line, avoidance of promissories)?

M. Budget:
    1. For production $ _____
    2. For printing/duplication $ _____

N. Miscellaneous notes:

PART 3: SIGN-OFFS:

_____ Project manager
_____ Marcom manager
_____ Product manager
_____ VP/Marketing
_____ VP/Sales
_____ President/CEO

News Release Worksheet

1. What type of announcement is this, e.g., to spotlight news, to use as a trade-show handout, local publicity for a personnel promotion or hiring, etc.?
   a. Product announcement
   b. Strategy announcement
   c. Financial announcement
   d. Acquisition announcement
   e. Personnel announcement
   f. Trade show summary

2. If a product announcement, is the price set and is product literature available to support the release?
   a. Is documentation available?
   b. Photos available?

3. If a strategy announcement, does the release need a rationale statement or "white paper" to support it?
   a. What photos or graphics are necessary to support this announcement?

4. What is the real reason for this announcement? i.e.,
   a. Is it a reaction to a competitor's move?
   b. Just an excuse for putting press kits in the trade show press room?

5. Where is this news item newsworthy?
   a. Only locally?
   b. Industry trades?
   c. National business press?
   d. Other?

6. If nothing else gets coverage or print, what is the minimum, single idea or happening you want covered? Express it in one declarative sentence with no adjectives.

7. Would quotes support the credibility of this announcement, or can it stand on its own? What should be said?

8. Is a sales figure necessary, or any other quantitative value that will substantiate the news?

9. Does the headline and introductory paragraph grasp that single idea or happening?

10. What attachments need to go with the release, or what other literature or information must be ready if the news media calls for additional information?

11. Does this news release require a Q&A for management and/or a rehearsal of answers?

12. Are important financial or investment implications present in this release, requiring it first be sent to your stock exchange representative or surveillance committee prior to distribution on the Dow Jones wire?

13. On the day of release, will the people cited in the "for additional information" line be present to take calls? Who else should be present to support the news announcement?

14. Are all unnecessary adjectives or promotional modifiers removed from the release?

15. Final check:
    a. Is there sufficient rationale to use a news release for this information, or is the newsworthiness suspect enough to use another type of communication?

Trade Show Management Checklist

This is intended to be a checklist guideline; it should be modified, adapted, added to, or shortened depending upon your organization's trade show participation. Leave appropriate space for the requisite information to be provided.

1. Show Summary—General Information
   a. Show name: _____
      (1) Exhibition Site: _____
      (2) Show dates: From: _____ To: _____
      (3) Exhibitor dates: _____ and hours: _____
   b. Specific target audience attending this show (description):
      _____
      (1) Is this audience a primary or secondary audience for us?
   c. Number of exhibitors: _____
   d. Number of attendees: _____
   e. Is this currently a budgeted show for us?   Yes ☐   No ☐

2. Show Exhibitor/Space Requirements
   a. Size of exhibit space required: _____
      (1) Can our current exhibit inventory handle this?   Yes ☐   No ☐
   b. When is space reservation deadline? _____
      (1) space reservation made? _____
   c. Space cost check authorized: _____
      (1) Date check request sent to accounting _____
      (2) Date check sent to show sponsor _____
      (3) Photocopy made: _____
         Sponsor address: _____
   d. Exhibitor registration deadline: _____
      (1) Attention of: _____
         Phone: _____ Fax: _____
   e. Check authorized: _____
      (1) Date check request sent to accounting: _____
      (2) Date check sent to exhibit registration: _____

    (3) Photocopy made: _____

       Address: _____

  f. Exhibit vendor to supervise installation?   Yes ☐   No ☐

  g. Exhibit vendor to supervise dismantle?   Yes ☐   No ☐

  h. Exhibit vendor to handle all shipping?   Yes ☐   No ☐

  i. Exhibit vendor to handle all show book order forms?

    Yes ☐ No ☐

3. Product and Services for Display

Item	Equipment Needed	Person Needed
1.		
2.		
3.		
4.		
5.		
6.		
7.		
8.		
9.		
10.		

4. Personnel Needed

Person	To Arrive	To Depart
1.		
2.		
3.		
4.		
5.		
6.		
7.		
8.		
9.		
10.		

  a. Deadline exhibitor/attendee list must be to show sponsor: _____

    (1) Completed: _____

5. Hotel Arrangements

  a. Hotel selected: _____

    (1) Per room rate: _____ Room type: _____

  b. Hotel AE: _____

    (1) Phone: _____ Fax: _____

    (2) Address: _____

    (3) Guest fax for use upon arrival: _____

  c. Reservations to be done by: _____

    Marketing _____ Sales _____ Travel _____

d. Number of company attenders: _____

e. Central billing approved by hotel?   Yes ☐   No ☐

   (1) Deposit needed?   Yes ☐   No ☐   Amount: $ _____

   (2) Check request sent to accounting on: _____

   (3) Check sent to hotel on: _____

   (4) Photocopy made: _____

6. Exhibit requirements

a. Size of exhibit space: _____

   (1) Orientation of front to entry: _____

   (2) Hall map attached: Yes ☐   No ☐

b. Pop-up ok? Yes ☐   No ☐

   Available when: _____

c. Exhibit vendor notified?   Yes ☐   No ☐

   (1) When: _____

d. CAD lay-out to arrive here on: _____

e. Number of demo stations: _____

f. Number of chairs: _____

g. Number of demo tables: _____

h. Number of pedestals:

i. Registration/reception counter?   Yes ☐   No ☐

j. Graphics required: _____

k. Other special requirements? (Please specify)

7. Exhibit Site Services and Shipping

a. Phone lines (specify requested numbers): _____

   (1) Data: _____

   (2) Voice: _____

   (3) Other (specify): _____

   (4) Phone order deadline: _____

   (5) Date check request sent to accounting: _____

   (6) Date check and form sent to show: _____

b. Electrical services needed:

   (1) Electrical order deadline: _____

   (2) Date check request sent to accounting: _____

   (3) Date check and form sent to show: _____

c. Labor services:

   (1) Exhibit vendor to subcontract labor?   Yes ☐   No ☐

   (2) Does show require exhibitor badges to gain preshow entry?

      Yes ☐   No ☐

   (3) Number of laborers needed: _____

   (4) Date/hours needed: _____

   (5) Date/hours needed: _____

   (6) "Letter of notification to use alternate labor" sent?

d. Drayage:
   (1) Date order form due: ———————————————————
   (2) Date order form sent: ———————————————————
e. Floral service?
   (1) Date order form due: ———————————————————
   (2) Date order form sent: ———————————————————
f. A/V equipment rental? Yes ☐ No ☐
   (1) Date order form due: ———————————————————
   (2) Date order form sent: ———————————————————
g. Computer rental? Yes ☐ No ☐
   (1) Date order form due: ———————————————————
   (2) Date order form sent: ———————————————————
h. Furniture Rental? Yes ☐ No ☐
   (1) Date order form due: ———————————————————
   (2) Date order form sent: ———————————————————
i. Hospitality suite? Yes ☐ No ☐
   (1) Date order form due: ———————————————————
   (2) Date order form sent: ———————————————————
j. Food and beverages? Yes ☐ No ☐
   (1) Date order form due: ———————————————————
   (2) Date order form sent: ———————————————————
k. Shipping services needed? Yes ☐ No ☐
   (1) Exhibit vendor to ship our materials? Yes ☐ No ☐
   (2) Selected shipper: ———————————————————
      (a) A/E: ———————————————————
      (b) Phone: ———————————— Fax: ———————————
      (c) Address: ———————————————————
      (d) Deposit needed? Yes ☐ No ☐
        1) Amount: ———————————————————
      (e) Date check request sent to accounting: ———————————
      (f) Date check sent to shipper: ———————————————
      (g) Photocopy made: ———————————————————
   (3) Items to be shipped separate of crates and exhibit (list):
   (4) Address for preshow shipment: ———————————————
   (5) Convention center address for shipment after set-up begins:
   ———————————————————————————————

8. Exhibit Graphics Requirements

a. Show theme: ———————————————————————
b. Corporation ID available for this size exhibit?
c. Products to highlight:
   (1) ———————————————————————————
   (2) ———————————————————————————

(3) ⎯⎯⎯⎯⎯⎯⎯⎯⎯⎯⎯⎯⎯⎯⎯⎯⎯⎯⎯⎯⎯⎯⎯⎯⎯⎯⎯⎯⎯⎯

(4) ⎯⎯⎯⎯⎯⎯⎯⎯⎯⎯⎯⎯⎯⎯⎯⎯⎯⎯⎯⎯⎯⎯⎯⎯⎯⎯⎯⎯⎯⎯

(5) ⎯⎯⎯⎯⎯⎯⎯⎯⎯⎯⎯⎯⎯⎯⎯⎯⎯⎯⎯⎯⎯⎯⎯⎯⎯⎯⎯⎯⎯⎯

d. Product ID available for this size exhibit?   Yes ☐   No ☐

e. Environmental enlargements?   Yes ☐   No ☐

   (1) Specify: ⎯⎯⎯⎯⎯⎯⎯⎯⎯⎯⎯⎯⎯⎯⎯⎯⎯⎯⎯⎯⎯⎯⎯

   (2) Deadline for inclusion with exhibit shipment: ⎯⎯⎯⎯⎯⎯

9. Promotions/Literature Needed

a. Our show theme: ⎯⎯⎯⎯⎯⎯⎯⎯⎯⎯⎯⎯⎯⎯⎯⎯⎯⎯⎯⎯⎯⎯⎯

b. Staff uniform: ⎯⎯⎯⎯⎯⎯⎯⎯⎯⎯⎯⎯⎯⎯⎯⎯⎯⎯⎯⎯⎯⎯⎯⎯

c. Specialty ad vendor notified?

d. Exhibitor directory

   (1) Copy deadline: ⎯⎯⎯⎯⎯⎯⎯⎯⎯⎯⎯⎯⎯⎯⎯⎯⎯⎯⎯⎯

   (2) Sent on: ⎯⎯⎯⎯⎯⎯⎯⎯⎯⎯⎯⎯⎯⎯⎯⎯⎯⎯⎯⎯⎯⎯⎯

   (3) To: ⎯⎯⎯⎯⎯⎯⎯⎯⎯⎯⎯⎯⎯⎯⎯⎯⎯⎯⎯⎯⎯⎯⎯⎯⎯

   (4) Phone: ⎯⎯⎯⎯⎯⎯⎯⎯⎯⎯⎯⎯⎯⎯⎯⎯⎯⎯⎯⎯⎯⎯⎯

   (5) Fax: ⎯⎯⎯⎯⎯⎯⎯⎯⎯⎯⎯⎯⎯⎯⎯⎯⎯⎯⎯⎯⎯⎯⎯⎯⎯

e. Show daily available?

   (1) Vendor: ⎯⎯⎯⎯⎯⎯⎯⎯⎯⎯⎯⎯⎯⎯⎯⎯⎯⎯⎯⎯⎯⎯⎯

   (2) Phone: ⎯⎯⎯⎯⎯⎯⎯⎯⎯⎯⎯⎯⎯⎯⎯⎯⎯⎯⎯⎯⎯⎯⎯

   (3) Address: ⎯⎯⎯⎯⎯⎯⎯⎯⎯⎯⎯⎯⎯⎯⎯⎯⎯⎯⎯⎯⎯⎯

   (4) Deadline for mechanicals: ⎯⎯⎯⎯⎯⎯⎯⎯⎯⎯⎯⎯⎯⎯

f. Ad agency alerted?

g. Trade journal preshow issue deadlines:

   (1) ⎯⎯⎯⎯⎯⎯⎯⎯⎯⎯⎯⎯⎯⎯⎯⎯⎯⎯⎯⎯⎯⎯⎯⎯⎯⎯⎯⎯

      (a) Mechanical deadline: ⎯⎯⎯⎯⎯⎯⎯⎯⎯⎯⎯⎯⎯⎯

   (2) ⎯⎯⎯⎯⎯⎯⎯⎯⎯⎯⎯⎯⎯⎯⎯⎯⎯⎯⎯⎯⎯⎯⎯⎯⎯⎯⎯⎯

      (a) Mechanical deadline: ⎯⎯⎯⎯⎯⎯⎯⎯⎯⎯⎯⎯⎯⎯

h. Specialty advertising/premium giveaways

   (1) Specialty ad vendor notified?

   (2) Type and quantity (list each):

i. Show literature needed (indicate quantity for each):

   (1) "What's New!" sheet   Quantity ⎯⎯⎯⎯⎯⎯⎯

   (2) Corporate capabilities brochure Quantity ⎯⎯⎯⎯⎯⎯⎯

   (3) Product Catalog   Quantity ⎯⎯⎯⎯⎯⎯⎯

   (4) Product info sheet A   Quantity ⎯⎯⎯⎯⎯⎯⎯

   (5) Product info sheet B   Quantity ⎯⎯⎯⎯⎯⎯⎯

   (6) Others (list each w/quantity)

j. Press kits   Quantity ⎯⎯⎯⎯⎯⎯⎯

   (1) Ship to: ⎯⎯⎯⎯⎯⎯⎯⎯⎯⎯⎯⎯⎯⎯⎯⎯⎯⎯⎯⎯⎯⎯⎯

   (2) Address: ⎯⎯⎯⎯⎯⎯⎯⎯⎯⎯⎯⎯⎯⎯⎯⎯⎯⎯⎯⎯⎯⎯

Legalities of Copywriting

Copy in advertising and collateral literature can sometimes put companies in legal difficulties. All it takes is for one customer to perceive that an advertising claim is false or misleading. In short, the customer claims that he or she bought the product based on the advertising and the copy's claim that the product or service would guarantee some result.

Specifically, advertising copy should not be overly promissory about product availability, product capabilities, or any other product claims that could fail to materialize. Don't say things that are not true. Also, don't make a claim or imply in promotions that your product or service will result in x, y, and z, i.e., all by itself. What if the customer doesn't follow directions or skips steps in implementing your service? That is the customer's fault, not yours—unless the customer perceives a promise or implied guarantee in the copy.

If your corporate attorney dislikes some of the copy for legal reasons, look upon that as a good opportunity to write more creatively. For example, saying "our product incorporates enormous potential" is risky, but less so when revised to say "our product incorporates surprising potential." Surprising really means nothing.

Avoid the following words in copy: profitable, profits, succeed, success, every, everything, always, all, power. These words are inherently promissory. To say your product or service will increase profits is unreasonable, because you can never know how well or how badly the customer will implement what you sold to him or her.

Use qualifiers such as help, assist, augment, or lend a hand. For example, instead of saying "our Acme widget will accomplish x, y, and z in your plant site," say "our Acme widget will <u>help you</u> accomplish x, y, and z in your plant site." You really lose nothing from the ad—except serious exposure.

Be increasingly careful with the following terms: turn-key, fully integrated, partnership. For example, "when you buy our ABC product, you can depend on us to be in partnership with you and your interests." Do you really want customers to think you are a partner ready to assist with loans, shipping, and other requirements of partnership?

If you have independent dealers, be careful about "implied agency." When producing mailers and other co-op promotions, add a disclaimer such as "To find out more about the Acme widget, mail the postage-paid reply card to your Acme dealer. As an independent, value-added consultant, your Acme dealer can provide complete information about Acme products."

The best rule of thumb: when in doubt, seek legal counsel. It's better to have your creative efforts "sanitized" than to suffer the consequences of lawsuits or FTC claims.

Legalities and Trademarks

In these tough economic times, few marketing issues are as important as protecting trademarks. Not only do companies have to watch out for counterfeiters, they also must police usage of their trademarks vigilantly. When properly protected, trademarks can lead to increased sales and market share. Losing them, however, can lead to much embarrassment.

A trademark can be any word, name, symbol, device, or design—or any combination thereof—that is adopted and used by a manufacturer or merchant to identify its goods and distinguish them from goods manufactured or sold by others. (A service mark is used to distinguish services.)

A company that registers its mark can prohibit others from using it anywhere in the country. Trademarks are among a business's most valuable assets—and they should be treated as such.

LOSING YOUR MARK

A company could lose its trademark by failing to renew its registration after 10 years, but that rarely happens. Allowing the trademark to become a generic term referring to the product rather than to the source of the product is more likely—and more difficult to prevent. Shredded wheat, aspirin, cellophane, dry ice, and escalator all were valid and enforceable trademarks that lapsed into common usage over time.

Some steps can be taken to strengthen trademarks, however. Marketing and advertising executives must ensure that the right trademark is chosen, that it is used properly, and that competitors and the general public do not misuse it.

Select a Good One

Choosing a good trademark is the first step in protecting it. Mere descriptive words are difficult to register and protect as trademarks. Thus, "Prime Beef" is less likely to be a valid trademark than "Kodak," a word coined by the company. (One notable exception is TV Guide, which remains protected, in part, because of the trademark owner's diligence.) Using a trademark on more than one product also is a good idea.

Use It Right

A trademark is an adjective and should not be used as a noun or verb. One should say, "Pass me a tissue" or "Pass me a Kleenex tissue"—not "Pass me a Kleenex." "I need to use the IBM computer"—not "I need to use the IBM." "Please make a copy," "Please make a photocopy," or "Please make a Xerox copy"—not "Please xerox this."

Businesses should be sure that they use their own trademarks properly; some companies even have usage guides for employees. They also should use their trademarks properly in all promotional materials. Marks should be in distinctive typefaces and bear the designation ™ for a trademark or ˢᴹ for a service mark if the mark is not registered with the U.S. Patent and Trademark Office. If it is registered, ® or "Reg. U.S. Pat. & Tm. Off." should follow the trademark.

In the court decision many years ago that found "aspirin" to be a generic term, the judge focused on the manufacturer's own label, which read "Bayer—Tablets of Aspirin." He stated that Bayer "itself recognized the meaning which the word had acquired, because the phrase most properly means that these tablets were Bayer's make of the drug known as 'aspirin.'"

Police Third Parties

Third parties that misuse a company's trademark should be informed of their error and asked—or warned—to stop. Policing competitors' advertising, newspaper stories, and even crossword puzzles can reveal such misuse.

Informational advertising that alerts the world to the company's trademark and sets up a policy against misuse may be critical to the trademark owner's attempts to protect its trademarks. Here are excerpts from some informational aids that trademark owners have published in an attempt to protect their trademarks:

- "The word 'Frigidaire' always ends with a capital ® (for the registered trademark designation)."
- "What's in a name? A lot . . . when the name is Kelly®. Kelly is a brand name for temporary help services provided exclusively by Kelly Services Inc. The following are registered trademarks of Kelly services Inc.: Kelly®, Kelly Girl®, Kelly Services®, Nobody Puts Temporaries to the Test Like Kelly®."
- "Don't confuse a weedeater with Weed Eater®. Sometimes people say they want a 'weedeater' when they really want a Weed Eater® brand trimmer. And, while a weedeater might be anything from a voracious goat to a little green creature from a gardener's nightmare, there is only one Weed Eater® brand trimmer. It's America's number one brand of trimmer—the one people ask for time after time."

- "Formica® is a special brand. 'Formica' is the name of a very particular product. It's both a registered trademark and a special brand name. As such, we ask that you use the name Formica® only when referring to our particular brand of products. This protects you as well as us. Because by properly using our name, whenever you ask for Formica brand, you'll be sure of getting the real Formica brand."
- "To all the writers and typists and proofreaders and editors who help us protect our trademark Kleenex® by always starting it with a capital K followed by l-e-e-n-e-x and following it with a proper generic—be it tissue, towels, or diapers—Kimberly Clark says 'Bless you!'"
- "Dear *New York Times:* 8 Down has us puzzled. Let's see, 6 Across is W-A-X-Y. That leaves us with a five-letter word for 'duplicate' beginning with the letter 'X.' Obviously, it couldn't be X-E-R-O-X. That's because 'Xerox' isn't a verb. It's our trademark. As a trademark, it should only be used as a proper adjective followed by the descriptive term, like a Xerox copier, a Xerox printer, a Xerox typewriter, or a Xerox duplicator. But you probably know this already. You of all newspapers are a stickler for this sort of thing. Which still leaves us with the original problem . . . a five-letter word for 'duplicate' beginning with 'X.' Xerox® is a trademark of Xerox Corporation."

BATTLING INFRINGEMENT

A trademark is a form of a monopoly, and owners have the right to stop infringers. Among the factors courts consider when deciding whether confusion exists between trademarks are:

- The degree of similarity between the owner's mark and the alleged infringing mark.
- The strength of the owner's mark.
- The price of the goods and other factors indicative of the care and attention expected of consumers when making a purchase.
- The length of time the defendant has used the mark without evidence of actual confusion.
- The intent of the defendant in adopting the mark.
- The evidence of actual confusion.
- Whether the goods, if they are noncompeting, are marketed through the same channels and advertised via the same media.
- The extent to which the targets of the parties' sales efforts are the same.

- The relationship of the goods in the minds of the public because of the similarity of function.
- Other facts suggesting that the consuming public might expect the prior owner to manufacture a product in the defendant's market.

Similarity Won't Play

The ability of a trademark owner to prohibit competing businesses from using identical or confusingly similar trademarks can be seen in a recent lawsuit filed by Kenner Parker Toys Inc., the owner of the Play-Doh trademark, against Rose Art Industries Inc., which sought registration in 1986 for the mark Fundough for its own modeling compound and related accessories.

The court that decided the case noted that a trademark owner may oppose the registration of any competing mark that—when used on or in connection with the goods of the applicant for a trademark—is likely "to cause confusion or to cause mistake or to deceive."

The test for likelihood of confusion does not focus on similarity of competing marks in the abstract. Rather, it evaluates objective evidence that the competing marks, when used in the marketplace, are likely to confuse the purchasing public about the source of the products.

The court said that "play" and "fun," in the overall context of these competing marks, conveyed a very similar impression. "Both are single syllable words associated closely in meaning. Particularly in the context of a child's toy, the concepts of fun and play tend to merge. In context, the prefixes "play" and "fun" seemed at least as similar as "tree" and "valley" or "island" and "valley," which the court noted had been held to be components of the confusingly similar marks Spice Tree and Spice Valley, in one case, and Spice Island and Spice Valley, in another.

In addition, the single-syllable suffixes "doh" and "dough" sounded the same. "In light of a modern trend to simplify the spelling of 'gh' words, consumers may even perceive one as an interchangeable abbreviation for the other," the court stated, noting some additional factors that support its view that Fundough would be an infringing mark:

- The marks Play-Doh and Fundough were used for practically identical products, namely modeling compounds and related modeling accessories.
- Both Kenner and Rose Art marketed their products in practically identical channels of trade, namely toy outlets.
- Both marks appeared on inexpensive products purchased by diverse buyers without exercising much care.

Finally, the court noted that the multitude of similarities in the trade dress of Play-Doh and Fundough products "crie[d] out for recognition." The color (dominated by yellow), size, and shape of the packaging for both products was the same. Comparable fictitious characters in a hat and a rainbow motif adorned the packaging of both products. And both products featured promotions—discounts, rebates, and the like—in a circle with serrated edges.

The trademarks themselves appeared in the same locations on both products' packages, and instructions and color charts were nearly identical. In its ruling in favor of Play-Doh, the court noted that "[t]hese trade dress features and more—original to Play-Doh—have appeared on products bearing the Fundough mark."

Complaint in Deep Freeze

Just how far can the trademark infringement theory go? Can it protect a novel marketing approach that a competitor imitates? That's the complaint Häagen-Dazs Inc. had several years ago when it filed suit against the producers and distributors of Frusen Glädjé ice cream.

Häagen-Dazs contended that the defendants packaged their product in such a way as to "cash in on the commercial magnetism of the exclusive marketing technique developed . . . by the family which owns and operates Häagen-Dazs." In particular, Häagen-Dazs focused on Frusen Glädjé's ice cream container, charging that the latter had duplicated several features in an effort to appeal to Häagen-Dazs customers and confuse them into believing that Frusen Glädjé was related to the Häagen-Dazs line. The specific features on the container were:

- The phraseology Frusen Glädjé used in reciting its product's ingredients.
- A recitation of the artificial ingredients not contained in the product.
- The manner in which the product was to be eaten to enhance its flavor.
- A two-word, Germanic-sounding name having an umlaut over the letter "a."
- A map of Scandinavia.

Häagen-Dazs contended that Frusen Glädjé intentionally packaged its product in a manner calculated to trade upon the "plaintiff's unique Scandinavian marketing theme." It sought a preliminary injunction to prevent Frusen Glädjé from continuing to use the allegedly infringing container.

The court did not see the merits of Häagen-Dazs's claim. The company's only trademark was for the name "Häagen-Dazs." It held no trademark, nor could it, on the so-called "unique Scandinavian marketing theme" it employed.

"This is simply a vehicle by which the plaintiff has chosen to market its product," the court said, ruling that the names Häagen-Dazs and Frusen Glädjé were "clearly distinguishable." Although it is true that both names contain two words to identify an ice cream product, the court did not find this to be unusual: "So do the names 'Louis Sherry' and 'Dolly Madison.'"

The court also noted that the Häagen-Dazs and Frusen Glädjé names seemed to be of Swedish origin, and, as appropriate in that language, an umlaut appeared over the letter "a." But, it concluded, that was a matter of grammar and not a basis upon which Häagen-Dazs could bring a trademark infringement suit.

The court found it equally apparent that the containers were clearly distinguishable "and would appear so to all but the most obtuse consumer." The coloring and designs of the containers, as well as the shape of the containers themselves, were so different "that only the most unobservant and careless consumer would mistake one product for the other."

Finding that Häagen-Dazs had failed to demonstrate even the remotest possibility of confusion at the consumer level as to the source of Frusen Glädjé's products, the court then rejected Häagen-Dazs's request for an order prohibiting Frusen Glädjé from using its container.

Source: Steven A. Meyerowitz, "Surviving Assaults on Trademarks" in Marketing Management, Vol. 3, No. 1, pp. 44–46.

Business Marketing's "Copy Chasers" Guidelines for Good Advertising

I. THE SUCCESSFUL AD HAS A HIGH DEGREE OF VISUAL MAGNETISM

On average, only a small number of ads in an issue of a magazine will capture the attention of any one reader. Some ads will be passed by because the subject matter is of no concern. But others, even though they may have something to offer, fail the very first test of stopping the reader in his or her scanning of the pages.

Ads perish right at the start because, at one extreme, they just lie there on the page, flat and gray, and at the other extreme, they are cluttered, noisy and hard to read.

An ad should be constructed so that a single component dominates the area—a picture, the headline or the text—but not the company name or the logo.

Obviously, the more pertinent the picture, the more arresting the headline, the more informative the copy appears to be, the better.

II. THE SUCCESSFUL AD SELECTS THE RIGHT AUDIENCE

Often, an ad is the first meeting place of two parties looking for each other.

So there should be something in the ad that at first glance will enable readers to identify it as a source of information relating to their job interests—a problem they have or an opportunity they will welcome.

This is done with either a picture or a headline—preferably both—the ad should say immediately to the reader, "Hey, this is for you."

III. THE SUCCESSFUL AD INVITES THE READER INTO THE SCENE

Within the framework of the layout, the art director's job is to visualize, illuminate and dramatize the selling proposition.

And the art director must take into consideration the fact that the type of job a reader has dictates the selection of the illustrative material. Design engineers work with drawings. Construction engineers like to see products at work. Chemical engineers are comfortable with flow charts. Managers relate to pictures of people. And so on.

IV. THE SUCCESSFUL AD PROMISES A REWARD

An ad will survive the qualifying round only if readers are given reason to expect that if they continue on, they will learn something of value. A brag-and-boast headline, a generalization, an advertising platitude will turn readers off before they get into the message.

The reward that the ad offers can be explicit or implicit, and can even be stated negatively, in the form of a warning of a possible loss.

The promise should be specific. The headline "Less maintenance cost" is not as effective as "You can cut maintenance costs 25%."

V. THE SUCCESSFUL AD BACKS UP THE PROMISE

To make the promise believable, the ad must provide hard evidence that the claim is valid.

Sometimes, a description of the product's design or operating characteristics will be enough to support the claim.

Comparisons with competition can be convincing. Case histories make the reward appear attainable. Best of all are testimonials; "They-say" advertising carries more weight than "We-say" advertising.

VI. THE SUCCESSFUL AD PRESENTS THE SELLING PROPOSITION IN LOGICAL SEQUENCE

The job of the art director is to organize the parts of an ad so that there is an unmistakable entry point (the single dominant component referred to earlier) and the reader is guided through the material in a sequence consistent with the logical development of the selling proposition.

A layout should not call attention to itself. It should be a frame within which the various components are arranged.

VII. THE SUCCESSFUL AD TALKS "PERSON-TO-PERSON"

Much industrial advertising, unlike consumer goods advertising, consists of one company talking to another company—or even to an entire industry.

But copy is more persuasive when it speaks to the reader as an individual—as if it were one friend telling another friend about a good thing.

First, the terms should be the terms of the reader's business, not the advertiser's business. But more than that, the writing style should be simple: short words, short sentences, short paragraphs, active rather than passive voice, no advertising cliches, frequent use of the personal pronoun you. A more friendly tone results when the copy refers to the advertiser in the first person: "we" rather than "the company name."

VIII. SUCCESSFUL ADVERTISING IS EASY TO READ

This is a principle that shouldn't need to be stated, but the fact is that typography is the least understood part of our business.

The business press is loaded with ads in which the most essential part of the advertiser's message—the copy—appears in type too small for easy reading or is squeezed into a corner or is printed over part of the illustration.

Text type should be no smaller than 9 point. It should appear black on white. It should stand clear of interference from any other part of the ad. Column width should not be more than half the width of the ad.

IX. SUCCESSFUL ADVERTISING EMPHASIZES THE SERVICE, NOT THE SOURCE

Many industrial advertisers insist that the company name or logo be the biggest thing in the ad, that the company name appear in the headline, that it be set in bold-face wherever it appears in the copy. That's too much.

An ad should make readers want to buy—or at least consider buying—before telling them where to buy.

X. SUCCESSFUL ADVERTISING REFLECTS THE COMPANY'S CHARACTER

A company's advertising represents the best opportunity it has—better than the sales force—to portray the company's personality—the things that will make the company liked, respected, admired.

A messy ad tends to indicate a messy company. A brag-and-boast ad suggests the company is maker-oriented, not user-oriented. A dull-looking ad raises the possibility that the company has nothing to get excited about, is behind the times, is slowing down.

What we are talking about is a matter of subtleties, but the fact remains: like sex appeal (which is not easy to define), some companies have it, some don't. And whatever it is, it should be consistent over time and across the spectrum of corporate structure and product lines.

Ketchum Public Relations— Pittsburgh's Crisis Marketing Message Action Plan (XYZ Corporation Assumes Filing 9:30 P.M., Friday)

Audience	Core Message(s)	Supporting Message(s)	Phone Calls	Press Interviews	Press Release
Board of Directors					•
Division Presidents	•		•		•
Regulatory Agencies	•		•		•
Plant Management	•		•		•
Key Customers	•		•		
Key Suppliers	•		•		
Key Shareholders	•		•		•
Industry Analysts	•		•		•
Sales Reps					
National Media					•
Local Media					•
HQ Employees		•			
Plant/Div. Employees		•			
Union Officials		•	•		•
Financial Community	•	•			
Other Customers		•			
Other Suppliers		•			
Other Shareholders		•			
Retirees					
Community Influentials	•				•

Letters	Meetings	Advertising	Responsibility	Timing
	•		Chairman, President	Before
			Chairman, President	Friday
			Law, PR*	Saturday
	•	•	Division President	Saturday
•			Division President	Saturday
•			Division President Bank Finance	Saturday
•			Finance, PR (Sr. Mgmt. Backup)	Saturday
			PR, Chairman, President	Saturday Sunday
			Division President	Saturday
			Release: PR Int.:**PR, Chairman, President	Saturday Sunday
		•	Release: PR Int.: PR, Division, President	Saturday Monday
•	•		Letter, Release: PR Meetings: Personnel	Saturday Monday
•	•		Letter: PR Meetings: Plant Manager	Sat., Sun., Mon.
•	•		Calls: LR*** Release: PR	Saturday
			Law, PR	Saturday
			PR (Sign:****Division President)	Saturday
		•	PR (Sign: Division President)	Saturday
			PR (Sign: Chairman, President)	Saturday
			PR (Sign: Personnel)	Saturday
			PR (Sign: Plant Mgr., Chairman, President)	Saturday

* Public Relations   ** Internal   *** Labor Relations   ****Signature(s)

Source: Reprinted with permission of Ketchum Public Relations/Pittsburgh.

Event Marketing Site Inspection Checklist

The following checklist is adapted from material provided by Serena Leiser, Director of Conference Services for the College of the Holy Cross in Worcester, MA, who has had considerable experience in corporate meeting planning. It is a thorough checklist for evaluating all aspects of the meeting/conference centers, from the meeting facility itself to the hotel rooms. You could organize an event without a checklist, but we suggest you avoid such risk.

PART 1: MEETING SPACE CHECKLIST

Obtain a complete floor plan of all public meeting space in the facility. While touring the facility make sure that all obstructions in the meeting rooms (e.g., pillars) are indicated on the floor plan. What is the total number of rooms when all movable walls are closed?

1. Physical appearance
   a. What is the general condition of the meeting rooms, e.g., carpets, walls, ceiling?
      (1) Are banquet tables and chairs in good condition?
   b. Can all meeting rooms be secured?
   c. Is the pre-function area adequate for registration and/or coffee breaks?

2. Access
   a. Are meeting rooms easy to find?
      (1) Is signage adequate?
   b. Are restrooms located conveniently to the meeting rooms?
   c. Where are fire exits in relation to meeting rooms?
      (1) Does the facility have a written emergency evacuation plan, and how often are employees drilled on the plan?
   d. Are passageways and doors to and from the facility, and within it, compatible with ADA rules for handicapped access?
   e. What is the accessibility of freight elevators to meeting rooms?

 f. Where is the banquet kitchen in relation to rooms being used for meal functions?
  (1) Is it close enough without being noisy?

3. Lighting and heating
 a. Are all meeting rooms well lighted?
  (1) Does the meeting room have individual light controls?
  (2) Where are they?
 b. Do all rooms have individual heating controls?
  (1) Where are they?
  (2) Make sure the ventilation system is on while you are evaluating the room. Is it noisy?

4. Phones and electrical
 a. Is there an adequate number of dedicated phone lines that can bypass the PBX so that computer/modem-based demonstrations will work effectively?
 b. Are there sufficient public phones in the area of the meeting rooms?
 c. Is there an adequate number of electrical outlets for access by laptop users?

5. Audiovisual concerns
 a. Do all rooms have built-in sound systems and are acoustics good?
 b. Do any rooms have furnishings that deter from any type of audiovisual presentations (e.g., mirrors, chandeliers, etc.)?
 c. Is ceiling height of the meeting rooms adequate for A/V presentations?

6. External noise
 a. Are the service corridors next to the meeting room carpeted to hold down noise?
 b. How many meeting rooms are serviced from this corridor and could the traffic be disturbing?

PART 2: AIRPORT CHECKLIST

1. Arrival
 a. Distance of gates to baggage claim
 b. Signage to baggage claim
 c. Distance of baggage claim to ground transportation
 d. Baggage carts available
 e. Porters available
 f. Signage for ground transportation
 g. Condition and appearance of airport
 h. Time from airport to hotel
 i. Cost of airport shuttle and taxi
 j. Does hotel have comp shuttle?

2. Departure

   a. Curbside check-in
   b. Porters available
   c. Signage to gates
   d. Food outlets
   e. Seating in gate areas
   f. Nonsmoking areas
   g. Lockers

PART 3: HOTEL CHECKLIST

1. Entrance

   a. Condition of carriage entrance
   b. Is entrance area cluttered?
   c. Is parking available at entrance during check-in?
   d. Is there a doorman monitoring traffic?
   e. Hours doorman is on duty
   f. Appearance and attitude of doorman
   g. Did doorman direct you to registration desk?
   h. Is valet parking available?
   i. Cost of valet parking
   j. Cost of self park

2. Lobby/front desk

   a. Condition of lobby
   b. Lighting
   c. Sufficient area for seating
   d. Noise level
   e. Signage
   f. Front desk appearance
   g. Uniforms
   h. Is there sufficient room for a large check-in?
   i. Front desk personnel attentive and informative
   j. Is front desk well lighted?
   k. Speed and accuracy of registration

3. Bell staff

   a. Is bell service available 24 hours?
   b. Is bell service attentive?
   c. Does bell staff explain room accommodations and service?
   d. Does bell staff point out fire exits?
   e. Does bell staff offer to get ice?
   f. Is bell staff neat, clean, well-tailored?
   g. Does bell staff put luggage on stand in room?

4. Corridors
a. Are corridors clean and well lighted?
b. Are room numbers visible?
c. Directional signage
d. Are there room service trays in hallways?
e. Are fire exits clearly marked (where is signage)?
f. Are hallways air conditioned?
g. Vending machine locations—are they well marked?

5. Departure
a. Bell staff
   (1) Courteous when called
   (2) Came within time given
   (3) Knowledgeable on transportation to airport
b. Front Desk
   (1) Was check-out area well organized (enough room for people waiting, stanchions, etc.)?
   (2) Was desk staffed sufficiently for number of people checking out?
   (3) How long was wait?
   (4) Was front desk clerk courteous?
   (5) Was bill correct?
   (6) If error on bill, was it handled in a courteous manner?
   (7) How long did actual check-out procedure take?
   (8) Was desk clerk knowledgeable on airport transportation?
c. Does hotel have express check-out, TV check-out?
d. Is a late check-out available?

6. Transportation to airport
a. Type used
b. Quality
c. Cost
d. Efficiency

7. Restaurant(s)
a. Type of restaurant
b. Capacity
c. Waiting time
d. Host/maitre d'
e. Menu displayed outside restaurant
f. Length of time from being seated until waiter's acknowledgment
g. Set-up of table
h. Overall cleanliness
i. Attitude and efficiency of personnel
j. Variety of menu
k. Cost appropriate for quality

    l. Waiter knowledgeable of menu items and preparation
    m. Waiter available when needed
    n. Nonsmoking section available
    o. Food prepared to any specifications
    p. All menu items available
    q. Length of time from ordering to being served
    r. Noise level of restaurant
    s. Water refilled
    t. Coffee refilled
    u. Ambience of restaurant
    v. Dirty dishes removed on a timely basis
    w. Bill presented on a timely basis
    x. Bill correct

8. Room service
    a. How many rings until phone answered?
    b. Attitude of person taking order
    c. Were all items ordered available?
    d. Were alternatives suggested for items not available?
    e. Was person knowledgeable on items on menu?
    f. Was approximate delivery time given?
    g. Did order come in time given?
    h. Professionalism of room-service waiter
    i. Did food come on tray or table?
    j. Was order correct?
    k. Was presentation pleasing?
    l. Were all condiments included?
    m. Was food still hot (cold)?
    n. Quality of food
    o. Value for price
    p. Gratuity included
    q. Any service charge

PART 4

1. Guest rooms
    a. What is first impression of room, is it inviting?
    b. Are nonsmoking rooms available?
    c. Air conditioning/heat controls and quality
    d. Safety locks and peep holes on doors
    e. Is lighting adequate and switches convenient?
    f. Drapes
        (1) Black out
        (2) Sheers
        (3) Smooth to open and close

    (4) Clean/torn
- g. Is furniture arrangement convenient?
  - (1) Desk with phone
  - (2) Comfortable place to read
  - (3) Place to sit to watch TV other than bed
- h. Phone
  - (1) How many and where
  - (2) Pads and pencils by each phone
  - (3) Phone books
  - (4) Instructions on phone charges
- i. Guest services directory
- j. City information guide
- k. Luggage stands
- l. Closet
  - (1) Adequate size
  - (2) Sufficient hangers, skirt hangers
  - (3) Regular or "hotel" hangers
- m. Is there a full-length mirror in room?
- n. Condition of bed linen
- o. Is there a third sheet?
- p. Extra pillows and blankets in closet?
- q. Is bed comfortable?
- r. Radio/clock/cable/in-room movies
- s. Mini-bar/prices
- t. What "extras" are in room?
- u. Is turn-down service provided?
- v. Is bathroom clean and well lighted?
- w. Are tub and sink discolored or cracked?
- x. Do stoppers in sink and tub work?
- y. Height of shower head
- z. Water pressure/temperature
- aa. Sufficient towels
- bb. Are towels within reach of shower?
- cc. Condition of shower curtain
- dd. Toilet clean, well functioning, and quiet
- ee. Are bath mat and rug provided?
- ff. Amenities provided
- gg. Are the following items in room or available from housekeeping:
  - (1) Iron and ironing board
  - (2) Bed boards
  - (3) Hair dryer
  - (4) Curling irons
  - (5) Non-allergenic pillows
  - (6) Lost luggage kits

De Bonis & Peterson Results/Efforts (R/E) Ratio™: Analysis of Marcom Results versus Effort Expended in Marcom Dollars

Before an analysis of marcom results versus marcom dollars expended can be completed, there are some basic assumptions which must be understood and accepted; these are discussed in Chapter 5.[1]

CASE SETUP AND DEFINITIONS

Deberson Manufacturing produces widgets and plans to launch an aggressive marketing campaign in the Southeastern United States. The marcom program supporting this marketing strategy is scheduled to take place in four sequential phases.

The *marcom mix* for each phase is based on the marcom objectives. The timeline for each phase could be weeks, month(s), quarter(s), or year(s), depending on the marketing strategy.

Phase 1 includes a leadoff public relations campaign built around sponsorship of a special cultural event, supported by targeted advertising in radio and trade publications intended to generate sales leads, and a follow-up direct mail fulfillment piece.

Phase 2 includes a continuing public relations campaign, an outbound telemarketing effort for a sales promotion which results in a second fulfillment piece being mailed.

Phase 3 is built around another sales promotion supported by a telemarketing campaign, additional trade ads, and support of another regional special event.

Phase 4 is targeted primarily at competitors' customers using a direct mail invitation to a regional industry trade show, supported by a sales promotion.

The **Revenue/Effort Analysis** is based on the notion that a behavioral return on investment (ROI) is defined as the ratio of results (purchasing behavior) to efforts (in this case, marcom dollars expended).

The Marcom Factor assesses behavioral ROI: did the target act based upon the marcom efforts? The marcom factor is derived through marketing research. For example, if four out of 10 buyers rated the importance of information received as a result of marcom activities to their buying decision as eight or higher on a 10-point scale ("1" being not at all important to the purchasing decision and "10" being extremely important), the Marcom Factor would be 40 percent. This is interpreted to mean that 40 percent of the sales made were as a result of or were significantly influenced by the marcom.

There are two results to efforts ratios which can be analyzed. One is revenue generated by marcom efforts; how much revenue was generated for each marcom dollar expended. And the other is profit generated by marcom efforts; how much profit was generated for each marcom dollar expended.

The analysis assumes a cumulative effect of marketing communications. The buyer in Phase 2 of the marcom campaign has already been exposed to one or more messages in Phase 1. The results/effort ratio shouldn't be calculated simply on the basis of the Phase 2 activities, but should amortize the results versus the efforts over both phases. This is the cumulative analysis calculated for each phase.

It also assumes that it is less expensive to acquire the first relationships in any marketplace, that the cost of acquiring subsequent relationships increases the further the company penetrates a market.

ANALYSIS

Phase 1—Deberson Widgets
Target: 100M businesses in the Southeast Region

Marcom Mix

1	2	3	4	5	6	7
Radio	Print	Direct Mail	PR	Special Event	Total	Σ Marcom
$33,000	$42,000	$35,000	$15,000	$7,000	$132,000	$132,000

Revenue/Effort Analysis

	11	12	13	14	15	16
	Units Sold	Marcom Factor	Marcom Sales	Revenue/ Unit	Marcom Revenue	Marcom Revenue/ Effort
					[13 × 14]	[15/6]
Phase 1	20,000	40%	8,000	$65	$520,000	$3.94

At the end of Phase 1, a total of 20,000 units had been sold. The marcom factor was 40 percent; 8,000 of the sales were the result of or significantly influenced by the marcom campaign. For each marcom dollar spent, $3.94 in revenue was generated.

Profit/Effort Analysis

	21 Marcom Sales	22 Revenue/ Unit	23 COG/ Unit	24 Net Profit/ Unit	25 Marcom Profit [21 × 24]	26 Profit Return/ Marcom Effort [25/6]
Phase 1	8,000	$65	$45.50	$19.50	$156,000	$1.18

For each marcom dollar spent, $1.18 in profit was generated.

PHASE 2—DEBERSON WIDGETS

Target: 80M non-buying businesses after Phase 1 in the Southeast Region

Marcom Mix

1 TE	2 Fulfillment	3 PR	4 Sales Promo	5	6 Total	7 Σ Marcom
$75,000	$19,740	$12,500	$17,500		$124,740	$256,740

Revenue/Effort Analysis

	11 Units Sold	12 Marcom Factor	13 Marcom Sales	14 Revenue/ Unit	15 Marcom Revenue [13 × 14]	16 Marcom Revenue/ Effort [15/6]
Phase 1	20,000	40%	8,000	$65	$520,000	$3.94
Phase 2	10,300	35%	3,605	$65	$234,325	$1.88
Cumulative Analysis					$754,325	[Σ15/7] $2.94

At the end of Phase 2, an additional 10,300 units had been sold. The Marcom Factor was 35 percent; 3,605 of the sales were the result of or significantly influenced by the marcom campaign. For each marcom dollar spent, $1.88 in revenue was generated. A total of $754,325 in revenue had been generated by $256,740 in marcom expenditures across the two phases. For each marcom dollar spent in Phases 1 and 2, $2.94 in revenue was generated.

Profit/Effort Analysis

	21 Marcom Sales	22 Revenue/ Unit	23 COG/ Unit	24 Net Profit/ Unit	25 Marcom Profit [21 × 24]	26 Profit Return/ Marcom Effort [25/6]
Phase 1	8,000	$65	$45.50	$19.50	$156,000	$1.18
Phase 2	3,605	$65	$45.50	$19.50	$70,297.50	$0.56
						[Σ25/7]
Cumulative Analysis					$226,298	$0.88

For each marcom dollar spent in Phase 2, $.56 in revenue was generated. A total of $226,298 in profit had been generated by $256,740 in marcom expenditures across the two phases. For each marcom dollar spent in Phases 1 and 2, $.88 in revenue was generated.

PHASE 3—DEBERSON WIDGETS

Target: 69,700 non-buying businesses after Phases 1 and 2 in the Southeast Region

Marcom Mix

1 Trade Ads	2 TE	3 Sales Promo	4 Special Event	5	6 Total	7 Σ Marcom
$45,000	$41,980	$13,450	$5,600		$106,030	$362,770

Revenue/Effort Analysis

	11 Units Sold	12 Marcom Factor	13 Marcom Sales	14 Revenue/ Unit	15 Marcom Revenue [13 × 14]	16 Marcom Revenue/ Effort [15/6]
Phase 1	20,000	40%	8,000	$65	$520,000	$3.94
Phase 2	10,300	35%	3,605	$65	$234,325	$1.88
Phase 3	7,800	25%	1,950	$65	$126,750	$1.20
						[Σ5/16]
Cumulative Analysis					$881,075	$2.43

At the end of Phase 3, 7,800 units had been sold. The Marcom Factor was 25 percent; 1,905 of the sales were the result of or significantly influenced by the marcom campaign. For each marcom dollar spent in Phase 3, $1.20 in revenue was generated. A total of $881,075 in revenue had been generated by $362,770 in marcom expenditures across the three phases. For each marcom dollar spent in Phases 1, 2, and 3, $2.43 in revenue was generated.

Profit//Effort Analysis

	21 Marcom Sales	22 Revenue/ Unit	23 COG/ Unit	24 Net Profit/ Unit	25 Marcom Profit [21 × 24]	26 Profit Return/ Marcom Effort [25/6]
Phase 1	8,000	$65	$45.50	$19.50	$156,000	$1.18
Phase 2	3,605	$65	$45.50	$19.50	$70,297.50	$0.56
Phase 3	1,950	$65	$45.50	$19.50	$38,025	$0.36
						[Σ 25/7]
Cumulative Analysis					$264,323	$0.73

For each marcom dollar spent in Phase 3, $.36 in profit was generated. A total of $264,323 in profit had been generated by $362,770 in marcom expenditures across the three phases. For each marcom dollar spent in Phases 1, 2, and 3, $0.73 in profit was generated.

PHASE 4—DEBERSON WIDGETS

Target: 61,900 non-buying businesses after Phases 1, 2, and 3 in the Southeast Region. These are companies that were brand loyal to a competitor and that required four marcom hits to convert.

Marcom Mix

1 Direct Mail $55,250	2 Sales Promo $32,500	3 Trade Show $7,525	4	5	6 Total $95,275	7 Σ Marcom $458,045

Revenue/Effort Analysis

	11 Units Sold	12 Marcom Factor	13 Marcom Sales	14 Revenue/ Unit	15 Marcom Revenue [13 × 14]	16 Marcom Revenue/ Effort [15/6]
Phase 1	20,000	40%	8,000	$65	$520,000	$3.94
Phase 2	10,300	35%	3,605	$65	$234,325	$1.88
Phase 3	7,800	25%	1,950	$65	$126,750	$1.20
Phase 4	13,650	60%	8,190	$65	$532,350	$5.59
						[Σ15/6]
Cumulative Analysis					$1,413,325	$3.09

At the end of Phase 4, 13,650 units had been sold. The Marcom Factor was 60 percent; 8,190 of the sales were the result of or significantly influenced by the marcom campaign. For each marcom dollar spent in Phase 4, $5.59 in revenue was generated. A total of $1,413,425 in revenue had been generated by $458,045 in marcom expenditures across the four phases. For each marcom dollar spent in Phases 1, 2, 3, and 4, $3.09 in revenue was generated.

Profit/Effort Analysis

	21 Marcom Sales	22 Revenue/ Unit	23 COG/ Unit	24 Net Profit/ Unit	25 Marcom Profit [21 × 24]	26 Profit Return/ Marcom Effort [25/6]
Phase 1	8,000	$65	$45.50	$19.50	$156,000	$1.18
Phase 2	3,605	$65	$45.50	$19.50	$70,297.50	$0.56
Phase 3	1,950	$65	$45.50	$19.50	$38,025	$0.36
Phase 4	8,190	$65	$45.50	$19.50	$159,705	$1.68
						[Σ25/7]
Cumulative Analysis					$424,028	$0.93

For each marcom dollar spent in Phase 4, $1.68 in profit was generated. A total of $424,028 in profit had been generated by $458,045 in marcom expenditures across the four phases. For each marcom dollar spent in Phases 1, 2, 3, and 4, $.93 in revenue was generated.

There would also be a customer maintenance and resolicitation program and rebuys from current customers. Both figures could be factored into this spreadsheet to assess the ongoing aggregate effects of all marcom efforts and the cumulative ROI.

NOTE

1. The work done by Don Schultz and Paul Wang at Northwestern University has provided a foundation for this analytical approach. Our thanks also to Lokesh Seghal of the Institute for Communications Research and Education (I-CORE) in Atlanta and Dr. Bruce Wardrep for their insights.

INDEX

A

A. C. Nielsen, 100
Accounting/finance departments, 272
Account management, by telemarketing, 192
Accounts payable department, 286
Acronyms, 73
Activities, interests and opinions (AIO),
113
Administrative phase, public relations,
219, 220
Advertising
advocacy, 224–225
budgets, 99–101
business and consumer compared,
90
collateral, at events, 182–183
collateral sales materials, 101–103
corporate, 224
creativity in, 88, 89
design of, 342–344
as direct marketing tool, 122
employee viewing of, 274–275, 276
functions of, 90
future media for, 103–104
guidelines for, 89, 342–344
media for, 94–99
message in, 89–94
paid, for events, 182
posttesting, 106
pretesting, 105–106
purpose of, 87–88
scheduling, 97–99
before trade shows, 163
Advertising agencies, 27–28
Advocacy advertising, 224–225
Aggressive acquirers, marketing to,
244
AIO (activities, interests and opinions),
113
Airports, for events, 349–350
Alcohol consumption, events, 175

All-we-can-afford method, budgeting,
100
American Marketing Association (AMA),
11, 77
Anderson, Mike, 181
Anderson Solone, Inc., 180
Anniversary mailings, 137–138
Annual reports
credibility of, 262
in crisis, 313
for employees, 276, 278
items in, 262
management in, 233
as marketing tool, 229, 234–236,
260–266
Appraisal phase, public relations,
219–220
Arrangement phase, public relations,
219, 220
Assessment phase, public relations,
219, 220
Asset players, marking to, 243
Associations, 11
AT&T, 224
Audience, 31–32
competition for, 33–34
for crisis communication, 302–303
infographics for, 34–35, 94, 113–114
marketing for, 35–36
for problem solving, 67
selection of, 342
Audience auditor, crisis team, 306
Audit. See Communication audit
Average frequency, advertising, 97

B

B. F. Goodrich, 224
Bankruptcy, 254
Belch, George E., 42n
Belch, Michael A., 42n
Bell, Alexander Graham, 187
Bell, Rivian, 258

Below-book-value buyers, marketing
 to, 243–244
Bernays, Edward, 213, 214, 227
Berra, Yogi, 208
Bierce, Ambrose, 283
Bill Communications, 12
Black and white simplicity questions,
 241
Blinking strategy, advertising, 99
BMA (Business Marketing Association),
 11, 42
BMC (bulk mail center), 131
Bogart, Leo, 107
Boilerplate descriptions, 322–323
Booths. See Exhibits
Booth traffic contests, 161–162
Boschee, J. A., 316
Bottom fishers, marketing to, 244
BRC (business reply card), 157
Budgeting
 advertising, 99–101
 for marketing plans, 21–22, 30, 37
 methods of, 100–101
Bulk mail center (BMC), 131
Bursting strategy, advertising, 99
Business advertising. See also
 Advertising
 compared to consumer, 90
 expenditures for, 99–100, 105
 functions of, 88
 infographics of, 94–96
 marcom integration of, 104
 measuring and evaluating, 105–106
 media for, 94–97
 writing strategies for, 90–94,
  334–335
Business Marketing, 11, 58n, 186, 266,
 342–344
Business Marketing Association (BMA),
 11, 42
Business reply card (BRC), 157
Buy and hold selling strategy, 233,
 237

                       C

Candidates forum, as community ser-
 vice, 293
Casual vendors, 272
Catalogs, 42, 101
CEO (chief executive officer), 25, 75
CFO. See Chief financial officer (CFO)

Chairman of the board
 agenda of, 24–26, 234, 261
 on investor relations task force, 236
Chapter 11 restructuring
 benefits of, 256
 marketing documents for, 255–256
 media communications of, 257
 of Service America, 258–259
 task force for, 254–255
Charity contributions, 288–289, 294–295
Chartists, marketing to, 243
Chase, Alexander, 267
Chesterton, G. K., 17
Chief executive officer (CEO), 25, 75,
 326
Chief financial officer (CFO), 26–27
 at communications audits, 272
 on investor relations task force, 236
 at marcom summit, 64
Close-end yes or no trap question, 240
Clutter, 5
Collateral, at events, 182–183
Collateral sales materials, 101–103, 105
College of the Holy Cross, 348
Collins, Tom, 3, 160
Communication, effective, 92–93
Communication audit, 23, 54–55
 CFO at, 272
 conducting, 57–60
 functions of, 57
 guidelines for, 56
 information sources for, 60
 by investor relations task force,
  236
 matrix, 60–61
 timing of, 57
Communications summit meeting. See
 Marcom summit
Community relations, 282–284. See also
 Community relations plan
 analyzing, 287
 benefits of, 275
 funding for, 285
 guidelines for, 284
 influential contacts in, 288
 press coverage of, 291–292
Community relations plan
 corporate support for, 288–289
 education activities in, 290–291
 ideas for, 292–293
 marcom integration of, 293–295
 measuring and evaluating, 295

objectives of, 285–286
reasons for, 283
Companies
corporate culture of, 27
department integration of, 5–6
marketing personalities of, 24–25
Company backgrounders, 163, 183, 260, 313
Company-generated events, 172, 174–175
Company profiles, 259
Company spokesperson, crisis team, 306
Competition, defining, 33–34
Competitive parity method, budgeting, 100
Compiled lists, direct mail, 126, 127–128
Completed transaction mailings (CTMs), 124
Computer programs, marketing to, 244
Consensus, summit meeting, 67–68
Consolidated lists, direct mail, 126
Continuity, advertising, 97
Contrarians, marketing to, 243
Cooperative lists, direct mail, 126, 127
Copy platform, 55
Copywriting, 334–335
Corporate acquisition programs, 24
Corporate advertising, 224
Corporate attorney, 26
in crisis, 308–309
in naming products, 71, 75
Corporate identity, 70–71. See also Logos
Corporate image advertising. See Public relations
Corporate style manual, 26, 69
Corporate takeover bids, 251–254
Creativity, in advertising, 88, 89
Credibility
of advertising, 95, 96
to investors, 252
Crisis. See also Crisis communication management
industry-wide, 306–307
media relations in, 309–311
Crisis communication management, 297–298. See also Crisis management team
audiences for, 302–303
contingency plan, 303–305

documents for, 310, 312–313
guidelines for, 298–299
marcom integration of, 312–314
measuring and evaluating, 314–315
perceptions in, 301
planning, 299–300
when restructuring, 254
Crisis description, 310
Crisis hot line, 257
Crisis location description, 310
Crisis management team
activation of, 305–306
members of, 300–301
post-crisis, 311–312
Crisis Q&A, 312–313
Cross-selling offers, 136
CSR. See Customer service reps (CSRs)
CTM (completed transaction mailings), 124
Current income investors, marketing to, 244
Customers
changing behavior of, 50
communication with, 246
educating, 36
perceptions of, 33
referred by employees, 275
relationship development, 154–155
retention of, 112, 135
telemarketing expectations of, 204
visits, 275
Customer service, telemarketing as, 190, 191
Customer service reps (CSRs), 104, 114, 271–272

D

Dartboard method, budgeting, 100
Database. See Progressive database
Database marketing. See Relationship database marketing
Dealers
concerns of, 173
crisis perception of, 303
expenditures for, 105
financial information to, 246
list of, 310
on product identity committee, 75
De Bonis, Susan J., 53
De Bonis and Peterson Results/Effort (R/E) Ratio, 50, 354–359

Deighton, John, 6n
Della Famina, Jerry, 87
Della Famina McNamee, 89
Designers, for logos, 79–80
Dialog Information Service, 77
Direct mail, 42
  budgeting for, 133–134
  cost of, 131
  expenditures for, 99, 105
  factors of, 124–125
  formats for, 133–134, 136–138
  functions of, 122, 135
  guidelines for, 122–123
  lists, 125–129
  marcom integration of, 135–138
  measuring and evaluating, 125, 138
  offer, 129
  postage for, 131–133
  to prospects, 134–135
  respondent profile, 123–124
  response options, 125, 129–131
  risk-reducers, 129–130
  with telemarketing, 189–190
  types of, 124
Direct response marketing. *See also*
  Advertising; Direct mail; Telemarketing
  advantages of, 119–120
  guidelines for, 120–Ä121
  media for, 122
  objectives of, 121
  strategy for, 121–122
  types of, 120
  use of, 121
Displays. *See* Exhibits
Distributors. *See* Dealers
Door-opener, sales device, 101, 102
Doyle, Arthur Conan, 19
Dreyfus Corporation, 257
Drucker, Peter, 20
Due diligence meetings, for initial public offering, 250
Dunn & Bradstreet Information Services, 110

E

Editors. *See* Press relations
Education, supporting local, 290–291
Effective frequency, advertising, 97–98
Einstein, Albert, 16
Eisenhart, T., 186

Emerging growth investors, marketing
  to, 245
Emerson, Ralph Waldo, 15, 70, 297
Employee name contests, 77–78
Employee relations, 267–268. *See also*
  Employees
  communication in, 225–226,
    274–276
  guidelines for, 268
  marcom integration of, 276–279
  measuring and evaluating, 279–281
  in restructuring, 256
Employees
  communicating with, 225–226
  evaluating, 270–274
  hiring, 275, 277
  motivating, 269–270
  recognizing, 275, 278–279
  surveys, 274, 279–281, 295, 314
Employee stock ownership plans,
  246
Erdos and Morgan, 260
Event marketing, 36, 167–168. *See also*
  Road shows; Seminars;
  Sponsorship events
  advertising collateral at, 182–183
  agenda for, 177–178
  alcohol consumption at, 175
  benefits of, 168
  competition analysis of, 170–172
  exhibit marketing compared to,
    168
  guidelines for, 169–170
  marcom integration of, 179–182
  in marketing information platform,
    173
  measuring and evaluating, 184
  problems of, 172
  at sales meetings, 179
  site inspection checklist, 348–353
  types of, 172
Events, to employees, 278
Exchange-listed loyalists, marketing to,
  244
Exhibit guides, 150
Exhibit marketing. *See* Trade shows
Exhibitor, 12
Exhibitor Show, The, 12
Exhibits
  costs of, 145
  graphics for, 332–333
  materials for, 145

message of, 146–150
modular systems for, 145
rental of, 146, 148–149
size of, 145–146, 329–330, 331
types of, 150
External perceptions management, 10,
14–15, 20, 171
Exxon Valdez oil spill, 216–217

F

Factors, problem solving, 66
Facts czar, crisis team, 305–306
Fair, as community service, 293
FCC National Bank, 115–116
Feedback, from marketing, 5
Festival, as community service, 293
Field sales reps. *See* Sales reps
Financial relations. *See also* Investor
relations
guidelines for, 229–230
marketing for, 228
Financial Relations Board, 247
Financial summary, for crisis, 310
Fireworks, as community service, 292
Five year planners, marketing to, 245
Flag display, as community service, 292
Flexible exhibiting capability, 146, 149
Flighting strategy, advertising, 98
Focus groups, 47–48
Ford Motor Company, logo for, 78
Frankel, Bud, 173, 186
Frusen Gl„dj„ 340–341
Fujitsu Microelectronics, 180–181
Fulfillment firms, 313
Fundamentalist investors, marketing to,
246

G

Galbraith, John Kenneth, 167
Gantt chart, 23
Gide, Andre, 54
Goldman, Jordan, 219, 227
Goodyear, 224
Gordon, Monte, 257
Government officials
communication with, 287
lobbying, 290
Grayson, Kent, 6n
Grizzard, Lewis, 4
Grove, Andy, 315

H

Häagen-Dazs Inc., 340–341
Herodotus, 62
Hill and Knowlton, Inc., 58n
Hodnett, Edward, 18
Holy Cross, College of the, 348
Home-town loyalists, marketing to, 244
Hook, Sidney, 167
Hospitality suites, trade shows, 161,
162
Hotels, for events, 350–353
House lists, direct mail, 126–127

I

Iaccoca, Lee, 233
Icons. *See* Logos
Ideal market position, 171
Ignon, Lance, 252
IMC. *See* Integrated marketing commu-
nications (IMC)
Incomplete transaction mailings (ITMs),
124
Indoctrination mailings, 136
Industry analysts, 36. *See also* Stock
analysts
Industry followers, marketing to, 244
Infographics, target audience, 34–35,
94, 113–114
Information
disclosing, 229, 231–232
managing, 234–236
in marketing strategy, 111–115
overload, 96
Informational advertising, 337–338
Initial public offering (IPO), 232,
249–251
Insider trading, 230, 232
Institute for Communications Research
and Education (I-CORE), 359
Integrated marketing communications
(IMC), 4, 6. *See also* Marketing
communications
defined, 8–9
to stockholders, 242–243
strategy components of, 9–10
Intel, Pentium chip error, 78, 224, 315
Internal objectivity, 14–15
International Exhibitors Association, 12
Internationalists, marketing to, 245
Interview, control of, 239–241

Investment advisers, marketing to, 244
Investor Relations Company, The, 243
Investor relations database, 247
Investor relations (IR), 235, 237
    analysts, communication with, 239–241
    approaches to, 238–239
    audiences for, 242–246
    development of, 246–248
    marcom integration of, 257–263
    measuring and evaluating, 263–264
    on-line, 242
    with takeover bid, 251–254
    when restructuring, 254–257
Investor relations logbook, 229
Investor relations message management
    task force, 236–237
IPO (initial public offering), 232, 249–251
IR. *See* Investor relations (IR)
Isuzu, Joe, 89
ITM (incomplete transaction mailings), 124

J

Joe Isuzu, 89
Johnson & Johnson, Tylenol tampering
    cases, 216–217
Junior Achievement, 292

K

Kaiser, Henry J., 18
Kalman, Jerry, 239, 266
Kennedy, John F., 298
Kenner Parker Toys Inc., 339–340
Ketchum Public Relations/Pittsburgh, 303, 345–347
Kettering, Charles, 17
King, Thomas R., 107
Knowledge, levels of, 18–19
Korda, Reva, 93

L

Langer, Suzanne, 41
Laser marketing, 120
Lasswell, H. D., 5n
Lead forms, for trade shows, 159–160
Lead response, in telemarketing, 190

Leave-behind sales device, 101, 102–103
Le Corbusier, Charles E. J., 13
Leiser, Serena, 348
Listening, 203
Lists, direct mail, 125–129
Lobbies, of building, 277–278
Lobbying, government, 290
Logos
    changing, 79
    and corporate identity, 70–71
    cost of, 79
    design of, 78–79
    at events, 183
    marcom integration of, 80
    measuring and evaluating, 80–81
    purposes of, 78
Lower-to-middle-price specialists, mar-
    keting to, 243
Low price/earnings investors, market-
    ing to, 245
Low-price specialists, marketing to, 243

M

Macro message, 84
Management, marketing of, 233
Management backers, marketing to, 243
Management Review, 316
MAP (Message Action Plan), 303, 345–347
Marcom. *See* Marketing communica-
    tions
Marcom factor, 355
Marcom mix, 354
Marcom research, 41–42
    analyzing, 47
    conducting, 46
    costs of, 49, 51–52
    design of, 46
    focus groups for, 47–48
    functions of, 50–51
    guidelines for, 42–43
    in marketing plan, 22–23
    measuring, 49–50
    need for, 15–16
    objectives of, 43–44
    by outside vendors, 16, 4–49
    posttest, 45
    pretest, 43, 45
    problem defined in, 44–45

report for, 47
sample for, 46
secondary data for, 45
sign-off at, 68
tools for, 46
Marcom summit, 62–63
agenda, 65–66
attenders of, 64–65
guidelines for, 63–64
problem solving at, 66–67
setting for, 65
subsequent, 68
Margin-elasticity elitists, marketing to, 245
Marketing
management, 232–233
sales v., 13–14
Marketing communications. *See also*
Marketing communications
program
defined, 4
to employees, 274–276, 323
expenditures for, 105
integration of, 4–10
target of, 55
Marketing communications professionals
information for, 29
learning, 11–12
role of, 10
teaching, 11
Marketing communications program.
See also Marcom research;
Marcom summit; Marketing
Information Platform (MIP)
budget for, 21–22
evaluating, 24
management chart, 23
measuring, 9
objectives of, 4, 22, 54, 55, 319
strategies of, 22, 320
Marketing customer information file
(MCIF), 116
Marketing department, 307–308
Marketing Information Platform (MIP)
confidential information in, 68
crisis plan in, 298
development of. *See* Communication
audit
event marketing in, 173
first draft, 23, 56–57, 63
function of, 55, 317

problem definition, 317–318, 324
project platform worksheet, 324–326
second draft, 63, 66
selling internally, 68–69
serializing, 68
situational analysis, 318–319
template sample, 317–323
Marketing News, 11, 105n, 186
Marketing plans. *See also* Marketing
communications program
marcom in, 21–24
sales input in, 273
Marketing staff, 29
Market research. *See* Marcom research
Market research firms, 16, 48–49
Markets. *See* Audience
Marston, John, 219
Maslow, Abraham, 169, 269, 281
Mass customization, 88
McClelland, David, 269, 281
McGraw-Hill Laboratory of Advertising
Performance, 141
MCIF (marketing customer information
file), 116
McKenna, Regis, 315
McLuhan, Marshall, 107
Media
advertising in, 88, 94–97
for direct advertising, 122–135
expenditures for, 99–100, 105
future, 103–104
scheduling, 97–99
selecting, 94–97
Media fact sheets, 257, 259, 310, 312
Media kits, 223
Media log book, 311
Media relations. *See* Press relations
Meeting space, for events, 348–349
Megatrends, 96, 108
Message
for advertising, 89–94
consistency of, 9
of exhibit, 146–150
explicit, 7
to financial market, 232–233,
235–236
implicit, 7–8
marketing strategies for, 320–322
relationship-building, 9–10
Message Action Plan (MAP), 303,
345–347
Meyerowitz, Steven A., 341

Michaelson, Gerald A., 14, 67
Micro-level message, 84
Miller, Cyndee, 107
MIP. *See* Marketing Information
    Platform (MIP)
Mission statements, 275
Mobil Corporation, 224–225
Monthly statement mailings, 137
Multichannel communication flow, 9

N

Naisbitt, John, 96, 108
Name badges, 158
Names, product. *See* Product names
Naples, Michael J., 107
Negative response option, 120
Net lifetime value (NLTV), 7, 112
Newsletters
    community and government, 294
    employee, 274
    sales, 101, 137, 179, 274
News releases. *See* Press releases
NLTV (net lifetime value), 7, 112
Noise, 5
Nonresponse mailings (NRMs), 124
Non-stock investment (NSI), 232
Northwestern University, 359
NRM (nonresponse mailings), 124
NSI (non-stock investment), 232

O

Objective and task, zero-based method,
    budgeting, 100–101
Objectives, problem solving, 67
OEM (original equipment manufactur-
    er), 303
Ogilvy, David, 90, 107, 305
Ogilvy and Mather, 93
One-step direct marketing, 120
Open-ended bait question, 240
Open houses, 293–294
Order-taking, in telemarketing, 190
Original equipment manufacturer
    (OEM), 303
Osborne, Adam, 246
OTC rebels, marketing to, 244

P

Packaging, marketing communication,
    8

Palmer, Ross, 259
Peckham, J. O., 100
People, in marketing communication, 8
P/E (price/earnings) ratio, 245
Percentage of sales method, budgeting,
    100
Perceptions, 8, 13–14
    in crisis, 301
    financial, 235
    management of, 14–15, 20, 171
    power of, 16–17
    problems, solving, 17–18
    research for, 15–16
Performance evaluations, 270
Peters, Tom, 8, 14, 235
Pfizer Pharmaceutical, 225
Photos, for crisis, 310
PIC (product identity committee),
    74–75
Planning, in marketing communication,
    8
Postage, direct mail, 131–133
Press kits, trade shows, 101, 162–163,
    333
Press relations
    for community events, 291–292
    in crisis, 302, 309–311
    at events, 182
    for financial communication, 248
    objectives of, 221–222
    strategies of, 222
    tactics for, 223
    at trade shows, 161–162, 163
Press releases, 214, 270, 291
    at events, 183
    of financial information, 248–249
    of restructuring, 257
    worksheet, 327–328
Press room, 311
Presumed guilt questions, 241
Price/earnings (P/E) ratio, 245
Pricing, as communication, 273
Pricing amendment, for initial public
    offering, 250
Proactive public relations, 217–218
Problem definition, problem solving, 66
Problem solving, 66–67
Product data sheets, 163, 313
Product definition, 32
Product demonstration, at trade shows,
    155–157
Product identity, 70, 71

Product identity committee (PIC), 74–75
Product information sheets, 163, 313
Production management charts, 23
Production schedules, 21
Product line expansion offers, 136
Product names
  employee contests for, 77–78
  guidelines for, 71
  marcom integration of, 80
  measuring and evaluating, 80–81
  selection of, 72–73, 74–77
  types of, 73–74
Program sessions, trade shows, 161, 162
Progressive database
  functions of, 111, 115–117
  hardware and software for, 109
  information on, 113–114
Project names, 72
Project platform worksheet, 324–326
Project worksheet, event marketing, 171, 348–353
Prospects, at trade shows
  hospitality suites for, 162
  marketing to, 158–159
  qualifying, 151–152
  types of, 151
Prospectus, for initial public offering, 249, 250
Psychographic data, 113
Psycholinguist, 75
Publications. *See also* Trade publications
  by company, 35
Public relations, 32, 42, 213–214
  credibility of, 221
  defined, 215
  emergency, 216–217
  expenditures for, 99, 105
  for financial information, 248–249
  guidelines for, 214
  internal, 225–226
  marcom integration of, 226
  measuring and evaluating, 226
  with media, 221–223
  objectives of, 214–215, 218
  phases of, 219–220
  proactive, 217–218
  tool selection, 218, 220–221
Public relations department, as touch-point, 114–115

Public Relations Journal, 266, 316
Public Relations Society of America (PRSA), 215
Public speaking, 156–157
Pulsing pattern, advertising, 98–99
Purge mailings, 138

Q

Q&A
  in crisis, 312–313
  for restructuring, 255
Quiet period, for initial public offering, 250–251

R

Race, as community service, 293
Rapp, Stan, 3, 119, 160
Rawl, Lawrence G., 217
Reach, advertising, 97
Reactivation mailings, 138
Reactive public relations, 216–217
Reception counter, trade show exhibit, 151
Receptionists, 270–271
R/E (De Bonis and Peterson Results/Effort Ratio), 50, 354–359
Red herring statement, for initial public offering, 250
Refer back offers, 137
Referral mailings, 126–127, 137
Registration statement, for initial public offering, 249
Relationship database marketing, 6, 108–109. *See also* Progressive database
  defined, 110
  guidelines for, 109–110
  hardware and software for, 109
  information gathering, 114–115
  information needed for, 111–112, 113–114
  marcom integration of, 117
  measuring and evaluating, 117–118
  for trade shows, 160–161
Relationship investing, 237–238
Relationship marketing
  customer retention in, 112
  exhibit marketing as, 153–155
  mailings, 137
  marcom in, 3–12

Relevant information, database market-
    ing, 113–115
Reporters. *See* Press relations
Research mailings (RMs), 124
Reselling offers, 136
Responder lists, direct mail, 126, 127
Response rate, direct mail, 125
Restructuring. *See* Chapter 11 restructur-
    ing
Results/efforts (R/E) ratio (De Bonis
    and Peterson), 50, 354–359
Retention materials, direct mail, 136
Return on investment (ROI), 5
Return-ratio buyers, marketing to, 244
Ritz Carlton Hotel, 269–270
RJR Reynolds Tobacco, 225
RM (research mailings), 124
Roadblocking strategy, advertising, 99
Road shows
    collateral for, 183
    for financial relations, 262–263
    guidelines for, 180–181
    seminar, 178
Robertson, Cliff, 224
Rogers, Will, 228
ROI (return on investment), 5
Rolling why question, 240
Rose Art Industries Inc., 339–340
Rosenbaum, Michael, 247, 266
Rosenbluth International Travel,
    116–117
Ross, Wilbur, 258
Rothman, Andrea, 107
Rothschild Inc., 258

S

Saarinen, Eliel, 78
Sale bulletins, 137
Sales
    marketing v., 13–14
    telemarketing support for, 191
Sales and Marketing Management, 12
Sales leads, 190, 192. *See also* Lead
Sales literature
    at events, 183
    expenditures for, 105
    at trade shows, 101, 157, 158, 163
Sales manager, 25–26
Sales meetings, 179
Sales reps
    communication with, 272–274

crisis perception of, 302
    at trade shows, 150–151, 158
Schopenhauer, Arthur, 17
Schultz, Don, 8, 359
Script, for restructuring, 255–256
Securities and Exchange Commission
    (SEC), 242
    concerns of, 230, 251
    guidelines, staying within, 231–232
    and initial public offering, 249
Seghal, Lokesh, 359
Segment-of-one communications, 4, 88,
    110
Seminars
    attending, 12
    marketing in, 175–177, 180–181,
        182, 183
Service America Corporation, 258–259
Shakespeare, William, 77
Share-of-market method, budgeting,
    100
Show dailies, 161, 333
Sign-off, Marketing Information
    Platform, 56, 68, 326
Single-source vendors, 272
Sitrick Krantz & Company, 252,
    258–259
Situation room, crisis, 305
Small float artists, marketing to, 243
Soliciting new accounts, in telemarket-
    ing, 191–192
Solone, Ray, 180
Speculating on the competition ques-
    tion, 240
Speculator relations, 237
Sponsorship events
    benefits of, 172
    company-generated, 174–175
    screening guidelines for, 173–174
    selection of, 172–173
Sprint, 224
SRDS (Standard Rate and Data
    Service), 128
Stand-alone sales device, 101, 102
Standard Rate and Data Service
    (SRDS), 128
Standards guide, 69
Stock analysts
    events for, 263
    interview by, 239–241
    restructuring communication to,
        257

Stockbrokers
  events for, 262–263
  marketing to, 242, 258
Stockholders, marketing to, 242–243
Stock market, 315
Stock valuation, 238
Strategic vendors, 272, 286
Strategy, problem solving, 67
Sun Tzu, 282
Suppliers, 246, 302
Surveys, employee, 274, 279–281, 295, 314
Synchronized management, 9

T

Tactics, problem solving, 67
Talent show, as community service, 293
Target market
  infographics of, 34–35, 94, 113–114
  profile, 319–320
Telemarketers
  characteristics of, 193–194
  compensating, 200–201
  fears of, 197
  hiring, 193–195
  listening by, 203
  mistakes of, 202
  monitoring, 198–199
  motivating, 199–201
  objections, handling, 197–198
  techniques for, 201–202
  training, 195–198
  voices of, 194–195
Telemarketing, 187
  advantages of, 188
  analyzing, 204
  costs of, 206–207
  with direct mail, 189–190
  as direct marketing tool, 122
  functions of, 190–192
  guidelines for, 188–189
  inbound, 190–191
  marcom integration of, 207–208
  measuring and evaluating, 208–209
  other media for, 207
  outbound, 191–192
  planning for calls, 203–206
  role of, 189–194
  time management for, 205–206
Thompson, J. Walter, 65

360 Designers & Producers, 148
Thurber, James, 31
Tombstone ads, 250, 260
Top-down method, budgeting, 100
Top-of-mind attitudes, 280
Total relationship marketing (TRM), 6
Touch points, 114–115
Trademark attorneys, 77
Trademarks
  defined, 336
  infringement upon, 337–341
  obtaining, 77
  purpose of, 78
  selection of, 336
  use of, 337
Trade press. See Press relations
Trade publications
  advertising in, 91, 95–97
  learning from, 11–12
  marketing in, 35, 42
  types of, 95–97
Trade schools, 290–291
Trade show literature, 101, 157, 158, 163, 333
Trade shows, 35–36, 42, 140–141. See also Exhibits
  assisting in planning, 294
  attendance for, 143–144, 164
  attending, 12
  benefits of, 141
  control of, 144
  costs of, 141, 145, 164
  during a crisis, 314
  event marketing compared to, 168
  expenditures for, 99, 105
  guidelines for, 142
  inquiry management at, 157–160
  items to bring to, 154
  management checklist, 329–333
  marcom integration of, 160–164
  measuring and evaluating, 164–165
  opportunities at, 153–155
  politics of, 162
  post-show follow-up for, 157, 158, 160
  potential of, 141, 143
  preshow promotion for, 157, 160, 163
  product demonstration at, 155–157, 164
  prospects at, 151–152, 164
  services at, 331–332

traffic management at, 157
Trade show staff, 150–155, 158, 160,
   330
Trade show staff handbook, 152–153
TRM (total relationship marketing), 6
TS/2, 12
Turnaround buyers, marketing to, 243
Tutorials, 175–177, 183
Twain, Mark, 309
Two-step direct marketing, 120
Typography, in business advertising,
   343–344

U

Underwriters, for initial public offering,
   249
Unique selling proposition (USP), 65,
   173
Unisys, 224
Universities, 177, 290–291
Upgrade offers, 136
U.S. Forest Service, 221
USP (unique selling proposition), 65,
   173

V

Value-added dealers (VADs), 303

Value-added resellers (VARs), 303
Vendors
   perceptions of, 286, 302
   types of, 272
Voices, telemarketers, 194–195
Von Clausewitz, General Karl, 140

W

Wallace, Sherwood Lee, 243, 266
Wang, Paul, 359
Watson, Thomas J., 11
Wayman Group, Inc., The, 99,
   105n
Werner, Lawrence R., 303, 316
What if questions, 241
Williams, Joe, 287
Wilson, Edmund O., 78
Wimmer and Dominick, 53
Winther, Eugene, 148
Wurman, Richard Saul, 107

Z

Zero-based budgeting method, 30,
   100–101
Zero-based marcom strategy, 55
Ziff-Davis's Computer Select CD
   Service, 77

AMERICAN MARKETING ASSOCIATION

The American Marketing Association, the world's largest and most comprehensive professional association of marketers, has over 40,000 members worldwide and over 500 chapters throughout North America. Its sponsors 25 major conferences per year, covering topics ranging from the latest trends in customer satisfaction measurement to business-to-business and services marketing, to attitude research and sales promotion. The AMA publishes 9 major marketing publications, including Marketing Management, a quarterly magazine aimed at marketing managers, and dozens of books addressing special issues, such as relationship marketing, marketing research, and entrepreneurial marketing for small and home-based businesses. Let the AMA be your strategy for success.

For further information on the American Marketing Association, call TOLL FREE at 1-800-AMA-1150.

Or write to

American Marketing Association
250 S. Wacker Drive, Suite 200
Chicago, Illinois 60606
(312) 648-0536
(312) 993-7542 FAX

TITLES OF INTEREST IN MARKETING, DIRECT MARKETING, AND SALES PROMOTION

SUCCESSFUL DIRECT MARKETING METHODS, by Bob Stone
PROFITABLE DIRECT MARKETING, by Jim Kobs
INTEGRATED DIRECT MARKETING, by Ernan Roman
BEYOND 2000: THE FUTURE OF DIRECT MARKETING, by Jerry I. Reitman
POWER DIRECT MARKETING, by "Rocket" Ray Jutkins
CREATIVE STRATEGY IN DIRECT MARKETING, by Susan K. Jones
SECRETS OF SUCCESSFUL DIRECT MAIL, by Richard V. Benson
STRATEGIC DATABASE MARKETING, by Rob Jackson and Paul Wang
HOW TO PROFIT THROUGH CATALOG MARKETING, by Katie Muldoon
DIRECT RESPONSE TELEVISION, by Frank Brady and J. Angel Vasquez
DIRECT MARKETING THROUGH BROADCAST MEDIA, by Alvin Eicoff
SUCCESSFUL TELEMARKETING, by Bob Stone and John Wyman
BUSINESS TO BUSINESS DIRECT MARKETING, by Robert Bly
COMMONSENSE DIRECT MARKETING, by Drayton Bird
DIRECT MARKETING CHECKLISTS, by John Stockwell and Henry Shaw
INTEGRATED MARKETING COMMUNICATIONS, by Don E. Schultz, Stanley I. Tannenbaum, and Robert F. Lauterborn
GREEN MARKETING, by Jacquelyn Ottman
MARKETING CORPORATE IMAGE: THE COMPANY AS YOUR NUMBER ONE PRODUCT by James R. Gregory with Jack G. Wiechmann
HOW TO CREATE SUCCESSFUL CATALOGS, by Maxwell Sroge
101 TIPS FOR MORE PROFITABLE CATALOGS, by Maxwell Sroge
SALES PROMOTION ESSENTIALS by Don E. Schultz, William A. Robinson and Lisa A. Petrison
PROMOTIONAL MARKETING, by William A. Robinson and Christine Hauri
BEST SALES PROMOTIONS, by William A. Robinson
INSIDE THE LEADING MAIL ORDER HOUSES, by Maxwell Sroge
NEW PRODUCT DEVELOPMENT, by George Gruenwald
NEW PRODUCT DEVELOPMENT CHECKLISTS, by George Gruenwald
CLASSIC FAILURES IN PRODUCT MARKETING, by Donald W. Hendon
HOW TO TURN CUSTOMER SERVICE INTO CUSTOMER SALES, by Bernard Katz
ADVERTISING & MARKETING CHECKLISTS, by Ron Kaatz
BRAND MARKETING, by William M. Weilbacher
MARKETING WITHOUT MONEY, by Nicholas E. Bade
THE 1-DAY MARKETING PLAN, by Roman A. Hiebing, Jr. and Scott W. Cooper
HOW TO WRITE A SUCCESSFUL MARKETING PLAN by Roman G. Hiebing, Jr. and Scott W. Cooper
DEVELOPING, IMPLEMENTING, AND MANAGING EFFECTIVE MARKETING PLANS by Hal Goetsch
HOW TO EVALUATE AND IMPROVE YOUR MARKETING DEPARTMENT by Keith Sparling and Gerard Earls
SELLING TO A SEGMENTED MARKET, by Chester A. Swenson
MARKET-ORIENTED PRICING, by Michael Morris and Gene Morris
STATE-OF-THE-ART MARKETING RESEARCH, by A.B. Blankenship and George E. Breen
AMA HANDBOOK FOR CUSTOMER SATISFACTION, by Alan Dutka
WAS THERE A PEPSI GENERATION BEFORE PEPSI DISCOVERED IT? by Stanley C. Hollander and Richard Germain
BUSINESS TO BUSINESS COMMUNICATIONS HANDBOOK, by Fred Messner
MANAGING SALES LEADS: HOW TO TURN EVERY PROSPECT INTO A CUSTOMER by Robert Donath, Richard Crocker, Carol Dixon and James Obermeyer
AMA MARKETING TOOLBOX (SERIES), by David Parmerlee
AMA COMPLETE GUIDE TO SMALL BUSINESS MARKETING, by Kenneth J. Cook
AMA COMPLETE GUIDE TO STRATEGIC PLANNING FOR SMALL BUSINESS, by Kenneth J. Cook
AMA COMPLETE GUIDE TO SMALL BUSINESS ADVERTISING, by Joe Vitale
HOW TO GET THE MOST OUT OF TRADE SHOWS, by Steve Miller
HOW TO GET THE MOST OUT OF SALES MEETINGS, by James Dance
STRATEGIC MARKET PLANNING, by Robert J. Hamper and L. Sue Baugh

For further information or a current catalog, write:
NTC Business Books
a division of *NTC Publishing Group*
4255 West Touhy Avenue
Lincolnwood, Illinois 60646-1975 U.S.A.